To forty-four years of History and Photography
with those outstanding characters "High on a Hilltop"

THE QUEEN OF TECHNICOLOR

THE QUEEN OF TECHNICOLOR

Maria Montez in Hollywood

Tom Zimmerman

UNIVERSITY PRESS OF KENTUCKY

Scholarly publisher for the Commonwealth,
serving Bellarmine University, Berea College, Centre
College of Kentucky, Eastern Kentucky University,
The Filson Historical Society, Georgetown College,
Kentucky Historical Society, Kentucky State University,
Morehead State University, Murray State University,
Northern Kentucky University, Spalding University,
Transylvania University, University of Kentucky,
University of Louisville, and Western Kentucky University.

Editorial and Sales Offices: The University Press of Kentucky
663 South Limestone Street, Lexington, Kentucky 40508-4008
www.kentuckypress.com

Cataloging-in-Publication data is available from the Library of Congress.

ISBN 978-0-8131-8257-5 (hardcover)
ISBN 978-0-8131-8259-9 (pdf)
ISBN 978-0-8131-8258-2 (epub)

This book is printed on acid-free paper meeting
the requirements of the American National Standard
for Permanence in Paper for Printed Library Materials.

Manufactured in the United States of America

ASSOCIATION of UNIVERSITY PRESSES

Member of the Association of
University Presses

CONTENTS

Introduction

It is January 30, 1944, in Washington, DC. Maria Montez, originally dubbed the "Mmmm Girl" by her studio and now known as "the Queen of Technicolor," is at the White House. Eleanor Roosevelt, who invited her for lunch and the presidential birthday balls to raise money to fight polio, sits opposite her. President Franklin D. Roosevelt is at the head of the table to her left. She came to Washington straight from Cleveland, the last stop on a national war bond tour she was headlining at the behest of the Hollywood Victory Committee. She has just finished filming a bit for *Follow the Boys* and is starring in *Gypsy Wildcat* for Universal Studios. *Ali Baba and the Forty Thieves,* another of her starrers, will open in theaters in two weeks. She has moved into Marlene Dietrich's former bungalow at Universal City and shares being queen of the lot with Deanna Durbin. Five and a half months earlier she married MGM contract player Jean-Pierre Aumont—currently an officer serving in the Free French Army in the Italian campaign.

At this moment Montez is an important member of her profession, her every movement covered by columnists all over the country. A native of the Dominican Republic, she may have arrived at Universal City four years earlier with a very thick Spanish accent and absolutely no acting experience. But now she is "the Queen of Technicolor" and the living embodiment of the federal government's Good Neighbor Policy to Latin America. And here she is at the White House, lunching with the first family and several Hollywood stars. The president of the United States invited her because he likes her movies.

Maria Montez's convoluted story of Hollywood success tells how the burning ambition of one woman combined with the specific needs of one of the smaller major studios and the particular spirit, interests, and needs of a time. Willing to do anything to achieve her goals, she aggressively made herself available to any and all writers and photographers, and was very clever in the persona she initially created. It did get her noticed, but the character she fashioned was so outlandish that it was hard to get beyond it and be taken seriously as a performer later in her career. She was perceived as a commissary actress, somebody who made dramatic entrances to nightclubs, proudly and vocally refused to wear a brassiere, dated every wolf in Hollywood, and was astoundingly self-absorbed—a reincarnation of silent movie era vamp Nita Naldi, a female version of the preening publicity hound Victor Mature. She was fun and outrageous to interview but always a personality, not an actress. In spite of all this, Maria did hit the pinnacle of success for a brief period with six Technicolor "Neverland" fantasies that had nothing to do with actual history or any other reality but took advantage of everything she had to offer and perfectly suited the wartime need for escapist entertainment.

The Neverland movies were gloriously fantastical, soaked in Technicolor, featuring derring-do, thrilling fight scenes, good guys, evil advisors, and Maria—often in a pool of some kind and always clad in skimpy, tight, and elaborate costumes designed by Vera West. The films were set in shining, colorful, make-believe Neverlands that existed only in the San Fernando Valley on the Universal lot. One group of the movies took place in a North Africa populated by bearded men on horseback and no Afrika Korps. The other group took place on tropical islands full of palm trees, exploding volcanoes, and lots of women in very brief attire. Japanese soldiers or warships were not even hinted at. There were always good guys being harassed by bad guys. In the Arabian fantasies the country was ruled by evildoers until the rightful leaders defeated them and reestablished proper government. Certainly, this could be cathartic for an audience engaged in war against the Axis. But the aim of the movies was pure escapism, allowing viewers to forget reality for an hour and watch the pretty woman and stalwart men. They were meant to offer audiences a respite from the worst conflict in human history that was right outside the theater door and mixed into all of their lives.

Besides being a gorgeous woman running about in fetching costumes, Maria was in fact a cultural touchstone during the war years. She became one of the primary national symbols of the US government's proclaimed Good Neighbor Policy, aimed at improving relations with Latin America. She was constantly referred to as Latin in the press. Much to the joy of Latin fans, she took seriously her role as an ambassador of goodwill with countries south of the US border, never caricatured her cultural heritage, never used her accent as a comic thing and, unlike any other Latin actress of the time, always played a queen, princess, or someone from the upper class.

In *Citizen Kane* the reporters combing the mogul's past were convinced they could understand him if they could only find out the meaning of the last word he spoke before dying: "Rosebud." They never found out. Maria demonstrated such overwhelming ambition and managed to successfully achieve such a seemingly unreachable goal that it is only natural to want to look for the "Rosebud" in her life.

But there is no single key to make Maria Montez's single-minded ambition and subsequent success easily understood. There is really no way to know where that fathomless well of desire came from. She never left a memoir, no correspondence exists where she explained it all, and everyone who knew her well is dead. Maria did give an important insight into what fed her deep belief in herself in a 1942 interview: "I am eemportant since I am five years old. . . . I cawm from eemportant people so that made me eemportant also." The writer poked fun at her accent, as was common at the time, but the meaning is obvious. She came from the highest echelon of first Barahona and later Santo Domingo society. It informed her self-image and helped to keep the fire of ambition well stoked. The imperiousness that marked most of her performances was not put on. It was her nature. Joan Crawford was as hyper-aggressive as Montez in her assault on the gates of fame. But she grew up on the wrong side of the tracks and no matter how famous she became she could always hear the train whistle. This was never the case with Maria. She came from important people and never lost the steadfast belief that she would get to the top of the Hollywood system—because that was where she belonged.

I think the closest we can come to finding a Rosebud in her life regards her relationship with her father, Isidoro Gracia Garcia. Her father was both a vibrant storyteller and the perfect example of someone who refused to give up on a dream until he finally attained it. Maria, his oldest and favorite daughter, was enthralled by her father; it seems that so much of the fuel for her active fantasy life, her burning ambition, and her single-minded dedication to realize her dream came from her admiration of her father and his colorful stories of his life. He was clearly her hero. Isidoro left her $20,000 ($381,505 in 2021's dollars) in his will, allowing her to leave her husband when she was twenty-seven to come to the United States and become a movie star.[1]

To comprehend why Maria Montez's ambitions to become a star actually worked, it is vital to understand the era in which she lived and worked. It is certainly remarkable she ever made a single movie. Unlike most of the other women helped by the Good Neighbor Policy, who were from Mexico or large South American countries, she was from the Dominican Republic, a place most Americans had heard of only because the US Marines and Navy occupied it from 1916 to 1924. She had never acted before. She had never even had a job before. She had married and become a homemaker, as was expected of the upper class in the small town of her birth.

Montez got a prominent agent in Louis Shurr and successfully signed a typical seven-year contract with Universal Studios, one of the minor Hollywood studios that specialized in quickly made B pictures. She had such a thick Spanish accent that she once lamented, "Even I cannot understand what I'm saying." Various internet sites claim that she lost her accent in the Dominican Republic and had to reacquire it to sound Latin American when she came to the United States. This is nonsense. She struggled the entire time she was in Hollywood to get her accent under control, not because she had any desire to hide her Latin American roots but so she could be considered for a broader range of roles. She had marvelous presence and her beauty was only enhanced on film. But her acting skills were rudimentary at best, and she had to be doubled if singing or dancing was called for.

There was another impediment to her achieving her goal. Besides a very thick accent and no acting training, as icing on the cake, she was twenty-eight years old when she first walked onto the Universal lot. That was so ancient for an ingénue with no stage or film experience that the studio turned her into a twenty-year-old by changing her actual year of birth, 1912, to a more youth-friendly 1920. But in spite of all these obstacles, somehow, within four years of arriving in Hollywood, she was at the White House celebrating the president's birthday with the Roosevelts and several members of Hollywood's elite.

Maria also had personal eccentricities that could either endear her to writers and co-workers or make her an object of ridicule. Known to have a particular dedication to St. Anthony of Padua, the Catholic patron saint of lost and stolen articles, she prayed to him often and always had a shrine to him wherever she lived. She was also a firm believer in astrologer Carroll Righter. She never made a move of any significance without consulting him and her astrological charts, and she constantly shared this with interviewers. Her husband, Jean-Pierre Aumont, wrote of her belief in ghosts and other worlds in his autobiography. Her niece Raina Paris noted that her aunt Maria, like her mother Teresita and her three other aunts, believed in many things unseen. She attributed it to the stories and legends of the island where they grew up. Of all her Universal co-workers Yvonne De Carlo seemed to understand Montez the best. She thought Maria lived in her own reality. You could join her and enjoy that bright, fantasy world with its scintillating hostess or stay on the outside and just scratch your head. But few at Universal had any interest at all in joining her in her world. None of Montez's closest Hollywood friends were associated with her studio.[2]

As will be explained in the text, from her arrival at Universal in June 1940 to her being announced as the lead in Walter Wanger's *Arabian Nights* in March 1942 Maria used the self-created Montez for Stardom club and five repeated antics to curry interest and favor with fans, photographers, columnists, and writers for movie magazines. She also managed to work her way into five national stories in 1941 to make moviegoers familiar with her. It was the antics and her creation of an interesting persona that people knew her for. Fans and critics did little note nor long remember the small parts and insignificant films Universal put her in at the beginning of her career. Until she appeared in a sarong in *South of Tahiti* in late 1941. This was followed by the six Neverland Technicolor fantasies that made her a bona fide star. Finally, all the crazy stunts and bombastic pronouncements took a back seat to how she appeared on the screen. Still, no matter how much money her movies made for Universal and how she outlasted Anne Gwynne, Evelyn Ankers, and the other women signed at the same time she was, she felt she was constantly at odds with her studio. She never felt Universal cared about her or took an interest in expanding the scope of her career by improving the parts she was offered or the actors she worked with.

Another significant factor in Maria's success was World War II. It was a total war. Almost every family in the nation had someone in one of the services. It took three and a half years and 407,316 dead and 671,278 wounded of the 16 million men and 360,000 women in uniform to go from initial disaster to unconditional victory. All the while the incredibly productive home front labor force, consisting of both men and an unprecedented number of women, supplied the US military and its Allies all over the world with the tools to fight that war and the food to keep them alive. Children from one end of the country to the next collected rubber, scrap metal, cooking fat, paper, and old clothes—all to take part in the prolonged effort to win the war. In the United States, rubber for tires and gasoline were strictly rationed, as was sugar and virtually everything else. The military had priority over all of it. But through it all, whether in an urban or small-town movie theater, on a ship at sea, in a jungle with a sheet for a screen, or in a blasted town somewhere in Europe, there were movies.[3]

Hollywood was at war like the rest of America. Tens of thousands of its workers were in the military. Still, not only were movies being cranked out faster than ever, the Hollywood Victory Committee sent stars to wherever the military was to entertain or just be with them. Films like *Wake Island* or *Thirty Seconds over Tokyo* were serious examinations of key events of the war. Many other films were pure escapism: sixty to ninety minutes to sit in the dark and immerse yourself in songs, silliness, or wild action. Trying not to think about what your son, brother, or husband—or daughter, sister, or wife—may be enduring. The country was hungry for diversion and movies provided it. Movie attendance grew every year during the war, finally topping out at over 80 million a week in 1946.[4]

Montez used the tools available to her in the 1940s. There were dozens of columnists and reviewers all over the country who wrote about her. Universal's photographers and shooters who specialized in the film world or worked for the several large-format photo-oriented magazines of the day took endless pictures of her. A score of movie fan magazines that publicized, criticized, and generally elevated Hollywood's stars eagerly featured her on their pages. All of these sources were constantly looking for content and Montez was always happy to accommodate them. Universal sent her on national tours to publicize her films. She visited soldiers at the behest of the Hollywood Victory Committee and on her own, as was expected of an actress at that time. The Hollywood studio system, and the massive publicity machine that went with it, is gone now. But in the 1940s it was at its apex. It was used as skillfully by Maria Montez as by anyone else in the history of Hollywood.

The Neverland movies were wildly popular. Her last three Hollywood films were not. Several independent producers had projects for Montez. All but one of these fell through, and the one film made was a complete disaster. She moved to France with her husband Jean-Pierre Aumont and made five more movies in Europe that had either very limited releases in the United States or none at all. Then on September 7, 1951, she took a very hot bath with reducing salts to ensure she retained the physical allure she needed to be the movie queen she always wanted to be and died at the age of thirty-nine (thirty-one, according to Hollywood). Maria was largely forgotten by Hollywood as the 1960s wore on to the 1970s. She was primarily remembered as a gay camp icon until her six Neverland films were released on DVD in the early 2000s and Vivian Perez and Luisa Peguero's *Maria Montez: A Dominican Star* website appeared to remind modern film fans who she was.

But for a short time, Maria Montez attained her implausible dream, becoming a genuine Hollywood movie star surrounded by a loving family. It was a complicated, difficult, rather astounding ascension. It involved her own singular ambition, the studio system, the vast network of columnists and fan magazines, the perfect timing of her arrival in Hollywood, and finally meeting exactly the right man. To steal a phrase from the Grateful Dead, it was a long, strange trip.

1

The Dominican Republic

The Dominican Republic occupies the eastern side of Hispaniola, the second-largest island in the Caribbean Sea. The western side is Haiti. It has one of the longest histories of any place in what would come to be called the Americas. Columbus stopped there on his first voyage in 1492. Santo Domingo, founded in 1496, is one of the first European settlements in the New World. The Tainos were the predominant people of the Caribbean islands. As was common with the native inhabitants of the Spanish Caribbean colonies, European diseases, especially smallpox and influenza, enslavement, and open warfare largely wiped them out. Spanish colonial demands that destroyed the natives' culture and self-determination finished the job. Those who remained largely intermarried with African and European peoples. Starting in 1503 African slaves who were put to work in the cattle ranches, agricultural fields, and mines on the island replaced the native population.

Haiti achieved its independence from France through a prolonged rebellion of slaves led by Toussaint Louverture. He was lured for talks by French forces, captured, and died in prison in France in 1803. The revolution was completed under the leadership of Jean-Jacques Dessalines, with Haiti declaring its independence from France on January 1, 1804. The Dominican two-thirds of the island was part of the Spanish Empire until 1821. The intention after declaring independence from Spain was to join with the proposed country of Gran Columbia, which encompassed most of northern South America, but Haiti annexed the rest of Hispaniola. It took another war of independence for the Dominicans to free themselves from the Haitians in 1844. The age of the *caudillos* followed. *Caudillismo* refers to the complete domination of a region or state by a particular *cacique*, or chief. When two or more such individuals arose in a country there was nothing but infighting over ultimate control. The Dominican Republic suffered several such periods of turmoil through the mid- to late nineteenth and the early twentieth centuries.

Various European countries and the United States vied to control the sugar and mining markets in the Dominican, which fluctuated wildly as world markets ebbed and prospered. This lasted into the new century as the country's economy and population suffered while the foreign debt reached untenable amounts. France, Germany, Italy, and the Netherlands all sent warships to the Dominican to collect money owed to their citizens. This prompted US president Theodore Roosevelt to issue his 1904 corollary to the Monroe Doctrine. The original document was aimed at keeping European nations from trying to establish or reestablish colonies in the Americas. The Roosevelt Corollary held that the US government would take the responsibility that the nations of Latin America would meet their financial obligations. For those who continued on the path of "chronic wrongdoing," the United States would be forced "to the exercise of an international police power."

The continuing political and economic chaos on both sides of Hispaniola caused the US Navy and Marine Corps to occupy Haiti in 1915 and the Dominican in 1916. Needless to say, the US attempt at nation building did not go over well among the people at whom it was directed. The Marines were finally withdrawn in 1924. Stability arrived in the Dominican at quite a price. Horacio Vásquez was elected president and the country entered into four years of prosperity. But he extended his reign by two years and then threatened to change the constitution so he could run for office again. This brought on another revolution, which led to Rafael Trujillo being elected president with a suspicious 95 percent of the vote. He would remain in office from 1931 to 1961. His friends would prosper, his enemies suffer. He even changed the name of the capital from Santo Domingo to Ciudad Trujillo (Trujillo City) in 1936.[1]

While all this political and financial chaos was sweeping so much of the country, the isolated southwestern part of the Dominican was beginning to grow. Isidoro Gracia Garcia arrived and began buying land to grow and harvest guayacan trees, whose hardwood was much appreciated in Europe and the United States. He was the quintessential early twentieth-century young man on the make. His family was originally from Teruel in the Aragon region of northeastern Spain. His soldier father was posted to Las Palmas, the largest city of the Spanish-controlled Canary Islands off the northwest coast of Africa. Here his two sons were born. Isidoro left the Canaries with his brother, Joaquin, first landing in Cuba and then moving on to the Dominican. They were not looking for day labor. They wanted to find land and set up their own business. Isidoro did exactly that in Barahona, where he met Teresa Maria Vidal Recio.

Her family had Dutch roots and was from the Dominican town of Bani. The family found themselves on the wrong side of a local political dispute

Fulfilling her father's request, Maria arranged for her three sisters Lucita, Adita, and Consuelo to join her in the United States, August 1944. Only the youngest, Teresita, remained in the Dominican.

and was forced to move west to Barahona. This fact would often be used by Universal Studios in its promotion of Maria Montez during World War II. Teresa was often referred to as a Dutch refugee. To World War II readers, that equated escaping from the Nazis. That was, of course, not the case. Political problems were endemic to the Dominican Republic all through the late nineteenth and early twentieth centuries. It was one of these upheavals that sent Teresa and her family first to Enriquillo and then on to Barahona.[2]

Isidoro and Teresa eventually wed and had ten children. Their second child and first daughter, Maria Africa Gracia Vidal, was born at 8:00 p.m. on June 6, 1912, in Barahona. The Africa part of her name was a salute to the Spanish city of Las Palmas on Grand Canary Island off the coast of Africa where her father was born. Her five brothers were Isidoro, Aquilino, Joaquin, Luis, and Jaime. Her four sisters were Adita (sometimes called Ada), Consuelo, Lucita (Luz), and Teresita. Isidoro and Maria were born out of wedlock as their father had to disengage himself from a relationship formed in Cuba before he could formally marry their mother.[3]

Once Maria Montez became a Hollywood star there was considerable interest in where this bundle of energy and aggression had come from. Charles Samuels set out to write the definitive article on Maria for *Motion Picture* magazine in 1946. He had been a newspaperman, news service reporter, press agent, and would eventually write biographies of Jackie Gleason, Clark Gable, and Evelyn Nesbit as well as co-author the autobiographies of Ethel Waters and Buster Keaton. In Samuels's 1946 essay on the life of Maria Montez he set out to find "the real secret of the success of the startling senorita who became famous as the most eccentric flower in the garden of wacks and wizards, goofs and geniuses, called Hollywood." To understand how Maria achieved success in the film capital, Samuels thought it was important to learn about her childhood and the events that formed her ambition. Like so many writers of the time he caricatured her accent in print. She told him, "But dolling, my youth was so dool. . . . It would be of no interest to anyone." But the writer was persistent, and after "much wheedling" he was sure he got the answers he was after. What he got was a lot of nonsense about her nonexistent life in the Canary Islands.

Maria told Samuels the story of the Sacred Heart convent school she supposedly attended from eight to seventeen. Suitably, in accordance with her Hollywood dreams, she claimed to have acted in and directed plays. Some of her summers were spent in the castle-like villa her father owned in the Canaries. She said she saw little of her parents as she grew up since her father was in the Dominican consular service and was assigned to one great European city after another. None of this is true, but it is a perfect example of her father's tremendous influence on her imagination and her enormous desire to make her life story sound more compelling, romantic, and cosmopolitan to US audiences than it actually was.[4]

Her widower, Jean-Pierre Aumont, finally got to the Dominican Republic in 1954, three years after his wife's death, after he had presented his recent films at a festival in Punta del Este, Uruguay. He met four of his brothers-in-law and Maria's mother for the first time. He spent a week with them in Barahona. Flor de Oro Trujillo, President Trujillo's daughter, came to one of the many events held in his honor. His reaction to the place is indicative of why Maria invented the Sacred Heart convent and her life in the Canary Islands. Aumont wrote that after seeing Barahona, "I couldn't succeed in imagining Maria's childhood in this tropical village."[5]

In spite of what she told Charles Samuels, Maria lived a life absolutely common for one of her class and place in the Dominican. A dutiful oldest daughter, she helped her mother raise her nine brothers and sisters as well as

Teresa's godson, whom she adopted when his parents died. She went through the eighth grade at a local school and married a safe, wealthy man at age twenty. It is not that she did not stand out in her hometown. She was always known as a smart, very expressive girl. When she was in third grade Maria was asked by her teacher to give a presentation on the three heroes of the Dominican revolution against Haiti—Juan Pablo Duarte, Francisco del Rosario Sánchez, and Matías Ramón Mella. Not content merely to recite, the nine-year-old gave a performance featuring physical and facial gestures. This got her thrown out of class but the kids loved it. When she was fourteen, Maria was chosen to welcome the pastor to the inauguration of Barahona's new Catholic church. She gave a short speech and presented the priest with a bouquet of flowers. She also gave performances on a stage she set up at her house. Her father was always one of the most enthusiastic audience members.

The young Maria dedicated herself to learning English. In her mind she planned to eventually move to Hollywood and get into the movies. To do this she simply had to speak English. She studied it in school and constantly read American movie magazines. Like many of her classmates, she sought out English speakers, especially those who worked for the local West Indies Sugar Company and lived in the Batey Central colony near Barahona. Knowing that her goal to reach Hollywood would also require a fetching figure, from grade school Maria was always dedicated to exercise, especially long walks around her hometown and playing baseball—in which, of course, she was the pitcher.[6]

Nice childhood memories, to be sure, but not the youth of the woman of the world Maria thought herself to be and wished to project. The Barahona of the early twentieth century was connected to the rest of the country only by ship. A road would not link the small city to Santo Domingo until the 1930s. This was simply not how Maria wished to portray herself and her surroundings. Her father's stories of his childhood in Las Palmas were so much more interesting.

Gracia was a very successful grower, so successful that he was appointed an honorary vice consul of Spain to the Dominican Republic. This was strictly an honorary title and was given due to his business success in the Dominican and because he was formerly a resident of Spain. It did authorize Isidoro to periodically perform official functions on behalf of Spain. But this was not enough for Maria. She claimed he was a member of the diplomatic corps, which is how he was portrayed in Universal's publicity machine and his daughter's fantasy re-creation of her youth.

William Gourley MacFeeters became the second important man in Maria's life in the Dominican Republic. He was the local representative of the

National Bank of New York (now Citibank), a key economic partner of the Dominican government. He lived up the street from the teenaged Maria, and though he was twice her age, he came to love her and asked her father for her hand in marriage. Her father consented, seeing MacFeeters as a good and stable man who would take care of his favorite daughter, now twenty. She had been raised to be the wife of an upper-class husband and that is exactly what she became. They married by proxy on November 28, 1932, while MacFeeters was in San Juan, Puerto Rico, having been transferred there by his bank. The union must have pleased Isidoro. His daughter's future was secure. He traveled with her to Puerto Rico, where the couple was married in a Presbyterian church, that being the religion of the husband. Isidoro was suffering from a weak heart and lived only a short time after the marriage.[7]

Perhaps to make sure she had her own money, perhaps because he had listened to his daughter's hopes of becoming an actress, Isidoro left his eldest daughter $20,000 ($381,505 in 2021) in his will. It was this nest egg that allowed Maria to pay for her trip to New York in 1939 when she left her husband to become a movie star. She told a British interviewer that had her father lived she would never have pursued a film career. Her mother did not approve of her daughter seeking a career. Maria would have stayed married to MacFeeters and been the wife her social class demanded. But her father did die and his favorite daughter eventually felt free to chase her Hollywood dream and had the money to do it.[8]

William MacFeeters is the perfect example of what happens when a Hollywood star sucks all the air out of the room. In all accounts of Maria Montez, he is dismissed as the old guy from Ireland who married the nubile seventeen-year-old Maria. She had to be seventeen because Universal shaved eight years off her life to make her twenty when she signed her initial contract. His name is usually inaccurately given as McFeeters, a small difference but indicative of how unimportant he is deemed to be in the tale of Montez. He is often identified as an Irish soldier who became a banker. Sometimes the couple is described as living in Belfast, other times in Santo Domingo or San Juan, Puerto Rico. It didn't really matter where. In the Hollywood story of Maria Montez, he was presented as just a deluded middle-aged man discarded by Maria after a year or so because she had been too young to know what she was doing when she married him. Plus, he stood in the way of her becoming a movie star.

MacFeeters could no more play a part in Maria Montez's life in Hollywood than James Dougherty could have a significant role in Marilyn Monroe's myth. They were both dismissed as guys who took advantage of young women,

Maria at seventeen, Marilyn at sixteen, by marrying them. Reality so often has nothing to do with the created universes of movie stars. It was claimed in many articles that Montez got her start doing plays when she lived in Belfast with her husband. This is not true. She was in Belfast only briefly when he took her to meet his family in 1936. If nothing else, MacFeeters certainly helped open the world to a young, inexperienced Maria. During their seven-year marriage they traveled extensively by first class to New York and Europe and lived well in various cities in the Dominican Republic and Puerto Rico.

This dismissal of MacFeeters is very unfair to one of the most substantial men in the Dominican Republic. He was a key representative of the National Bank of New York, which was critically involved in the finances of the island nation. William Gourley MacFeeters was from Raphoe, a small town in Donegal near Belfast. He was born March 13, 1893, the oldest of five children of William and Elizabeth MacFeeters. He became a part of the Irish diaspora of the nineteenth and early twentieth centuries. He sought his fortune in Canada, immigrating to Winnipeg, Manitoba, in 1912. MacFeeters joined the Royal Flying Corps on February 11, 1918, under short service, or for the duration of the war. When he entered service in Toronto three months later, he became a clerk for the aviation cadets in the newly christened Royal Air Force. After mustering out in November 1919, he decided to move on to the United States. MacFeeters, now listed as a bank accountant, swore he was neither an anarchist nor a bigamist, and immigrated to Chicago. He eventually came to New York City and got a job with the National Bank of New York in 1920. The bank was in the process of expanding into the Caribbean and Central America. MacFeeters, who spoke Spanish, was sent to the Dominican Republic. He remained there, mostly working out of the capital, Santo Domingo, with time spent in Barahona, San Pedro de Macoris, and San Juan, Puerto Rico, until moving to La Paz, Bolivia, after World War II.

All we know of what Maria felt about her union with MacFeeters are her various comments in interviews and writings that she married too young and too spontaneously. But she was twenty and the marriage was by no means a rushed affair. There were no children from a union that lasted seven years. It seemed more a cultural expectation than anything else. The only indication we get from what MacFeeters felt about all this was the fact that he divorced Montez from Puerto Rico. Maria once asked interviewer Charles Samuels not to write about him in the article he was preparing about her life. "But do not mention my ex-husband's name, plizz," he quoted her. "Every time it ees mentioned, he writes me angry letter. Let the poor man rest in peace, yes?" Interesting choice of words. MacFeeters clearly was just a thing of her past.[9]

One thing that is certain is Maria was kicked up a notch in Dominican society and had a chance to experience the wide world beyond Barahona thanks to her marriage to the banker. Their home was given as Santo Domingo (renamed Ciudad Trujillo in 1936) whenever they traveled. This was the capital of the Dominican Republic and of far more importance in the country than the isolated agricultural center that was Barahona. Whenever they traveled, they were in the first-class section of the ship. Maria had come from a leading family in Barahona and married one of the wealthiest, most influential men living in her country. She always did imperious well in her films and came by it naturally from the life she led before she left the Dominican Republic. It would, however, affect her relations with the crew on the sets as she was filming. In the beginning she tended to treat them as servants.

Thus Maria, by birth and by marriage, was at the apex of the social structure in the Dominican Republic. Yet in spite of all that, it is evident she already had a considerable fantasy life and was frustrated by her circumstances. Montez biographers Margarita Vicens de Morales and Vivian Perez both tell the story of a married Maria meeting some friends from Barahona in Santo Domingo. They spoke a bit, then went their separate ways. Two hours later those same friends saw her in a jewelry store pretending to be an American tourist. The friends tried to say hello to her but she behaved as if she did not understand what they were talking about. Whatever her position in Dominican society, it was not the life she dreamed of.[10]

Maria's seven-year marriage to William MacFeeters certainly served to open the world to her. Prior to her marriage she had rarely left Barahona. Their delayed honeymoon trip to New York was incorporated into MacFeeters having to report to the central headquarters of his bank in September 1933. He and his wife, listed as Mary MacFeeters and traveling on an English passport, sailed on the S.S. *Caracas* bound for San Juan and New York. They had a much more extensive vacation in 1936 when MacFeeters took his wife back to his hometown in Ireland. On the way they toured through France and England. All of this would be part of the Montez creation. She included this trip on the biographical data sheet she filled out for Universal when she first arrived at the studio in June 1940 and mentioned it often in interviews she gave over the years. Just like the fantasy about the convent school in the Canary Islands, her actual European travels were aimed at presenting her as a sophisticated, cosmopolitan citizen of the world—not a girl from an isolated agricultural town in the Dominican Republic that was not even connected by highway with the capital until Maria was a married woman.[11]

When the couple returned to New York from Europe in February 1937, MacFeeters reported to the National Bank and then returned to his job in the Dominican. Maria stayed in New York by herself for five months before returning to Santo Domingo and her husband in July. There is no record of what Maria was doing for those months on her own in New York. Clearly, she emerged with a better understanding of Manhattan. When she left her husband and returned to the city in May 1939 to become a movie star, she at least knew the various nightspots and restaurants that would allow her to be seen and possibly to meet the sort of producer who could start her on her way. Plus, in those five months in New York she found out she could get along on her own.

Elizabeth Russell, a friend of Montez from New York, was her roommate when she first moved to Los Angeles. She wrote a screenplay called "A Star in Gemini" about her friend that is the closest thing we have to a personal memoir about Maria. The title comes from both Montez and her astrologer Carroll Righter thinking she was the perfect Gemini in that she has a split personality: part good, part bad. Russell has Maria romantically arriving in New York escorted by the character patterned after her lover, Englishman Claud Strickland, who brought her up from the Dominican. (There will be more about Strickland later.) It is interesting that Russell, who knew Maria intimately in New York and Los Angeles, would make Strickland such a key part of Montez's arrival in the United States. It demonstrates how vital Russell considered him to be in her friend's life. It also is indicative of how completely overlooked another important man in the Montez saga has been.[12]

Maria came to New York via Palm Beach, Florida, escorted by millionaire yachtsman Thorne Donnelley. He had been cruising through the Caribbean since December 2, 1938, fishing and visiting Cuba, Puerto Rico, Haiti, northern South America, and the Dominican Republic on his yacht *Mako II,* commanded by Captain Frank Seabrook. Donnelley was a very wealthy man, not given to hanging out in dockside dives. His wife and two daughters were with him, and he gravitated to the highest society of the places he landed. Somehow on this extensive voyage he met Maria MacFeeters, and she was added to the ship's entourage. She had clearly made up her mind to finally leave MacFeeters and make the attempt to conquer Hollywood, and Donnelley gave her the method to carry out the initial part of her plan. They arrived in the boat's home port of West Palm Beach, Florida, on April 21, 1939. Maria was examined and admitted to the United States on an eight-month visitor permit. She was listed as being married, with her husband living in "Trujillo," Dominican Republic. Donnelley had to pay a $10 tax because he failed to furnish a manifest for his alien passenger. From West Palm Beach the *Mako II* made its way north to New York, arriving on June 3.[13]

Montez is often portrayed as living with a Bavarian count and countess in New York. It was the sort of story she would have told, as it would put her in with European royalty. In reality she was still living on the *Mako II* when she left New York for Universal City a year later. Her host Thorne Donnelley was one of those rich young men with a guaranteed income in life dedicated to making his own way in both business and sporting endeavors. He was born in Chicago in 1896 into the family that owned R. R. Donnelley and Sons Company, which printed most of the telephone directories in the United States. The company also operated in the direct-mail and cartography fields. Donnelley inherited a $6 million trust fund ($123,131,000 in 2021 dollars), though he had little to do with the family company. After serving in the US Navy during World War I, he started the Donnelley Radio Telephone Company and from 1939 to 1940 constructed several radio stations along the shores of the Great Lakes to improve ship-to-shore radio communication to better safeguard shipping. During World War II he stored the *Mako II* at the Daytona Beach Boat Works and rejoined the US Navy. He was instrumental in developing the art of photographic interpretation, which played such a huge part in gathering intelligence for the war in the vast Pacific Ocean.[14]

Donnelley was what was described at the time as a sportsman. He did not seem to have a job he had to report to. He was very involved with hunting, hiking, and auto racing, but his favorite pastimes were boating and fishing. He loved his yacht the *Mako II.* It was no small putting-about boat. It was a Gloucester-type motor vessel built in 1937 and requiring a crew of five. The boat's several cabins were described as "beautifully and comfortably equipped." It had a length of eighty feet and a breadth of sixteen and a half feet.[15]

Donnelley also enjoyed the Hollywood crowd. Errol Flynn lived on the yacht for a time in 1939. Donnelley was known to love the company of beautiful women and Maria certainly fit the bill there. She apparently lived on the yacht during most of her time in New York. Donnelley left no memoir, so there is no way to know what their relationship was. He is totally absent from any of the stories Montez told Hollywood writers about her early days in the United States. Donnelley certainly threw many parties on the *Mako II* and it was at one of them that Maria first met model/actress Elizabeth Russell, who became such a close friend. This is how Russell has her character first meeting Maria in "A Star in Gemini," but the boat's owner or whoever threw the party that brought them together is never mentioned in the screenplay. According to Russell, it was their great curiosity about the world as well as a shared Catholic upbringing and deep belief in astrologist Carroll Righter that made them such fast friends.[16]

One wonders if MacFeeters still harbored hopes of saving his marriage. He flew to Miami on February 5, 1940, and went on to New York two weeks later. His stated reason for coming to the United States was to confer with National City Bank vice president J. H. Durrell on Wall Street. If he did seek out Maria, there is no record of it. The destruction of the marriage had certainly not been his idea. It is possible only to speculate what the conversation might have been if they did meet in New York. It is known that after a month he traveled to San Francisco for a two-month stay in California. He left New York on May 18, shortly before Maria got on a train for Los Angeles to come out to Universal City. MacFeeters returned to Ciudad Trujillo. He never saw his wife after that and divorced her from San Juan in June 1941. The entire scenario is just a further demonstration of Maria's will. She left her home, family, and marriage to get into the movies. Nothing was going to deter her from that goal. Any man she became involved with in her future would be a part of her scheme to succeed in Hollywood.

Her first task in New York was to make friends with the owners and maître d's of the nightclubs and restaurants that would draw the Hollywood people Maria hoped to impress. Along the way she met several designers, illustrators, and photographers who wanted to use her as a model. She only said yes to one of the major designer/illustrators of this era, McClelland Barclay, whom she met at the El Morocco nightclub. The illustration Barclay made of her displays a beautiful young woman in a bathing suit lying next to water with a flower in her hair. What he said attracted him to Maria was that she was "the perfect cosmopolitan woman." Her lovely features did not mark her as any particular race or nationality.[17]

In the midst of trying to ingratiate herself with the nightclub people, Maria was living on the *Mako II*. The boat was anchored at 23rd Street in Beach Head, giving her easy access to the part of Manhattan she craved. Life was not dull for Maria. She fell in love with English stockbroker and member of the peerage Claud Dobree Strickland. Despite having absolutely no acting experience, she acquired a prominent agent in Louis Shurr, who lived in New York and was primarily a Broadway theatrical agent at that time. But he did connect Broadway clients with Hollywood producers looking for fresh talent. He got Teresa Wright signed up with Samuel Goldwyn for *The Little Foxes* shortly after he signed Maria. He was the perfect agent for the Dominican neophyte. As his client Bob Hope noted, "If you were his client, he believed in you so fervently that you could believe in yourself. . . . When you had a hit, it was your hit."[18]

Maria and her loyal agent Louis Shurr at the Mocambo, July 11, 1944.

Teresa Wright had at least been co-starring in the wildly popular *Life with Father* on Broadway for several months. Maria had no experience at all. When asked why such a top agent would sign someone so green, George Lozzi, a former agent and friend of Louis Shurr who became a major producer, responded, "Was she beautiful?" When informed that yes, Maria was stunning, he replied, "For Louis and the Hollywood of 1940 that would have been plenty." Louis Shurr was not the only fellow connected to Hollywood who thought a pretty face was sufficient. In a profile Pete Martin wrote on Ava Gardner, he reported that after MGM's Louis B. Mayer first saw some film of her sent from New York and heard her deeply rural southern accent, he said, "She can't act, she can't talk. She's terrific! Get her out here"—and signed Gardner to MGM.[19]

Maria's friend Felix "Fefe" Ferry, owner of the Monte Carlo nightclub, introduced Maria to Shurr. Soon after this another friend told her George Schaeffer of RKO Studios was going to be at the 21 Club. Maria got dressed to the teeth, collected Louis Shurr, and headed over to 52nd Street. Schaeffer was given the full blast of her flirtatious charm and expressed interest in signing her for RKO at $100 a week. But first he wanted her to take acting classes as well as classes to tone down her accent. Soon after Maria met Schaeffer, Ferry alerted her that Universal producer Joe Pasternak was going to be at his club so she showed up, once again escorted by Shurr. Pasternak wanted to sign her right then to a seven-year contract with six-month options for $150 a week. He didn't require her to take any classes and would provide a train ticket to Los Angeles. Maria began to plan her move to Universal City, where she could actually begin living out the Hollywood dreams that had fueled her imagination since she was a girl.[20]

The first part of Maria's plan had worked beautifully. Rather than go to Hollywood like every other movie-struck girl, she went to New York, found an agent who would introduce her to a producer, and came to Hollywood with a contract already in hand. It took her a full year of working at it, but she had consciously set out to get discovered and she was. Once signed by a major studio, her next task was to figure out how to get noticed, how to stand out from the horde of comely women constantly being signed by the Hollywood studios.

The year 1940 was the height of the studio system. Eight movie factories dominated Hollywood. The five major majors were MGM, Paramount, Warner Brothers, 20th Century Fox, and RKO. The three major minors were Universal, Columbia, and United Artists. The Big Five were perfect examples of vertically integrated corporations. They conceived, produced, created, distributed, and exhibited their product. The three major minors produced, created, and distributed their films but had no theater chains in which to exhibit them. United Artists was unique in that it was the home of independent producers who came to the studio with their own ideas. Columbia and Universal primarily produced B movies with periodic forays into A features. When Maria MacFeeters arrived on the Universal lot, the studio was almost exclusively producing B movies that would be shown in independent and second-run theaters scattered all over the United States. They were always on the lookout for beautiful young women who could distract the audience from the simplicity of the scripts being churned out by the studio. It was an added benefit if she could act, but by no means a prerequisite.[21]

In one sense, Maria's timing could not have been better. She was in a perfect position to take advantage of the blossoming Good Neighbor Policy, the federal government's effort to develop better relations between the Americas. The Germans had worked hard to improve their position with Latin American nations and the US government wanted to stop them. There were German agents all over Latin America, doing everything they could to enlist the southern nations as allies to the Nazis. Obviously, the US government was determined to fight German inroads into the Americas as strongly as possible.

Franklin Roosevelt's determination to improve relations among the nations of the Americas went all the way back to his 1933 inaugural address, when he proclaimed he was committed "to the policy of the good neighbor." He would renounce the right to unilaterally intervene in the internal affairs of other nations, so often practiced in the first three decades of the twentieth century, at the Montevideo Conference that December. The process of non-intervention in the internal affairs of Latin American countries and seeking to improve trade between the two Americas was kicked into high gear when the Office of Coordinator of Inter-American Affairs was created in August 1940 with Nelson Rockefeller as its director. Hollywood was signed up to help in the fight through the Office's Motion Picture Division, originally under the direction of Jock Whitney.[22]

They certainly had their work cut out for them. President James Monroe had declared the Monroe Doctrine in 1823 to end further European adventures in the Americas. It was not meant to interfere with the few colonies that still existed at that time, but it did mean an end to additional efforts to colonize or recolonize the Americas. From the Latin American perspective, it was evident the United States was proclaiming itself to be the dominant power in the region. After the Spanish-American War of 1898 Spain was gone as a colonizer, only to be replaced by the United States. The 1904 Roosevelt Corollary to the Monroe Doctrine held the United States would be responsible to European countries trying to collect monetary claims from Latin American nations. Therefore, the United States became the international policeman in the Western Hemisphere.[23]

The dichotomy between North and South America from the southern point of view is perfectly set up in *Ariel,* one of the most famous essays in Latin American literature, written by Uruguayan José Enrique Rodó in 1900. He used characters from Shakespeare's *The Tempest* to explain the sharp distinction between the two Americas. Latin America is represented as the soulful, passionate, aesthetic Ariel and the United States as the crass, materialistic Caliban. The south felt alienated, completely misunderstood, belittled, taken advantage of, and treated with no respect by the United States. This lack of respect and understanding felt by those south of the United States border extended to their portrayal in American movies with Latin characters. They were generally represented as stereotypically hot-blooded, highly emotional, and extremely loyal—if not too smart. If a Latin woman was offered the choice between a Latin and an Anglo man, she always chose the Anglo.

Hollywood played a part in supporting the Good Neighbor Policy, with several actresses being given a chance in the film industry as a result. Carmen Miranda was the most successful; Maria Montez was second. Lupe Vélez, Mona Maris, Olga San Juan, Movita, Margo, Elena Verdugo, and others were part of the program. But Hollywood's initial efforts did nothing but aggravate Latin filmgoers. They perpetuated the same old stereotypes spiffed up by Technicolor. *Down Argentine Way* (1940) was so full of obnoxious Latin stereotypes that a movie theater in that country showing it was actually burned down. Carmen Miranda may have been the most successful of the Latin stars brought into the system by the Good Neighbor Policy, but her crazed, ludicrously passionate presentation and fracturing of the English language with her caricature of a Latin accent infuriated many Brazilians because it did nothing but maintain North American stereotypes. When she returned for a concert tour in Brazil in July 1940 she was poorly received by the people who had been her oldest fans and was booed off the stage at a charity event she had organized. She did not return to Brazil until 1955.[24]

The Motion Picture Society for the Americas helped give advice for reducing stereotypes to North American filmmakers, and these certainly lessened over time. But throughout the war, in all of Latin America's newly wired for sound and recently built theaters as well as in the existing houses, with the exception of Walt Disney's animated and live-action *The Three Caballeros*, the favorite Hollywood fare were the key films of the period, not the movies specifically made with a Latin theme. J. D. Spiro reported on the rise of Latin women in American films and the problems Hollywood movies were having south of our border in a nationally published piece for Sunday supplements. After describing the new careers of Maria Montez, Nina Orla, Ilena Martínez, and Esther Fernández in the United States, he goes on describe what Latin Americans want from North American movies. "Much of Hollywood regards the new trend of films aimed at Latin America as a mistake. Most, including Latin performers, think Hollywood should keep turning out excellent pictures with their established stars and not try to deal in Latin characters or backgrounds. Efforts in the past have led to loud and frequent complaints of 'careless misrepresentation in characterization and story, lack of discrimination in casting and incredible errors in costumes and setting.'" As a case in point Spiro cites *Down Argentine Way,* which did well in the United States but was hated in South America.[25]

Proving the point, none of the Hollywood wartime films that were most popular in Latin America had any sort of Latin theme. Among them were *Mrs. Miniver* (1942), about the English standing up to the Germans, Ernst Lubitsch's masterful comedy *To Be or Not to Be* (1942), *Pride of the Yankees*

Universal often presented Maria as a stereotypically steamy Latin woman in her initial portrait sittings.

(1942), about Lou Gehrig, the romantic *Random Harvest* (1942), Mitchell Leisen's psychological musical *Lady in the Dark* (1943), Tay Garnett's *Mrs. Parkington* (1944), which told the arc of a woman's life, and Charles Vidor's take on Chopin, *A Song to Remember* (1945). Europe, with the exception of England, was largely a lost market to the Hollywood studios after 1940. Latin America was wide open and received unprecedented attention from Hollywood. The studios even paid for the wiring for sound of many theaters.

US films typically claimed 70–90 percent of Latin American screens, depending on the country.[26]

Maria Montez may have been the latest beneficiary of Hollywood's attempt to be a Good Neighbor but before she reported to the studio, she had to improve her resident status. She had been in the United States on a visitor's visa. She had to update her status to permanent resident. To do this, she took the Santa Fe Railway out to the coast and headed for Mexico. This was necessary because she had to cross the border and reenter the United States through the port of entry at San Ysidro, then an independent town bordering San Diego and just north of Tijuana, Mexico. She entered the United States alone as Mary MacFeeters, née Gracia, twenty-eight years old, under the Dominican quota. She used as a reference English actress Elizabeth Earl, who had been signed by Warner Brothers and had passed through San Ysidro several months before Maria. She gave the address of the same apartment building claimed by Earl at 137 South Peck Drive in Beverly Hills. Her permanent place of residence was given as Trujillo City and her most recent address Thorne Donnelley's yacht *Mako II* in New York City.[27]

Once her immigration status was in order, Maria was free to travel north to Los Angeles and report to Universal. She was part of a recently signed contingent that *Variety* would come to call a "Crop of Screen Sirens" because "Glamour Girls [were] Still Potent Bait." The article covered recent signings by all the studios. Besides Maria, described as a "South American looker," Universal had also signed Broadway's Carol Bruce, Texas-born model Anne Gwynne, former Salinas, California, telephone operator Kay Leslie, eighteen-year-old Mexican "pepper pot" Nina Orla, who was a dancer in New York nightclubs, and British star Anna Lee.[28]

Maria arrived in her new city alone. She had a major agent in Louis Shurr, but that was it. There was no mentor/producer helping to guide her career, and unlike scores of Hollywood hopefuls from Gloria Swanson to Myrna Loy, Ginger Rogers and Yvonne de Carlo, Montez did not have a mother single-mindedly pushing her career while watching out for wolves. She also had absolutely no acting experience. The only things she had were her natural beauty and a singular, laser-focused determination to succeed. Initially she stayed at the Beverly Wilshire Hotel in Beverly Hills before finding an apartment in that city with her friend from New York Elizabeth Russell. She had her foot in Hollywood's door. Now she had to make an impression and get on the screen.

2

Universal City

The Universal Studios that welcomed Maria Montez to its San Fernando Valley lot was four years into its latest transmogrification. Like so many of the early film companies, it was started by a salesman who stumbled onto the phenomenon of projecting movies. It was founded by Carl Laemmle who was born in the kingdom of Wurttemberg, in what would become Germany, in 1867 and immigrated to the United States in 1884 with $50 in his pocket. He initially settled into the German Jewish community in Chicago, where he found work as a bookkeeper, later settling into the clothing business. He eventually began operating a string of nickelodeons, and later organized a film exchange network.

Laemmle quickly determined that the real money lay in distributing and producing the product to be projected in his nickelodeons. In 1909 he moved to New York and started the Independent Moving Pictures Company (IMP), which immediately came into conflict with Thomas Edison's General Film Company. Edison, every bit as controlling a mogul as Cornelius Vanderbilt, Andrew Carnegie, or John D. Rockefeller, sued anyone who was making movies with his patented filmmaking equipment without being a member of his "Trust" and paying to use his equipment.

On April 30, 1912, Laemmle merged IMP with five other film companies to form the Universal Film Manufacturing Company with Laemmle as its president. Initially Universal made its movies around the Fort Lee, New Jersey, area, as did so many of the other early film companies. All that changed when Colonel William Selig demonstrated what a far better location Los Angeles was. You could film outdoors all year long, and there was an ocean, an island, mountain ranges, prairies, desert, and a growing city all in close proximity. As icing on the cake, Edison and his trust agents were a continent away. Selig's Polyscope Company had shot its first film in the Los Angeles area in 1909. Six years later, Laemmle opened Universal Studios on 235 acres of farmland in the San Fernando Valley slightly northwest of downtown Los Angeles to consolidate his operations.

As usually happens in a new industry, the movie business went through a period of shakeout in the 1920s. What had been a crazy mélange of dozens of independent companies filming all over Southern California coalesced by the mid-1930s into eight major studios with several smaller niche studios such as Walt Disney, Monarch, Monogram, and Republic Pictures. The eight major studios were divided into five "major majors" (MGM, Paramount, 20th Century Fox, Warner Brothers, and RKO) and three "major minors" (Universal, Columbia, and United Artists). The key difference was that the five majors were perfect vertically integrated corporations in that they owned theater chains to show their product while the minors did not. Universal made a variety of films at its San Fernando Valley lot. There was a late effort to acquire its own theater chain through leasing existing houses, but the Depression put an end to that idea. As a result, the majority of the studio's films were shown in independent houses in cities and small towns all over America. Universal was Carl Laemmle's fiefdom and he became so famous for hiring relatives and refugees from Europe that he inspired poet and cultural observer Ogden Nash to observe, "Uncle Carl Laemmle / Has a very large faemmle."[1]

Part of that "faemmle" was his son, Carl Jr., and his nephew William Wyler. His son, made production chief of the studio in 1928, determined that Universal had to make complex, grade A movies if it was ever to do battle with the major majors. He hit it big with the film version of Eric Maria Remarque's best-selling novel of German soldiers in World War I, *All Quiet on the Western Front* (1930). The film not only made a star of Lew Ayres; it was nominated for four Academy Awards and won Best Director (Lewis Milestone) and "Outstanding Production" (now called Best Picture) in the 1929–1930 awards.

The desire to produce class A pictures largely evaporated along with Laemmle's ownership of Universal following the financial disasters of *The King of Jazz* (1930), *Magnificent Obsession* (1935), *Sutter's Gold* (1936), and *Show Boat* (1936). Carl Laemmle lost control of his studio when he was unable to combine quality productions with solvency. He had taken out a $750,000 loan from the Standard Capital Company, a Wall Street firm that specialized in making loans to struggling companies. Laemmle sold his studio on Universal's twenty-first anniversary, March 14, 1936. With the $5,500,000 sale, Standard Capital Company's president, J. Cheever Cowdin, became the new head of the studio, with Laemmle associate R. H. Cochrane serving as company president while Charles R. Rogers was made production chief. Along with one of the largest lots for Hollywood production, Standard

Capital also received controlling interest in the corporation's fifty-two distributing organizations and subsidiaries located throughout the world. The name Universal was retained for the making of films.[2]

Cochrane and Rogers did not last long. Universal kept right on losing money under Standard Capital's ownership. After two years the duo was replaced by Clifford Work as production chief, although his background was not in making movies but in exhibiting them, and Nate Blumberg, who was also in exhibition rather than production, as president of the company. J. Cheever Cowdin continued to control the finances out of New York. Under their leadership Universal finally regained both solvency and the need to start taking on new contract players for all the productions the studio was planning.[3]

Following the Laemmles out the door were many of the other Europeans Uncle Carl had put on the payroll. The new Universal was cut to the bone in an effort to make it profitable. Luckily for the new ownership, Deanna Durbin, who had been dropped by MGM when it felt it could only retain the services of her or Judy Garland, not both, became wildly popular. She was instrumental, along with all those great creepy horror movies the studio made and the organizational skills of the new management, in saving Universal from closing. Durbin, of all the Universal contract players, had her own unit, led by Joe Pasternak, producing her films. But the new regime concentrated primarily on producing grade B features, serials, and newsreels. The few class A films that emerged from Universal in this period were generally the work of visiting producers or directors, who were often forced to use studio contract players since Universal helped fund their films.

Maria Montez was not immediately headed for any of those rare A features. Universal had to figure out just what it had in this obviously beautiful woman. She was a contract player, under salary to the studio but with absolutely no experience. She first had to get settled. After initially staying at the Beverly Wilshire Hotel, Maria found a nice two-bedroom apartment in Beverly Hills with her New York friend Elizabeth Russell, who was determined to give up modeling and make it as an actress.

Russell had a taste of filmdom when she first came to Hollywood in 1936 at the behest of her friend Zazu Pitts. She won a few parts at Paramount, but returned to New York and her modeling career when her option was not picked up in 1938. She had married Rosalind Russell's brother, John, in 1929 and had a son, John Knight Russell. They were divorced in 1937 during her first sojourn to Hollywood. After her divorce and with her friend Maria going out to Hollywood, Elizabeth decided to give the movies another try.

She returned to the Paramount lot in 1944 and was the model for the painting of Mary Meredith who becomes the evil haunting spirit of Windward House in the classic ghost story *The Uninvited.* But her most memorable moments on the big screen occurred initially due to her friend Maria.

Peter Viertel was writing *Saboteur* for Alfred Hitchcock at Universal when he met Maria. His mother, Salka Viertel, had been an actress and screenwriter in Vienna before immigrating to America in 1928. She became a screenwriter for MGM, specializing in films that starred her friend Greta Garbo. Every Sunday at her house in Santa Monica Canyon she held parties for fellow European exiles and Hollywood friends passionate about current events. It would have been exactly the crowd Montez wanted to be part of. Peter Viertel's friend RKO producer Val Lewton asked if he knew a woman who looked feline for a picture he was preparing called *Cat People.* Viertel asked Maria, and she suggested her roommate Elizabeth Russell. On a double date—Viertel with Maria and Russell with Austrian count Friedrich von Ledebur—Peter urged Russell to go see Lewton. She met with Lewton and the two clicked. Much like Leo G. Carroll with Alfred Hitchcock, Ward Bond and Jack Pennick with John Ford, William Demarest with Preston Sturges, and Woody Woodpecker with early George Pal, Russell became part of Lewton's stock company. She appeared in small parts in virtually every film Lewton produced at RKO.[4]

Maria helped get her friend's career in gear, but at Universal she was just another in a long line of inexperienced contract players the studio signed over the years. The studio had a set protocol for grooming their new contractees for life in front of the movie camera. Maria's first job at the studio was to fill out a biographical data form to help Universal publicize its new player. The document, from John Joseph's publicity department, asked the new player to "please answer all questions fully and frankly" on the form since "writers of special publicity features generally find 'angles' for stories in facts, experiences, hobbies and individual likes and dislikes." Maria did her best but much of the form was left blank and she never once had to use the back of the page "for additional information" on any of the questions.[5]

She noted three names on the first page. Her professional name was already Maria Montez, chosen because her father's favorite entertainer was the nineteenth-century dancer and entertainer Lola Montez. Her birth name was Maria Gracia and her legal name was Maria MacFeeters. She was living at the Beverly Wilshire Hotel. She came clean on her birth date, listing it as June 6, 1912. It must have been the studio that changed it to 1920 to make her officially twenty years old when signed. Maria prematurely checked off "divorced" when it came to marital status and left everything blank relating to her former husband. Also blank was anything having to do with her youth in Barahona. She listed her birthplace as "Dominican Republic" but started the often-quoted fantasy that she went to school at the nonexistent "Sacred Heart convent in Santa Cruz on Tenerife" in the Canary Islands.[6]

Another commonly told story that emerged from her data sheet was that she tried to run away from the convent to return home but only got so far as the pier when school officials found her. The constantly repeated fantasy that her father, Isidoro Gracia, was in the diplomatic corps came from Maria listing his occupation as "Spanish Consul and Delegate of Embassy" rather than rancher. This was purely an honorary position. He was never an official of either the Spanish or Dominican government. This led to invented stories of her having lived all over Europe while her father was in the diplomatic corps and her meeting William MacFeeters when Isidoro was supposedly stationed in Ireland. There was one straightforward answer in this section. When asked what was the lowest period in her life, "when things looked blackest," she answered, "When my father died."

Montez always wanted to project an urbanity and appreciation of the wider world. She wrote that her father served as consul in Shanghai. Her athletic diversions were riding and swimming. Her interests other than sports were dancing, reading, and writing. She had a collection of antique jewelry and Goya prints. For clothes preferences she listed evening dresses, which she liked to wear to dinner parties and in café society. She spoke Spanish, French, and English and had visited Spain, England, France, Ireland, Scotland, the West Indies, the Canary Islands (in this one case, only in her dreams), and the United States. Asked what brought her the greatest satisfaction, Maria answered, "Coming to America."

What Maria makes very evident on the studio's biographical data sheet is how thrilled she is to actually be in Hollywood. Harking all the way back to the plays she made up as a girl in Barahona, her first ambition is listed as "acting." She lists the "high period" of her life as "Coming to Hollywood" and when asked "What do you like or dislike most about Hollywood?" she answered, "I like all of Hollywood" and "all the beautiful people around." One thing that might have given Universal pause was her note under "What was your first job?" She wrote, "Modeling for McClelland Barclay," which occurred when she was twenty-seven. Maria listed her favorite actors as Paul Muni and Greta Garbo, but regarding her own stage or screen experience, she wrote, "None." Asked, "Who or what was responsible for your start in pictures? How did your start come about? What breaks did you get? (Please explain fully)," she responded simply, "Joe Pasternak."

The Universal publicity department released the first "Maria Montez—Biography," gleaned from her data sheet, to the press in September 1940. After listing her legal name, birthplace, and date, nationality as "Spanish," height, weight, and coloring as "reddish brown hair, brown eyes," it starts off with prominent artist McClelland Barclay choosing her as "the true cosmopolitan woman." It establishes her upper-class credentials by moving on to the story of her diplomat father, Dutch mother, and the fantasy Sacred Heart convent, since like "all daughters of well-to-do Spanish families, Maria was early in life sent to convent school." There is no mention at all as to why her father's name was Gracia and hers MacFeeters. The biography just has her completing school at Sacred Heart and traveling through Europe until she finally arrives in the United States, where "she quickly made friends" and, forsaking her upper-class background, "discovered a new ideology which people termed 'economic independence.'" After modeling for Barclay, she was introduced to Joe Pasternak, who flew her out to Universal to take a screen test. Other aspects included are her nine brothers and sisters, collection of Goya prints, antique jewelry ("claimed to have once been part of fifteenth century Queen Isabella's crown jewels, famous in the story of Columbus"), her love of swing and opera music, her admiration for the writing of Spanish author Vicente Blasco Ibáñez, French authors André Maurois and Alexandre Dumas, and Englishman William Shakespeare, and that she enjoys reading, piano, swimming, and horseback riding. At the end it is noted that her first role for Universal will be opposite Johnny Mack Brown in *Trail to Paradise* (later changed to *Boss of Bullion City*). Her age is never mentioned, only that her birthday is June 6.[7]

Gossip columnist Hedda Hopper had a friend at Universal who let her see a stack of biographical data sheets. Maria's original was not in the stack, but a subsequent sheet filled out in 1941 after she had appeared in several small parts was. In this Maria wrote of how she was trying to get used to being on sets and on film. There was also a question asking what the contract player's parents wanted her to be. Maria responded, "A wife," which is what she had indeed become, fitting in exactly with the expectations of her class. It was the life she lived for seven years with William MacFeeters, until after her father died and she had been exposed to the world far beyond the Dominican and finally decided to throw it all over to become a movie star. She was only starting out as she filled out the Universal paperwork, but she knew where she was heading and her parents' wishes had nothing to do with it.[8]

Several things happened to new contract players after they finished their initial biographical data sheet. The next step was also an initiative of John

Ray Jones photographs Maria at the Universal portrait studio, 1940.

Joseph's publicity department. It was necessary to have eight-by-ten-inch glossy photos to submit to newspapers and magazines along with the biography sheet. Maria immediately trekked over to the portrait studio, run by Ray Jones. He had been the head of Universal's stills department since the shakeup in 1936 forced out so many of the Eastern Europeans that had been part of the Laemmle regime. Polish-born Jack Freulich had been brought over from the major photographic distributor Underwood and Underwood to head Universal's portrait studio from its inception in 1920. Ray Jones was one of his assistants from 1929 to 1932, when he quit to freelance at Paramount, Fox, and Columbia for four years before returning to run the department.

Jones and Maria hit it off immediately. She realized how important glamour shots would be for her career and trusted Jones to bring out her best in photographs. In a 1941 article he wrote as a guest columnist for Paul Harrison, Jones argued for the importance of still portraits in the success of an actor. He thought they might eventually take the place of screen tests in determining the suitability of perspective contract players and the development of versatility for established actors. As an example of the part still photography could play in a career, he cited the case of Maria Montez. Over one thousand

In this studio portrait from her first sitting, Maria's right arm is pulled well back to emphasize her breasts and give a hint of cleavage.

photos at a cost of $35,000 had been shot of her "before she ever played an important role." He credited the portraits he took of her in the sarong she would wear in *South of Tahiti* with convincing producer-director George Waggner to give her the part.[9]

One of the most commonly used photographs from these early sessions showed Maria in a dark bra top and full skirt leaning back on a pillow. It was printed on *Yank* magazine's pin up page. The photo also wound up in the *Albuquerque Journal* Sunday movie section. The caption writer perfectly summed up why so many of Jones's photos of Maria worked so well, noting, "That come-hither look is one of the obvious reasons for the rise to stardom of Universal's lovely Maria Montez." Jones was able to translate all of the sensuality he saw in one of his favorite subjects to photograph. When subjects showed up at the portrait gallery, they were first taken in to makeup and then to the dressing room, where the clothes for the session would be waiting. The lights would be set up at either one of the walls of the studio, a blank drape or a set piece mock-up, depending on what the publicity department wanted from the session. Universal's publicity department had been instructing Jones to simplify his backgrounds since the majority of the photos would be printed in newspapers. The eight-by-ten-inch negatives would be developed in the studio lab and a proof print created. The chosen images were then taken to a roomful of women who would retouch the negatives, removing any flaws in the sitter, however slight. Finished prints would be made from the retouched negatives, to be sent to magazines or newspapers, in response to fan requests, or to be exhibited at theaters showing the actor's movie.[10]

The first session in Jones's gallery set the template for the early photos of Montez released by Universal. The first group of portraits stressed her sensuality and Spanish roots. She is wearing a white dress with scooped neckline and a black mantilla. In the second group she has on a flowered sunsuit with a deep V neckline, and her shoulder-length hair is brushed well off her face. In the third setup she is in a dark-colored dress whose top has a tie that comes up around her neck, leaving her sides and back bare. She is clearly not wearing a bra. The leaning-back pose stresses both her breasts and, thanks to a fill light, her dark hair hanging away from her back. She is wearing the topaz bracelet she brought from the Dominican Republic.[11]

All three setups accentuate Maria's beauty. Universal was clearly preparing her to be presented as a glamour girl. She looks at the camera with a languid expression, bedroom eyes, and no smile. This is just not how comediennes or innocent ingénues were presented to the public. All of the photos are from the waist up and there is an obvious emphasis on her blatant sexuality. Studio photographers were largely precluded from showing cleavage by the Motion Picture Production Code, generally referred to as the Hays Office after its original administrator Will Hays. It had originally been set up by the major studios in 1930 to censor their movies and publicity. Its rules became more strongly enforced when Joseph Breen was appointed in 1934 to administer

From Maria's first sitting with Ray Jones, 1940.

the office and forcefully apply the dictates of the code. So, breasts had to be covered, cleavage retouched out.[12]

The Montez photos were perfect examples of how to circumvent the code by the subtle exposure of breasts. The third group with the dark dress shows a side view. The key light on Maria's face and upper body illuminates her breasts without exposing any cleavage. The deep necklines of the other two dresses hint at cleavage without directly showing it. This type of shot was not uncommon for studio portrait photographers of the time. When Jones had to show that Gloria Jean was now eighteen and no longer the child star she had been, she was posed in a tight bra top to a sunsuit and shot from the side. The photo perfectly shows off her breasts without showing any skin. Rules may have been set down by the Hays code, but there was always a way to dance around them.[13]

Montez's second session with Ray Jones followed the same pattern as the first. She is once again lying on a divan with a dark-colored midriff top and a light-colored skirt. Her right arm is drawn sharply back to make her chest more prominent. It is a three-quarters view of her, which aims the left breast directly at the camera while the right breast is in profile. There is no cleavage on display, but her breasts explode out of the photograph. It's all in the lighting, clothing, and body angle. The retouchers narrowed her waist on the right side by scratching the negative. The second group taken in that session continued the Spanish theme. This time she is wearing a white mantilla that sets off her dark hair perfectly. The makeup people and retouchers made certain there were no flaws of any sort visible on her face. The photos that came out of the studio portrait galleries were never meant to be pictures of people; they were pictures of glamorous movie stars. Jones's products were photos of Maria Montez, certainly not of Maria Gracia or Maria MacFeeters.

The beauty of Montez and the skill of Ray Jones in transferring it to photographs would be continuing hallmarks of her career. A perfect example came four years after her initial sessions with Universal's chief portraitist. *Screenland* magazine did an article on tall girls in the movies. The text largely concerns Rosalind Russell and Alexis Smith. The mention of five-foot-seven Maria is a story of her father telling her to be proud of her height, to "accept it as a mark of superiority." Accompanying the article is a Ray Jones photo of her looking impossibly elegant in a long black gown with lace appliqué on the bodice. The caption reads, "Another stately lady, Maria Montez: tall, but so terrific!" Three of the six photos depict tall women in bathing suits, but it is the single pic of Maria that expresses the most obvious sensuality. Photographs of Montez were at least as important to her career as her films.[14]

Roman Freulich, Jack's younger brother, joined Ray Jones in the photo studio in 1940 and shot many portraits of Montez. Ed Estabrook took both portraits and numerous "candid" photos of her away from the confines of Universal City. George Hurrell placed her in his *Esquire* portrait series, the Esky portrait postcards, and the datebook he produced for the magazine. Jack Albin, Gene Lester, and Bob Wallace were only three of the "specials" who shot for movie magazines that always looked forward to working with Maria

In another trick of the photographer, once again Maria's right arm is pulled well back to make her braless breasts more prominent.

Perfectly lit Ray Jones portrait stressing Maria's Latin roots.

because she was so cooperative. She put forth a huge effort to make every photographer she worked with happy, believing that happy photogs made better pictures. They were far more integral to introducing and revealing her to the public than the minimal exposure she received in her earliest movies.

The portrait studio was part of the publicity department, so it should be no surprise that the flak emanating from Universal matched the photographs. In her early days the studio labeled her the "Mmmm Girl"—a takeoff on her name and the perceived delectability of their new contract player. In reference to her home island and to take advantage of the Good Neighbor

Policy, she was also referred to as "Dominican Dynamite" and the "Caribbean Cyclone." In a nationally released blurb, Universal called Montez its "Spanish beauty." The studio started using the sobriquet "the Queen of Technicolor" after *Arabian Nights* was released in early 1943.[15]

Universal never complained when columnists invented even more seductive ways to describe Montez. Allusions to her Latin heritage were common. To Associated Press writer Amy Porter, she was a "new and luscious movie girl from Santa Domingo." To the *Oakland Tribune,* she was one of the "Latin Lovelies" out to conquer Hollywood. To columnist Sheilah Graham, she was "the South American threat." Jimmie Fidler was not that interested in her nationality. He thought she deserved "the most-theatrical-personality-in-Hollywood-award." One year later he expanded his view, writing, "She is as temperamental as a lynx with a toothache, as determined as a pit bull, as uninhibited as a monkey in a zoo and as egotistical as George Bernard Shaw." Comparing her to silent vamp Nita Naldi, he also thought "she is a throwback to old Hollywood days when sensationalism was the rule."[16]

Universal was doing its duty by its new contract player. The studio helped pave the way for her initial contacts with columnists. Her biography sheet was circulated among Hollywood scribes and all members of the multifaceted Hollywood publicity machine, as were the photographs taken by Ray Jones. Studio heads had already decided to put her into a harmless western movie called *Boss of Bullion City* to see if she could act at all and, more important, how she registered on film. As did all the studios, Universal also set up well-publicized dates with known men about town and other contract players so its recently signed actors would be mentioned in columns and photographed for newspapers and fan magazines. This early in her career Maria was completely unknown, so she was strictly mentioned as the girl some well-known man was with.

The first time Maria was mentioned in the *Los Angeles Times* was in its "People Are Talking" section: she was seen with Tim Durant, "sportsman" and friend of Charlie Chaplin on June 9, 1940, at the Paragon Room of the Victor Hugo restaurant shortly after she arrived on the lot. A month later Broadway columnist Dorothy Kilgallen reported that MGM's chief production designer and former husband to Dolores del Rio, Cedric Gibbons, was "wooing another Latin lass, Maria Montez." According to Harrison Carroll and Jimmie Fidler, by November she was the "Gal Pal" of Universal's recently divorced Mischa Auer; the two were spotted at Bill Jordon's Bar-Music on Beverly Boulevard and the Pirates' Den on La Brea, where Auer amazed the crowd by playing the piano with two grapefruits. Later that month the *Los*

Here Ray Jones accentuates both Maria's eyes and the fullness of her left breast. The studio photographers were not supposed to show cleavage, but Jones gets a hint of it here.

Angeles Times has her at a large party at Leo Carillo's house in Santa Monica Canyon with Auer, several other Universal stars, and William Boyd, Joel McCrea, and Mickey Rooney.[17]

All this hype followed the studio's tried-and-true method of introducing a newly signed ingénue to prospective audiences. Universal had lots of experience introducing women contract players to movie fans. *Variety* did an article on how new movies were being delayed by the scarcity of new faces, except in the Valley. "Universal has been second to none of the majors in building new players." The program for integrating new contract players into the studio was much the same for Anne Gwynne, Peggy Moran, Marie McDonald, Evelyn Ankers, Elyse Knox, or Carol Bruce, who were signed about the same time as Montez. The only difference was Maria was not native to the United States. She was a "Good Neighbor." For starters, her accent had to be reduced. Then the studio would have to find her niche: the role that would set her in the public mind. Because of her accent, there was the further decision to be made of whether she was going to be allowed to develop into a general-purpose actress or become an ethnic stereotype like 20th Century Fox's Carmen Miranda or Universal's own Lupe Vélez.[18]

But that was the studio's job. Most of its new contract players left it up to Universal to control their publicity and mold their image. Not so Maria Montez. She was convinced she had to get noticed immediately if she were ever to advance her career. She was not content to leave her future and lifelong dream to a business entity that had more pressing concerns than the career of one minimally paid contract player. She had had the drive and single-minded dedication to leave her family, a life of privilege on the island of her birth, and her husband of seven years to trek to the United States to become a movie star. She had no intention of relying completely on Universal to advertise her presence.

In the earliest days of her career, as Maria was in the process of deciding the course of her self-promotion, she met Henry Rogers at a nightclub. If anyone could give her competent advice about furthering her career, he was the man. His nascent career as a Hollywood publicist had recently gotten a major boost when he managed to get a young Rita Hayworth the cover of *Look* magazine on February 27, 1940, as she was filming *Strawberry Blonde*, the film that would kick her career into another gear. He did this by assuring *Look* that besides having an important movie coming out, she had won a nonexistent award for being the best-dressed actress when off-screen.

In the 1940s, most publicity, like casting, was handled by the studios themselves rather than outside specialists. Meeting Rogers gave Maria a unique opportunity to speak with someone outside the publicity department at Universal who understood how to build up her name recognition. He certainly understood what a publicity agent could do for someone in Hollywood, as well as the profession's limitations. He did not know Montez and had never worked with anyone from Universal. But when she asked him how to get recognized, he gave her key advice: "To interest the papers—you've got to be one of two things—important or unusual. You're not important, so be unusual, be the exception. Step out and tell the world 'I'm the great Montez, the most beautiful creature in Hollywood and the best actress.' Step out and say, 'Look at me.' They'll look alright." Maria wanted to know what reaction she could expect. "The reaction will be who-the-hell-does-Montez-think-she-is! But they'll talk Montez. I don't give a whoop if they praise you or damn you. Just let them talk about you. Then it's up to you."[19]

Montez met Rogers soon after her appearance in *Boss of Bullion City.* She was still feeling her way in Hollywood at that time. The quick bit of advice he gave her fell in a fertile field. It fit in perfectly with her natural inclinations and nascent plans to break out of the herd of Hollywood ingénues and become a star. She rapidly set about figuring out how to become "the exception" Rogers spoke of. The ideas she began to develop turned into the several themes Maria would repeat over and over again with indefatigable determination. Film historian Jeanine Basinger caught the Montez spirit perfectly when she observed, "As a character says in *'Arabian Nights,'* looking at her, 'She is a young moon, mounting the stairway to the stars.'" Indeed, Basinger commented, Montez was mounting that stairway "by stomping right on up."[20]

Montez took stock of herself and concluded that the two things she had to sell were an alluring physicality and a playful personality. The easiest thing to start selling was her physical presence. She was five foot seven, statuesque for a woman of that era. Her figure was almost perfect by American standards—thirty-five-inch bust, twenty-four-inch waist, and thirty-four-inch hips. By constant exercise and careful dieting, she kept her weight around 120 pounds. All this might seem like arcane, worthless fandom knowledge. But it was what was going to get Montez onto the screen. She understood right from the beginning that she knew nothing about acting for a movie camera. She always was aware of what a liability her accent was. With time she planned to overcome these two obstacles. Meanwhile, she had to get noticed. Her face, body, and personality would be her tools to make Universal, Hollywood, and America conscious of her.[21]

The first thing she had to deal with was her pronounced accent. In this she had the full backing of the studio. Several columnists at the time, especially Sheilah Graham, thought it was fake and she was trying to take advantage of the current interest in Latin actors. This is ridiculous. She had fought to control her accent in English ever since she arrived in New York. She had several language coaches supplied by the studio over the years. Attending speech classes before it signed her was one of the demands made by RKO when she spoke with that studio in New York. Universal had agreed to put

An effort to show her cultured side while keeping her sexy: Jack Albin's photo for a fan magazine taken at Maria's apartment.

that off until she was on the lot. But Montez found her accent such an obstacle that she felt she had to "distract producers from that with my looks and clothes and manner."[22]

This was not an attack on Maria's ethnicity. Americans in 1940 had scant patience for actors in major roles having serious accents. Sidekicks were expected to be colorful and a pronounced accent was often part of their character, but not so stars. Greta Garbo, Marlene Dietrich, and Ingrid Bergman made it to the top echelon of Hollywood because they were able to minimize their accents and be intelligible to most Americans. Even the Germans who escaped the Nazis only to wind up playing them on Hollywood screens, such as Conrad Veidt, had to tone down their Teutonic accents. Paul Lucas was Hungarian and had an understandable accent that allowed him to play all manner of Europeans. For all the extensive buildup she received from Paramount in 1938, Francesca Gaal never could reduce her accent sufficiently and soon disappeared from Hollywood. Mexican-born Dolores del Rio was able to make the transition from silents to talkies because she had only a mild accent. Statuesque model Anne Gwynne impressed the Universal people when she first auditioned for them in June 1939 but was told she had to take diction lessons to lose her Texas accent. Over in Culver City, newly signed Ava Gardner spent hours with an MGM language coach working to lose her incomprehensible rural North Carolina accent. The first thing Julia (later Julie) Adams had to do before she was signed by Universal in 1949 was lose her pronounced Georgia accent. The same was true for Atlanta-born Evelyn Keyes. Carmen Miranda and Lupe Vélez were the exceptions to the rule. They used their accents to comic stereotypical effect. It was part of their act.[23]

While continuing to work with a language coach, Maria decided to start her own fan club to increase her recognition. She called it the Maria Montez for Stardom Club. Universal, like all the other movie studios, had a very well-used mailroom. Since one of the biggest requests the studio received was for pictures of the stars, boxes of photographs were in a cabinet with the names of contract players and the number and type (portrait, publicity, or fashion) of the prints. The studio noted the amount and kind of mail players received as a way to judge their popularity with the all-important fans. If the letters were not requesting a photo, they might be commenting on one of the stars, a recent role the star had played, or how the star looked. It was all kept track of by the studio publicity department, which reported its findings to the front office. It was not an easy thing to move fans to write to the studio when you had appeared only briefly in obscure movies. Maria wanted to keep her mailbox active, so she started writing letters to Universal from the Maria Montez for Stardom Club and encouraged her newfound fans to follow suit.

Maria creating her own club was not exactly a well-kept secret. Hedda Hopper observed, "Maria Montez had to get attention before she got a career." In one of her longer Sunday columns, called "She's a One-Woman Avalanche!" the columnist examines how "this Latin American bundle of nerve and determination" first got attention in Hollywood. It certainly was not from appearing in her first few movies, since "you had to watch awfully close in order to see her . . . and she was bad—wow!" According to Hopper, her first recognition came from camping out at the portrait studio and starting the Montez for Stardom Club. Suddenly letters started arriving at the mailroom "asking when they would really see her. She began to get good parts. Many letters she wrote herself."[24]

Taking Henry Rogers's advice to heart, Maria set out to "be unusual, be the exception." She fastened on five themes that most actresses either did not talk about or would have thought ridiculous. Columnists and fan magazines were only too happy to publicize the themes because they were so unusual and she was so intriguing. Pete Martin wrote an article for the *Saturday Evening Post,* "Dominican Dynamite," that covered this period. In the ultimate testament to what great copy Maria was always sure to be, he noted that if Los Angeles city editors were ever faced with a slow news day, they barked at their reporters, "'Get out to Beverly Hills and see that Montez dame!' Nor do the reporters often come back empty-handed. For, though Maria is a ball of fire in the studio, in her own drawing room she is Halley's comet colliding with a super nova."[25]

Her spirited antics outside studio control drew interesting responses from two of her fellow contract players. Anne Gwynne wished she had followed Maria's example. "I wish I had been more insistent on better pictures. Maria Montez complained about absolutely everything and told me not to be so cooperative. They made her a star, and I'm sure her demands had a lot to do with it." Rosemary de Camp also completely sympathized with Maria's dedication to self-promotion, believing Universal did not do enough to publicize her and her unique talents. Remembering the studio's treatment of Montez, she said, "Oh, poor child, you know they really used her very badly. . . . They wouldn't treat her well and she was constantly angry." Whether envious or sympathetic, Maria's fellow Universalites understood her dedication to self-promotion.[26]

The good news was that just as Maria's career was starting, Universal, like all the other studios, was encouraged to keep working by the federal government despite the US entry into the war. The studios were expected to work closely with the Office of War Information's Bureau of Motion Pictures to help the government explain to the American people the nature of the enemy, what the war's aims were, and how it was necessary that the populace support the war by working in defense plants and buying war bonds and stamps. Hollywood had to help the government convince the public that this was a war to maintain the national existence and protect the American way of life. To play its part in both instructing and entertaining Americans as well as producing films for the armed services, the film industry was declared an "essential activity" by the federal War Manpower Commission. Granted, it was number twenty-nine of thirty-one, but it was there. L.A.'s other great industry, the building of airplanes, was number one. To remain an "essential industry" the studios had to create new stars the public wanted to see. Montez was determined to be one of them.[27]

The first theme Maria started working on to make her an exception was something she had all to herself. However minimal her actual screen time may have been, she was quickly acknowledged as the finest commissary actress of all time. Vern Haugland wrote an entire column about the spectacle that was Maria having lunch at the Universal commissary. He observed, "Dining, for Maria, is an intensely dramatic experience. She puts tragedy into the slicing of a steak, and she butters bread with wild abandon. There's passion in the way she consumes a dessert." The performance with her food was always mesmerizing and often accompanied by costume changes. "Yesterday it was a pair of white shorts and bra and a great deal of exposure. Today she is the lady in green—a long, svelte green gown, with green tie rag, and a large green picture hat." The Universal male component was always aware of her presentation. "Andy Devine . . . gasps, then squeaks at Brad Crawford, 'Look, look; here comes la Montez.' Charles Boyer, solemn, serious, stares as long as politeness will allow. Hugh Herbert kittenishly calls, 'Woo, woo, oh Maria.'"[28]

The female component was also aware of Maria's antics. In 1942 Marjorie Lord, who would go on to television fame as Danny Thomas's wife in his popular sitcoms in the 1950s and '60s, was a newly signed Universal contract player with considerable experience on the stage. She watched Montez enter the cafeteria with awe. Like everyone else, Lord went to the cafeteria to get a bite to eat and have a conversation after a long morning of making movies or preparing to make one. She knew Montez was a "wheeler, dealer. She had a very strong personality. She came into the cafeteria like a star. Notice me, notice me! She wanted all eyes on her and if they weren't, she found a way to make them look." Lord never saw anything else like it in her long career.[29]

Montez quickly realized she had a winner with her commissary antics. Not only did her behavior get her known around Universal, a number of magazine articles based on interviews with her appeared. In one of his syndicated national Sunday newspaper pieces, Dee Lowrance wrote how Hollywood might be facing a manpower shortage due to the war, but "they won't ration glamor." He noted the many new attractive actresses cropping up at all of the studios. One of them was Maria Montez. Lowrance saw her as "another young thing with more than the usual gifts as to face and figure." He thought what really set her apart was her own campaign for stardom, part of which started with her first visit to Universal's commissary. He described her arriving alone and starting to read one of the trade papers. "As her eyes perused the news, her face reflected her reactions—smiles chased themselves across her mobile face, frowns, grimaces, moans etc. followed rapidly. Every so often a silvery giggle startled the room. . . . Soon everyone was saying, 'Who is she?' and the studio started putting her in pictures in self-defense." As Louella Parsons summed up, Maria "was never born to bloom unseen."[30]

Many of the earliest fan magazine articles on Montez stressed the brilliance of her commissary performances. Freelance movie scribe John Franchey wrote several pieces about her. In *Movies* magazine in March 1942, he delighted in describing her commissary antics as "a show comparable to changing the guard at Buckingham Palace." A wag dubbed her the "Commissary Cornell," referring to Broadway great Katharine Cornell. When the performance is finished, she sits sidesaddle in her chair with her legs crossed, fumbles in her purse, leaves a handsome tip, and "sweeps" from the room. Franchey wrote that Montez came for lunch while shooting *South of Tahiti* "in a sliver of Paisley wrapped around her hips, a form-fitting flowery bra adorning the upper torso and a very intellectual volume under her arm. Waitresses do double takes, leading men choke on their roast beef, and jaded producers perk up." To cap the performance, she is paged for a telephone call.[31]

Franchey also described the second theme Montez developed: her equally spectacular entrances into nightclubs. In a 1942 article in *Silver Screen* he called this practice "a work of art" with staging "right out of De Mille." Carole Landis might "prance smilingly" into Ciro's in a satin evening dress, creating "what might be called a minor furor." But when Maria comes in: "You glance up and there she is, standing atop the landing, caparisoned in one of those black how-does-it-stay-on-without-straps dresses. . . . She stands there ten seconds, maybe, as if she had never been in Ciro's before and was, you might say, casing the joint." The band goes out of tune; oohs and aahs sweep the place. All the wolves in the restaurant perk up. "Waiters turn around to look, the supreme compliment." Photographers prepare their flashguns. Montez descends the two steps into Ciro's, "gliding gracefully over to the best table in the house, the headwaiter leading the play and her escort tagging along behind her." And all this dramatic flair from an actress who had only played small parts in five largely forgettable movies. When Franchey asked Maria if her behavior was an act she replied, "Of course it is." It was just another aspect of the wildly-desirable-woman image Montez created and continued to perfect.[32]

Showing up at the Mocambo with an established star, in this case Rudy Vallee, was a sure way to attract photographers, February 10, 1941.

Part of this act was intended to catch the attention of people that could be beneficial to her career. In late 1946 she told Dan Reeve, who had taken over Harrison Carroll's column while he was on vacation, that when she was in a club, she watched to see who entered. If someone like David Selznick or Samuel Goldwyn came in, she would go out and make a new entrance herself. She claimed to have made twelve entrances to the same place one night, with photographers snapping away each time. After *Arabian Nights* she was able to tone down the act since she now was starring in important movies that made a lot of money for Universal. "Don't think, though, that I didn't work for it."[33]

Sheilah Graham was one columnist who was never a fan of Maria. Having found out that her name was MacFeeters when she came to Universal, the writer thought she was probably a fraud, with an Irish American rather than a Latin American background. But even Graham could appreciate how Montez used nightclubs. In an April 1941 column she wrote, "Maria Montez, who says she comes from Spain—the studio says Puerto Rico—makes at least six entrances and exits every time she goes to Ciro's. She draws attention to herself with exotic clothes and an accent that is much too good to be true. Rumor hath it that her real moniker sounds Irish. But what difference does it make as long as Maria's non-screen behavior draws the important attention to her personality?" Three months later Graham was still in awe of how successful Montez was at drawing attention to herself in spite of a paucity of screen time. The columnist noted that Maria "looks through six fan magazines, finds her portrait in all of them and says, 'It's not enough.' Pretty good considering she's never yet made an important film." *Hollywood* magazine could only concur, noting that Montez was "the ranking entrance-maker in town."[34]

A third tactic that garnered the unknown actress a good deal of attention was Maria's often-told stories of how to keep "Holly-wolves" in line. This was an offshoot of her constantly noted penchant for appearing at nightclubs with a wide variety of men. Columnists in both the newspapers and fan magazines constantly ran pieces on who was out with whom. Maria gave them plenty of opportunities as she struggled for recognition prior to her starring role in *Arabian Nights.* Mischa Auer was her official Universal escort; they were reported on from May to November 1941. She was also linked with "sportsman" Baron Gerhardt von Wurnabund. There were photos of Montez on the town with Franchot Tone, Walter Pidgeon, Orson Welles, Rudy Vallee, Bruce Cabot, Pat DiCiccio, Stephen Crane, actor and narrator Truman Bradley, world traveler and eventual character actor Austrian count Frederick von Ledebur, Pulitzer Prize–winning playwright and member of the Algonquin Round Table Marc Connelly, Warner Brothers press agent Bob Taplinger, Hollywood Plaza Hotel owner Joseph Drown, and German international soccer player Kurt Kruger. Plenty of ink emerged about her relationship with Claud Strickland in the columns, but no photos since he was flying for the Royal Air Force in England. When Swiss bandleader Teddy Stouffer came on the scene the photographers and columnists kept pace. Her relationship with Jean-Pierre Aumont was followed avidly, if suspiciously, in the columns and fanzines.[35]

Since Montez was known to be such a serial dater, it should not have come as a complete shock that she would find a further way to exploit going out with so many men. This third tactic emerged about the time *South of Tahiti* was opening across the country in October 1941, in an article that would constantly be referred to until she married Jean-Pierre Aumont. The Gene Schrott essay appeared in *Motion Picture* magazine and featured a picture of a smiling Maria lying in bed in her nightgown, talking on a phone, with the caption, "Who's Afraid of Hollywood Wolves?" Photos of five said subjects—Gordon Oliver, Franchot Tone, Mischa Auer, Bruce Cabot, and Jean Negulesco—

appear on the right side of the page. The whole point of the piece is that Montez does not shy away from such wolves, nor is she in any way intimidated by them. Her attitudes toward dealing with men were very conservative, indicative of her time and ethnic background. Maria thought men should make passes at women, should be aggressive in their ardor. It was completely up to the woman to control the situation after the initial pass. Women friends often warned her about going out with prominent wolves, but she always ignored them. She found "Holly-wolves" much tamer than their continental counterparts. Their main problem, she contended, is they do not understand how to approach a woman. They must learn to be subtle and to take advantage of the situation—such as music, moonlight, and the mood of a woman. She believed "a man is never a wolf until a woman makes one of him." A woman lures a man to her and "deliberately assumes that 'come and get me' attitude. So, when you get to the bottom of it all, you can't blame the men."[36]

This pronouncement was followed by a self-penned article called "Are Men Such Fools?" and another done with her friend Gladys Hall, "Me and Men." She continued the theme of subtly controlling men in these articles. Women should not try to dominate or rule men. She describes her mother telling her, "You may be beautiful someday, Maria, and you may do important things. But never forget that you are first of all a woman, and that the world belongs to men. Do not try to take it from them. Let them give it to you—it is easier that way." It seems curious that as aggressive and demanding as Montez was concerning her career, she would espouse such conservative views of relations between the sexes. But the upshot was that a woman had to control the man in any relationship without making it obvious. Whether he was a wolf of the old school or a mild-mannered man, it made no difference. The woman had to be actually in charge while letting the man think he was. Her success with Holly-wolves became so widespread it made its way into a Jimmie Fidler column about Carole Landis, who had moved into a beach house next to Cary Grant and Randolph Scott. "Asked whether she could handle this situation, Miss Landis quipped, 'If I can't, I'll take lessons from Maria Montez.'"[37]

Montez continued her conservative advice to women that she learned from her mother in "How to Dress for a Man," another article she wrote. She argues it is the natural course of events that a woman dresses herself for a particular man, concluding, "If a woman does not please the man she wants to please in the way she dresses, what is there in store for her but unhappiness?" She suggests choosing feminine clothes with good, simple lines. Hats that make you feel beautiful. Be sure the colors are right for you, and wear jewelry "according to the preference of the man." A woman has to choose the correct presentation because all men want a woman "to look pretty, desirable, and sophisticated, too."[38]

All of this discussion of controlling men was part of Maria's campaign to stress her desirability and uniqueness. Maria wrote of dealing with wolves in South America, Europe, and the United States. It was exceedingly rare for a woman to speak of such a broad experience with men at that time. *Motion Picture* brought up the article several times, including in its "Glamour Issue" and the article, "Romance Is Rationed, Too: Don't Feel Sorry if You Haven't a Date Saturday Night—the Stars Are in the Same Fix." The magazine noted that Maria overcame this dearth of suitable dates by spending a lot of time at USO shows surrounded by soldiers. She, of course, has no trouble handling the room full of men since she can so easily control wolves.[39]

Montez was in New York when the article about her lack of fear of wolves appeared. After attending an Armistice Day premiere of *International Lady*, she spoke with author and syndicated humorist H. Allen Smith. He titled his article "La Montez Tells Women in General of Holly-Wolves." He makes reference to the revealing photographs that appeared in *Life* and then describes Maria as "tall, slender, with appropriate bulges and an accent." She is part of Hollywood's answer "to the demand for Latin American cultural identity." But what concerns him is her saying that all anyone wants to talk to her about is her being a specialist on dealing with Holly-wolves. Maria even spoke of writing a book on the subject, as she had already told columnist Harrison Carroll. Smith is loath to have such secrets get out. When he expressed his concern, she said, "Me, I am crazy about men. I am not a shrinking vine, but I would go crazy without the men. My book, I am only trying to get everybody like that. You see?" He certainly did see, and he worried about the effect of her telling all the other women of the country how to handle men. He was certain it would have a drastic effect on relations between the sexes in the United States. Smith declared he had a good mind to write in protest to Nelson Rockefeller, who was in charge of the government's efforts to grow the Good Neighbor Policy in Latin America, and see if he couldn't get him to can her opinions.[40]

The fourth part of the Montez drumbeat for attention was to accent how uniquely and dazzlingly gorgeous she was. The crescendo of the supposed self-worship came out of her first viewing of *Arabian Nights* and immediately became identified with her. The story went that she was watching the movie at a Universal screening and loudly exclaimed, "When I see myself on the screen, I am so beautiful I scream with joy." Whether this was spontaneous or purely calculated, it became one of the most popular quotes from la Montez.

This was not a phrase that one could imagine being uttered by Anne Gwynne, Teresa Wright, Joan Leslie, Joan Crawford, or any other woman in Hollywood since the days of the vamps in the silent era. It was Montez. She had been engaging in public self-worship ever since she arrived in Hollywood. When she was signed to play island woman Melahi in *South of Tahiti,* Montez explained to Sheilah Graham, "I play Dorothy Lamour—with oomph." She told her friend and columnist May Mann, "All day long I think up new ways of getting new publicity," and there is not much point in being coy about it. Using a variation on the *Arabian Nights* observation, she tells Mann that when she sees herself on the screen, "I look and I look. And I say that gorgeous creature. She is the most beautiful girl I have ever seen."[41]

When talking to the Associated Press's Robert Myers for his nationally published Sunday column, Maria admitted, "I'm sensational." This was the tenor of the interview; as Myers noted, "Maria and I had a talk one day about Montez, and I must report that at no time did Montez tire of the subject. Nor, as a matter of fact, did I." The author wrote that she was one of the "Sweater Girls." When she removed her coat in the Universal commissary to be interviewed, Myers commented, "Everyone smiles when Montez takes off her coat. That's showmanship." But no matter how tight the sweater, Montez wanted him to know, "I'm sensational—but proper as hell." Columnist Erskine Johnson also got the full treatment. "Maria Montez was talking about everything from Maria Montez to Maria Montez. Not conceitedly, mind you, but shrewdly. And there's no smarter damsel in Hollywood than Maria."[42]

Look magazine's February 23, 1943, article on her is a perfect example of how she presented herself and how she used her physicality to push along her career. The four key photos of the piece show Montez getting out of her car, with her dress fallen away sufficiently to expose the entirety of both legs and "her creamy shapeliness"; lying back on the car seat fully clothed but with her legs tucked to her chest in what looks like coital bliss; eating lunch with much cleavage on display in her *South of Tahiti* sarong; and lying on the floor looking over fashion sketches with designer Chadounne. The essay retells the standard nonsense created about her past. Her evident self-obsession is once again compared to Victor Mature. She proclaims, "I am the great Montez" and should possibly be rationed like meat or sugar, and "Did you ever see anything as wonderful as I am?" She described her first commissary performance where she delightedly read the *Hollywood Reporter* by noting, "I was quite sensational that day."[43]

Columnists often wallowed in Maria's uninhibited nature. When *Life* magazine did an article on Hollywood columnist Sidney Skolsky, one of the key photos is of the writer lighting Montez's cigarette from his own. She is in a black embroidered nightgown, showing some cleavage. For the caption to the photo, he wrote, "Maria Montez firmly believes that a woman should look her best in the bedroom. How do I know this? She told me so, and then I went to see for myself."[44]

This was the only one of the five themes that started to create fallout by 1943. In a January 31, 1943, interview with John Rosenfield, he listened to her sing her own praises. He thought she had gone about as far as this tactic would allow. "So far Miss Montez hasn't over-played her hand, although her methods are treacherous. Most correspondents dislike a too aggressive bid for publicity more than Garbo-Ginger-Jean Arthur inaccessibility." She has gotten away with it to this point because the scribes "find Maria Montez a warm and friendly personality and so far have been willing to abet her daring game." One month later Jimmie Fidler felt the time had run out on Maria's endless self-promotion. He wrote one of his "Confidential Communiques" to Maria: "Your egocentric outpourings to the press were getting attention at first, but you've carried them too far." Montez certainly paid attention to what was being written about her. In April she was telling columnist Erskine Johnson, "I talked to everyone. They thought I was a conceited fool. I don't mind them thinking I am a fool, but not a conceited fool."[45]

The *Look* article where she spoke so enthusiastically about her own beauty drew blowback in the letters to the editor column two months after the article appeared. Of the four responses, three of them condemned her often stated self-worship. Private R. N. Owens wrote, "I'm sure she could find a lot of men who could resist her if she would wander down Texas way. We have plenty of beautiful women there—but they don't believe in telling us so themselves."[46]

The criticisms led her to rethink the self-glorification she had been using up until that time. According to *Variety,* the Universal publicity department was being inundated with mail, especially from soldiers, making fun of Maria's bragging about how beautiful and desirable she was. The industry's leading journal claimed John Joseph's department "is doing a big tremble act with Montez fireworks in offing." Maria was quick to see the act was wearing thin. Whether or not there was a huge nudge from her studio, Montez changed tactics. Besides telling columnist Erskine Johnson she feared being thought of as "a conceited fool," in a March 1943 article in *Movie Show* magazine Maria admitted to Elizabeth Wilson, "Perhaps I am too egotistical." In New York that same month she "wearily" told the local correspondent for *Motion Picture,* "I'm tired of being sensational. . . . I want to get away from these mad publicity stunts and settle down to being a real actress."[47]

The fifth of Maria's themes really set her apart as "unusual." Film historian Jeanine Basinger described Montez as having "a perfect oval face, dark eyes, smooth, clear skin and a thick mane of hair. She was tall (five feet seven), full-bosomed, and had astonishing coloring." It was certainly common for actresses of the 1940s to speak about their skin and hair. But the "full-bosomed" thing—unlike almost all other female film players of her time, Maria was willing, even eager, to talk about and display the magnificence that was her breasts. The 1950s is generally thought of as the age of breasts in American movie history, with Marilyn Monroe, Sophia Loren, Jayne Mansfield, Mamie Van Doren, June Wilkinson, and many others "busting out all over." But there were stirrings in the 1940s.[48]

Lana Turner is at the top of this list. She was the original "Sweater Girl." Columnist and wit Dorothy Kilgallen did one of her "Voice of Broadway" columns on "things I never expect to see." Two of them were "Maria Montez refusing to talk for publication" and "Lana Turner in a padded evening dress." Jane Russell, whom Bob Hope described as "the two and only," spent the war years as a spectacular pair of breasts in photographer George Hurrell's memorable portraits for *The Outlaw* and dozens of magazine articles. Carol Landis was featured in a seemingly infinite number of pin up shots in bathing suits and clinging gowns. These women certainly used their breasts to garner attention and columnists quipped about them. But the women themselves tended not to directly talk about them no matter how much attention they attracted. Not so Maria.[49]

Jane Russell was a teenager completely in the hands of a man obsessed by her breasts. Howard Hughes thought deeply about Jane's breasts, constantly planning ways to exploit them. He urged photographers to emphasize them, dreamed up the type of costumes she should wear, even designed a special bra for them. Maria's campaign was strictly her own creation. In "A Star in Gemini," Elizabeth Russell's screenplay about her friend and former roommate, she has her Maria character explaining to astrologer Carroll Righter that what the audience wants is cheesecake. She pulls up her dress to display her legs, then pushes out her chest and tells him how lucky she is to have such a beautiful bosom. Montez thought most American girls made the mistake of emphasizing the wrong aspects of their bodies. She did admire them for being so casually pretty and able to hold onto their youthful looks. But, she told Courtenay Marvin of *Screenland,* her North American sisters were too concerned about the size of their hips. "Maria deplores . . . the attention and concern we lavish on hips instead of the bosom. A beautiful bosom, she points out, is a most important asset as the South American woman recog-

Maria on-stage with Doodles Weaver in January 1942. As an air jet blows her skirt up, the expression on her face is indicative of her early days in Hollywood, when she would put up with almost anything for publicity. The back of the image is stamped *Modern Screen* magazine, photo by Bob Beerman.

nizes." Montez then goes on to describe a series of exercises to help the bust and gives advice on how to choose the proper bra and clothing "to accent if this part of your figure is beautiful, to gracefully conceal if it is not."[50]

She spoke in the same vein to Ida Jean Kain in a syndicated column called "Your Figure Madam." When Kain asked Maria how a woman should carry herself, she responded, "I have never seen a woman who stood and walked gracefully who did not have a beautiful bosom. It seems to develop the muscles which have to do with the bust." Her measurements at this time were given as 34-23-35.[51]

She also emphasized her breasts by becoming one of the "Sweater Girls"—a sartorial choice subsequently banned by the Breen censorship office. One of the most famous pictures in her early career was taken by *Life* magazine's Peter Stackpole, showing a braless Maria in a tight sweater on a cold L.A. morning. The photo helped gain her national attention, given the popularity of the publication. Studio photographers such as Ray Jones and his assistant Roman Freulich were largely precluded from showing cleavage by directives from Joseph Breen of the Hays Office. To overcome this, the angle of the woman's body could be arranged so as to show off the breasts, as was often done with Maria. When George Hurrell set up his own photography business separate from the movie studios, he did not have to present his subjects as dictated by the Hays Office. He snapped the single sexiest photo ever taken of Montez at his studio on Sunset Boulevard. She is on the floor in a leopard-skin wrap with so much cleavage in view that her breasts are barely covered.[52]

In a note in *Modern Screen* magazine under the headline "Photo Phobias," it is noted that Hollywood stars react differently to the candid camera when out on the town. Rita Hayworth and Dorothy Lamour may be addicted to low-cut gowns, but when a photographer approaches, they shift an arm or find some other way to cover their breasts, while "Maria Montez wriggles into a more revealing position." This propensity is on display in the dozen photos that appeared of her when she was gathered with several other ingénues around the pool on the 1941 cruise to premier *The Sea Wolf.* [53]

Peter Stackpole was certainly not the only photographic recipient of Maria's skillful employment of her ample breasts to garner publicity. Gene Lester was one of the many "specials" who took photographs for the numerous movie magazines. He first came out to the West Coast in the late 1930s to shoot for *Radio Guide* magazine. He was soon taking pictures of Hollywood celebrities for publications as varied as *Photoplay, Look,* and (as West Coast correspondent) for the *Saturday Evening Post.*

Early in 1941 Lester was sent by *Photoplay* to Maria's apartment in Beverly Hills to do some photographs of her. When he arrived, lights and cameras in hand, she emerged from her bedroom stark naked. After registering his surprise, Lester, dedicated magazine photographer that he was, did not whip out his camera and start snapping away. He simply explained to Montez that she had to put on something as there was nowhere he could legally sell nude pic-

Maria, a big proponent of "a beautiful bosom," hated wearing a bra, as she demonstrated for Jack Alpin when he visited her for some photos at her Beverly Hills apartment, 1941.

tures of her. She retreated to her bedroom and soon called Lester in. He said he found her lying on her bed in a diaphanous dressing gown that was essentially transparent. "We should have a picture of my figure," she insisted. Lester had her pose at the window in profile, which rendered her nude in silhouette. When he printed the picture, Lester used a darkroom technique called "burning" to add light to relevant parts of the picture so it would be dark enough to show no detail, thereby allowing it to be published. It was from this session that the commonly available photo of Maria lying on her bed reading a horoscope magazine in a nightgown emerged. The collar of the gown is flipped up on the right side, clearly exposing her full breast and dark areola. This was a photo for his archives. No movie publication in the 1940s would ever have published such a revealing photograph.[54]

Columnists and movie journalists joined with photographers and Maria in emphasizing her breasts. She was famous for eschewing the use of a brassiere. Pete Martin wrote a long piece on her for the *Saturday Evening Post* that hit all the highlights of the Montez presentation. He saw her as "easily the outstanding exponent of uninhibited self-expression." He runs through the commissary period and the taming of Holly-wolves. When Martin said he would like to send a photographer to take some pictures, Maria observed, "I fit a sarong pretty well." When it came to wearing that sarong, he included a quote from an Earl Wilson column where she assured him, "Brassieres! My dear fellow, I have never used them. I have no need for them, thank Gawd."[55]

Sidney Skolsky wrote a piece called "Puts Her Best Points Forward" where he noted that GIs call Maria "The Bra Woman" because she rarely wears one and doesn't need it. He also explains her love of massage, that she takes sunbaths in the nude, and of course, that she slips off her black nightgown when she is ready to fall asleep—again in the nude. Earl Wilson slightly altered the nickname to "Bra Girl," noting, "She was wearing a revolting amount of clothes" when he interviewed her for a column three months later. He had been horrified to hear she was not going to do any more cheesecake. On the contrary, Montez replied. She told him that many of her friends called her "the Bust," and Wilson could expect to see more cheesecake in her upcoming movies. Terrific, he thought. Why would she quit it when she was so successful at it?[56]

The rest of the press certainly continued to pay attention to Maria's "best points." *Modern Screen* magazine printed the response of Edith Head, Paramount's multiple Academy Award–winning costume designer, who was asked which Hollywood stars had the most beautiful curves "between the neckline and the waist?" She named Dorothy Lamour, Veronica Lake, Ginger Rogers, Ann Sheridan, Joan Bennett, Olivia de Havilland, and Betty Grable. The outraged editor of the "Good News" section responded, "What? No Lana Turner, Lauren Bacall, Maria Montez, Paulette Goddard, Linda Darnell or Jane Russell? My goodness." A year later in the same magazine in the gossip column "Here's Hollywood" attributed to "Weston East," there was a piece about former juvenile actress Diana Lynn, noting that she was growing up. At a party given by David O. Selznick she wore a low-cut evening gown held up by one shoulder strap. Demonstrating how completely Maria had become shorthand for overt sexuality, East noted, "It would have been daring even on Maria Montez."[57]

Many people have dismissed Montez as just another pretty airhead because of her outrageous behavior. Her actions seemed so goofy and her pronouncements so fantastically self-absorbed it was hard to take her seriously. But, as with Hamlet, there was a method to her madness. She followed Henry Rogers's advice and her own inclinations in a single-minded drive to achieve recognition. Soon after she finished shooting the fifth of the six Neverland movies, *Gypsy Wildcat,* in December 1943, Maria sat down with her columnist friend May Mann and explained just how she rose from obscurity to the Neverland franchise. The piece was called "Maria Montez' Frank Advice to Movie Struck Girls." The article is not so much an advice piece as a fairly detailed account from Montez's point of view of just how she made it in Hollywood. She was actively trying to change her career and the perception of her by this point, so to her mind this was a historical article. It shows Maria to have been perfectly focused, creative in her planning, and utterly lucid about how she got where she was and how she wanted to move forward from there.[58]

Montez starts the essay by noting that everyone's pathway to stardom is different. She can only speak of her own. Before she ever got to Hollywood she asked herself three questions. "First, did I have an unusually photogenic personality? Second, did I have a driving force within me to be successful? Third, did I have any talent or aptitude for acting?" Obviously, she answered herself in the affirmative.

She did not come directly to Hollywood because the place was already knee deep in beautiful women who wanted to be in pictures. Instead, she went to New York. Her plan was to be seen in all the right places in New York "to cultivate the acquaintance of columnists and photographers. I dressed to appear spectacular." This would also bring her to the attention of the owners and maître d's of the major nightspots. "I figured this to be sound advertising and merchandising." She met an important agent (Louis Shurr) who wanted to represent her. She made it evident she wanted to be signed by one of the studios while in New York; she did not want to go out to the West Coast and be dragged from office to office hoping for the best. She "wanted to sign with the studio where I would have the best opportunity. So, I studied the list of contract players and stars at each of the studios, and chose Universal because there was no one there who conflicted with my type."

After signing in New York, Maria went to Los Angeles where she set her own publicity machine in motion. "When I reached Hollywood, I continued my policy of being seen often in public, and with people who would be of help to me through my being seen with them. I chose my clothes carefully and gave careful attention to my hairdos and my appearance." She worked constantly to improve her English and acting ability. At least twice a year she tried to get back to New York to renew her contacts with columnists, newspaper reporters, and magazine editors. She concludes, "Guiding my career is a business with me. . . . I managed to develop a girl named Maria Montez into prominence here where competition is keen and thousands do not succeed. . . . It is still hard work, a never-ending job. . . . And I love it; every minute of it."

The theme of the article is succinctly summed up in Maria's words "Movie stardom is a matter of complete concentration, just like success in any endeavor." Part of that endeavor is to get noticed. Here is where men come in. Maria's advice is, "Go to all of the right places with the wrong men!" By this, she means the sort of wolves who want to have their picture in the newspaper. "Your name will be mentioned with theirs in the columns. Overnight you become a personality that is known." As previously noted, she followed her own advice in quite the dedicated fashion. Maria Montez was linked with well-known Hollywood wolves. Her name was in the papers as a desirable young woman even if she had not yet appeared on screen.

Maria also offered advice as to the importance of columnists and movie writers. "You depend on their assistance completely to help you! Always have an interesting story to tell. Figure out new ones and keep several in mind. For the photographers—dress, so they cannot resist taking your picture!" Her entrances to nightclubs were well planned. "If I was groomed to look spectacular when I made an entrance at a night club, it was because I had planned it so." Entrances to the commissary were no different. She advised, "Never go to the studio looking like a hobo. . . . Make yourself an interesting personality. Remember every time you enter the studio, every time you enter the commissary for lunch, you are on the stage. Eyes are watching you. You must give a performance that will be pleasing. An actress cannot afford to 'let down.'" Columnist Jimmie Fidler, for one, thought she lived this ideal. He noted, "Maria Montez looks off-screen just like you'd imagine a movie actress should look off-screen."[59]

She claims in her "Advice to Movie Struck Girls" that one such entrance led to two producers seeing her one night after her astrologer, Carroll Righter, advised her to go to Ciro's and make an entrance in a stunning gown. This led to her role in *That Night in Rio* and testing for *Blood and Sand.* At that time, she had only done two walk-ons and one cowboy movie at Universal. Montez credited her entrance and general presence at the nightclub with capturing the attention of the 20th Century Fox producers. She was already signed up for *Moonlight in Hawaii* and *Raiders of the Desert* but, she claimed, when Universal saw her tests for Fox it led the studio to decide to feature her in *South of Tahiti.* That film clicking, coupled with how she looked in *That Night in Rio,* led to her home studio deciding to cast her in Technicolor features. All because she wore a great gown and displayed herself for two producers at Ciro's.

Given all this discussion of how to dress, it should be no surprise that Montez next advises her readers to never discount the power of cheesecake. "Some girls have talent. Some have legs. Girls must capitalize on them, as they do their brains. If you have legs, then let them be seen in your pictures." She

Maria makes her entrance at the Mocambo, September 1942.

certainly took her own advice to heart. There are not that many photographs of Maria in a bathing suit, but there are lots of photos of her showing off her legs.[60]

Maria had little to say about her studio in the extensive article with May Mann regarding how she made it in Hollywood. She concentrated exclusively on her own actions. While Maria was busily finding ways to publicize herself, Universal joined in the fight to publicize its new contract player. More important, however, it was struggling to find out where she ultimately fit. The studio decided right off that their Latin American starlet would not be defined by her ethnicity, as was the case with Carmen Miranda. She could not sing or dance, so those options were moot. Glamour seemed to come naturally to her, but how to exploit that? What sort of part could she be put in that would cause moviegoers to keep coming back for more? Universal had to find out if its new player was worth renewing after the first six months of her contract passed. So the studio started throwing Maria against the movie screen to see where she might stick.[61]

The studio wasted no time getting Maria into her first film. Universal specialized in B movies, and there were always plenty of productions in process or planning. In August 1940, two months after arriving on the lot, Montez was getting off Calhoun's Traveling Emporium wagon and meeting Johnny Mack Brown in Bullion City. He was one of the myriad cowboy stars heading his own series in the early 1940s. He did his first western film for MGM but soon found himself at Mascot Studios, Supreme Pictures, and eventually Universal. His chief western success would be with Monogram. But during his brief tour with Universal, he was assigned to a quick "oater" to be called *Boss of Bullion City* (originally *Paradise Valley*). The two-week shoot took place at the historical Iverson Ranch in Chatsworth. Films had been produced there since *The Squaw Man* in 1914 and would continue into the television age with *The Lone Ranger, Gunsmoke,* and *Bonanza* in the 1960s. *Boss of Bullion City* would not be one of the more memorable movies filmed at Iverson.

Brown stars as Tom Bryant, who arrives in Bullion City to open a newspaper with his pal Burt (played by perennial sidekick Fuzzy Knight). He quickly discovers the crooked sheriff has been staging robberies throughout the territory with his outlaw deputies. When a large shipment of gold is set to leave town, Bryant takes it from the Express Office to keep it out of the hands of the bad guys. He finds out that Mike Calhoun (Earl Hodgins) has sold his Emporium wagon and is going back east with his daughter, Linda (Maria Montez). The only person he told he was carrying $15,000 was the evil sheriff. Bryant assumes the sheriff will rob the stagecoach and sets out with a posse to prevent that. He successfully thwarts the robbery as homesteader Martha Hadley (Nell O'Day) rides up to help. Bryant makes sure the good deputy arrests the sheriff and the stagecoach continues on its way. Bryant saves both the gold and Mike Calhoun, exposes the evil sheriff, and earns the love of the brave, hard-working, skilled-riding, straight-shooting Martha. All in an hour.

You are wondering how Maria Montez wound up on a horse-drawn wagon with a name like Calhoun. The script explains she had been in a Mexican convent school since she was a child. Thus the accent. When she is

In *Boss of Bullion City,* "Linda (Maria Montez) decides to stay in Bullion City with Tom Bryant (Johnny Mack Brown)," according to the snipe.

introduced to the Mexican owner of the town saloon, they immediately begin to speak Spanish. It is the only time in any of her American movies that Montez spoke her native language.

Maria is no more than adequate in the fourth-billed role in this standard oater. But she looks magnificent, is dressed beautifully, and seems like absolutely no one else in the basic western town of Bullion City. As will be the case in *The Exile,* her last film at Universal, she seems to have nothing to do with her surroundings. There are three female characters in *Bullion City*. The daughter of the saloon owner dances to the accompaniment of her three musician brothers. Nell O'Day is a homesteader wearing simple western working clothes who can ride like the wind and shoot very accurately. In stark contrast, Maria is clearly a convent-bred, high-class woman—even if her father is a traveling peddler. The class differences among the three women are never mentioned, but it could not be more obvious. Maria was not yet the princess or queen she would so often be in her later films, but she clearly was from a higher social class than the other women. She is the only one allowed to pitch a fit in the movie. Her natural imperiousness comes through even though she is merely getting off her father's wagon. No one had to teach her how to project that. She was from the highest class in Barahona and married into the highest echelon of Dominican society. Her past carried over into her film career.

Following her fairly substantial part in *Bullion City*, Montez was soon given a miniscule one and a half minute walk-on in *Lucky Devils* in early September 1940 and a set-dressing part in the more substantial *Invisible Woman* in October. In the former, Maria is in a bathing suit after being picked to be the Mercury Newsreel "Bathing Girl of the Week." She won out over Andy's (Andy Devine) girlfriend, Gwendy (Janet Shaw), who says, "What does she have that I wish I had?" Maria, in her tight bathing suit, leans over her and says, "Size 34." As she leaves, she says a flirtatious good-bye. Andy watches her go. "Gee, she has a beautiful voice," he wistfully says.

A few weeks later Maria was filmed as a member of a group of models standing with Kitty Carroll (Virginia Bruce) who answered eccentric inventor Professor Gill's (John Barrymore as part of his prolonged, sad decline) advertisement to become the eponymous heroine of *The Invisible Woman*. The film was very successful for Universal, making \$659,600 on a \$269,062 negative cost. Maria had very little to do with this windfall. She has no dialogue in either of the two scenes that feature the models of the Continental Dress Company. In both scenes she wears very elegant gowns. In the second scene she at least gets a close-up two-shot as the chastised manager of the shop explains the new, more moderate rules of the company. Maria does a good job looking surprised.[62]

By December 1940 Maria had been on the Universal lot for almost six months. She was making dramatic entrances to the commissary and to nightclubs all over Los Angeles while the studio was still trying to decide what to do with her. Filming of newly signed comedians Bud Abbott and Lou Costello's movie *Buck Privates* was scheduled to begin in the middle of the month at Universal City. The comedy duo had largely stolen *One Night in the*

Maria in *The Invisible Woman* with title character Virginia Bruce.

Tropics, their first film for Universal, in supporting roles. But there was no particular reason to expect their first starring film would be anything other than just another comic quickie coming off the studio assembly line. *Daily Variety* was often used by the studios to plant notes about their upcoming films. On December 19, 1940, Hollywood's key publication connected Montez to a film for the first time, announcing she had been added to the cast of *Buck Privates.* A month and a half later, the original one-sheet movie poster was published by *Variety.* Maria was listed as one of "a bevy of Hollywood scintillating lovelies." As it turned out she was not in what would become one of the biggest hits Universal had ever had, bringing in over $4 million. The studio had an outside offer that seemed to promise to aid Montez's career far more than just being one of the "bevy of Hollywood scintillating lovelies."

20th Century Fox had decided to update the 1935 Fox Studios film *Folies Bergère de Paris* and, in the spirit of the Good Neighbor Policy, switch the setting from the French capital to Rio de Janeiro. It would be called *That Night in Rio.* Needing Latin women to be part of the film, Fox requested that Universal allow Maria to report to them as a loan-out. This was common under the studio system. The requirements of a new film sometimes demanded someone different than the home studio had under contract. A loan-out would then be sought from another studio. The benefit to the loaning studio was that its contract player was known to be in demand. Another boon was that the requesting studio always paid more than the usual pay level of the loaned player. The loaning studio kept the difference in salary. In *That Night in Rio,* Maria would play a South American dancer named Inez and be photographed in Technicolor. The filming was scheduled to run from November 15 to the first week of January. No one at Universal had any reason to believe the two knock-about burlesque performers that were Bud Abbott and Lou Costello would produce anything special with *Buck Privates.* But the studio jumped at the chance to see how Montez looked in Technicolor.

As of 1941, Universal had never filmed anything in what came to be called three-strip Technicolor. Part of Carl Laemmle Jr.'s effort to produce A pictures had been the studio's one foray into process 2 Technicolor. *The King of Jazz* (1930), starring Paul Whiteman, was a wild mélange of musical acts in very subdued, greenish color. Process 3 was a revelation. It was far more vibrant than any of the previous attempts. One drawback: while the third process was gorgeously soaked in color, it was also incredibly expensive. Universal was just a few steps up from poverty row and never had the necessary funds for such an undertaking. Not only was the film stock itself expensive and scarce, the producing studio had to rent special cameras as well as camera operators from the Technicolor company. The process required much stronger lights than was the case with conventional black-and-white film, and required the hiring of a color specialist for the lighting. Universal would not make its first Technicolor film for another year and a half, when the studio began filming *Arabian Nights* in June 1942.[63]

20th Century Fox was one of the five major major studios. Montez must have been thrilled when she first arrived on the lot in the Rancho Park section of West Los Angeles. Production chief Darryl F. Zanuck had one of the sharpest minds in the film industry. He also had far more money to throw at his films and some of the largest stars in Hollywood under contract. *That Night in Rio* would star Don Ameche in a double role as Baron Duarte and an American entertainer who impersonates him, with Alice Faye as his wife and Carmen Miranda as the chief entertainer at the nightclub they all attend. It was partially meant to repair some of the damage caused by *Down Argentine Way* (1940), which caused riots in some theaters in Argentina for its absurdly stereotypical view of the United States' Good Neighbors. Montez is in only one scene and is listed eleventh in the cast list as "Inez."[64]

She would make the most of her short time on the Fox lot. Montez used one of the ploys that had worked for her at Universal. Edmund Hartmann, a studio writer when *Rio* was being filmed on the lot, remembered her entrance to the cafeteria. She entered in a revealing dress and carefully surveyed the room. If she saw no producers who could help her career, she left. Regardless of how she came into the cafeteria, there is no record that Zanuck tried to inveigle Montez into the 4:00 to 4:30 sex romp he held every day in his office when he was "in conference." As a gorgeous loan-out she was exactly the sort of woman he would have tried to lure to his bed. But it was unlikely she would have acquiesced to his desires had he offered. He had nothing to do with her home studio and she would have seen Zanuck as just another Holly-wolf, albeit a highly placed one.[65]

Maria's part in *Rio* was small but she did get a close-up and dialogue in her only scene in the film. She is in none of the dancing scenes with the other chorus girls. At first all you see is Maria's legs as she walks backstage. A large box being carried by two men blocks her upper body. But the baron recognizes those legs from a past encounter and strikes up a conversation with her. The scene lasts less than a minute, but Montez looks gorgeous in Technicolor and is wonderfully flirtatious with Ameche as he lustily remembers their time together in Pernambuco. She runs up the stairs when the perpetually agitated Carmen Miranda arrives and pitches a fit. Their time on screen together is very brief, but in that time, Maria made the far more famous star look undernourished. Montez had great legs and was very generous about putting them on display. In *Rio,* she was put in the shortest possible dancer's costume Fox could get past the Hays Office. Her naturally auburn hair caught the light perfectly and her features looked much more attractive than they ever had in the programmers Universal had put her in. It is interesting to compare her appearance in the low-rent Universal B movie *Lucky Devils* and the Fox A movie *That Night in Rio.* Everything in the Fox film is perfectly lit and cleverly staged. *Lucky Devils* was a pure assembly-line programmer. Montez is indifferently presented and her scene is not milked for its inherent sexiness and comedy. *Rio* proved that when properly lit and costumed, Maria was a knockout.[66]

Montez must have made a positive impression on the producers at Fox. The bullfighting film *Blood and Sand* starring Tyrone Power was scheduled to begin shooting in January 1941, immediately after *That Night in Rio* was completed. Fox was having a hard time casting the role of Dona Sol. She was a very wealthy woman who lures Juan (Power) the bullfighter away from his loving wife, Carmen (Linda Darnell). The part called for someone who was imperious, gorgeous, and preferably could dance. Initially Zanuck wanted Carole Landis for the role but she refused to dye her trademark blonde hair black. The studio then pursued Hedy Lamarr, but MGM refused to loan her

Two ambassadors of the Good Neighbor Policy, Maria and Carmen Miranda, on the set of *That Night in Rio.*

out. Many more actresses were considered: Mona Maris from Argentina, Jane Russell, Gene Tierney, and Dorothy Lamour.

The studio went so far as to make a screen test of Maria Montez in the role of Dona Sol. The first two scenes she could have handled with ease. They both took place at the temptress's home and involved considerable dialogue. In the first scene she seduces Juan; in the second she deals with his wife coming to confront her. Carmen loses and Juan stays with Dona Sol. It is the third scene that helps explain why Fox convinced Columbia to loan them Rita Hayworth instead. Juan is at a nightclub with Dona Sol. His former friend and current rival Manolo (Anthony Quinn) asks her to dance. She consents, and the sensual dancing the two engage in makes it evident the wealthy woman is moving on to a new matador. This called for a talented dancer. The scenes in the film are mostly in close-up as the couple falls in lust on the dance floor. This was not something Maria would have been capable of. The part was a major boost to Hayworth's career and helped set her screen persona.[67]

Maria was finally able to take a break after *Rio* wrapped. She flew back to New York to spend time with friends and renew her acquaintance with eastern columnists. A *Life* magazine article on the Latin invasion that featured Montez arrived on the newsstands of the country while she was in New York. Two months later, on May 23, 1941, *Variety* reported that Universal would "retie Maria Montez" seven weeks ahead of the expiration of the option on her contract. She may not have starred in anything yet, but by mid-1941 things were starting to look up for the actress now being referred to by columnists as "la Montez."

3

National Stage

In a column about newcomers to the screen in 1941, Sheilah Graham had to give grudging admiration to the indefatigable Montez. The columnist described her as a girl who "has the facility of corralling publicity. For a girl who has made five 'B' films only, Maria receives tremendous attention from reporters and cameramen—particularly the latter. If her acting measures up to her sex appeal, Maria, who was born in the Dominican Republic should have quite a film career." Graham summed up how Montez had garnered all that attention although she had never starred in a movie. The Montez for Stardom Club, along with her relentless pursuit of columnists and fan magazines and being willing to pose for any photographer who asked, coupled with the efforts of the Universal publicity department, had helped garner some of the preliminary attention Maria was seeking. She had been in several forgettable Universal features, generally as little more than part of the scenery. Her biggest film was her loan-out to 20th Century Fox for a small but memorable part in Technicolor for *That Night in Rio.* Graham argued it was past time for her to find a part in a movie that would justify all the attention she had been getting.[1]

By mid-1941 Montez, who took the columnists' words very seriously, knew she was little more than a curiosity: "a commissary actress," a maker of great entrances at nightclubs, someone who was constantly seen on the town with different men, and a famous controller of wolves. She may have been fodder for endless columns printed in newspapers and fan magazines, but she wanted desperately to be a bona fide movie star, not just some photogenic oddball. Maria knew she was moving along too slowly in her film career. She was completely cognizant of the fact that she had to get the process in high gear. Maria was perilously close to thirty years of age and despite her notoriety Universal seemed loath to give her any kind of meaningful role. She needed the sort of national press that could elevate her above all the other beautiful, aggressive starlets who inhabited Hollywood and grab the attention of both her studio and the public.

The year 1941 would be the one Maria worked her way onto the larger stage. She edged her way into five national stories that provided ink, photos, and lots of attention from coast to coast. It would also be the year when Universal finally found the right niche for Montez by putting her in a sarong for a seventy-eight-minute B movie called *South of Tahiti.* She was fourth on the cast list and only spoke a mish-mash of pseudo South Seas dialects. But she was in a sarong—and the public ate it up.

The year had gotten off to a positive start for Maria. She had moved up to a speaking part with a very popular actor, Don Ameche, in an A movie at Fox that showed off all her obvious charms in stunning Technicolor. On the strength of the word of mouth generated by that movie she got the first of the national spots that would help rev up her career. Montez was contacted by *Life* magazine to be the subject of one-third of an article being prepared for the February 3 issue that would be called "Latin Ladies: Hollywood Is Invaded by Talent from South of the Rio Grande." It was a common theme for articles at that time and became the first way Maria worked herself into national stories. The Associated Press, *Oakland Tribune,* Amy Porter, and Paul Harrison in his syndicated column published similarly themed pieces, not only promoting the newly signed actresses but playing a part in the Hollywood-supported Good Neighbor Policy.[2]

Montez was generally included in these articles, but to appear in *Life* was something special. Not only was it one of the most popular periodicals in the country, it was easily the most prestigious photography-based magazine. The photographs for the piece were taken by Peter Stackpole, one of the original five photogs hired for the magazine, which had debuted on November 23, 1936. He had come to the magazine's attention following the brilliant work he had done on the construction of the Golden Gate and Bay Bridges in San Francisco. He became *Life*'s West Coast photographer and naturally covered numerous Hollywood subjects.[3]

"Latin Ladies" included Carmen Miranda from Brazil and Mona Maris from Argentina as well as Maria. Miranda was seen as the most experienced performer of the three, while Maris was the most serious and Montez the newest and sexiest. Being the sexiest naturally meant Maria wound up with the bulk of the photos. Each of the three women had an individual portrait. Montez was the only one showing cleavage. Stackpole shot not only that portrait, but also a six-photo series of her dancing the rumba in a black bra top and shorts. Also included was a still from 20th Century Fox backstage on the *That Night in Rio* set featuring a spectacularly leggy Maria towering over a seated Carmen Miranda as they talk. It makes for quite the contrast.

This was the sort of national attention that could only help a career. Stackpole, much like Universal's photographer Ray Jones, enjoyed working with Montez. She was not only beautiful but more than willing to do most anything for a photographer. He next photographed her when *Life* published an article called "Hays Office Cracks Down on Cinema's Sweater Set" two months later for the April 14 issue. This was a perfect topic for a photo-based magazine that wanted to feature sexy photos of women without being too obvious about it. Publisher Henry Luce was determined that *Life* remain a classy, family-friendly magazine. *Pic* and *Click* were oversized photo-oriented magazines that ran far more risqué photos than would ever be found in *Life*. *Look* was somewhere in between. The sweater article came from the decision of the Breen motion picture censorship office to dissuade the growing use of tight sweaters and visible cleavage on actresses. There were six photos of young actresses wearing sweaters, with the legend "yes," "no," or "maybe" under each picture. There was one yes, one maybe, and four no's. Maria was the most spectacular of the no's. The photo had been taken on a chilly morning by the fountain at the Garden of Allah Hotel on Sunset Boulevard. Maria, unlike the other women, is clearly braless, with her left arm pulled back sharply to make the sweater even tighter, showing very evidently erect nipples. It was about as blatantly sexual as *Life* was going to be.[4]

Stackpole contacted Maria a third time when he needed to add a sexy component to an article being prepared about W. C. Fields for the May 12 issue. When he met her again, the photographer asked Montez if she had any response to the photo in the sweater-girl article. She responded that she received over two hundred letters after the photo ran. Fields quipped that the letter writers should have been weaned by now. All that out of the way, Stackpole snapped several photographs of Maria in a very short sunsuit and high heels, being pursued by Fields in exercise clothing with his trainer running along next to him. In another photo the actress is lifting a prop dumbbell, once again making her breasts quite prominent.[5]

The Stackpole article on the sweater ban propelled Montez into her second national event of 1941—the great Hollywood sweater ban. The opening salvo in the sweater war came from Joseph Breen, head of the Hays film censorship office, when he officially notified the studios he was banning the use of tight sweaters on their actresses on April 2, 1941. Pete Harrison in his *Harrison's Reports,* aimed at independent theaters across the country that were not under the control of the five major majors, succinctly spelled out the problem as Breen saw it and its preferred outcome. In his April 19, 1941, report, Harrison wrote,

Maria demonstrating what the Hays Office declared the danger of sweaters at the Garden of Allah's pool, April 1941.

> In recent months we have noted a marked tendency to inject into motion pictures shots of low-cut dresses and costumes, which expose women's breasts, as well as "sweater shots"—shots in which the breasts of women are clearly outlined and emphasized. All such shots are in direct violation of the provisions of the Production Code, which states clearly that the more intimate parts of the human body must be covered at all times, and that they should not be clearly and unmistakably outlined by the garment. In the future, any shots in which women's breasts are partially or wholly exposed in any sweater or shots in which the breasts are clearly defined will be rejected. This is important.[6]

The furor had been slowly brewing since Lana Turner took a walk down the street wearing a tight sweater in her first movie, *They Won't Forget* (1936). This certainly helped set Lana's career as a bombshell. A few months earlier she was just a junior at Hollywood High School skipping class to have a Coke at the nearby Currie's Ice Cream shop when she was discovered by *Hollywood Reporter* founder Billy Wilkerson. In the official story this was changed to the more upscale Schwab's Drugstore, where she was sipping a malt. Wearing a sweater. The inclusion of the sweater story was a deliberate effort to make her sexy right from the start. Her sweater fame became ubiquitous. Five years after Lana took her walk, cartoonist Bernard Thompson drew a caricature map of the MGM lot. A clothesline with two sweaters hanging on it with the breasts indelibly imprinted on them is labeled "Lana Turner's Wardrobe."[7]

Not surprisingly, Hollywood's columnists jumped all over the sweater controversy. Even before the ban, Hedda Hopper noted, "It used to be leg art that got over young beauties in the magazines. Now it's sweaters. And don't think it's the studios who are trying to keep those pictures out of circulation, 'cause they send 'em in." A month after the ban, Hopper noted that angry sweater manufacturers were wondering why Hollywood was so intent on ruining their business. Jimmie Fidler chimed in with a condemnation of the ban. "It looks as if the Will Hays office is censoring pictures with (1) cotton in its ears, (2) wearing blinders, and (3) a distorted conception of evil. The newest edict, banning photographs and movie scenes of girls wearing sweaters, is sublimely ridiculous." The same preoccupation with women's breasts showed up in a joke popular at the time. What are the three reasons girls wear sweaters? The answer: the first is to keep warm.[8]

Maria was right at home in this tempest in a teapot. She was never shy about exploiting her breasts and she took complete advantage of this national opportunity. Montez had been part of the biggest article on the subject in *Life* magazine. Then Sheilah Graham put her right in the middle of the controversy: "Maria Montez is a leader of the local sweater set and also has the facility of corralling publicity." In a later column she compared "actresses vs. sweater girls" regarding which were more valuable in the "matter of Motion Picture Esthetics." Maria was compared to Anne Baxter. Montez and all the other Sweater Girls lost in all five comparisons. Louella Parsons wondered if the Hays Office's preoccupation with sweaters might expand into banning sarongs. She noted that this would go particularly hard on Dorothy Lamour and Maria Montez. But in spite of all her exploitation of her own breasts Maria wanted columnist Robert Myers to know "I'm sensational but proper as hell."[9]

The third opportunity for national exposure came Maria's way right in the middle of the sweater battles. Warner Brothers had a scheme in mind to have a special premiere for one of its new films and Louis Shurr got her included. A favored gimmick that developed in the late 1930s was to have the grand opening of a movie in the city where it took place. This garnered enormous publicity nationally and sent the city where the premiere occurred—which was not used to having Hollywood stars walking its streets—into a frenzy. MGM premiered *San Francisco* in that city in June 26, 1936, *Gone with the Wind* in Atlanta on December 15, 1939, and *Young Tom Edison* in the inventor's childhood home of Port Huron, Michigan, on February 10, 1940. 20th Century Fox got into the act when it premiered *To the Shores of Tripoli* in San Diego, just south of the Marine Corps base at Camp Pendleton on March 24, 1942. Warner Brothers eventually cornered the market on the practice, premiering *Dodge City* in Dodge City, Kansas, on April 1, 1939, *Virginia City* in Reno and Virginia City, Nevada, on March 16, 1940, and *Santa Fe Trail* in Santa Fe, New Mexico, on December 13, 1940.

Warners continued its 1940 run of out-of-town premieres when someone in the studio offices got the idea to open *The Sea Wolf,* based on the Jack London novel about a maniacal sea captain, on the ocean liner S.S. *America,* traveling north from Los Angeles to San Francisco, on March 22, 1941. The premiere was held in the ship's theater. Several of those watching, including Maria, were seen running for the restrooms due to the rough seas. Once the ship docked in San Francisco, Mayor Angelo Rossi officially welcomed the entire troupe at a press reception and breakfast aboard ship. Joining the mayor as honored guests were Charmian London, the writer's widow, Hobart Bosworth, who starred in the first version of *The Sea Wolf* in 1913, and the star of the current film, Edward G. Robinson. Fans, who paid $10 for adults and 50 cents for children, were let in after the news conference ended. The stars signed hundreds of autographs while the fans' admission fees were donated to the San Francisco Community Chest fund. The *San Francisco Chronicle* noted that the stars with the numbest hands by the end of the fiesta were Edward G. Robinson, John Garfield, Charlie Ruggles, Mary Astor, Jane Wyman, Susan Hayward, Alexis Smith, and Priscilla Lane.[10]

After mingling with their fans, the Hollywood visitors and the press there to cover them traveled by bus to tour Valley of the Moon, Jack London's ranch in Sonoma County. They were guests at a barbeque luncheon hosted by Charmian, with entertainment provided by a Mexican orchestra in traditional garb. Following the lunch several of the stars of the film were driven to the Sebastiani Theater in Sonoma to introduce a special showing of *The Sea Wolf.*

Such excursions were obviously meant to publicize both the current film and the stars of the studio. But they were subject to interlopers joining in the fiesta. Louis Shurr made certain that Maria would be part of the excursion. She obviously would not be included in specifically Warner Brothers–related events, and not that many fans knew her to ask for an autograph. But she could show up at the open events staged for photographers and she was there to talk to journalists. Maria made the most of the experience. She was not on the *America* to take a cruise to San Francisco. She was there to be seen. She was working at making America conscious of Montez.

As usual, Maria completely understood the nature of the event and how she could exploit it. Edward G. Robinson had the bravura role as the psychotic captain in *The Sea Wolf.* But it seemed obvious to Maria that most of the photographs would be of the younger, handsomer John Garfield. She therefore made every attempt to be near him in group pictures. For the photographs taken around the ship's swimming pool, she wore a black bathing suit with ample cleavage on display. It seems evident that Warner Brothers was trying to feature its recently signed starlet Alexis Smith. But Maria managed to join in virtually every photo taken around the pool. Her simple beauty made her stand out in every one. The most commonly used photo of the event featured Warner contract player Ronald Reagan in the pool about to throw a beach ball to Maria. When *Film Fun* ran a series on the events on the ship it called the piece "A Sight to Sea." A long descriptive paragraph described the junket. Maria was featured prominently in four of the five photos that ran with the article. The largest was of her catching her dress as a sea breeze blew it so that it billowed up over her nylons and underwear. As in the four others, Montez is smiling fetchingly at the camera.[11]

Movie Life did not run the Reagan photo. Instead, it used a half-page photo of Maria, Marguerite Chapman, and Alexis Smith lying down on the side of the pool. From the pose, it's clear that breasts are the point of the picture. Chapman has her left arm largely covering hers, Smith covers hers by pointing at the camera, and Maria has her left arm under her breasts to make them even more prominent. She is also on the left side of the photo, which runs from left to right, making her the dominant element in the picture. Alexis Smith looks good. Maria looks delectable and draws the viewer's attention. This could not have been Warner Brothers' intention, but it was never revealed how galling this must have been to the studio's front office.[12]

Silver Screen followed suit in showcasing Maria. The largely unheard-of Universal ingénue was in two of the five photographs on the all-photo page. In one she is sitting with Warner Brothers' publicity chief Bob Taplinger,

The *Film Fun* article included two more photos of Maria in her bathing suit and only one of Alexis Smith—in a group photo. Montez was described in the text as "one of the Warners beauties at play." This could not have made Warner Brothers' publicity department happy.

wearing, naturally, a very low-cut gown. In the second, she is in a group picture with all the Warners' players who were in the movie or had been invited on the voyage. She is sitting next to John Garfield. On her other side is Warners' glamour girl Alexis Smith.[13]

Montez already knew the dozens of columnists and film commentators who sailed on the *America.* She had recovered from the previous night's

Maria at her writing desk preparing a Western Union telegram, her face reflected in a prewar portrait of Claud Strickland.

seasickness by morning and was eating breakfast in the ship's dining room when *San Francisco Chronicle* scribe Herb Caen, recognizing the friend of all columnists, asked the "eyeful zow-er" what she was doing on a Warner Brothers cruise. Maria was rarely at a loss when a clever quip for a journalist was called for. She told him, "It's all part of the good neighbor policy." Caen noted, "Then you're from South America?" No, corrected Maria, she was from Universal Studios.[14]

Interspersed with the photo sessions for *Life* magazine and the oceangoing premiere of *The Sea Wolf* occurred the fourth, more complicated aspect of Maria's war for recognition. It lasted all of 1941, and while it garnered lots of publicity it was one of the most controversial aspects of Maria Montez's early life in Hollywood. She claimed to be engaged to a fighter pilot in Britain's Royal Air Force named Claud Dobree Strickland. The idea of the flamboyant Hollywood actress being in love with a daring RAF fighter pilot was romantic perfection. The columnists ate it up. But all this was coming from "the greatest commissary actress of all time." The question concerning Strickland was not so much whether Maria was engaged to him, but if the pilot existed at all. In this case, Maria was a victim of her own aggressive clamoring for any sort of publicity. A major school of thought, stated most completely by the *New York Times,* held that the pilot was nothing more than a publicity device invented by Maria and her studio to garner space in newspapers and magazines.

The first mention of Strickland as a man in Maria's life was in a December 30, 1940, column by Jimmie Fidler. He noted that "Holly-wolves" might as well leave Montez alone since the anklet she never took off was a present from "her real heart," RAF pilot Claud Strickland. By April 1941 Erskine Johnson was reporting that Montez and Strickland planned to wed once her divorce from William MacFeeters became final. Universal made the engagement "official" when it sent out a blurb printed nationwide on June 18 claiming the couple had met in London two years before, then again in New York when she was a model for McClelland Barclay. Their actual marriage depended on the war, as Strickland was currently a flying officer (equivalent to a first lieutenant in the US Army Air Force) in a London defense squadron.[15]

The ante was upped another notch when Harrison Carroll noted in his July 25 column, "That rather vague English fiancé of Maria Montez may turn up soon in the flesh" as he was trying to get a leave to come see her in August. Hedda Hopper agreed in her column four days later. Jimmie Fidler noted that Maria had dashed off to New York in "a sudden sprint" to meet the visiting Strickland. All this was possible because William MacFeeters had divorced Maria in June in Puerto Rico, where they had officially been married, under a local law allowing the dissolution of a marriage that produced no children in five years. All the rumors of visits from England were dashed when the Associated Press released a photo on November 7 showing Maria, still on the *South of Tahiti* tour of the East Coast and the South, holding her stomach and looking devastated, with the caption, "RAF fiancé alive?" The article notes that Strickland had been shot down and Montez thinks he is a prisoner of war. The Associated Press released a blurb titled, "Actress Learns Fiancé Is Nazi War Prisoner." It held that the actress had received a telegram from the flyer's mother to that effect. Five days later a photo of Montez in an Atlanta hospital had the caption "Has Bad Luck in Large Doses." Not only was she suffering "from a generally run-down condition," she had also recently heard that her fiancé was missing in action.[16]

By February 1942 it had become accepted belief that Strickland was a prisoner of war in Germany. *Screen Guide* magazine stated it in a caption under a photo of Maria at a nightclub. Jimmie Fidler noted the same thing in his column of March 17. The following month *Movie Life* magazine published a photo of Montez reading a letter next to a photograph of Strickland, with the caption noting he was a POW. But as Hedda Hopper's

News service photo, "Believes Missing RAF Fiance Alive," November 7, 1941.

legman (researcher) Jaik Rosenstein noted, "Cynicism is the legman's occupational disease. He doesn't believe in Santa Claus—or in movie stars." It was a disease shared by many columnists. The real capper of suspicion of the whole Strickland story came by way of the *New York Times* nine months after he was first reported missing by his supposed fiancé.[17]

On August 23, 1942, the *Times* published an article called "To the Rear of the Class, Baron Munchausen." It is an exploration of the grandiose exaggerations, à la Baron Munchausen, engaged in by press agents. The *Times* flatly reported that Claud Strickland was a make-believe creation used to get Maria's name and picture into the news. He is dismissed as a complete fabrication, "one of that rich stock of personalities whose function is to get names, real names, into the news. . . . Mr. Strickland has a 'living' counterpart in almost every studio press department, in the imagination of almost every freelance press agent."[18]

Jimmie Fidler wrote of the actress's anger over the Munchausen article, "Maria Montez is making threat [of a lawsuit] over a New York news dispatch that her much-publicized 'heart' Lt. Claude [*sic*] Strickland, reportedly a war prisoner in Europe doesn't exist at all." This dismissal of the RAF pilot became the accepted belief in writing about Montez and Strickland. In a May 1943 article in *Photoplay* magazine on the dearth of men in Hollywood due to the war, the relationship between Montez and Strickland was dismissed as the result of the actress not having enough dates. "Some unkind observers," noted *Photoplay,* "pointed out that this was merely a face-saving device to cover up the lack of eligible men on her list."[19]

The rejection of the truth of the Strickland story continues into more recent things published about Montez. In *The Glamour Girls* (1975), James Robert Parish and Don Stanke note that Maria was "allegedly bereaved" over his disappearance, and state that after he was reported to be a POW, "for whatever reasons, the Maria-Strickland liaison soon thereafter disappeared from the realities of life." The Wikipedia biography of Montez notes that she was reported to be involved with Strickland, "but it was later revealed that this was a publicity stunt." This was repeated in the Wow.com and Peoplepill.com biographical entries on Montez. In the *Mediatico* blog on Latin American, Spanish, and Portuguese media cultures, the author of a piece comparing Maria Montez with female impersonator Mario Montez has her expanding her career by agreeing to various publicity stunts, "including a fake RAF boyfriend." In the 2014 Dominican-produced biopic *Maria Montez: La Pelicula* (Maria Montez: The Movie), there is a scene in which the unknown starlet Maria hears on the radio that a pilot named Claud Strickland has been shot down and is missing. She immediately gets on a radio show by proclaiming this complete stranger to be her fiancé. The character playing Louis Shurr nods in appreciation of her cleverly using a real event that she has nothing to do with and getting a publicity bonanza out of it.[20]

Maria herself talked openly and enthusiastically about Strickland to interviewers. In a discussion of her love life, she told Louella Parsons that William MacFeeters had been a mistake of youth but "I love Claud Strickland." She described their relationship to her friend May Mann in a manuscript

Maria signs photos—and shows off her legs. Note the photo of Claud Strickland in his RAF uniform on the desk.

being prepared soon after Montez became involved with Jean-Pierre Aumont in April 1943. She told Mann she was surprised she could love again. MacFeeters was not her first love. She was impressed with him and had been raised to believe she had to conform to expectations regarding marriage and domesticity. She then created a load of nonsense about initially coming to the United States at seventeen. A talent scout from Warner Brothers wanted to sign her, but her parents said no. At nineteen she was back again on a fishing trip to Cuba and Mexico. She was married by this time, but soon separated from him. Then she launches into how she met a "handsome young Britisher" and fell in love truly for the first time. This is typical of Montez's stories, an odd combination of things made up to make her seem a cosmopolitan citizen of the world and things that actually happened. She goes on to say that they both needed to get divorced before they would be able to marry each other. This was exactly what happened. She did not start talking to columnists about Strickland until both of them were divorced.[21]

In preparation for the article that became "Second Love for Maria," she was talking to an actual friend in May Mann, not just a writer. However fuzzy she might have been about peripheral details, Montez was as honest as she ever was in discussing her feelings. Mann noted, "Maria is not the conceited young egotist that she has been pictured. Much of her publicity has been intentional." Montez spoke of how poor an image Jean-Pierre Aumont had of her before they actually met, thinking her "dreadful . . . so conceited." When she met Aumont, Maria admitted, "My life was so empty." She was crushed by the death of Claud Strickland, her lost love. As she explained, "Any girl if she will admit it, is desperately lonely if she isn't in love." Then she met Aumont.

> I am so surprised. I am so happy. To discover that a girl can fall in love twice. I thought it wasn't possible for me to fall in love again. Perhaps I could explain. For so many many months I have been so unhappy. So unhappy before I discover I love Jean Pierre and he loves me. . . . The man I was to marry was lost in the war. I would wake up in the middle of the night so homesick. I longed so much for him. To think that I am in love again the second time. So happy and so in love. It seems too wonderful.[22]

There was one aspect of the whole Strickland episode that was brought up only by Jimmie Fidler. He had something of a love-hate relationship with Montez. She was always good copy, but he didn't seem to trust her at all. In October 1941—just three weeks before photos of her mourning Strickland appeared—Maria met Teddy Stauffer when she was at the Mocambo with Louis Shurr. Born in Switzerland, Stauffer was yet another elegant European man. He had been dubbed Germany's swing-king or its Benny Goodman as the leader of his band the Teddies. Maria gave her phone number to Stauffer at the Mocambo and they started dating the next night. According to him they spent a romantic night at her small house on South Camden Drive in Beverly Hills while Addinsell's *Warsaw Concerto* was on repeat on her record player.[23]

Maria at Ciro's "with famous bandleader" Teddy Stauffer, published in *Hollywood* magazine, March 1942.

It was a short-lived relationship. Maria's affair with Stauffer seems to be a classic case of love on the rebound. In March 1942 Stauffer had to go to Tijuana for the same reason Maria had; he was an alien on a visitor pass who wanted to become a permanent resident. But he was not able to upgrade his visa and was forced to stay in Mexico. Ken Morgan noted that tongues were wagging all over Hollywood about Montez trying to get Stauffer's release from Mexico so they could get married. He assured his readers, "T'aint so." Stauffer was never able to get a permanent resident visa and finally wrote to

Maria that he could not reenter the United States so their relationship was doomed. He remained in Mexico and eventually became one of the founders of Acapulco as a major resort. He dated Rita Hayworth and was married to Faith Domergue and later Hedy Lamarr.[24]

Montez and Stauffer were often snapped at a table at one of the major nightspots in Hollywood and became accepted as a couple. Fidler's column on March 17, 1942, noted, "Nice of Maria Montez not to break her engagement to RAF Wing Commander [*sic*] Claude [*sic*] Strickland because he's a German prisoner, but what's she gonna do about local and real love, Ted Stauffer?" The relationship was also hinted at by *Photoplay* magazine in its October 1943 issue. Montez's stories about Strickland were seen as examples of the "white lies" told by Hollywood people. The magazine, accepting Strickland as a real person, wondered how could she fall in love so quickly with Jean-Pierre Aumont when her previous love might be languishing in a German POW camp? Because the heart changes, the magazine reasoned. She wasn't lying about Strickland. She just loved him and then didn't.

Maria invented the Sacred Heart Academy in the Canary Islands to make her childhood seem more cosmopolitan than it was in the remote agricultural section of the Dominican Republic where she grew up. There was no such academy and she never set foot in the Canary Islands. But she did not invent Claud Strickland. He was a very real person and he had an equally real relationship with Maria. She was often photographed in her bed at the start of her career and visible on the nightstand was a photograph of Strickland, at first in prewar civvies and later in his RAF uniform. For an article called "Magic Maria," *Movie Life* ran a photo of Montez reading a letter next to a photo of the pilot in his RAF uniform with the caption "Her fiancé Captain [*sic*] Claude [*sic*] Strickland is a prisoner in Germany." There are numerous photographs of the actress wearing the anklet presented to her by Strickland that Fidler wrote about in his column. The report that she dashed off to New York because she was sure Strickland was coming was true, the mix-up due to a mistake in a cablegram. The cable company printed "darling" as "sailing" and she thought he was on his way to New York.[25]

The real Claud Strickland gave up his prosperous life to go on active service in the Royal Air Force as soon as England declared a state of war with Germany. At age thirty he flew a Hawker Hurricane fighter plane in the 615 Squadron in defense of London during the Battle of Britain in the summer and fall of 1940. He was, in Winston Churchill's memorable phrase, "one of the few" to whom "so much" was "owed by so many." He died a very real death on a raid over Belgium on October 27, 1941.

Claud Dobree Strickland was born to Claud Hugh Strickland and Una Clara Bell Strickland in Tewkesbury, Cheltenham District, Gloucestershire, England, on March 29, 1909. After attending university, he became a stockbroker. A very wealthy young man, bilingual in English and Spanish, he traveled to the east coast of South America prior to his 1934 marriage to England's leading model, Lady Marguerite Rose Bligh. They separated in 1940. In November 1937 Strickland received his certificate from the Royal Aero Club, which trained wealthy Britons to fly in case of war, at which time they would be brought into the Royal Air Force. He took a final extended vacation to the United States before the war, arriving in New York on January 26, 1939. The New York World's Fair, "The World of Tomorrow," opened on April 30, 1939, and was undoubtedly one of the lures that brought Strickland to the city. After spending time in Manhattan at the Ritz Carlton Hotel, he flew south to Palm Beach, Florida, then returned to New York. Somewhere in this time period he met Maria MacFeeters and they fell in love. He was back in England in time for Britain's declaration of war on Germany on September 3, 1939, following the German invasion of Poland.[26]

Maria claimed that she and Claud Strickland were engaged. There is no question that they had a relationship. Strickland spoke Spanish, had considerable experience in Latin America and, if his first wife was any example, he loved beautiful women. The stockbroker was exactly the type that appealed to Montez. He was tall, suave, and European. Despite all the arranged dates at Hollywood nightclubs, Maria never had a relationship of any length with a North, South or Central American. Strickland is a main character in Elizabeth Russell's screenplay about Montez. She has them arriving in New York together on a steamship from Central America and Strickland introducing Maria to Louis Shurr, who would become her agent. Russell claimed that Maria's initial attraction to her second husband Jean-Pierre Aumont was because he looked so much like Strickland.

Key dates in their lives line up perfectly. Maria started talking about being engaged to Strickland only after his divorce in February 1941 and hers on June 8 were final. Montez announced his being lost in action soon after it happened. She was in Atlanta on a publicity tour for *South of Tahiti* when Maria claimed Strickland's mother contacted her that he was missing in action. She must have been informed by someone that Strickland was missing as soon as his plane disappeared. Hedda Hopper wrote that Montez identified the missing pilot as the nephew of the Earl of Dudley. Strickland's father was actually the ninth Earl of Darnley. Whichever one got the name and relationship wrong, clearly Maria knew the pilot's story.[27]

While Maria was trying her best to get screen time at Universal, Claud Strickland was flying Hurricane fighter planes for the 615 Squadron of the RAF, known as "Churchill's Own" after the future prime minister. After being called up on September 3, he was sent to the RAF training squadron to transition into flying high-performance military aircraft. Strickland initially flew in the defense of London, then moved with the squadron to defend the docks at Clydebank to the west of Glasgow. They were redeployed to the London area again to participate in the Battle of Britain. Following that epic aerial battle, the 615 took part in raids on the German-held coasts of Belgium and France.[28]

On the night of October 27, 1941, Strickland and several other pilots were sent on what the RAF called a "rhubarb" mission. This involved raiding the enemy coast, seeking out targets of opportunity. Strickland was sent to the "single man's" side—meaning the more heavily defended Belgium rather than the "married man's" territory, France. His plane was hit by anti-aircraft fire and Claud Strickland was killed in the subsequent crash. He was buried in the churchyard of the small Belgium town of Bredene. The mission was entered into the squadron's log book.

> The usual dawn patrol gave way to an early morning rhubarb operation to the seaplane basin at Ostend where two HE 59s were destroyed on water and a third damaged on land. Several gun positions were attacked including the C.O.'s old friend on the hanger roof. The ground defense put up a tremendous amount of flak and unfortunately, F/O Strickland and Sgt. Petts were both shot down. Claude [*sic*] was tremendously popular and his keenness and pluck were a byword. Petts, too, in his quiet way, was very much liked by us all.[29]

Claud Strickland died at age thirty-one. The well-connected columnist Jimmie Fidler was the only one to pass on an unofficial London report that Flying Officer Claud Strickland, "Maria Montez' real heart" was killed in action in his July 26, 1942, column. Just as Maria was old at twenty-eight to be trying to break into the movies, Strickland was ancient at thirty-one to be a World War II fighter pilot. Maria was never interested in frivolous, shallow men. As would be the case with Jean-Pierre Aumont, Strickland was not willing to sit comfortably on the sidelines while his country was engaged in a war for its very existence. (The International News Service did not issue a blurb on Strickland, who was "missing and believed dead," until November 14, 1942.)[30]

All the suspicion as to the reality of the flyer became moot with Maria's marriage on July 13, 1943, to Jean-Pierre Aumont. *Photoplay* published an article called "Lush, Latin and Lethal" just prior to her marriage. Strickland was mentioned in the piece. Perfectly summing up the Hollywood press's view of Montez, the author noted, "The beloved was an RAF officer, of course. He could scarcely have been less and done justice to Maria's idea of the fitness of things." The two opposite views of Strickland's existence were noted, as was the fact that Maria hotly denied that he was a figment of her imagination. But with the arrival of Aumont, "the two schools of thought have vanished into thin air."[31]

But Strickland's name was brought up one last time in Hedda Hopper's column of September 21, 1945. After mentioning Maria's pregnancy, she asked the question, "Who says Maria Montez isn't sentimental?" The columnist went on to note, "If her baby is a boy, he'll be christened Jean Claude Aumont. First name for husband and second for her great friend RAF pilot Claude [*sic*] Strickland, who lost his life over the English Channel during the war." Maria had a daughter so the point became moot. But this did in fact become the name of Jean-Pierre Aumont's first son with Maria Pavan who was born in 1957.[32]

The fifth publicity event that was so key to Montez's making her mark on the national scene involved America's most famous and prestigious university, Harvard. It would not be the first time the university would be exploited for publicity by Hollywood. This checkered history goes back to the Ann Sheridan affair. The *Harvard Lampoon* dubbed the actress, known as the "Oomph Girl," as one of forty or so actors "least likely to succeed." Sheridan responded by calling the *Lampoon* "the saddest idea of a magazine" and "a pale copy of *Captain Billy's Whiz Bang.*" Not content to just let it lie, *Harvard Lampoon* president W. Russell Bowie Jr. responded with staggering snobbishness and pomposity. "As a graduate of a remote Texas kinder garden School [North Texas State Teachers College]," he said, "Miss Sheridan is not qualified to offer any intelligent criticism of the *Lampoon*, which caters to a somewhat different class. In view of this, Miss Sheridan's opinion of the Lampoon is of supreme indifference to its editors." In a perfect example of "town versus gown," the Brockton police force invited Sheridan to their annual ball on May 13 to apologize for "the embarrassment offered you by certain ill-mannered young men of Harvard."[33]

Next to show up at the prestigious university was starlet Marjorie Woodworth. In May 1941, her publicist somehow convinced the editor of the *Harvard Lampoon* to ask her to the university's spring dance. He said she would never show up but would send some sort of joke gift like a cast of her leg. Of course, she did come to the dance. Photographers snapped away for the fifteen minutes she stayed. They also snapped away when she sat with legs crossed on the lap of the statue of John Harvard. Some students expressed

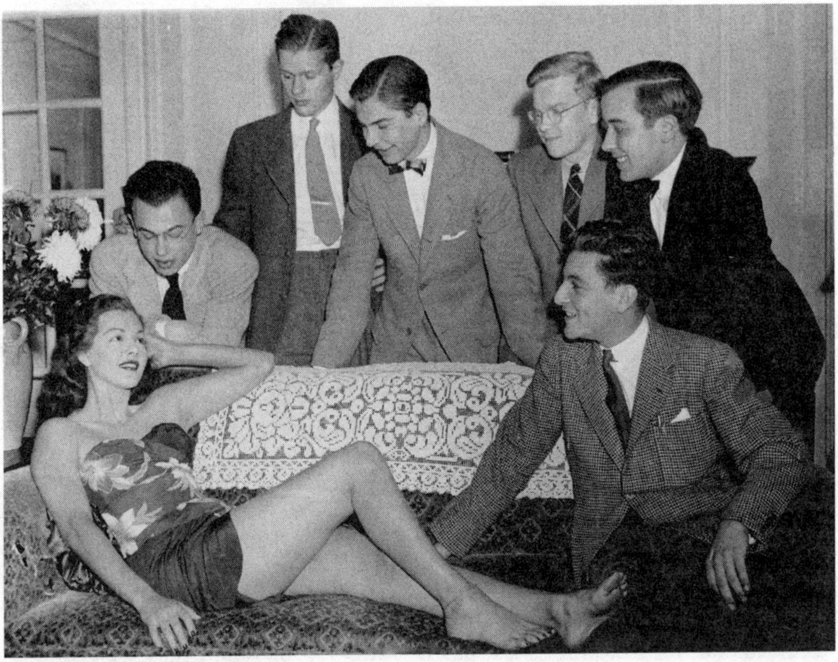

Maria at Harvard in her slendang (sarong), Bertram Benedict at her feet. Strickland's anklet is on her right ankle.

their dim view of the proceedings by throwing tomatoes at the visiting Miss Woodworth as she departed.

Bertram Benedict was responsible for setting in motion the next Hollywood travesty aimed at the delicate elitists of Harvard. He was already exotic to his freshmen friends as he was one of the very few Southern Californians in his class. As icing on the cake, his stepfather was in the movies. Howard Benedict had worked in the RKO publicity department before becoming a producer for Universal Studios, specializing in Sherlock Holmes films. The committee members for the freshman dance thought they could make a real splash if they could convince their classmate Bertram to get his father to send a real live movie star to their dance. When Howard got the request from his son, he contacted Universal's publicity department, which told him Maria Montez was due to be in Boston to appear onstage at a local theater for the opening of *South of Tahiti.* Universal knew she was up for anything that would get her name in the papers, so she was ordered to appear at the Harvard freshman dance.

Young Benedict and the rest of the Dance Committee met Maria at the train station on October 30, 1941. They were accompanied by scores of press photographers and reporters who, once they had snapped the actress's arrival at the station with the welcoming committee, happily repaired to her Copley Plaza hotel room. She changed into her sarong from *South of Tahiti* and posed for more photos with Bertram and his fellow committee members. Universal representatives on the East Coast had been wildly successful in stoking the interest of the local press. Several of the photos were taken by the various news services and received national play. Bertram Benedict was in most of them—an eighteen-year-old looking perplexed by both the gorgeous woman in the sarong and the frenzy she created.

That evening when he went to her hotel to escort the actress to the dance, Bertram was aghast to find her dressed in a diaphanous white gown that made it blatantly evident she was not wearing a brassiere. While he remembered admiring the sight, he tried his best to explain to her that she would not be allowed into the dance wearing a dress that revealing. Maria went back to her room and came back in a non-see-through dress. Still without a bra. They headed to campus surrounded by Universal flacks and a horde of photographers. Benedict never did have much of a chance to talk to Montez. Like most people who spoke to her away from a sound stage, he remembered her accent as quite pronounced but easily understood. When they were denied entrance to the dance itself due to the commotion created by the press, Maria was incensed. They were asked to leave the premises. Bertram remembers she kept saying, "Don't you worry baby, I'm going to sue them" as they were escorted out. It was the exact reaction the press wanted. Here was the imperious Montez flying off the handle as expected, given the public persona she had created. Benedict went on to the dance alone and Maria went back to her hotel, mission accomplished.[34]

But the fiasco did not end there for Bertram Benedict. The next day he was summoned to the dean's office to find a table laid out with the numerous newspaper articles and photographs of Montez in her sarong, supposedly taken on the way to a Harvard dance. The dean explained in no uncertain terms that Harvard was not amused by this kind of publicity and unless it was terminated immediately Benedict would be looking for a new university to attend. He put in a frantic call to his father back at Universal to call off the Harvard campaign. Fearing for his son's future, he did just that. Meanwhile, the *South of Tahiti* caravan moved on.[35]

One often-repeated myth of Maria's Harvard visit was printed in the *American Magazine* and dozens of articles and columns that mentioned her Cambridge excursion. It was reported that she visited Harvard to keep a date with a freshman and the secret got out—999 more guys eagerly waited to dance with her. Supposedly she happily did a turn on the floor with all of them. A thousand eager freshman guys. Like the whole rest of this goofy adventure, the dance marathon was a creation of John Joseph's publicity department. It was perfect. What red-blooded American eighteen- or nineteen-year-old would not want to dance with that stunning Hollywood star, Maria Montez, who was supposed to be about their age? Of course, the Maria being publicized—a fun-loving, nightclub-hopping party girl—would love to dance with a thousand teenage strangers. It was all nonsense. The last thing in the world Montez had any interest in doing was wasting her time dancing with the entire freshman class. She was there for publicity, period, and there was nowhere in America in 1941 that offered as easy a path to national publicity than Harvard. She used the opportunity perfectly. An example of this that portrayed Maria as the self-possessed scrapper she delighted in came from Hedda Hopper. The columnist explained that in light of the tomatoes hurled at Marjorie Woodworth, Montez went to Harvard prepared. She had two crates of ripe grapefruits in her car "and was ready to let 'em have it if they started any monkey business."[36]

The next stop on the *South of Tahiti* publicity tour was the Georgia Institute of Technology (Georgia Tech) in Atlanta. The situation could not have been more opposite the zoo at the Harvard dance. Renan Moreira, the Latin American correspondent for the student newspaper the *Technique*, interviewed Maria and wrote of her as no writer who was a native of the United States ever did. The Universal publicity department stayed in the background. Montez wore a white dress with a scooped neck and a mantilla for the interview. Moreira was clearly taken with his subject, admiring "her virginal figure, attractive personality, and sweetness of speech." He also noted even though it was a short, late-afternoon visit, "all of the students who happened to be in the campus trailed Maria's steps, some wishing they had bigger eyes, some using their imagination widely."[37]

Maria had stated her desire to pose with the Harvard football team. That did not work out, but she had better luck with the Georgia Tech squad. She opted for a skirt and jacket rather than the white shorts and sweater she had planned for Cambridge. Naturally she wore high heels and was talked into donning a leather football helmet. She took several photos running with a football in the midst of the Georgia Tech backfield and later kicking a football in her heels. They are some of the most unusual photos ever taken of Maria, and they certainly were not the image Universal wanted to present of her. Unlike the photos of the Harvard onslaught, the football photos were published only by the *Atlanta Constitution* and the Georgia Tech newspaper.[38]

Maria running with the Georgia Tech backfield. The caption read, "Instead of 'Dream Backfield' this picture could well be called a backfield with a dream. The dream is Miss Maria Montez, the beautiful Latin movie star, who made a trip to the Tech campus recently." (Courtesy of the Georgia State University Library, Special Collections.)

After Atlanta, Maria would continue her *South of Tahiti* tour by visiting Variety Club chapters, or "tents," with stops at a charity banquet in Charlotte, North Carolina, hosted by Pat O'Brien, and on to Cincinnati and Dayton, Ohio, where she was welcomed as "Universal's . . . new Sarong Girl from South America." Even this early in her career Montez made a point of contacting local film distributors and theater owners, wanting them to be on her side in her self-perceived war with Universal for recognition.[39]

Maria capped off these five national events with one of the most important fanzine articles of her career. *Motion Picture* magazine ran a score of articles featuring Montez over the course of her career, but none had more impact than the December 1941 piece by Gene Schrott called "Who's Afraid of Hollywood Wolves?" It presented her as beautiful, desirable, cosmopolitan, and always in charge. Schrott wrote that she created a buzz from the first time she set foot in Ciro's nightclub. People wanted to know who she was. "She radiated youth and beauty and animation. She was a lady from head to toe. But she was a lady who wasn't afraid of life or men or any obstacle she might bump into." Her lack of fear of "Holly-wolves" and her ability to tame them became an integral part of the Montez persona.[40]

One aspect of her life that Maria took seriously, although practically no one else did, was her writing. She was always insistent on trying to display a serious intellectual side. She had a rhumba song copyrighted that was used in a show. She wrote two novels, "Forever Is a Long Time" and "Reunion in Lilith," and a self-help book called "Hollywood Wolves I Have Tamed." None of these were published. Montez had more success with her poetry. She was a guest at the fourth annual poetry conference of the California Federation of Chaparral Poets at the Hollywood Chamber of Commerce on May 15, 1943. She followed Robert Service of "The Shooting of Dan McGrew" fame as a speaker. Her poem "Twilight" earned both national and international recognition. It won an award from the Manuscripters Club, a Los Angeles writers' organization, and was also published in *Baho Rueo, revisita literaria latinoamericana* in 1943. Her poetry also extended to songwriting.[41]

Montez took her poetry seriously and had success with it outside of her Hollywood career. But when she tried to read some of it to a writer for the *New York Sunday Mirror,* she was treated as a ridiculous simpleton, "a little girl who had just been permitted to run a lunch party for grownups." Three of the poems are printed. They are a bit flowery for North American taste, but they are serious works by someone who knows how to express herself. To the *Mirror* writer she was just "a poem with legs." The accompanying photo illustrates that idea. Much like Universal the newspaper just wanted Montez to quit trying to be a complete person and show her legs. Her experience with the *Mirror* rather than her reading to the Chaparral Poets summed up her Hollywood experience as regards her writing.[42]

All of her courting of national news sources was helping to raise Maria's profile, but it would do no good if Universal could not find where, if anywhere, she could fit in the movie firmament. The studio recognized what a fireball it had in its employ. Dan Kelly, the chief of talent at Universal and the oldest casting executive in point of service in Hollywood in 1943, thought, "She is the most ambitious woman I've seen in a quarter of a century in Hollywood. Nothing short of hell and high water can keep her from being a star." But what sort of star? The studio kept placing her in small parts in different kinds of movies to see how she performed and what sort of role registered with the public.[43]

In January 1941 she was scheduled for a brief part in the canteen section of Abbott and Costello's *Buck Privates.* It would have been a chance to see how she performed in a modern comedy. The switch to *That Night in Rio* had amply demonstrated she was able to say lines with a comedic flair. So

Blonde Maria in costume for *Raiders of the Desert.* She appeared as a blonde only in *Moonlight in Hawaii*; by the time filming started for *Raiders* she was back to her natural hair color.

Universal pulled her from *Buck Privates* to appear in *Moonlight in Hawaii* as the eighth-listed cast member, playing the part of a hotel hostess named Ilani. Filming was delayed when Maria's part had to be extensively rewritten. Originally Ilani was supposed to be a comic character, described as "a professional Hawaiian from Brooklyn." With Montez slated for the part it became smaller and sexier. She was supposed to look like a Hawaiian, but in her first scene, where she puts a lei around the neck of Pete the cruise director, he tells his bandleader friend, "She's got a funny accent for a native." The bandleader responds, "It's a slight mixture of Castilian and Brooklynese." She is presented as both worldly wise and in charge of herself in her other two brief scenes.

In the meantime, the studio had Maria test for the leading role of Claire Ledeux in *The Flame of New Orleans.* Marlene Dietrich had been cast in the part but was threatening to leave the production due to her unhappiness with Bruce Cabot as the male lead. The problems were worked out, however, and Dietrich stayed with the picture.

Moonlight in Hawaii finally started filming in March 1941. By this time Ilani had become a blonde non-native girl working at the hotel. Adele Mara, born Adelaide Delgado in Detroit, was turned into a blonde when she moved to Republic Studios in 1942. But Mara had light skin and practically no accent. Attempting to Anglicize Maria by dying her hair blonde while she still retained her thick Spanish accent was ridiculous. *Moonlight* and several portraits from Ray Jones's studio provide the only evidence that Universal had briefly lost its mind.[44]

Moonlight in Hawaii

Moonlight in Hawaii starts with Pete Fleming (Johnny Downs) deciding to leave the singing quartet he is part of and become a tourist guide. He is on a cruise ship escorting the wealthy Mrs. Effie Floto (Marjorie Gateson) and her three nieces to Hawaii. The other three members of the quartet stow away on the ship and later move into a Hawaiian hotel room. The group eventually gets a chance to sing with the hotel band, led by Clipper Conovan (Mischa Auer). They hope to get their own radio show, and would-be singer Toby Spencer (Jane Frazee) suggests they audition for her father, a pineapple grower. But he is in a business dispute with his partner, who owns a canning company. Neither can afford to carry on business alone so each decides to try to woo and marry Mrs. Floto. All of this wooing is complicated by the delectable Ilani (Maria Montez) who works at the hotel. It winds up that Mrs. Floto marries bandleader Conovan, the two tycoons resume their partnership and sponsor the radio show for the musicians and, of course, Pete and Toby fall in love.

Moonlight in Hawaii was a typical sixty-minute entertainment of the kind Universal cranked out by the dozen for the small-town and independent

Maria vamps hotel guest Leon Errol in *Moonlight in Hawaii.*

theaters that were its chief customers. The *Film Bulletin* dismissed it as an "inconsequential musical for duals," meaning it was fit only to be the second of a double-feature program. The only thing to recommend the "flimsy little musical programmer from Universal" was "a bevy of beautiful girls, including the torrid Maria Montez." *Weekly Variety* was equally unenthusiastic, finding it a "tiresome musical" and a "haphazard concoction." The eternally upbeat *Hollywood Reporter* at least concluded that theater owners should find it "entertainment enough to pleasantly amuse customers of all houses."[45]

Universal's director of advertising and publicity, John Joseph, wanted to get some positive word sent out about the studio's ingénue Maria Montez. In one missive she was described as a "sultry Latin beauty signed by Universal recently" who "has a chance to demonstrate her allure as 'Ilani'" in the movie. In another blurb from Joseph it was noted that the "appearance of Santo Domingo's sultry siren, Maria Montez, as an alluring, if spurious, Hawaiian" kept attracting too many men to the set to ogle her. Director Charles Lamont said it was two hundred guys at last count. He had to establish a limit to the number of visitors because of Maria. The blurb did not point out this was only her second speaking part for the studio.[46]

So at least Maria was garnering a small bit of publicity from *Moonlight.* You have to admire Joseph's dedication to his job. Maria was primarily used as a beautiful object that passed through various scenes, uttered a few lines that confused and bothered all the men, and disappeared. The blonde hair simply did not go with the few words that came out of her mouth. It was abandoned along with any further useless attempts to Anglicize her with the end of the movie. As with Columbia's tinkering with the looks of Rita Cansino/Rita Hayworth, Universal wanted Maria to seem less Latin. But there was no hiding that accent or Maria's desire to be an embodiment of the Good Neighbor Policy. Maria's hair went quickly back to its natural auburn color.

Two weeks after wrapping *Moonlight in Hawaii* Montez was being fitted for an Arab costume for another sixty-minute quickie called *Raiders of the Desert.* Her hair was still blonde when Ray Jones took his portraits, but that was changed by the time filming started. The movie was one of the fourteen "Aces of Action" adventure comedies from Universal that featured the team of Richard Arlen and Andy Devine. The costumes were the one thing the Hays Office warned Universal about. The censors sent their stock line that the costumes "should at no time be revealing." Maria's certainly were not. Her part was slightly larger in this film, with a few more lines. She moved up from sixth on the cast list to fourth. This would be the first time she would appear in the genre of movie referred to as an "Eastern" around the Universal lot. Or, more irreverently, a "tits and sand" epic. She would be an Arab named Zuleika. It was the first time she co-starred with Turhan Bey who, along with Maria and Sabu, would be the key "exotics" used by Universal. They would go on to more significant work later in their careers. It was also her introduction to Andy Devine, who would join her in the more lavish *Ali Baba and the Forty Thieves.*

Raiders of the Desert

The brief story of *Raiders of the Desert* starts with Dick Manning (Richard Arlen) and Andy McCoy (Andy Devine) stowing away on a ship they think is headed for California, but is really going to Arabia. They meet Alice Evans (Linda Hayes) on the ship and follow her to Libertahd, a modern city created by an American philanthropist named Jones in the middle of the desert to bring American ideals of democracy to the area. Sheik Talifah is determined to bring the city under his command and smash the ideals professed there, which he believes are warping the minds of his people. Hassen (Turhan Bey), posing as Jones's aide but really a spy for Talifah, aids him in this. Together Hassen and Talifah arrange to smuggle guns into Liberthad to their supporters but they are taken by the townspeople who, with the help of legionnaires, defeat Talifah's men and ensure Jones's continued rule. Dick and Alice return to America together while Andy has to leave his love object, Zuleika (Maria Montez) in Libertahd with her boyfriend.

Moonlight in Hawaii at least had the energetic singing of the Merry Macs to bring it some attention. *Raiders* had nothing. Besides the tepid notices in the trade papers it was scarcely reviewed anywhere around the country as it started to appear on the screens of secondary theaters after July 25, 1941. It appeared at the Noble Theater in Anniston, Alabama, where the *Star* newspaper, no doubt primed by the Universal press book, optimistically noted, "Maria Montez, sultry Latin actress, is prominently featured." *Variety* found her to be "a fickle desert cutie." The *Los Angeles Times* briefly noted the film under new releases, commenting, "Maria Montez is attractive as an oasis charmer." As the national press was still dealing with the juicy story of what her relationship with Claud Strickland really was, Maria's career on film was just limping along.[47]

As Zuleika, Maria did little more than show up in very concealing Arab garb. She even speaks some pseudo-Arabic to explain why she has such an accent. She appears in four short scenes as someone for Andy Devine to pant over. She already has a man, but Devine goes to her house three times to serenade her with his banjo and enrage her inamorato, who keeps dumping water on him from the second floor—a rather hackneyed effort at comic relief. *Raiders* did little more than continue to impress Universal with how well Maria registered on film.

On June 18, 1941, two weeks after *Raiders* wrapped up, Montez showed up on the set of *Bombay Clipper*, another hour-long black-and-white aspirant to B movie status. Ranked fourth in the cast again, she plays Sonya Dietrich Landers, who is aiding her husband, a spy in the employ of foreign powers. These "powers" are never named as the Germans since *Clipper* was filmed in the era of strict neutrality prior to the bombing of Pearl Harbor. But it is clear

Maria with a gun in *Bombay Clipper.* She wouldn't have another until *Tangier.*

what country the spies are working for. Much of the movie takes place on what is referred to as the Bombay Clipper, one of the Boeing 314 seaplanes that were the first aircraft to commercially connect the United States with Europe, Hawaii, and Asia by air. It was a groundbreaking airplane featuring sleeping compartments and a dining lounge that was aimed strictly at the extremely wealthy. There never was an actual Bombay Clipper that flew from Bombay to Singapore to Manila. It was simply a perfect movie conception in that it was flying from one exotic place to another while offering a minimal set to concentrate the action and minimize production costs.[48]

Even the most completely B of B movies had to be submitted to the Hays Office. It had little to comment on regarding the *Bombay Clipper* script. There were guns involved, so as always, "at all times gruesomeness must be avoided when characters are shown dying or being shot." The censors warned the studio to be careful how the reporters are presented as the "newspaper profession is particularly sensitive as to the manner in which its representatives are portrayed on the screen." They also warned that when a woman's luggage was being searched for the diamonds, "no intimate undergarments, such as panties or brassieres, should be shown."[49]

Bombay Clipper

Jim Wilson (William Gargan) is a foreign correspondent in Bombay used to traveling the world looking for stories. His fiancée, Frankie Gilroy (Irene Hervey), has been left at the altar twice and is sick of waiting for him. Jim tells his boss at Amalgamated News Service that he is going back to the States to marry Frankie. He is offered a desk job in the San Francisco office if he will do one more investigative piece involving a mysterious shipment of Indian diamonds leaving on the Bombay Clipper. He and Frankie are married on the Clipper by the captain but start fighting again when she discovers he is doing one more job. Jim has discovered that a royal gift of jewels given by India to England are on the plane, being sent to the United States to be cut and used as diamond heads for precision tooling for the war effort. After landing in Singapore, Jim gains possession of the diamonds, but they are stolen from him on the airplane and he is tossed out the door of the Clipper by the thieves. He manages to grab hold of the strut on the step the plane uses for landing and takeoff and is rescued by Chundra (Turhan Bey), who turns out to be an agent for the Indian government. The captain announces that no one will be let off the airplane when it lands in Manila. Dr. Landers, the leader of the foreign agents, hijacks the plane with the help of his wife (Maria Montez) and arranges to land it next to a submarine. Jim and a passenger defeat the hijackers and a discredited pilot, who was wounded in the fighting, manages to fly the plane safely to Manila.

Once again, Maria is barely in this movie. She is adequate playing the newly married wife of the foreign agent who is out to steal the diamonds. She holds a small pistol on the pilot as her husband takes the diamonds from the foreign correspondent. She has a brief scene in which she explains how she met and married Dr. Landers in Constantinople. She is also a witness to Jim and Frankie's marriage. And that's it. The most that can be said about Maria's part in *Bombay Clipper* is that she looks fine in the limited time she appears onscreen. She is not singled out in the trade papers' reviews, which found the movie fit only to be the "secondary feature" on a bill.[50]

This time Maria had almost a full month before she had to report for her next film. She spent an afternoon with Ampelio Gonzalez, the president of the Latin Riding Actors Association, who falsely declared Montez was a former Miss Central America, and mentioned a proposed Miss Latin America contest to be held August 3 at the Verdugo Woodlands in Glendale. Who knows how much veracity any of this had? The point is that anything to do with Latin America could depend on Maria for support. Right after this Maria was taken to the Spanish-themed Santa Barbara Festival by *Spot* magazine. This was during her brief time as a blonde and in the midst of her Sweater Girl phase. The photos represent this as well as the Spanish gown she wore to the Fiesta Ball. The accompanying article explains she is still largely unknown except in all the smart Hollywood nightclubs. Universal is dedicated to changing this and she will be "accorded the Hollywood publicity buildup." According to the magazine she was right at home at the Fiesta, having gone to many of them in her "native" Spain. Maria was ever the good sport; there is a photo of her on the beach in a bathing suit and another in pants and sweater riding a donkey. Montez went from the fiesta back to Los Angeles to prepare for *South of Tahiti,* which would start filming in late August on the Universal lot.[51]

While Maria was completing her small parts in *That Night in Rio* and *Moonlight in Hawaii,* Universal was thinking of giving her the title role in one of their many horror movies, *Captive Wild Woman.* From the short studio-planted blurb in the *Hollywood Reporter* it seems the studio was actually thinking of starring her as the Paula Dupree half of the gorilla-woman creature that results from a mad doctor's experiments with applying human female hormones to a gorilla. Needless to say, things don't go well. It was finally made in 1943 with Burnu Acquanetta in the role. About this time someone in the vast Universal organization said out loud, what do you suppose Montez would look like in a sarong? Prophetic words, whoever uttered them. It so happened the studio had another film in the works that had need of someone who could sport a sarong fetchingly.[52]

The thought of Montez in a sarong was certainly part of the studio's ethnic perception of her. Every other Latin actress from Lupita Tovar and Dolores del Rio to Armida and even a young Rita Moreno would spend time in the South Seas playing an island girl clad in the short, off the shoulder, figure-hugging sarong. The vision of Montez in a sarong brought her the most attention she ever got from both Universal's front offices and from the columnists and reviewers. *Variety* reported as early as May that Montez would soon be starring in a picture with a South Seas background. For the first time she would be on the cover of a magazine representing one of her movies. *Spot* featured Maria in her cleavage-baring red slendang (Universal's name for a sarong) crouching down next to the leopard Nisa on the cover of its January 1942 issue.[53]

Finally, there was a swell of interest in a role she was going to play. Ray Jones had done a series of portraits of her in the sarong that very much

Maria in her slendang with what the snipe calls "a jungle thespian" on the beach at Palos Verdes in *South of Tahiti.*

impressed the casting department. Once the decision was made to place Maria in *South of Tahiti,* Universal distributed the photos to whoever would take them. They led to a short piece by the United Press published during the filming of the picture called "'Battle of Sarongs' on in Film City." The article, developed by Universal, proclaimed, "Maria Montez new challenge to Dorothy Lamour." Right from the start Maria was presented as a hot, scantily dressed "shapely charmer." "Latin-American with a vibrant figure and an

Ray Jones's photos of Maria in her slendang had caused an unprecedented stir, so Universal was very keen on making the most of *South of Tahiti.* Here Maria is conferring with her director, George Waggner.

intriguing accent, Miss Montez had been groomed for such a role for a year." Her costume was fallaciously said to be "a scanty sarong made entirely of gardenias that must have caused Hays office censors to raise an eyebrow."[54]

The sarong sure did wonders for Dorothy Lamour. The brief costume Vera West designed for Montez and the scintillating way she filled it out did the same thing for her. The sarong would cling and expose—but not so much that it upset the Hays Office. Universal chose to call the garment a slendang, which it claimed was the proper name for it. It was the first time Montez was in a film that lasted seventy-eight minutes and the first time she left the Universal lot to film some exteriors: south of Los Angeles at Dana Point in

Orange County. She was still fourth on the cast list, but had a much larger part with considerably more dialogue, albeit in a mostly made-up language. The filming went so well and Maria looked so incredible in the slendang that this was the film in which Universal chose to place the card "Introducing Maria Montez" in the credits, even though it was actually her seventh film. Maria in her sarong is the chief feature in the one-sheet movie poster created to advertise the film. It was reworked for an announcement in *Film Bulletin.* Maria, "The Screen's New Blaze of Excitement" and "the Mmmm Girl," is still the most prominent image on the poster. The title the copy editor for the *Cleveland Plain Dealer* came up with for its review of *Tahiti* was "Maria Montez Is the Newest Sarong Girl."[55]

The Hays Office always had its hands full when a South Seas adventure movie came up, and *South of Tahiti* was no exception. Four amended copies of the script were submitted before it was finally passed. The basic story was acceptable. The problems, as usual, had to do with sex and violence. Too many sailors were killed by the leopards. The snake should be eliminated as it upsets children and local censor boards often take them out. The native girl's raiment also needed attention. "You understand, also, that the costuming of your heroine and the other native girls must be adequate at all times." It must not be "suggestive of women of loose morals." And by all means, the men must wear undershirts. Melahi (Maria) must not lie down on a mat with a man. Plus, the dialogue is full of "sex suggestiveness" and must be altered. It took two months, but Universal finally got its certificate of approval.[56]

South of Tahiti

Sailors Bob (Brian Donlevy), Chuck (Broderick Crawford), and Moose (Andy Devine) argue with Larkin (Henry Wilcoxon), the captain of their boat, over the shares of their last pearl haul. They steal the boat and wind up on an unchartered island to the south of Tahiti. While Chuck and Moose are away searching for water, Bob meets princess Melahi (Maria Montez) and her pet leopards. He is taken to the high chief of the village, Kawalima (H. B. Warner), and is told he may stay so long as he abides by the community's laws. Bob is all for this since he is attracted to Melahi. Chuck and Moose are willing to go along until they see the natives sacrificing pearls in a ceremony. But Bob is warned by the true power behind the throne, Tahawa (Abner Biberman), that white men are not welcome on the island.

While Bob is trying to teach Melahi to speak English, Moose and his native girl, Tutara (Armida), find a wrecked airplane in the jungle. The sailors hope to use the parts to repair their ship, but Melahi is afraid she will then lose Bob. Chuck talks Moose into stealing the pearls but Kawalima discovers the plot. They run out of the tomb where the pearls are to find their ship has been set on fire by Melahi. Captain Larkin arrives on the island with a crew to steal the pearls. Bob warns Kawalima, who tells him that Tahawa is going to marry Melahi and will be the next king. Bob feels like a chump and joins in Larkin's plot to steal the pearls until he learns the evil captain has kidnapped Melahi for insurance. Bob, Chuck, and Moose join with Melahi's leopards to defeat Larkin and his men. When Bob and Melahi go back to the temple, they are captured by Tahawa, who plans to kill Bob and proclaim himself the new king. But Kawalima arrives and sets the leopards on Tahawa, who is killed. A party is held for Bob and Melahi and Chuck, Moose, and Larkin all reluctantly toss pearls into the fire of sacrifice.

The original title for *South of Tahiti* was *White Savage*—but that was saved and used a couple of years later for another Montez film. The first title fit perfectly with the history of Maria's character. Bob, the white sailor stranded on the island, first encounters her as she leads her leopards along a jungle trail. The trailer for the movie notes he is "at the mercy of a primitive wild woman and her savage hoard." But as the movie unfolds it turns out she is actually white. She was in a plane crash as a child that killed her parents. Universal was obviously excited by the possibilities offered by *South of Tahiti.* It was released before *Bombay Clipper,* although that movie had been completed one month before *Tahiti* started filming. The notes prepared by Universal for the press book that was sent to theater owners all over the country refer to "the screen's fiery, new tropical find, Maria Montez." As usual, *Daily Variety* got it immediately. According to that periodical, the slendang "is something like a sarong, only more so. Or less so." Even the *New York Times* got it. Its reviewer noted that Universal had concocted a collection of clichés passing as a movie that is "an inducement to get Maria Montez out of street clothes and into a sarong." It was the first time her studio went all out to publicize a part played by Maria. Coupled with the slendang, it worked.[57]

The *Boston Traveler* was equally taken with *Tahiti*'s star, if not with the movie. It is such a witless rehash of every single trope in the often-visited island genre the reviewer wondered if Universal meant it to be satire. Maria is another story. She is remembered as "the personable starlet who had the Harvard freshmen agog on her recent Boston visit." Costumed in a slendang—and don't you call it a sarong—"she is a tasty dish, who sings as

Main Street in downtown Los Angeles was home to several second-run theaters where you could find many movies that never received the Motion Picture Production Code seal. Here the "reel" view of the South Seas, *South of Tahiti,* is the second feature to the "real," or at least more salacious, view.

well as she looks." It is evident what the copy editor thought of the film. The review is titled, "Maria Montez at Lux."[58]

Part of the "Production Data from Universal Studios" John Joseph sent to Joseph Breen on *South of Tahiti* was "Information on Personalities": "Black eyed, exotic, beautiful and [as] tempestuous as the role she plays in this picture, this Latin-American lovely, brought to Hollywood from South America by the Universal Studios, receives an ideal introduction to audiences in this country as the jungle princess, Melahi."

This was the first time Universal urged theaters to prepare promotional setups in the theater lobby for one of Maria's films. The studio suggested a tropical theme with palm trees and Hawaiian music. Theaters could contact a bookstore about getting a map of the South Pacific. In a true sign of those very different times, theaters were urged to contact the local high school or college's costume design class to have a contest for the best design of a sarong, with the winning sketches to be shown in the theater lobby. As a real topper, they could have a beauty contest with girls wearing a sarong. The prize would go "to the girl most nearly approaching the measurements of Maria."[59]

If you were going to be a sarong woman, you simply had to get along with animals. With Dorothy Lamour it was usually monkeys. With Montez Universal upped the ante. She was always surrounded by various types of jungle cats. *Tahiti* was the first time she co-starred with things stealthy and furry, but it would certainly not be the last. The studio released several stills that were picked up by newspapers around the country showing Maria in her slendang with cats of varying size and ferocity. She appeared in full color on the cover of *Spot* magazine in her red slendang with her arm around a leopard. Universal got further mileage out of the cats when John Joseph, the head of publicity, invited national columnist Paul Harrison out to the lot to meet Olga Celeste, who trained the leopards for *South of Tahiti.* Her work was cut out for her on this film because in spite of all the publicity, Montez did not much care for the leopards. When one of the cats, which was supposed to be circling ominously in the background, bounded up and tried to play with Brian Donlevy, Maria quickly absented herself from the set. Olga stepped right in and calmed everyone down, saying these large cats are just like kittens, always up to mischief.[60]

As for Maria, she was far more comfortable with smaller versions of the cats—cubs, in fact. Another set of photos to advertise *South of Tahiti* was taken by the pool of the Beverly Wilshire Hotel. Roman Freulich, who did both studio portraits and off-lot photos of Universal's players, was sent to shoot Maria playing with tiger cubs. For this series, Maria is posed in a short sunsuit lying on an outdoor lounger that perfectly shows off her legs. The anklet given to her by Claud Strickland is very much in view on her left ankle. Crawling all over her are three very young tiger cubs. They are friendly balls of fur, nuzzling her face, licking her toes, and generally behaving exactly like you would expect a trio of cubs to behave. Maria clearly loves it, laughing as the cubs climb all over her. It is one of the best series of nonformal portraits ever taken of her. She looks exactly as presented by her publicity: young, gorgeous, good-natured, and perfectly happy to be a sarong girl who enjoys playing with jungle animals.[61]

The photo shoot at the Beverly Wilshire mirrored Maria's performance in *South of Tahiti.* There is none of the imperiousness evident in *Boss of Bullion City.* She is all sweetness and light, clearly delighted to be in a first-rate role at last. Universal got around her accent by having her speak some sort of pseudo-

Roman Freulich photo of Maria with what the snipe assures us is "her souvenir" from *South of Tahiti,* "a tiny striped 'cat'" at the Beverly Wilshire Hotel.

Polynesian language. There are several scenes where Brian Donlevy is trying to teach her English. It's an uphill battle. But she is so sparkling that the audience could care less what language she speaks. It's plain to see why this movie finally put her on the cinematic map. Her only other performance to register the same level of sweetness would be as the "good" sister in *Cobra Woman.*

When Universal released a page of Montez photos, called "Slendang Girl," to publicize *South of Tahiti* for Sunday supplements all over the country on November 16, 1941, four of the six pictures featured her and jungle cats. Five show Maria in her slendang. Universal made a very big point in the advertising for *Tahiti* that the true name of the garment as worn in Malaya and the Dutch East Indies was slendang, not sarong. Universal's take on the garment was considerably briefer than what would be found in Indonesia. The studio pushed the exotic factor for all it was worth, noting Maria is from the Dominican Republic, had been a model for McClellend Barclay, never cooks for herself, and keeps lion cubs as pets. It stressed that her accent is her own. One of the photos shows her in a slendang, standing on her tiptoes to accentuate the lines of her legs and body, speaking into a recorder as she reads her script in order to check her enunciation. Another shows Maria surrounded by luggage as she packs for her promotional trip to publicize *South of Tahiti*—"so the public would not get the idea Maria lives in slendangs."

Another way of publicizing *South of Tahiti* was stressing Maria as the new sarong girl in town. *Screen Guide* published an article subtitled "Montez Shows Lamour That Two Can Play at Her Game." Dorothy Lamour is pictured on the left, scowling in her sarong with her legs severely crossed and raised, covering her body. Maria, on the right, looks fantastic lounging on a rock with her physique on display. There are Jack Albin photos of Montez playing the piano and a conga drum, another of her looking radiant in a nightclub, and a still from *Tahiti* in her slendang. She looks new, fresh, and exciting in all of the photos. The article is some fantasy about what a gamble this is for Maria since she has "a background of serious dramatic study abroad, in New York, and in Hollywood." You wonder who fed the publication that. It does return to reality by noting, "her studio feels that Maria will find a short cut to stardom by exploiting her physical attractions in native costume. Her fiery, voluptuous beauty in '*South of Tahiti*' seems to prove their case." In that they were correct. *Tahiti* led to the six Neverland movies that made Maria's career.[62]

Author Tom DeVane captured just how important *South of Tahiti* was to Montez's career. In January 1942 he wrote an article for *Hollywood* magazine called "Glamour Is Her Dish." He noted that she might have just finished her first starring role wearing a slendang in a "Dorothy Lamourish" role in a South Seas island movie, but she was already known as a movie star. Maria explained to him how she had achieved this. She credited her father with teaching her to think and to plan. She applied his advice to breaking into Hollywood. "My first three months here I was out every night. I deliberately set about making my face known. I danced my feet off—but always I was photographed and always I was mentioned in the gossip columns, until finally people begin to say, 'Who is this Montez anyway?' That is what I wanted. I am a glamour girl without even setting foot in front of a movie camera!" *South of Tahiti* would change all that.[63]

Besides the slendang, Universal was able to make some mileage out of having Montez "sing" for the first time in one of her movies. The song "Melahi" played over the credits and Maria "sang" it twice in the movie. It was issued as a song sheet, its cover image featuring Maria in her slendang with flowers in her hair leaning against a tree next to Brian Donlevy as they look into each other's eyes. The film's director, George Waggner, wrote the lyrics with music by Frank Skinner. It was to be "sung slowly." It is quite the ode to love and Melahi.

> Melahi, flower of the jungle night, calling to me o'er a sea of blue
> The moonlight, sifting through the palm trees
> Seems to bring me nearer the magic that is you.

Terrific publicity for the movie—only Maria had to be dubbed. Martha Tilton, who sometimes sang with Benny Goodman's band, was hired to sing the song.[64]

The impact of Montez in her slendang was nicely summed up by Sidney Skolsky in a 1944 column that was largely about the glory that was Maria's breasts. He tore himself away from her chest long enough to note the big break in her career. "Her fan mail started when she appeared in a sarong. The picture was *'South of Tahiti'* and letters poured in from exhibitors stating that the public wanted to see more of her. It was admitted that she was no great actress. But who cares?"[65]

South of Tahiti put Montez in direct conflict with the established and original sarong queen, Dorothy Lamour. But *Screen Guide* thought Montez could hold her own as long as wartime priorities did not interfere. Cloth, like everything else, was rationed. But as long as Universal could secure a priority for the material, she could slip on one dazzling sarong after another and continue to make box office news. The magazine expressed one fervent wish, "Here's hoping she can always get that priority [for the sarong material]." That "fervent wish" was shared by Keith Wilson in his syndicated Sunday filmdom article where he was wondering, "Who's queen of the smokies?" After *Tahiti* and the latest cache of Ray Jones photos, he thought the "newest claimant" for the hot, sultry title is "Universal's Maria Montez, a product of Santo Domingo."[66]

Two months went by while Maria was back east publicizing *South of Tahiti* on her first publicity tour. Before she left, she paid a visit to the MGM lot in Culver City to read for the role of Cesca for the upcoming film *Tortilla Flat.* As was the case with *Blood and Sand,* it would have meant a significant part in a loan-out to one of the major studios in moviedom. She lost out to Betty Wells. She also read for the roll of Maria in *For Whom the Bell Tolls* at Paramount. She commented on this plum role, "Whether I get the part of Maria or not is of little consequence. But I believe that since most of the characters of Hemingway's book are Spanish types, Spanish actors should be allowed to portray some of the roles." Ever conscious of her role in the Good Neighbor Policy, she thought this would increase the value of the movie in South American markets and aid in furthering goodwill between the Americas.[67]

The *Tahiti* tour was the whole reason she was available to "dance" with the Harvard freshmen. It also gave her the opportunity to show up in Detroit for the November 19 world premiere of Abbott and Costello's third service comedy, *Keep 'Em Flying.* It was held at Detroit's five-thousand-seat Fox Theater, one of the finest movie palaces in America. Universal wanted to have as many contract players as possible to celebrate the latest effort from the hottest duo to ever walk its lot. Maria joined the film's co-stars Carol Bruce, Dick Foran, and Martha Raye in support of Abbott and Costello. The premiere was being broadcast coast to coast and a reception at the Ford Motor plant followed the premiere.

In this period Montez appeared on a magazine cover for the first time in the April 1941 issue of *Film Fun.* She is presented in a stereotypical Latin fashion with castanets in her hands, a deeply scooped bra top, and a very colorful skirt slit up the middle to expose her legs. There is a straw mat behind her. The picture is titled "Perky in the Straw." *Film Fun* was essentially fifty pages of pin ups. Not quite *Life,* but she was on the cover. With a magazine cover on the stands, *That Night in Rio* coming into theaters, and a small part in *Moonlight* that did not require her to be on set constantly, Universal decided to include her in a group of studio players sent to entertain at the Legislative Ball at the Sacramento Memorial Auditorium on April 23, 1941. Appearing at the ball celebrating California's state legislators with the likes of Phil Silvers and Kathryn Grayson could only help promote the studio's contract player.[68]

On December 10, 1941, filming commenced for *The Mystery of Marie Roget.* Alfred Hitchcock's *Saboteur* was shooting on the lot at the same time. *Saboteur* was written by Peter Viertel, whom Montez had dated for a time. She had been considered to play "a femme spy in the picture." It would have been a minor role in an admittedly big movie, but Universal had greater things in mind for her after *South of Tahiti.* In *Marie Roget* she was back to a one-hour movie filmed entirely on the Universal lot, but at least she would be top billed in the opening credits and second billed in the closing. The screenplay, by

Michael Jacoby, was loosely based on an Edgar Allan Poe story of the same name. The studio was obviously very impressed by the reaction to Montez as an island girl, but it had her scheduled for *Marie Roget* when it was still unsure as to her niche. In fact, she had wangled the part away from previously cast Peggy Moran just a few days before shooting was to start. Moran had been practicing the French song she was to sing, which had to be written out for her phonetically as she did not speak the language. Forty years later she was still suspicious how Montez got the part. She certainly was not a fan. She recalled, "We always considered her a little bit of comedy relief in a way, because she put on such acts."[69]

However she did it, Maria got the part. This time Universal would try her out in a gothic horror story as a nineteenth-century cabaret singer. All of her recent antics nationally were not ignored as she was touted for her new role. Louella Parsons, who always liked Montez, noted that although "her pictures at 'U' have not held up with her off-screen publicity," she has learned from her experience at college. "Maria Montez' jaunt thru Harvard must have given her a taste for the classics, for Universal's sultry siren will abandon her sarong for a fling into chiller-drama in Edgar Allan Poe's '*The Mystery of Marie Roget.*' Bet the Harvard lads never dreamed Marie would be bringing 'literature' to the screen but since their life-sized study of the Montez' measurements on that recent trip, they'll probably be voting for her to do Dickens next."[70]

The Mystery of Marie Roget

The Poe story starts out in 1889 Paris. The town is obsessed with the disappearance of musical comedy star Marie Roget (Maria Montez). Police inspector Gobelin (Lloyd Corrigan) is being pressured by Henri Beauvais (John Litel), French minister of naval affairs and a friend of the Roget family, to find out what happened to her. The inspector pulls his medical officer friend Paul Dupin (Patric Knowles) into the case. A woman's body with a mutilated face is found in the Seine. It is thought to be Marie, but she shows up while Gobelin and Beauvais are at the Roget home telling Marie's grandmother Cecile (Maria Ouspenskaya) and sister Camille (Nell O'Day) of her supposed death. Camille and Marcel Vigneaux (Edward Norris) become engaged, but the engagement is just a ploy by lovers Marie and Marcel, who plan to murder Camille, who is set to inherit 1 million francs from her grandfather's estate.

Cecile hires Dr. Dupin to escort Camille to a party as she fears she will be murdered there for her money. That night, Marie and Marcel argue when he hesitates in killing Camille. Marie disappears again. When another body without a face is found in the river, Marcel confesses to killing Marie but says he did so to save Camille. He is released after being supported by Dr. Dupin at his arraignment. That night Gobelin learns from Scotland Yard that the first woman found in the river was the wife of Marcel. Gobelin and Dupin find out that Marcel has eluded police surveillance and is loose in Paris. They rush to the Roget home just in time to stop Marcel from killing Camille. Marcel escapes out an upstairs window; Gobelin pursues him across the Paris rooftops and kills him.

Universal must have realized its mistake immediately. There was none of the flurry of articles, photos, reviews, and fan letters generated by the very dark role Maria was given in *Marie Roget* compared to the avalanche of interest that greeted her after *South of Tahiti.* Louella Parsons even titled her column about *Marie Roget,* which was just being filmed, "Maria Montez to Abandon Sarong for Role in Thriller." Maria's accent is very much under control, but again her "singing" was dubbed, this time by Dorothy Triden. No one wrote about the period costumes Maria wore, and this time Russian-born Maria Ouspenskaya owned the leopard. Sadly, Ouspenskaya died tragically in bed in a fire ignited by a cigarette in 1949. She never left a memoir. It would have been interesting to know what one of the most classically trained actresses in Hollywood in the 1940s thought about both Maria and this trite take on Poe's story. The only thing the two actresses had in common was a pronounced accent and a devotion to Carroll Righter and his astrological charts.[71]

At best, Maria was mildly noticed in what was dismissed as a quickie take on a serious story. Even *Variety* and *Hollywood Reporter* were hard put to work up much enthusiasm. At least the *Reporter* noted, "Miss Montez is briefly glimpsed as the attractive Marie." Bosley Crowther in the *New York Times* dismissed *Marie Roget* as "a dreary, aimless film, devoid of logic or excitement or even a shadow of suspense." For once it is hard to argue with him. The only thing to recommend *Marie Roget* is the atmospheric camera work of Elwood Bredell, who would later lens *The Killers* (1946).[72]

Fellow cast members had varying impressions of Maria this early in her career. Nell O'Day, who played with Maria in both *Marie Roget* and *Bullion City,* thought she was "intelligent and charming" and remembered they "got on very well." But like columnist Jimmie Fidler, O'Day commented, "She was not popular with the staff and crew because she thought of them almost as servants. She treated the dressers and other people from the wardrobe department as though they were maids!" Early in the game, Montez told her she did not want to be an actress, she wanted to be a "pair-sone-ality." Edward Norris, who played the murderer Marcel, knew the "people on the lot resented her, because of her holding things up." But the two of them "got along very well, I liked her very much, I thought she was underrated." Enjoying Maria's sparkling personality while recognizing the continuing problems she had with the studio, crew, and directors was common among those who knew her at the time.[73]

Maria's second Christmas in Los Angeles was imminent. Her entire family was still at home in the Dominican Republic. She had just finished *Marie Roget* and was talking to Teddy Stouffer, another displaced person in L.A. with no family, about the season. He started telling her about the great ski resorts of Europe he had visited so often before having to leave the continent. Maria pointed out that Sun Valley, Idaho, had recently opened as America's leading ski resort. They decided to head out to Idaho for Christmas in the snow. Stouffer was a skilled skier but he enjoyed taking Maria down the beginners' run and "holding her, feeling her warmth and excitement and happiness." On Christmas Eve Maria and Stouffer sat around an open fireplace singing carols in several different languages. It wound up being a wonderful Christmas for Montez. She was in a new environment for her with someone she loved who appreciated her for the sweetness of her nature that could blossom when she did not have to constantly put up her created Maria Montez front. She left right after the New Year to return to Universal and the renewal of her constant war for stardom. Stouffer stayed to work as a ski instructor.[74]

The year 1941 had been a good one for moving Maria's career along. In December she was back in *Life* with a photo taken at Atlanta's Paramount Theater by candlelight since there were lighting restrictions due to the demands of defense-related industries using so much of the local Tennessee Valley Authority–generated power. On December 1 her contract option was picked up by Universal for the third time. Claud Strickland was missing in action and the Japanese would bomb Pearl Harbor six days after her option was picked up. While Maria flourished the world war got worse and far closer to home.

For its part, Universal had been both surprised and encouraged by the reaction to Maria in a sarong in *South of Tahiti.* As she finished *Marie Roget,* the studio was preparing a part for Montez that would get her back to the South Seas. Abbott and Costello were getting ready to start filming *Pardon My Sarong* on March 2, 1942—two months after *Marie Roget* wrapped. Maria was slated to play the chief's daughter. This time she would not be wearing anything like the heavy period costumes that covered the increasingly famous Montez form from her neck to her ankles in her previous film. She would be back in a sarong.

4

Arabian Nights

Joe Pasternak had taken a good look at Maria in New York, very much liked what he saw, and recommended that Universal sign her. But looking good in person and having that beauty register on film are two different things. It was up to the studio to arrange screen tests and time in the portrait studio for its new contract players. Then to work them into small roles to see how they looked and performed on-screen. If these three steps worked out, it was up to the studio to find a niche for new actors—a created personality and filmed persona that would fit them and keep moviegoers coming back to see them.

In the case of Clark Gable, MGM immediately sent him to Howard Strickling, the studio's publicity manager, to create his image. He took one look at the physically impressive Gable and decided the former oil field worker should be presented as a man's man. Gable fell into the orbit of director Victor Fleming and started hunting, fishing, and riding motorcycles in earnest. He had never had the time, interest, or money to seriously indulge in these pastimes before he signed with MGM. Fans loved him in he-man roles: a daring aviator in *Test Pilot,* an aggressive newsreel cameraman in *Too Hot to Handle,* the stalwart first mate and leader of men in *Mutiny on the Bounty.* No one had much interest in seeing him as a nineteenth-century Irish politician, and *Parnell* was a total failure. Universal was faced with the same challenge with Maria Montez. She had been up on the screen and clearly she filmed very well. But where did she fit?[1]

Universal tried Maria out in westerns, spy thrillers, and gothic mysteries. But it was when she was put on a sarong for *South of Tahiti* that the studio was inundated with letters from fans and the national press finally noticed her on-screen. Louella Parsons wrote that she had been "publicized in so many nightclubs, I began to think she was a professional diner-outer. . . . Now one film, '*South of Tahiti,*' is released, [and she is] well enough known to be invited to Red Cross drives and visit Yale" (actually Harvard).[2]

The outrageous behavior Maria engaged in for publicity and for pressing Universal into giving her parts that so enraged Peggy Moran when she lost out for the lead in *Marie Roget* was viewed differently among the women signed by the studio at the same time. Anne Gwynne thought, "If I'd followed Maria Montez's lead, I'm sure the Studio would have given me better opportunities." Kathryn Adams, who did several B movies and serials for Universal between 1940 and 1942, enjoyed her time there and everyone she worked with. "Except for Maria Montez [who] was not a pleasant person. She was one of the exceptions." Classically trained Gale Sondergaard, who was at Universal from 1941 to 1947 and co-starred with Maria in *Gypsy Wildcat,* agreed with Kathryn Adams; she could never stand what she perceived as Montez's very unprofessional behavior. In a review of a book about Ray Jones, Mimi Couch recalled many of the Universal stars featured in the book whom she had known as a contract player at the studio. Of Montez, she remembered, "She was a fiery and beautiful Latina who refused to wear a bra in her films."[3]

The varied views of La Montez held by her fellow contract players had one common theme: she was fanatically devoted to establishing herself. But the important thing was what the executives at Universal thought of her. They recognized that *The Mystery of Marie Roget* was clearly a step in the wrong direction for the Montez persona following *Tahiti,* so the obvious move was to get her back in a sarong. Luckily for all concerned, the next Abbott and Costello comedy was about to go before the cameras. Titled *Pardon My Sarong,* it called for the surprisingly successful duo to move beyond the service comedies that made them one of the most popular comedy teams in films and broaden their horizons. Bing Crosby and Bob Hope over at Paramount were already popping up all over the world in their "Road to" movies. Why not have Abbott and Costello do the same thing and why not bring a sarong-clad Montez along for the ride?

It is indicative of how excited the heads of Universal were about Maria's prospects that in the original cast list released by Universal's publicity department she was scheduled to play Luana, the chief's daughter. This would have made her the second female lead in the next movie of the kings of the studio. The story line had the comedy duo inadvertently driving the bus they stole off the end of a pier when they take a wrong turn. They sign up to crew on a yacht race to Hawaii but wind up on the proverbial uncharted tropical isle. Obviously, Abbott and Costello would be the focus of the movie. The main secondary male role would be the yachtsman. The main female role was his love interest, and that part went to Virginia Bruce. The second female lead was the chief's daughter, who had to marry Costello when he was mistakenly perceived as the legendary hero who would lead the natives to reconquer their haunted temple in the mountains. Maria's princess was third billed on the cast list, after Abbott and Costello and Virginia Bruce. When Maria was removed from the part, it went to Nan Wynn. The only other island girl part of any significance was Ferna. She had several lines but was primarily a character created to pursue Lou Costello. This would have been too small a part for Maria after the splash she made playing the female lead in *South of Tahiti*. It went to Marie "The Body" McDonald.[4]

Montez did start out filming *Pardon My Sarong*. While she was listed only as a cast member in the blurbs sent out by the studio for the release of *Bombay Clipper*, which was released after *South of Tahiti* in January and early February 1942, she was being touted as the studio's "sarong girl" and currently filming the part of a South Seas princess by late February. A March 1942 Associated Press piece about how several studios were preparing musicals "as a war antidote" noted that Universal planned to make *Pardon My Sarong* with Abbott and Costello. It would be "another South Seas-er, with Maria Montez, the poor man's Dorothy Lamour." This is an interesting take as Virginia Bruce had female top billing just after the comic stars. But she, of course, was not going to be wearing the sarong that needed to be pardoned.[5]

Columnist Jimmie Fidler was invited out to the set as the filming commenced. He noted that George Raft was also visiting the *Sarong* set but immediately lost interest in the proceedings when he learned that neither Virginia Bruce nor Maria were on the set. When Montez did arrive, Fidler noted that she came in "wrapped in a sarong and thirty-seven pairs of male eyes (the entire crew and Raft)." All of this changed with the studio blurb released to the press on March 27, 1942, noting that Walter Wanger was scheduled to film *Arabian Nights* starting in May and it would star Jon Hall, Sabu, and Maria Montez (in that order).[6]

The agent for that change was independent producer Walter Wanger and his second planned movie under his contract with Universal. In 1942, Wanger was in his second term as president of the Academy of Motion Picture Arts and Sciences and the producer of such key films as *Stagecoach, Foreign Correspondent,* and *The Long Voyage Home.* He was an outspoken proponent of films having substance and meaning, not just being popular entertainment. Universal, the king of the B pictures, may have seemed an odd choice for someone with Wanger's sensibilities. But the Universal of 1941 was changing. He was exactly what Universal was looking for under the regime of J. Cheever Cowdin and Nathan Blumberg. Money had been rolling into the studio, thanks to the skill of the new management, the wildly popular films of Deanna Durbin and Abbott and Costello, the various established monsters, and the successful series of weekly serial films produced there. By 1941 Universal was poised to once again begin making the sort of A movies that Carl Laemmle Jr. had produced eight years before. Both Cowdin and Blumberg believed in the producer-unit method as the best way to create A-level films. Alfred Hitchcock was brought in to film *Saboteur* and Gregory LaCava to do *Lady in a Jam*. Wanger was bringing along *Eagle Squadron*.

Wanger had been distributing his films through the choice of most independent producers, United Artists, since the summer of 1936. Their relationship produced several fine films. He worked with director Fritz Lang on *You Only Live Once* (1937), John Cromwell on *Algiers* (1938), John Ford on *Stagecoach* (1939), and Ford again on *The Long Voyage Home* (1940). The trouble was United Artists had considerable difficulty with its leadership. The demand for its mostly A-level product was high, but the profits were way down. UA did not have its own theater chain, unlike the five major majors, and had difficulty getting its films onto the best screens around the country. This cut down on the producer's profits. It is significant that David O. Selznick, one of UA's staunchest producers, released *Gone with the Wind* through MGM. Universal may not have had its own theaters either, but it did have one of the best lots for Hollywood production and a much more established distribution system. Plus, the studio wanted Wanger badly and, unlike United Artists, it very much wanted to film *Eagle Squadron*.

Wanger's alliance with Universal allowed him to work as a studio unit rather than the semi-independent producer he had been. Under the terms of his agreement with the studio, Wanger was in charge of producing the film, but since the studio was financing it, he used its lot, its personnel, its stars, and its widely established distribution system. He brought production designer Alexander Golitzen along with him and Universal signed him to a long-term contract. They got right to work on *Eagle Squadron*. It told the story of American pilots who traveled to England to join the Royal Air Force before the United States was actively involved in World War II. The film starred established Universal performers Robert Stack, Diana Barrymore, Jon Hall, and Nigel Bruce. One of the most successful directors on the lot, Arthur Lubin, helmed the film, while Stanley Cortez filmed it before moving on to his next project, *The Magnificent Ambersons* (1942), for Orson Welles. *Eagle Squadron* was standard wartime fare, its only new wrinkle that it featured Americans in England's air force. Wanger was president of the Academy of Motion Picture Arts and Sciences, involved with the Office of War Information, and an outspoken advocate of movies playing an important role in explaining the reasons for the war and Americans' duty to play their part in winning that war. He also knew that people needed to relax and be entertained. That is where he put his prodigious filmmaking abilities next. He wanted to make a Technicolor extravaganza out of the tales of *The Arabian Nights*. His effort proved so successful it led to an additional five Neverland fantasies starring the newly created team of Maria Montez and Jon Hall. Turhan Bey summed up their popularity and need: "They were pure escapism, and there is nothing wrong with that. There was a war on, and films like this were great for morale."[7]

Wanger, like several other Hollywood producers, realized that as the war stretched into its second and third year, audiences were tiring of war films. They wanted distracting entertainment. He had wanted to do an alternative take on the often-filmed stories of *A Thousand and One Nights* since the mid-1930s. He planned on calling his film *Arabian Nights* and eventually came to believe it could be done justice only in Technicolor. This would create new challenges for Universal. The studio had never done a film in the three-color process. It was very expensive, requiring the studio to use highly restricted color film, special cameras and cameramen from the Technicolor Company, and an astounding number of lights. The company stipulated that its technicians had to accompany the cameras to check the color balance on the set and to generally oversee that the process was used properly. One of the major problems was that Technicolor film was in short supply due to the many training movies being created by the military. But Wanger's vision of old Baghdad was a colorful and grand one. He just had to convince Universal to ante up and create one of its periodic A movies.[8]

The effort certainly paid off. Costing slightly over $1 million to make, the film brought in over $4 million and four Academy Award nominations. It also set the template for the five following Neverland films, all of which vibrated with expensive color. A spreadsheet was prepared for Wanger to differentiate the costs involved with shooting the film in Technicolor rather than black and white, assuming 145,000 feet of negative. The difference in negative cost would be $26,012. It would be $2,184 just to rent the cameras. The Technicolor camera crew would add another $9,300. Cutting the negative would be the same for color or black and white, but protecting the master positive print would add another $1,762. Overall, the added cost of shooting *Arabian Nights* in color would be $44,190 ($1,117,000 in 2021's dollars). All this was just the cost of filming. In order to save money in other aspects, it was suggested that black-and-white rush prints be used. Large interior sets should be avoided to cut down on construction costs and lighting requirements. Rehearsing time should be held to a minimum. The studio was urged

Arabian Nights was nominated in four categories at the 15th Academy Awards, held at the Coconut Grove, March 3, 1943. Maria is pictured with George Frazier, who covered the entertainment world for *Life* magazine. (Courtesy of the Academy of Motion Picture Arts and Sciences.)

to "select a director and a cameraman who will make satisfactory speed in photography." But costs and problems notwithstanding, Wanger, one of the most successful producers in Hollywood, was going to make Universal swallow the pill. He wanted his tale of the 1,001 nights to be vibrant with color. Universal bit the bullet, partially because Fox had demonstrated just how spectacularly its star photographed in Technicolor.[9]

It was Universal's decision to have Montez play Sherazade (as they spelled the traditional Scheherazade) in Wanger's film. The studio certainly went to work to spread the word about *Arabian Nights.* News of the casting of the upcoming movie first showed up in the *New York Times* March 24, 1942. Richard Hays in his "Along Film Row" column for the *Seattle Times* followed three days later to report that Wanger would follow *Eagle Squadron* with *Arabian Nights* and that the cast was set on Montez-Hall-Sabu. Four days later, Edwin Schallert, chief Hollywood correspondent of the *Los Angeles Times,* announced that producer John Anthony Dunham wanted to make a movie revolving around the Spanish-themed Santa Barbara Festival in California that would star Maria Montez. He followed this with, "Incidentally, she is to have the primary part in *'Arabian Nights'* with Jon Hall and Sabu."[10]

Columnists gave the movie considerable free publicity during its filming. Schallert did another column where he noted Universal was so happy with the film that it intended making Maria, Hall, and Sabu "a sort of eternal trio, or triangle, or something like that." He concluded, "Evidently it is thought that *'Arabian Nights'* will make the group thoroughly popular." Schallert was joking. He knew full well that every studio loved to create teams of actors that would bring fans back to see their latest creation. Their next two films, *White Savage* and *Cobra Woman,* were both in preparation. It was Maria who stood out to most of the visitors to the set. The correspondent for *Showmen's Trade Review* showed up and saw her waiting in costume while the technicians prepared the scene. He described her as "very easy to look at and helps the eye muscles open the eyelids."[11]

Photos were released featuring Montez. In one she is braless in a shoulder-baring white dress with a caption about dancing in New York nightclubs, posing for McClelland Barclay, and organizing the Montez for Stardom club. In another she is in the fringed bra top and headdress she wears in the film. This caption reads, "Maria is the exotic and eccentric young lady all Hollywood talks about." In its August 1942 issue *Screenland* printed a photo of Maria and Jon Hall in their costumes, noting that *Arabian Nights* was being filmed in Technicolor.[12]

John Rosenfield published one of his Sunday essays about the new star just as *Arabian Nights* was being released nationally. He pointed out that she was currently known "to such sections of the public as inspect leg art in magazines and remember whose legs they are," but that *Arabian Nights* would make her a star. Rosenfield wrote that her success came as a result of a "cold-blooded strategy" to break into Hollywood. He noted she signed with Universal because that studio did not have any exotics with an accent. She

Ray Jones photo of Maria in her *Arabian Nights* costume. This was one of Universal's most requested pin ups.

then went on to work with any photographer who had film, became the supreme commissary actress in town, and figured out how to make spectacular entrances to nightclubs. In *Arabian Nights,* he enthused, the studio had figured out how to get her as naked as possible and still pass the Hays Office.[13]

Universal could do this because the lady herself completely understood her initial appeal. She told Rosenfield, "I never saw such a beautiful woman on the screen as me. . . . To date I have given the movie audiences sex. From now on I propose to combine sex with drama. My beautiful body—the upkeep has been terrific." But she would continue to work on that "upkeep." She had been her own publicity department for two years and now it was finally paying off. Two more films were planned by Universal with Maria continuing to challenge the Hays Office. Rosenfield thought she could get away with being so outrageous because the scribes find she has "a warm and friendly personality." Her interviews "and the pictures she is willing to pose for make lively copy—not to say lovely." He concluded that with the release of *Arabian Nights* audiences would soon know Maria as well as they did Greer Garson.[14]

Apparently Walter Wanger was not completely convinced. One of the constant undercurrents in Elizabeth Russell's screenplay "A Star in Gemini" was the actress's uncertainty over keeping the leading role in *Arabian Nights.* She had fought hard within Universal to get the part. But other actresses, such as Simone Simon, were being tested. The studio had unsuccessfully contacted Fox to see if Gene Tierney was available. In Russell's screenplay, Maria is convinced that neither Universal nor Wanger believes in her ability to play the leading role. *Silver Screen* summed up the immediate challenge in playing the leading lady in its synopsis of the movie. "Yes, she was beautiful, Sherazad, so beautiful that no man could look at her but to desire her." The character had to be successfully portrayed as eminently alluring to several men and worthy of being a queen or the movie would not work at all. It is known that besides his interest in Simon and Tierney, Wanger's attention had been very much captured by Burnu Acquanetta. This is why columnists all over Hollywood started writing about a feud between Maria, "the Caribbean Cyclone," and Acquanetta, "the Venezuelan Volcano," stressing, as the nicknames suggested, their perceived Latin volubility.[15]

This supposed "feud" tells a lot about the ethnic, racial, and sexual mores of 1940s Hollywood as well as Maria's clear-eyed evaluation of her career. The Hollywood press loved nothing more than creating "feuds" between the people they covered. Sometimes it was played for laughs by both sides, such as Jack Benny and Fred Allen. Other times it was real, as between Bette Davis and Joan Crawford at Warner Brothers. It worked better for women because it fit the stereotype of the day that a woman could not get along with another woman if a similar goal, or a man of any sort, was in play. There is no doubt that Wanger expressed interest in Acquanetta. She was a newly signed Universal contract player who had initially been hired on July 20, 1942, to play the role of a "Virgin" in *Arabian Nights* for one week at $235. By August 10 Wanger's interest got her elevated to the role of Ishya, one of the leaders of the harem. In this she joined Rosemary Dempsey, Pat Starling, June Ealey,

Burnu Acquanetta, described in the snipe as "Universal's sensational new film 'find,'" in her *Arabian Nights* finery. Walter Wanger certainly agreed.

and Virginia Engels. Her dark skin set her as what would have been called at the time an "exotic" type. It was a northwestern European–centric term. It spoke of darker skin, differently shaped eyes, the "brown-skinned girls" of sea shanties. Acquanetta realized this early in the game and after hearing President Roosevelt's talk about pan-American relations she decided to present herself as a Latin American. She became a model for Harry Conover and later John Robert Powers, posing as a Latin American woman. She eventually signed with Universal, whose publicity department dreamed up the "Venezuelan Volcano" appellation.

It all blew up when she could not produce any identification as a South American for the Screen Actors Guild when she attempted to sign up. She then "admitted" to being a Native American, specifically, an Arapahoe originally from the Wind River Indian Reservation in Wyoming. It was said that Burnu Acquanetta meant "burning fire, deep water" in her native language. The story went that her Arapahoe mother and part Cherokee, part Caucasian father both died and she was adopted and taken to Norristown, Pennsylvania. Ever nimble, Universal took it in stride. The studio declared she would be "the first female full-blooded Indian to be featured in the movies." The *Milwaukee Journal* was a bit harsher in its judgment. The photo that accompanied the article about the changes in Acquanetta's story labeled her the "perpetrator of Hollywood newest film hoax."[16]

The Acquanetta-as-an-Indian story was what Universal was going with during the filming of *Arabian Nights.* She was one of the few harem girls singled out for photographs in her costume by Ray Jones. She was a beautiful woman, photographed magnificently, and seemed to be headed for bigger things. Wanger released publicity statements that he was thinking of pairing her in a film with Charles Boyer following her introduction in *Arabian Nights.* Until the producer received a handwritten letter from Norristown, Pennsylvania, sent on September 11, 1942.

> To whom it may concern:
>
> This is to certify, that Burnu Acquanetta, as she calls herself is a plain Negro girl of Norristown, Pa. She is Miss Mildred Davenport of 1211 Willow St. Norristown, Pa. Her parents Mr. and Mrs. Robt Davenport *are living.* She is no Venezuelan. Her parents are Americans and she was born in Norristown. She has lied a great deal to get where she is. This is a very true statement.
>
> Send her back to Norristown Pa. She is a colored American girl. We all knew her well and Charles Boyer will soon find out.
>
> Her Friends and classmates of Norristown, Pa.[17]

The production code of that era is generally cited over its concern for violence and sexuality. But it also specifically prohibited miscegenation, which was defined as "sex relationships between the white and black races." If Acquanetta was from Venezuela, a Latin woman could still get the guy.

There might have been a chance if she was an American Indian. It would probably have to be a western movie, but it would have been possible. But as a Black woman, forget it. Black men at the time were generally relegated to roles as comic relief, menials, servants, doormen, manual workers, sleeping car porters, or tribesmen. Black women were almost exclusively maids and absolutely never the love interest of the inevitably white leading man. Acquanetta did not get the lead in *Arabian Nights* and never made the film with Charles Boyer Walter Wanger had in mind. While the studio did not admit to her being Black, it was common enough knowledge that when *Jet* magazine published a piece about her in 1952 it was simply accepted that she was Mildred Davenport from Norristown. As far back as July 1950 the *Los Angeles Sentinel,* the city's entry into the thriving Black press of the time, referred to her as the "beautiful Negro screen actress Mildred Davenport, known professionally as Acquanetta."[18]

Word of the conflict over the leading role got out, of course, and columnist Erskine Johnson wrote, "Maria Montez and Burnu Acquanetta, Universal's new find, can get along without each other very well." Sheilah Graham, never a fan of Montez, wrote, "Acquanetta, the Indian girl, is said to be feuding with Miss Montez on the Universal lot. Their quarrel is probably about who wears least in their films." Maria always downplayed any animosity between the two. When Louella Parsons brought it up, Maria logically responded, "Neither one of us is important enough to have a feud. Now, if it were Hedy Lamarr and Marlene Dietrich, it would be a different matter. Besides, I play the lead in '*Arabian Nights.*' I am Sherazade and Acquanetta is one of six girls—just a small part. Acquanetta is just starting and I wouldn't do anything to hurt her. It wouldn't be fair." She went on to say she hardly knew Acquanetta. She thought she was an Indian, though she did not have the sharp nose Maria believed was a hallmark of First Nations peoples. "She is dark and quite pretty. Maybe she is a Venezuelan Indian," Maria concluded.[19]

After a few small roles at Universal, Acquanetta was tapped to play the title role in *Captive Wild Woman* (1943), in which mad scientist John Carradine turns a female ape into a woman. She played the part without having any dialogue. Next year she was back in the same boat, playing the title character in *Jungle Woman.* From Universal, Acquanetta moved on to Monogram for a brief time but was soon out of films. She eventually married Jack Ross, a Phoenix, Arizona, car dealer. She appeared on the small screen doing her husband's ads for local television and eventually hosted her own local television program in which she introduced the Hollywood movies of her youth.[20]

Maria elaborated on why she would not have a feud with Acquanetta in an interview with Dick Mook for his "Pictures on the Fire" column in *Silver Screen* magazine. The author made fun of her accent as she insisted she was not feuding "weeth Eendian girl" and did not even know her. She reiterated that if she ever did feud with someone, it would be "some wawn eemportant." Then she explained why. The answer would explain the ruling ideal of her life from the Dominican Republic to New York and Los Angeles and on to Paris. "I do not have to feud weeth unknowns to be important. I am eemportant seence I am five years old. . . . I cawm from eemportant people so that make me eemportant also." Throughout her life she would continue to live as an upper-class woman no matter the size of her parts or where she lived or whom she was with.[21]

There was another casting decision on *Arabian Nights* that spoke to the strict color line that existed in 1942 in Hollywood and in the United States in general. Sherazade needed a maid, called a "dresser" in the cast list. Even in an Arabian fantasy the part went to a Black woman. Chosen for the small part was Jeni LeGon, whose name is scarcely remembered today. Like Kenny Washington breaking the color line in the National Football League in 1946 with the Los Angeles Rams, when Jeni LeGon signed a contract with MGM in 1935 she became the first Black woman to sign with a major film studio. But major studio contract or not, she still was not allowed to eat in the cafeteria. MGM brought her in as one of the leading tap dancers of her era. But the studio could not figure out how to incorporate an obviously Black woman into their musicals and dance extravaganzas. It would not be possible to make her the love interest of Andy Hardy the way they did with other recently signed ingénues like Lana Turner, Donna Reed, Esther Williams, or Ann Rutherford. MGM eventually bought out her contract, making her available for stage work in England, starring roles in all-Black independent films, and to play maids for various Hollywood studios.[22]

Peggy Satterlee, who played one of the six court Virgins, joined Jeni LeGon in having a small part in the Technicolor Arabian desert. Whereas LeGon was one of a crowd in a few of the production stills distributed in advance of the film's release, Peggy Satterlee was in several singles in her harem outfit and in a score of cast photos, looking great with a smile that lit up her lovely face. Satterlee's career was destroyed not by the limitations Hollywood imposed due to race or because she lacked talent, but because she was one of two underage girls who charged Errol Flynn with rape. The trial started in January 1943, just as *Arabian Nights* was coming out in theaters. Whatever future she may have had in film evaporated with the savaging she

Maria and the Virgins. Peggy Satterlee is leaning against Maria.

received on the stand by defense attorney Jerry Geisler. Flynn was found not guilty.[23]

In the twenty-page, full-color program for *Arabian Nights* available in theaters showing the film, Acquanetta and Peggy Satterlee are very well illustrated. There are more photos of the harem girls than of the principal actors. Of the three of those, Maria got the full page while Hall and Sabu had to share a page. Jeni LeGon is nowhere to be seen. The same was true of another program that was printed on newsprint paper in sepia and called *Movie Classic Close-up: Arabian Nights.* Even more than the beautifully printed theater program, this twelve-page giveaway concentrates on beautiful, scantily clad women. Several photos of Maria, Peggy Satterlee, and Elyse Knox (who went on to a career as a Universal scream queen in several horror movies) are featured. Jon Hall and Leif Erickson were there, but the emphasis was on all those beautiful women. The war was not ignored. GI favorite Frances Langford was pictured with her husband, Jon Hall, and Maria, naturally in costume, was illustrated adding to Universal's scrap-collecting wagon. Wanger wrote a note to Maurice Bergman of Universal's publicity department in New York praising the program. The only thing he wanted to make clear was that "the picture was conceived artistically by Alexander Golitzen" and that he would like the studio "to build up Golitzen wherever possible."[24]

Other cast members were given their own publicity. Sabu had just signed a contract with Universal after appearing in several eastern-themed films for the Rank organization in England, whose huge fantasy-themed films were on hold for the duration of the war. There simply wasn't the money or the space to film them in England. Selar Shaik was discovered in Mysore, India, by documentarian Robert Flaherty, who needed someone to realistically play the title role in his film *Elephant Boy.* Sabu actually was a *mahout,* or elephant boy. He had been working with his father on the enormous beasts ever since he could walk. Orphaned at seven, Selar was completely amenable to working for the Korda Brothers. It was Alex Korda who decided the very young Indian actor needed a single name. He came up with Sabu and it stuck for the rest of his life. His older brother Dastagir went with him to England. Their names got all screwed up by English customs officers. Dastagir was registered as the family name with Shaik as the older brother's name. Sabu went on to do *The Thief of Baghdad* and *The Jungle Book* before coming to Universal. In the downtime between takes on the set he could often be seen reading aviation books with the expectation he would eventually join the army air force.[25]

Leif Erickson had the US Navy waiting for his services as soon as he completed work on *Arabian Nights.* He was playing the evil, phony caliph who steals the office from his brother, played by Jon Hall. He was the bad guy in the film who had to be vanquished so Hall and Montez could ride off together across the desert sands before "The End" shows on-screen. Universal dreamed up a publicity piece to be given to any newspaper that would print it in which Erickson chose his favorite glamour girls who would make the perfect harem. No fool, he had Maria and the film's chief dancer, Carmen d'Antonio, in his harem. He did go outside Universal to round out the list. He included Alice Faye, Judy Garland, Rita Hayworth, Veronica Lake, Hedy Lamarr, Dorothy Lamour, Ginger Rogers, and Ann Sheridan. He would soon find himself surrounded by pin ups of his "harem" in barracks and on ships. He departed "Baghdad" to serve as a combat photographer in the Pacific theater, was shot down twice, received two Purple Hearts, and photographed the Japanese surrender on the battleship *Missouri* in Tokyo Bay.[26]

The Neverland movies were strictly meant to be escapist fantasies for a nation involved in a total war. In that regard they were brilliant. An integral part of all six of the Netherland movies were the comic relief players. They were as much a part of Neverland as Maria being rescued. In *Arabian Nights* the funny antics largely came by way of veterans Billy Gilbert and John

Qualen. Gilbert was literally born backstage at the Hopkins Opera House in Louisville, Kentucky, where his parents were appearing. He went on to a long career in vaudeville before being lured out to Hollywood by comedy maestro Hal Roach. Probably his most famous part was as the befuddled process server in *His Girl Friday* (1940). In *Arabian Nights* he played Ahmad, the owner of the circus where Maria danced and Sabu was an acrobat. After doing small comic bits all through the movie, he emerges as a hero when he saves Jon Hall, the rightful caliph, from being killed by the top bad guy.

John Qualen had a forty-year career in Hollywood. He often played Scandinavian-accented characters as part of John Ford's stock company. He came by the accent naturally. He was born in Canada but his parents were both Norwegian. He's probably best remembered for dramatic roles such as Lars Jorgensen, who loses his cattle and his schoolteacher wife to the Comanche in *The Searchers* (1956), Berger the Norwegian involved with the underground in *Casablanca* (1942), and Muley, who had been tractored out in *The Grapes of Wrath*. In *Arabian Nights* he was at his seriocomic best as a very frustrated Aladdin. He kept looking all over the place but could never find that lamp. He was also one of the people who kept ignoring Shemp Howard, of Three Stooges fame, as Sinbad when he started to tell stories of his days as a sailor. Also of note was the talented and stunningly sinuous Bella Lewitzky being brought in to do the Dance of the Single Veil.

Arabian Nights was an enormous production by Universal standards. After the preliminary costume fittings and portraits, the cast and crew gathered at Universal City on June 29, 1942, to start shooting. The dreams Maria had had ever since her Barahona girlhood were finally coming true. She was going to star in a Hollywood movie for one of the eight major studios. Whatever anxiety she felt over the perceived lack of support from Universal, Walter Wanger, and the rest of the studio front office would have to be overcome by Maria's reliance on her looks and attitude to see her through. Maybe she still could not act, but she knew she was going to look fabulous not doing it.

The vast majority of the movie would be filmed at Universal City. Second units were taken to Kanab, Utah, as well as Bryce and Zion National Parks. Maria's riding double Babe DeFreest went to Kanab in her place along with forty crew and fourteen other cast members. The most careful costume preparation involved Montez's exotic wardrobe. It was perceived as one of the chief lures of the movie, so Vera West made what Universal's press book called "an exhaustive study of traditional Arab costumes." She certainly did this but, as West observed, "We are called upon to do a great deal of research for period gowns or costumes. . . . From these emanate style influences which

Jack Albin, who had gone to Maria's apartment to take some of the sexiest photos of her early career for *Screen Guide* magazine, was sent to the *Arabian Nights* set to photograph her in her breakout role.

can be modernized and afford striking and original designs." Emphasis on "modernized." This resulted in a series of costumes made primarily of transparent chiffons and gauzes that consisted of thirteen pieces weighing a grand total of six pounds, eight ounces—slightly less than one average single feminine outfit. Part of the savings was in the veils they did not have to supply their star. Maria was slated to do the Dance of the Single Veil rather than the Dance of the Seven Veils.[27]

The press book for *Arabian Nights* makes it very evident Universal had big plans for Maria. The only name on the cover is Walter Wanger's. That changes with the interior. There are several photos of Montez in her Arabian finery and group pictures of the starring trio. One of the articles prepared for theaters to clip and send to local newspapers was an advance piece called "'*Arabian Nights*' Lauded as Fascinating Entertainment." It promised, "Rarely has any cinema venture been anticipated with livelier interest," and one of those interests was "glamorous Latin star" Maria Montez. There was also a feature article, "Maria Montez Has International Off-Screen Role." Besides being president of the Academy of Motion Picture Arts and Sciences, Wanger was also a key man in the Motion Picture Division of the Office of the Coordinator of Inter-American Affairs. He had a special slant on Montez. In the article Wanger is quoted as saying that she was picked from several actresses being considered for the part "mainly because of her personality and ability." But also because "she is an unofficial ambassador of goodwill, and as her fame spreads on the screen, she is fast becoming one of our most formidable influences in furthering the good-neighbor policy of the Americas." Maria is quoted as saying, "Anything I might do on or off screen, to inspire further friendliness among the countries of this hemisphere makes me very happy." Wanger must have been gratified when he received a letter from *Look* magazine's Hollywood office containing an article from the *Des Moines Sunday Register Magazine* called "Maria Montez, the Little Latin Dutch Girl Plays the First Good Neighbor—Scheheherazade." The writer noted, "No Arabian, Senorita Montez symbolizes Latin America's alliance with the United States in the war against the dictators."[28]

Further suggested submissions for local newspapers included an advance feature, "Maria Montez Wins Hollywood Acclaim in '*Arabian Nights*,'" that proclaims Maria "as a potential successor to the great glamour girls of all time." It includes Hedda Hopper's observation that she is a throwback to the colorful showmanship of the great silent stars. There are several photos of Montez in costume and with the various players, including the harem girls. Another article involves those pics of Maria in her costumes. "Soldiers Beg for Montez Pictures" concerns the medical detachment of the 108th Infantry Regiment "somewhere abroad" (Hawaii at that time). The soldiers had already been sent a batch of photos but wanted new ones of her dressed as Sherazade.[29]

The boosting of Maria continued in the "Showmanship" section. This concerned various ways for theaters to promote the film. It was noted that Max Factor had a national campaign featuring Montez and a line of perfume called "Arabian Nights" that would be available at the time of the film's release.

The harem girls deserved their own display. It was suggested that theaters place photographs of the girls in a shadow box with cheesecloth scrim in their foyer. Flashing light bulbs would accentuate the display as well as burning incense and a "huge eunuch" who could be hired to guard the harem girls. Another suggestion was to "Select Mmmm Girl." The press book reminded the theaters, "Maria Montez was nationally publicized as the "Mmmm Girl" and demonstrates "plenty of Mmmm in '*Arabian Nights.*'" It was actually suggested that theaters get local guys to "splash bulletin boards in their schools with pictures of Montez as Sherazade." Local high school girls who most nearly compared with Maria could be chosen to appear at banquets, rotary luncheons, and finally at the theater for a contest to pick the winning Mmmm Girl. "The rivalry between schools would pack your house."[30]

The studio chose one of its most experienced directors in John Rawlins to helm *Arabian Nights.* He had been directing since 1929, and specialized in the action B pictures and serials that were Universal's forte. The cinematographer was Milton Krasner, who filmed everything at the studio except westerns and serials and eventually moved on to filming Technicolor extravaganzas for 20th Century Fox. W. Howard Greene was brought in to operate the unique Technicolor cameras. The script went through several hands. Wanger had been interested in making a film from *A Thousand and One Nights* since Harold Lamb took a crack at it in 1936. Different scripts with various approaches followed in 1937 and 1941. Michael Hogan got screen credit for the story and screenplay for the 1942 film. He was an Englishman who was fresh off writing *Rebecca* for Alfred Hitchcock. "A rather excited woman" named Rhoda Rosker confronted Adolph Schimel in Wanger's office in July claiming to be the author of the story being used by the production company. Wanger responded that he had never heard of her and "she is probably some crack-pot." But he did direct Schimel to look into the claim. It went nowhere. True Broadman was given credit for additional dialogue.[31]

The ongoing world war did interfere with filming *Arabian Nights.* Kanab was not the first choice for shooting second-unit photography. The original plan was to film around the White Sands Monument near Alamogordo, New Mexico. The White Sands Service Company wrote Universal on March 24, 1942, informing the studio of the difficulty of transportation out to White Sands from Alamogordo and suggesting that it should plan to shoot after 4:00 p.m. given the glare during the day. The Southern Pacific Railroad wrote on the 28th to inform Universal that shooting in its chosen area would be difficult since "some sort of war plant" was being built and there was practically no accommodation available anywhere near White Sands. Additionally, transportation in the area was extremely restricted. It turned out the construction was the Alamogordo Bombing and Gunnery Range, which opened on May 14, 1942. The first atomic bomb exploded there July 16, 1945.[32]

On August 19 the railroad wrote again concerning the change in plans to film around Kanab. The closest the movie company could get to Kanab was Cedar City, and it would then be necessary to take a bus eighty miles to get to the site. Two baggage cars were to be assigned to the company, provided they were not required for military traffic. The railroad further warned Universal that under the rules of the Office of Defense Transportation it would not be possible for the railroad to provide a second section or special train for the movie company.[33]

The war also impacted the sets. The government put a limit of $5,000 on new construction for individual films. Construction material was in short supply everywhere as the building of the Arsenal of Democracy had priority over everything domestically. Universal had its massive back lot with all kinds of standing sets that could be reworked into an approximation of Baghdad. The big challenge was going to be how to thriftily build the desert palace of the evil brother of the caliph. The brilliant solution was to build a large, fur-lined pool surrounded by several tents. Not only was it cheap to construct, it also gave Sabu a chance to frolic in the water with various handmaidens and Maria a place to take one of her many filmic baths. This was all the brainchild of Alexander Golitzen, Wanger's art director. Universal had a nice distribution of responsibility in making its movies. The producer concentrated on the story and the people who would bring it to the screen. Golitzen took care of the physical aspects of the movie. Wanger was so pleased with his art director's ideas that he made him associate producer on the film. He also made sure the credits for art direction included Golitzen along with Jack Otterson, who was headed for the US Army as soon as filming was done. The number of extras who would normally populate the sets was reduced because of the war, and those still available wanted to double their day rate from $5.50 to $10. Scenes that were originally slated to include 1,000 extras found that number cut down to 250.[34]

Both Walter Wanger and Universal understood that one of the major draws to the movie would be Maria Montez running around the colorful sets in the brief, pseudo-Arabian costumes whipped up by the studio's costume designer, Vera West. Ray Jones spent many hours in the portrait studio photographing Maria in the outfits she wore in the film. On one of these occasions, Ray's seven-year-old son John was in the studio helping his dad prepare the sets for the day. Maria came in wearing one of her costumes. John had seen all sorts of actresses in his dad's studio, but he was stunned by how beautiful Montez was in person. And she was so friendly. Maria took one look at John and said, "What a cute little boy." She sat down and put him on her lap and talked to him about his life while his father positioned his camera and prepared to take the photos. She finally told John she had to go to work now. John went to watch his dad take the photos. He was still stunned. Not only was Maria incredibly beautiful, she was such a nice lady.[35]

There were few problems coming Wanger's way from the Hays Office. The censors warned about general considerations rather than specific problems with the submitted script. As always, they warned against "undue gruesomeness" in the torture and battle scenes. They warned the producer to be careful of "sex suggestiveness" in the harem scenes or with the female slaves. They also warned the film must never suggest that women could be presents and to "please exercise great care with the costuming of all women throughout this production." These warnings were taken very seriously by the studio. Not only did they need Breen's approval, they also knew that local censorship boards would just clip parts of the film they found objectionable, thereby making those reels useless. Breen's notes on the film carried real weight.[36]

Arabian Nights

Arabian Nights starts off in a harem in Persia with an overseer reading a story to a group of six eager, underdressed young women. The story is of Sherazade (Maria Montez), the chief dancer in Ahmad's (Billy Gilbert) wandering circus. She catches the eye of Kamar (Leif Erickson) the brother of the caliph, Haroun al-Rashid (Jon Hall). Kamar's attempt to overthrow the rule of his brother fails and he is captured. When Haroun goes to visit his brother, who is being put to death by slow torture, he is forced to flee and is wounded when Kamar's supporters attack him. Acrobat Ali Ben Ali (Sabu) finds Haroun, discovers his identity, and hides him in the circus troupe. Haroun takes one look at Sherazade and immediately falls in love.

Kamar assumes Haroun is dead and takes the throne of Baghdad. His grand vizier Nadan (Edgar Barrier) schemes with the captain of Kamar's guard (Turhan Bey) to find the missing Sherazade for Kamar. He is successful, but the guard decides to sell the entire troupe, including Sherazade, into slavery. They escape when the troupe's strongman dislodges the chain holding them at the slave market. They are discovered by Nadan's troops at the river and he blackmails Sherazade into poisoning Kamar in order to free Haroun, whom she loves. Ali learns of the scheme and with his fellow performers manages to free Haroun, who then demands they free Sherazade. Ali is sent to bring the troops still loyal to Haroun to the tent city in the desert where Kamar is holding Sherazade. Kamar quickly captures Haroun along with the circus troupe that went to help him. Only now does Sherazade learn the true identity of Haroun. The two brothers start fighting with swords. Meanwhile, Ali and the loyal troops arrive and a battle begins with Kamar's men. Kamar is about to deal a death blow to Haroun when Nadan kills him. As the greedy vizier prepares to kill Haroun, he is stopped by the circus owner, Ahmad, and killed by the circus strongman as he tries to escape. With Haroun victorious and having won the hand of Sherazade, the circus troupe and all the loyal subjects celebrate Haroun's return to his rightful position as caliph of Baghdad.

It was immediately obvious that Walter Wanger had created just the sort of movie audiences wanted in late 1942. The evil despots taking over the land of the freedom lovers could certainly be seen as standing in for Nazis and Japanese imperialists, but only if you were mistakenly looking for real-world meaning in the film. *Arabian Nights* was pure escapism for a nation at war. Bright color and exotic sets, a gorgeous woman strutting about in brief costumes, and good triumphing over evil. The box office was excellent. Universal chalked up $3,453,416 in sales on a movie that cost $904,765. On top of the major profits, *Arabian Nights* drummed up four Academy Award nominations—extremely rare for a Universal film. Frank Skinner was nominated for Best Score, Drama or Comedy. Both Otterson and Golitzen were nominated for Best Art Direction. The nomination also included Interior Decoration by Russell Gausman and Ira Webb. Milton Krasner, William Skall, and W. Howard Greene were up for Best Cinematography, Color. Among the nominees for Best Sound was the Universal sound department, directed by Bernard Brown. Let's hope the old saw that it's an honor just to be nominated was enough. *Arabian Nights* did not bring home any Oscars.[37]

The critics largely saw the movie for the high-spirited escapist fantasy it was meant to be and Maria was generally singled out as the chief fantasy object. The trade papers were never the best source for revealing the quality of a movie. Their reviews were far more oriented to how well the picture would do for theater owners than to any critical evaluation of the quality of a film. Plus, the trades relied on ads from the major studios and were never keen to criticize their products. Nonetheless, they were unanimous in thinking America's theaters had a sure bet with *Arabian Nights*. The *Hollywood Reporter* found it "exquisite": "No finer Technicolor has ever been seen on the screen than in this magnificent realization of the extravagant pageantry of the mystic East." The periodical was sure the movie would "make Maria Montez a star in her own right."[38]

Variety found the film full of "flesh, fantasy and fun . . . designed to beguile the mind away from more sober and somber matters." The newspaper thought "Walter Wanger's '*Arabian Nights*' should find a hearty and prosperous welcome wherever it may be billed." Jon Hall is singled out for his "strong, manly role." Maria is mentioned as the "arrogant and spirited" dancing girl. The *Showmen's Trade Review* noted to theater owners, "If your customers like spectacle . . . this will come as close to giving the ultimate in satisfaction as any film that ever occupied your screen." Montez was rated "a sumptuous morsel of femininity."[39]

Newspapers across the country generally praised *Arabian Nights* for its consuming fantasy. The *Pittsburgh Post-Gazette* thought, "A more generously packaged holiday gift the movie-goer could not want." As for Maria, she is "sultry and supple as she performs a dance that is a distinctive contribution to the choreography of the erotica." The *San Diego Union*'s Don Short rated the movie as one of the outstanding pictures of the year, noting it had been held over for a second week in that city's spacious Spreckels Theater. In Dallas, the *Morning News* lauded the film's brilliant Technicolor and noted that *Arabian Nights* was not Maria's first movie, "nor will it be her last. She is a resplendent eyeful with her brazen body, her baby face and her Titian-tinted tresses." W. Ward Marsh in the *Cleveland Plain Dealer* was also very impressed by the Technicolor in the movie but found the acting wanting. Ah, but certain concerns were more important than thespian considerations. Marsh observed, "Mr. Hall has the body beautiful and Miss Montez is as shapely as they come with a face lovely enough to make the most case-hardened misogynist retract all his former vows and vote for this newcomer."[40]

The magazines also had fun with the movie. *Life* ran a two-page piece on the making of *Arabian Nights* before it was released. It featured four pictures of Maria in her harem costume by photographer Mark Kaufman and enthused that "she does the Dance of the Single Veil." Noting her membership in the Sweater Girl union outlawed by the Hays Office, *Life* noted, "Law-abiding Maria simply took off her sweater and donned the two-piece harem costume." *Time* ran a picture of Maria with its review and noted it would be just another old-time sheik picture except for "1) sleek Maria Montez, 2) Technicolor." The reviewer enjoyed the lighthearted approach to the subject matter but thought it was the first two points that would bring in the audience. *Photoplay* saw the main draw as Technicolor and thought Montez "makes a believable Sherazade." *Modern Screen* loved the movie and thought people ought to flock to see it as it is the "type of picture that seems sure to grow as scarce as 1A males before we get through with Hirohito, Hitler, Mussolini et.al. That is the extravaganza." This was due to central casting not only doubling its charge for each extra but also losing people to the military, the Douglas and Lockheed aircraft factories, and the strict government limit of $5,000 on new set construction coupled with the scarcity of material. *Hollywood* got right to the point in its piece "Streamlined Fantasy." The one page is illustrated with Maria in her "Arab" finery, the desert pool, and the six Virgins in their fetching costumes.[41]

There was, of course, one negative review. The always reliable Bosley Crowther of the *New York Times* wrote movie reviews for the leading American newspaper. This is ironic in that he obviously hated movies, Hollywood, and most things west of the Hudson River. As Walter Wanger declaimed in a letter to Byron Price, the director of censorship in Washington concerning the *Times* reviewer, he "represents an exclusively metropolitan point of view bounded on one side by '21' and on the other by the Museum of Modern Art." In his review Crowther chided Wanger for making a "gaudy spectacle" that has nothing to do with the true stories of the *Arabian Nights*. There may be lots of "swearing by the Prophet's beard" but the movie is more like a standard western than the original tales it is supposedly based on. While Crowther conceded, "It all looks highly sensational in Technicolor," he dismissed Maria Montez as playing "the beauteous dancer with the hauteur of a tired nightclub showgirl." In general, "the creative talent was lacking. It stands as costumed horse-opera and not much more."[42]

One aspect of the filming of *Arabian Nights* that did not wind up in the press—except for a few jibes from Jimmie Fidler—was Maria's continuing problems with the crew on her films. She had not yet begun to express, loudly and repeatedly, a desire to appear with someone other than Jon Hall as a co-star. It was the crew she could not get along with. She had spent her life as a member of the upper class in a highly stratified society. The whole egalitarian bent of society in the United States was completely foreign to her. "A Star in Gemini" has Montez fretting over the lack of confidence the producer and studio have in her while receiving small tortures from the set people. She receives a burn from a hairdresser, the makeup used is too dark, she is clipped in the nose by a clapper as a take is to begin. She claimed all this was done on purpose and she threatened to sue.

The ever-helpful Jimmie Fidler wrote a column titled "Montez Gives Set Workers Cold Shoulder." He noted that many Hollywood personalities are very successful at selling themselves to the public, but "are foolish enough to antagonize the little people with whom they must work. I'm thinking just now of Maria

Montez, a girl who has succeeded better than most in courting the favors of the newspaper and magazine scribes. She's worked hard at that—much harder (and I think more skillfully) than any paid press agent she could have employed." But the "high-handed, inconsiderate tactics" she uses on the crew are "short-sighted" and "inexcusable." Fidler understands that "Miss Montez is still a Hollywood newcomer and can be excused a few mistakes. I hope she will be big enough to take this criticism that I'm dishing out as well-meant—and profit by it."[43]

Montez certainly had the capacity for growth. Whether it was taking Fidler's criticisms to heart or simply recognizing that what she was doing was not working, she made an effort to change her approach to working with the people on the crew. When she wrote "Maria Montez' Frank Advice to Movie Struck Girls" for the August 1944 issue of *Screenland* magazine with May Mann, two of the seven photos showed her having coffee with the crew and buying a bond from the studio's self-appointed bond salesman. In the article, she advises, "When you go on the set to make a picture, always acquaint yourself with the crew. Make them your friends. They are experts . . . [and] can do so much to make working pleasant."[44]

Trouble with people on the set and her suspicions of her own studio notwithstanding, *Arabian Nights* was a watershed in Maria's career. Set director Alexander Golitzen summarized the impact. "That picture *made* Maria Montez . . . and she became a regular 'star' on the Universal payroll." Her gain in status was marked by *Motion Picture* magazine. An article in its February 1942 issue about chef George Mardikian and the joy of cooking with glassware was illustrated by "Universal's brown-eyed Spanish senorita," who was brought in to sip his coffee. In the magazine's December issue nine photos of Maria illustrated the article asking, "Are you star material?" The caption read, "Maria Montez, who posed for the exclusive photos on these two pages, has proven that she's definitely star material. That is the reason why Universal is starring her in Walter Wanger's *'Arabian Nights.'*"[45]

Silver Screen magazine drew the same conclusion in its September 1942 issue as *Arabian Nights* was being filmed. "Fame for Maria" described Sherazade as "a part every actress in Hollywood was trying to get. It means from now on she will be a star." There are two stills from the film, not surprisingly of Maria in her harem girl finery. This seems like an article generated by Universal. It has all the studio bio stuff about her father as Spanish consul and the convent upbringing. The article even manages to get in a note about her youth. The caption for a photo of her lying in bed playing with a teddy bear reads, "Still has several dolls and teddies and such from her not-so-distant childhood." In reality she was thirty at this time.[46]

Montez certainly aimed to grab all the perks that went with starring in a blockbuster movie. The five tables near the bar were the premier places to sit at "Prince" Michael Romanoff's restaurant on Rodeo Drive in Beverly Hills. The rest of the seats were in the back room. Sheilah Graham interviewed Pancho, the headwaiter, about this dilemma. He had operated several restaurants and never had a problem like those five tables. Regulars in the front room included Merle Oberon, George Raft, Fred Astaire, and James Roosevelt. Greta Garbo did not care where she sat. "But someone like Conrad Veidt or Maria Montez, if you put them in the back room they refuse to come here again." Pancho also noted that although photographers were banned from the restaurant, Maria managed to bring in a photog disguised as a guest. Those five seats were such a misery to Pancho that he declared, "If I had my way I'd burn them all."[47]

The columnists all agreed with the assessments of *Motion Picture* and *Silver Screen.* In her yearly roundup Sheilah Graham featured Maria in "Younger Girl Players Now Get Film Breaks." Dee Lowrance wrote his columns for Sunday supplements. When he said to "take a look at the stars for '43," he included Montez, who had become a bona fide leading lady after being "one of those sometimes-seen young actresses whose pictures—mostly in leggy poses—are found in newspapers and magazines but whose image was not to be found often on the screen itself." Kate Hollidax of the Associated Press also noted Maria as someone who had come to the fore in 1942. She wrote, "In *'Arabian Nights'* Montez not only proved to be a champion glamour girl but also "an acting threat."[48]

It is a great example of how one role can lift an actor out of the struggling mob and make him or her a star. Two weeks before the start of filming for *Arabian Nights,* Maria was fulfilling a demand Universal made only of its broad roster of starlet contract players who had not found their way to the top. On Sunday, June 7, the studio sent out Maria, Anne Gwynne, Evelyn Ankers, Jane Frazee, Marie McDonald, and Elyse Knox to "pose in costumes and brevities" at the Ambassador Hotel's Camera Gardens for a group of amateur photographers. The photographers would submit their favorite photos to Universal, where they would be judged by portrait studio head Ray Jones. All just another part of the publicity machine, but after *Arabian Nights* it would no longer be the kind of assignment in which the studio would include Maria Montez.[49]

A month later, with filming on *Arabian Nights* well under way, the advancement of Maria's place in Hollywood was evident. Maria and Jon Hall were to serve as judges of the final contestants in the USO's Victory House in downtown Los Angeles' Pershing Square beauty contest on the Fourth of July 1942. It was a national holiday, so *Arabian Nights* would not be filming. Hall dropped

Maria's success in *Arabian Nights* resulted in demands for her autograph. She was always happy to comply with this hallmark of stardom.

out, but Maria showed up to judge the bevy of beauties vying for the title of Miss Victory of 1942. These wartime extravaganzas always drew huge crowds to the park and the bond-selling facility at Victory House did a land office business. A US Army Air Force B-25 celebrating the Jimmy Doolittle raid on Tokyo in April was also on display in Pershing Square if the bathing beauties were not enough to bring in crowds to buy bonds. As icing on the cake, Miss Victory was guaranteed a chance to wear a harem outfit in the movie. Universal released a photo of Montez in a conservative business suit evaluating the bevy of bathing-suited beauties. Wide World released a photo of four of the entrants showing up on the *Arabian Nights* set in their bathing suits with Maria looking on in her Arabian finery. They are labeled as "candidates for movie roles."[50]

Just after the filming of *Arabian Nights* wrapped, Maria's new place in the studio hierarchy was solidified by a magazine article and two events on the Universal lot. Montez was no stranger to *Silver Screen* magazine. It included several pictures of her in its piece on the *Sea Wolf* cruise. She demonstrated how to apply skin cream in the November 1941 issue. She was still doing makeup in the June 1942 issue, where she demonstrated how to apply paint-on hosiery that simulated stockings and it was noted she would be seen in *Pardon My Sarong.* The September 1942 issue constituted a major step forward for Maria when she was featured in the previously noted article "Fame for Maria." Two of the seven photos are from the movie the fan magazine assures its readers will make her a star. It was quite a different take from her previous appearances in the publication. La Montez was being celebrated as a bona fide movie star. *Arabian Nights* was the last time in her career she would not get top billing in one of her movies.[51]

Her stock on the Universal lot was also on the rise. On September 24 Maria was chosen to award trophies to the winners of the studio's annual tennis tournament. Six months later Universal made a very big deal about the fact that Maria was moving into Marlene Dietrich's former bungalow on the lot. The studio provided *Showmen's Trade Review* with a photo of producer Paul Malvern carrying its now certified star over the threshold of the bungalow. Maria claimed that one of the reasons she first signed with Universal was because it did not have an actress of her type, meaning an "exotic" glamour girl. This was inevitably reported as not having a glamour girl on the lot. In 1940 Dietrich was very much in evidence. By 1943 she was gone, and both her glamorous position and her bungalow now belonged to Maria Montez.[52]

Montez had a month off between the end of filming *Arabian Nights* and the start of *White Savage.* The main thing she did was travel to San Francisco a week after the studio tennis tournament for a huge bond rally being supported by Universal at San Francisco's Civic Auditorium on September 30. She garnered some "Good Neighbor" press upon her return to Los Angeles by being one of the many Latin stars to attend the premiere of the Mexican film *Ay Jalisco no te rajes* (Ah Jalisco, Don't Back Down) on Main Street downtown at the city's premier Spanish-language theater, Frank Fouse's California, and the recently reopened Roosevelt on October 8.[53]

Now that she was a certified star, Maria was featured in a variety of magazine stories in November. Montez's contribution to an article in that month's issue of *Cosmopolitan,* "My First Date," was a completely bogus story about a date with her cousin Don Luis in a moonlit garden in the Canary Islands—chaperoned, of course, by a younger sister. In *Collier's* she was part of a piece about how nine Universal players cope with wartime gas rationing. The article included photos of Marlene Dietrich, Abbott and Costello, and Deanna Durbin, but the largest picture was of Montez on a scooter. *Movie Stars Parade* celebrated her as the "M-mm-mmm Girl Montez" with five photos and an essay about her huge ambition, her nightclub entrances, Claud Strickland, and her role in *Arabian Nights.* While she was appearing in print all over the place,

Maria at the Beverly Wilshire Hotel for Frederick Sprague's exhibition of his portrait of her.

she was in person at the Beverly Wilshire Hotel, where a crowd of two hundred had gathered to see the unveiling of Maria's portrait by Frederick Sprague. In the crowd was Dutch painter Ernst van Leyden, who would also paint her. The *Los Angeles Times* referred to her as "Universal's glamorous Latin star" in its review of the exhibit. On November 22, in the face of all this positive news, Universal had the good sense to pick up the option on Maria's contract.[54]

It was clear to Universal even as *Arabian Nights* was still being filmed that it had hit upon a winner in combining Maria Montez, Jon Hall, and Sabu. During the filming it was announced by *Daily Variety* that the next two films starring the trio were in the works. This overruled Louella Parson's early prediction that after completing *Arabian Nights* Universal would star only Maria in something called *North Star,* about a sarong-wearing movie star stranded in an Alaska army camp. Instead she would be back in a sarong in *White Savage,* using the discarded original title for *South of Tahiti.* (In the original movie attached to the title, Maria's white parents were killed in a plane crash and she was raised by the island chief. So in the beliefs of the time this would make her a "white savage." In the later movie the appellation seemed to describe the German-born evildoer played by Thomas Gomez, who was intent on robbing the island of the wealth of jewels in the sacred pond.) Her co-stars would return. Jon Hall had been making a specialty of beefcake in South Seas island movies all the way back to John Ford's *The Hurricane* in 1937. His first film was the 1935 MGM version of *Mutiny on the Bounty,* where he played an uncredited Tahitian native. This was certainly fitting since his mother was a native of the island and his uncle James Norman Hall co-wrote the book the movie was based on with Charles Nordhoff. Sabu had been making a specialty of playing athletic sprites since his earliest films with Alexander Korda.[55]

Universal had finally figured out what to do with Maria Montez. The two things she could do well on film were act imperious and look gorgeous. Of all the Latin actresses who were brought to the screen in the spirit of the Good Neighbor Policy, she was the only one who was constantly being starred as royalty. Her studio had finally found her niche: to be a foreign princess, to be dressed as suggestively as possible, and to not have to say too much. *Arabian Nights* set her on the track and led rapidly to *White Savage* and four other very popular Neverland fantasies.[56]

White Savage had several things to set it apart from Maria's other movies. For one, she was to receive her first screen kiss. She had leaned down and gone cheek to cheek with her bearded boyfriend Abdullah in *Raiders of the Desert,* but this would be her first actual kiss. A similar publicity ploy earned an enormous amount of attention for Deanna Durbin when she received her first kiss from Robert Stack in the appropriately titled *First Love* (1939). It was a very big move for Durbin in showing she was transitioning from being a kid with a big voice to a young woman with a big voice. She had always projected a virginal wholesomeness in her previous four films. An example of the worldwide popularity of both her and the movie is that Anne Frank put up two photos from *First Love* in her part of that crowded, hidden annex in Amsterdam where her family and others were trying to elude the Nazis.[57]

Maria's first kiss certainly never garnered anything like the publicity splash that Durbin's did. In a blurb that started appearing in August 1943, Universal claimed Montez was kissed nine times in *White Savage,* but that only the ninth kiss really counted for much. The studio claimed she had made a study of screen kissers and found them wanting. "'Most of them,' she explained, 'act as if they had one eye on the time clock.'" Universal knew that Maria, whom it claimed had married at seventeen, never projected virginity. Even in the small bit parts in her first movies she was clearly a worldly-wise woman, not a girl.

Studio photo of Maria in her sheerong for *White Savage.*

Of course, when Durbin made *Three Smart Girls* (1936), her first movie at Universal, she was only fourteen years old and looked it, if she did not sound it. At the time of *White Savage* Maria was sold as twenty-two by the studio even though she was actually over thirty. Columnist Paul Harrison noted that during the filming of *Arabian Nights* she was never kissed, "even though she is the oomph, woomph, wow and whistle girl of the season." Montez just didn't have virginal in her limited thespian's toolbox. The closest she ever came was as the good sister in *Cobra Woman.* But there she was in her tight sarong. She seemed like she had already been kissed. Probably a lot. But give Universal credit; it was in there pitching.[58]

The other thing the studio pushed with both hands and feet was the "fact" that Maria was not wearing a sarong. Dorothy Lamour wore one of those and was as certified in the public mind as the "Sarong Girl" as Lana Turner was as the "Sweater Girl." When Hedy Lamarr came slinking into *White Cargo* as Tondelayo, she did so in a "lurong," according to MGM. Maria in *South of Tahiti* wore a slendang. Two years later she was in a "sheerong" for *White Savage.* This worked a lot better than the first-kiss gambit. News outlets thought there was a lot more interest in Maria wearing brief, clinging costumes than getting kissed. Montez did her part and kept gamely referring to the garment as a sheerong. In another blurb supplied by the studio, she was quoted as saying, "I am a native princess in '*White Savage.*' No princess would think of slipping into one of those shoddy sarongs." The sheerong was defined as a sheer sarong. It was "sheer for its gauzy transparency and ong because of its tropical derivation."

Frederick Othman was one columnist who went with the studio's line. In his November 5 essay, "'Sheerong,' New Dream Garb for Maria Montez," He noted the value of the clinging costume, whatever it was called. "As long as a garment has the minimum of yardage, is wrapped around a beauteous lady, and has a name which ends in 'ong,' the cash profits are guaranteed." The sheerong as designed by Vera West for the "s-a-n-sational" form of Montez is "in the traditions of Minsky strip tease . . . leaving her in a little something vaguely reminiscent of a bathing suit out of the world of Buck Rogers." This was exactly the sort of publicity Universal lusted after. Not one word about her acting or if the movie made any sense at all. It was purely about how delicious Maria looked in the costume created for her. *Screen Guide* listed all the things Montez was doing wrong to break into movies, but that nonetheless had been successful for her. It asked, "What has Maria Montez got that the average girl doesn't? We'll say she has self-confidence and plenty of 'sheerongery.'"[59]

Othman and *Screen Guide* notwithstanding, most reviewers didn't bite. They kept referring to it as a sarong. Not that they complained. Leading movie magazine *Photoplay* enthused, "Look, she's got it on again! Montez and that sarong!" Lee Mortimer in the *New York Daily News* couldn't care less what they called the thing. Like many other reviewers he just thought, "Maria Montez is grand in '*White Savage,*' beautiful, shapely and enticing."[60]

Montez had been back on the Universal lot since October 24. Arthur Lubin, who was to direct *White Savage,* had never worked with Technicolor film. He set up a sound stage to do brief Technicolor tests of the trio of principal actors. The bulk of color stock was going to the military for training films but the studio had managed to corral enough of the rare film to keep the Universal trio in its glowing tones. Initially it had seemed the studio had no choice but to do the follow-up to *Arabian Nights* in black and white. Once the Technicolor stock had been secured for *White Savage* it was clear Lubin would have to up his game to show mastery of the complicated film stock. Once he showed what he could do with Technicolor on his initial foray with the process, Universal assigned him to do the large-scale color epic *Phantom of the Opera,* which won two Oscars in 1944.

This would be Lubin's first outing with Montez. He would later direct her in *Ali Baba and the Forty Thieves.* They did have their dramatic blowups, but he generally had good relations with Maria. He remembered her as "a very, very beautiful girl" who "became extremely popular" but "was very temperamental." Speaking of the Hollywood of his time, he noted she "was not a particularly good actress, but if you are photogenic you don't have to be too good an actress." It would be on *White Savage* that Maria would have two of her temperamental epic eruptions that Lubin remembered so well. The first happened after she had been sitting around freezing while waiting for her scene. She felt she could not eat or drink anything "because I have to take care of the body beautiful. In that sarong, they call it a sheerong, it will show even if I just eat an olive." When they were finally going to film her scene, Maria wanted her hair and makeup attended to. Lubin told her she was holding up production. She loudly pointed out that she had been sitting around the set for hours. "I knew I will have to tear something, or I will keel him. I cannot tear off my sarong because then I would be nude, so I tear off my wig." In fact, she tore it in half—and that was the end of filming for the day.

The second explosion occurred after another long day of shooting when Lubin got upset with Maria because she kept flubbing her lines. Not one to suffer criticism with equanimity, Montez looked right at him and yelled, "Lubin, you are full of shit," and stomped off the set. Producer George Waggner went after her to try to calm her down. He told her not to be so upset because "all directors are full of shit." The next day, everyone showed up at Universal City and the movie went on. But it gave the studio another story about the tempestuous "Dominican Dynamite."[61]

Filming on *White Savage* commenced on October 31, 1942. Russell Gausman and Ira Webb designed the movie to be shot on redressed existing sets at Universal City. Portions of the movie were filmed in Laguna Beach. Lubin was the studio's leading director at this time. He was also working with

Maria and Jon Hall wait while cameras and lights are adjusted on the *White Savage* set.

what had become a very hot trio. *Arabian Nights* was a huge hit, and the public was already being prepped for the second installment of the Montez-Hall-Sabu franchise. George Waggner was one of the major producers on the lot, and he seemed responsible for bringing in fledgling screenwriter Richard Brooks. *White Savage* would be his first produced screenplay. He had little good to say about the experience, thinking, at best, "it was just the sort of light entertainment in which audiences sought escape from the war and other troubles." It did help launch a career that would see him go on to write and direct deeper fare in *Blackboard Jungle, Cat on a Hot Tin Roof, Elmer Gantry,* and *In Cold Blood.*[62]

Two weeks before *White Savage* began filming, the script was sent to the Hays Office for approval. Typically with the Neverland films, complaints had to do with sexual matters. Breen threatened to withhold certification if "the suggestion of a sex affair between Tahia and Kaloe (Montez and Hall) which is indicated in the fade out on page 72" was kept in the script. There was also concern over how the island girls would be dressed. "Here (page 10) and elsewhere throughout the script it is imperative that the costumes of Tahia and the other native girls be adequate." The producers were also instructed, "It is unacceptable to show the fish hook caught in Tahia's posterior, and the business of Kaloe removing the fish hook must be handled carefully." These problems, as well as close-ups of Tahia in a blue costume and two girls sitting around the campfire wearing costumes that "were quite breast revealing," were all taken care of and *White Savage* received the Motion Picture Production Code's certificate of approval on April 7, 1943.[63]

White Savage

Temple Island is ruled over by Princess Tahia (Maria Montez), who controls a gold-lined, jewel-filled pool that is the source of the island's wealth. Unfortunately, in the island town of Port Coral, Sam Miller (Thomas Gomez), a white merchant of German antecedents, covets the jewels, going so far as to strangle a white fisherman who learned of them. Miller wants to steal the jewels for himself and is working on getting Tahia's brother Tamara (Turhan Bey) to help him. Kaloe (Jon Hall) is a shark fisherman who wanted to get the rights to fish the waters around Temple Island but found out from his friend Orano (Sabu) that the princess will not allow it. Seeing a beautiful young woman in town, Kaloe tries to pick her up and complains loudly about Princess Tahia and how awful she is. Unbeknownst to him, it is Tahia he is speaking to—she winds up tossing him into the bay.

Orano arranges a meeting between Kaloe and Tahia, but it goes poorly; she banishes him from the island, believing he is only interested in the fishing rights, not her. Eventually he worms his way into her good graces, and she tells him of the pool of jewels. Kaloe warns Tahia not to trust Miller. The merchant cheats Tamara out of the deed to Temple Island in a crooked card game, but Kaloe forces his way into the game and wins back the deed. As Tahia is set to announce her engagement to Kaloe, Miller shows up with the dead body of Tamara, claiming he was killed with Kaloe's knife, and the fisherman is arrested and imprisoned. Orano frees him and with the help of Tahia the trio convinces one of Miller's hoods to admit his boss is behind the killing of Tamara. Learning of his exposure, Miller and the rest of his mob sail to Temple Island to steal the jewels. When they explode the sacred pool with dynamite, an earthquake ensues, which kills them and devastates the island. But Tahia has the deed to the island back, the jewels are safe, and she happily falls into the arms of Kaloe.

White Savage was certainly not the equal of *Arabian Nights* in its story or production values. But it was as wildly popular as its predecessor, thanks to the chief selling points of the glorious Technicolor look of the film and the ogle-

From this marquee of the Uptown Theater in Kansas City, Missouri, it is evident where the emphasis is with *White Savage*. (Courtesy of the Academy of Motion Picture Arts and Sciences.)

worthiness of Maria in her sheerong. The studio-produced press book ran a suggested review to be used if small-town newspapers did not have their own reviewer. The movie was proclaimed as being set "in the tropical seas, but the time is before the Japanese started their evil work." On the same theme, it's noted that "the picture is a complete escape from the more serious things of our times."

The ads for *White Savage* promised "the spectacular stars of '*Arabian Nights*' in the screen's titanic tropical thrill!" as well as "Thrills untamed! Savage excitement! Pagan love!" The return of the trio concept was used in several newspapers. *Daily Variety, Motion Picture Daily, Hollywood Reporter,* and the *Jefferson City (Missouri) News and Tribune* all pointed out that Universal had developed a successful trio that pulled in an audience. Richard Hays, writing for the *Seattle Daily Times,* noted the continuation of the Montez-Hall-Sabu team as well as the other two high points: "If there is anything more eye filling than Maria Montez in a sarong, it is Maria Montez in a sarong and the Technicolor." The *Omaha World Herald* concentrated on Maria's contribution. "As an ocular feast, Miss Montez would probably lead your hit parade. As an actress, she is still learning. When and if her histrionics lifts to a par with her anatomical standing, she'll be the screen's leading lady." Rudolf Elie Jr. in the *Boston Herald* was primarily taken with the movie's Technicolor, the "conspicuous" Montez, and the excellent villainy of Thomas Gomez. Universal's ads featured a full-length illustration of Maria in her sheerong and portraits of Jon Hall and Sabu.[64]

It was up to Lee Mortimer in the *New York Daily Mirror* to perfectly grasp the whole point of *White Savage.* He loved the Technicolor and admired Maria, finding her "grand . . . beautiful and shapely and enticing. She can also act." As for the movie, "After an epidemic of war films, '*White Savage*' is what the public has been yelling for." Don Short made the same observation in the *San Diego Union.* He found the movie "a deviation from the long list of war pictures." It also gave the audience a chance to appreciate Maria, who is "more alluring than she appeared in '*Arabian Nights.*'"[65]

As usual, Universal filled the movie with talented supporting players. As the evildoer who kills the princess's brother and tries to steal the jewels out of the sacred pool, Thomas Gomez is at least a vague tie to the lethal chaos of which *White Savage* was meant to be an antidote. Although he plays a character named Sam Miller, he is portrayed as a German in the movie. He is eminently hissable. Bella Lewitzky, who performed the extensive "native dances" in the film, was another positive aspect of *White Savage.* She did the same in *South of Tahiti, Arabian Nights, Ali Baba and the Forty Thieves, Cobra Woman,* and *Gypsy Wildcat.*

There is no real comic relief in *White Savage* as there had been in *Arabian Nights.* What little laughs there are come from Hall not recognizing Montez as the princess and the general antics of Sabu. The other primary character actor is Warrensburg, Missouri's favorite son, Sidney Toler, at his Charley Chan best as Wong the trader. Turhan Bey returns to the Neverland fold as the princess's doomed brother who very nearly loses control of the island to Gomez in a card game. All in all, a much more somber outing in Neverland than the previous journey.

On the negative side, the animosity between Maria and Jon Hall began to seep out into the press. *Photoplay*'s Cal York was at Frances Langford's house interviewing her about her recently concluded tour of Alaska and the Aleutian Islands with Bob Hope. Langford's husband, Jon Hall, came home from the *White Savage* set and York and Langford began trying to get him to talk about his relationship with Maria. They got stories of her needling Sabu "out of his Indian calm," and of the consequences of Maria repeatedly blowing her lines, causing Hall, wearing heavy chains, to have to climb seven times up and down a stairway. He finally protested to Montez, who responded,

"Listen Mr. Hall. I'm not reading the line wrong. I have a photographic mind." When Hall retorted that he thought her mind "had been overexposed," Maria completely blew up at him, much as she had at director Arthur Lubin, yelling at him that he was "full of shit" and storming off the set. But it all calmed down. Bella Lewitzky danced wonderfully, the volcano exploded to punish the evildoers and keep the islanders on the straight and narrow, and all was right with the world.[66]

Universal was not a film company to want to change what had proved to be a winning combination. The studio picked up Maria's option once again after *White Savage* as *Cobra Woman* was preparing to go before the cameras. When the studio found a duo or trio that clicked with the audience, more movies were guaranteed to follow. After Abbott and Costello hit it big by joining the US Army in *Buck Privates* (1941), they were soon joining the US Navy and finally the US Army Air Force. Later they went through every monster in the Universal fold after *Abbott and Costello Meet Frankenstein* (1948) clicked. The same was true of Basil Rathbone and Nigel Bruce in the Sherlock Holmes series. Audiences clearly loved the Montez-Hall-Sabu trio no matter what sort of Neverland they were put in. Still, reality was out there rearing its problematic head. Sabu was now nineteen and had chosen American rather than British nationality. He was subject to the draft and had received his notice to report for a physical. There seemed to be little doubt he would pass it just fine. Two months after *White Savage* was completed, cameras rolled on *Cobra Woman.* It would be the trio's third movie in ten months and its last.[67]

5

Queen of Technicolor

Cobra Woman had initially been conceived as a starrer solely for Maria. But as *Arabian Nights* demonstrated how well the Montez-Hall-Sabu trio worked together, it was rewritten to accommodate all three actors. Yet ever since the photos and news items were released to publicize the opening of *Arabian Nights,* it was evident Montez was the chief selling point of the trio. This is when Universal came up with a name that stuck. *See* magazine helped alert the world when it called its two-page illustrated article on Maria "'Queen of Technicolor': Title Is Found for Dominican Starlet Maria Montez." The concentration on Montez was evident in Universal's advertisements for *White Savage.* The four-page ad in *Variety* featured a full-page color ad of Maria in her sheerong simply labeled "She." Newspaper ads had her in the sheerong with the blaring caption, "untamed! Tahia!—Daughter of Eve . . . With A Soul of Satan!"[1]

With the completion of *White Savage* and while *Cobra Woman* was still being worked on, Maria headed off for her February 6, 1943, Hollywood Victory Committee–sponsored appearance at the basic training and medical corpsmen school based at Camp Grant in Illinois. She then took the train to New York to appear on the Cresta Blanca Winery–sponsored *Carnival* radio show. *Arabian Nights* had started appearing in theaters across the country in January, so this time she was arriving in New York as the star of a major Technicolor movie and the latest hot young thing. When she got off the train she was rushed by a group of newsmen and photographers. Arriving at the same time was Hollywood veteran H. B. Warner and lively young actress Bonita Granville. A *New York Sun* reporter covering arrivals at Penn Station was surprised at how Montez got all the attention of the numerous newspeople. Warner had been a leading man in silent movies and was still doing considerable work as a supporting player at sixty-six years of age. He had done over one hundred movies, from playing Jesus Christ in Cecil B. DeMille's *King of Kings* in 1927 to the island chief in *South of Tahiti* in 1941. Granville had already done forty films by age twenty and had recently appeared as Bette Davis's obnoxious niece in *Now Voyager.*[2]

The *Sun* writer has Montez posing for the photographers with "plenty of teeth" and telling the scribes that while there was a place for glamour girls during the war, she "would even like to play roles fully clothed." She then signed a number of autographs and disappeared in a taxicab. Warner and Granville, considerably more down to earth people, even if they were in the movies, just went to the Waldorf Hotel, where the reporter eventually caught up with them for an interview. The title of the piece perfectly caught Maria's new standing in February 1943: "Star Arrives in Technicolor: Maria Montez, 'Sheerong Girl' of Films, Is Mobbed—Two Veterans Unmolested."[3]

Maria was in New York to reconnect with all the East Coast columnists and to appear on the *Carnival* radio show that would be recorded on the night of February 10, 1943. It was Maria's first time guesting on a major American radio program. Oscar Levant and George S. Kaufman were the masters of ceremonies. In the radio ads it was noted that the guest would be "Maria Montez!!! Hollywood's exotic new glamour girl."[4]

Three days after appearing on the Cresta Blanca–sponsored show, Maria was to be photographed in the sheerong she wore in *White Savage* for the *New York Daily News.* Julia McCarthy, one of the paper's scribes, interviewed her after the photo session. She noted that Montez "panthered out of the dressing room encased in this swatch of dry goods." She also observed the marked effect Maria had on all the men in the room. McCarthy recorded the photographer as saying, "Gosh dang." All the other men just stared. The reporter attributed this reaction to, besides the form-fitting sheerong, "her deliberately friendly attitude. She thinks it's good business." She saw Maria as someone who might be appearing in goofy movies but was completely self-aware and on the job at all times. When McCarthy asked her what the thing was that she had on and where was it worn, Maria logically answered, "It is a sheerong. They are worn on Universal Pictures lot in Hollywood, where I make '*White Savage*.'"[5]

After the sheerong discussion and Maria noting her appearance on the Cresta Blanca *Carnival* show, McCarthy turned to how well Montez always seemed to be dressed. Never at a loss for words, Maria had a very contemporary explanation for her excellent clothes sense. "'If girls don't dress up lovely,' she says in that fascinating, broken Ingliss, 'why, soldier say? What do I care if Japs get her—just look at the old bag!'" Rather harsh, but right in line with her continuing campaign to trumpet her own beauty and desirability.[6]

Montez also took the time to sit down with Hyman Goldberg, the renowned "girl specialist" for the New York afternoon newspaper *PM* in her room at the Sherry Netherland. The publication was known for its use of

When *PM*'s columnist Hy Goldberg went to interview Maria at the Sherry Netherland in Manhattan, he took along photographer Jack Downey who, of course, asked the always-cooperative star to show off her legs.

photographs, so naturally Goldberg did not go alone. Fitting in with tradition, of the three pictures of Maria that accompanied the piece, two concentrated on her legs. The importance of the article is that it was one of the opening salvos in Maria's efforts to change the direction of her career. In a brilliant ploy to both ratchet up interest in her current movie while at the same time trying to advertise where she wanted her career to go, Maria bemoaned the fact her latest movies were getting her "nakeder and nakeder." In *White Savage,* the film she just completed, she noted, "I wear less than ever." She hoped Universal would "let me make a movie with clothes on." Once again demonstrating that she was not only in on the joke but had created it, she freely admitted to her self-publicizing past. "It isn't true that I believe I'm the most beautiful women in the world. I just said it because I knew the papers would print it."[7]

Montez went on to complain to Goldberg that she was never taken seriously. He asked her if she considered herself as intelligent as she was beautiful. This was a key point with Maria. "More," she said, "I am very well read. I just finished a book by Lloyd C. Douglas." She is referring to the author whose novel *The Robe* was on the best-seller list at that time. She also noted she has been studying English for two and one-half years and it "burns the hell out of me" that some people keep saying she is from Brooklyn and no one would ever tell her what's wrong with the place. Goldberg chose to remain mum on the subject.[8]

By March 1943 she was already complaining about her studio not using her well and wanting to do movies in which seeing her body was not the only reason for attendance. But she was still at the point where she was so happy to be starring in films that she would take what Universal assigned her even if she thought the role restrained the actress she wanted to become. Those days were numbered. One month later she expressed a variation on the same complaint. In a caption to a photograph of her distributed by the Newspaper Enterprise Association national news syndicate she said she wanted to do a comedy.[9]

Maria's return to Los Angeles was in preparation for the filming of *Cobra Woman,* the third movie in the Montez-Hall-Sabu series. It was the third of the six Neverland films made but the fourth one released. *Ali Baba and the Forty Thieves* would be the fourth of the six made but the third one released. Universal had several other films in the pipeline for the trio in spite of Sabu passing his army physical. The hope always was that the US army would postpone induction to give an actor time to finish a film. The studio was planning to shift the nature of Neverland after *Ali Baba* for an espionage thriller. It was to be called *The Flame of Stamboul,* written by Richard Brooks, who had done *White Savage.* Paul Malvern and George Waggner took turns producing the Neverland fantasies. *Stamboul* was Malvern's, and Waggner was set to do the follow-up, *Zorya,* being written by Ralph Stock. According to Universal, *Stamboul* was to be an Axis spy movie based in Turkey. The stated reason it was not ultimately made was for fear of upsetting that neutral nation. *Zorya* became *Gypsy Wildcat* and dealt with gypsies in an indistinct past in some vaguely eastern European place that caused no problem with the Allied war effort.[10]

While preparing her costumes, studying her lines, and trying to figure out how to play a dual role as a good sister and a bad one in *Cobra Woman,* Maria was scheduled for a March 2 appearance on Bob Hope's radio program. The two had an immediate connection in that Louis Shurr represented them both. It is indicative of Hope's wartime activity that only 9 of the 144 episodes of his Pepsodent radio show originated from NBC's studios on

Sunset Boulevard. The other 135 were broadcast from various military bases. In this case the radio crew traveled to Camp Cooke, an enormous base near Lompoc, California, where the army trained mechanized forces. Montez was familiar with the area, as she had visited the Marshallia dude ranch located there before the war. The ranch was condemned and became part of Camp Cooke. As usual on her radio appearances, she was the butt of many of Hope's lustful jokes, but she gamely hung in there. It was one of the most popular radio programs on the air and was a very nice follow-up to her Cresta Blanca appearance.[11]

There was a constant effort at the time to bring the war into a story, no matter how tangentially. The "Today's Radio" columnist in the *San Antonio Express* did just that when he noted Maria's upcoming guest spot on the Hope show. He printed a story sent to him by one of his listeners who had received a letter from her pilot brother in North Africa in which he noted that he did not mind so much when the Germans shot at him, but he was very angry when a bombing raid disrupted his favorite radio program. For the pilot's sake the columnist hoped the Germans would take the night off for Hope's March 2 show, since the comedian was going to bring "the dark-haired and sultry-eyed Maria Montez to the microphone as his guest star for the evening," and the writer was sure the pilot would not want to miss that.[12]

Soon after her appearance on Bob Hope's show, Montez received a letter from Teddy Stauffer telling her that he was stuck in Mexico. The Immigration Service was not allowing him to reenter the United States. The two had been writing steadily for months but now there was no choice other than to break up. Maria had written him that her "faithfulness has no limits." As any man would, Stauffer reveled in the sentiment. But he knew he was trapped in Mexico, at least for the duration of the war. He wrote her, "After all these long months apart, I feel we can never come together again as we once were." He invented a woman who wanted to marry him and said, "We have nothing to be sorry about, but I feel there is nothing left for us." Stauffer remained in Mexico the rest of his life. Maria soon met John-Pierre Aumont.[13]

There were other, more cheerful things on her schedule. On March 9 she had her first appointment as a guest of the Theta Sigma Phi women's journalism sorority at Brittingham's restaurant at the CBS radio complex on Sunset Boulevard. The Universal press releases had Maria being the guest of honor at the sorority. This was not the case; she was one of several invited guests. But this was an important event to Maria. She was the author of several published poems and loved the idea of being recognized as a writer. Two weeks later she was at Grauman's Chinese Theater for the premiere of *Young Mr. Pitt*

Maria as the good sister in *Cobra Woman.*

with her new love, Jean-Pierre Aumont. The *Los Angeles Examiner* ran a photo of them captioned, "Two of the most watched film celebrities were this romantic twosome."[14]

Montez emerged from her new Universal bungalow on April 19 to start shooting *Cobra Woman,* with Jon Hall and Sabu ready to play their established Neverland roles. The script had already been submitted to the Hays Office for approval. The censors' first note was to be expected. They had seen some costuming stills and warned, "You are no doubt aware of the difficulties encountered with films of this sort, because of the type of costumes worn by the native women. We urgently advise that you consult your costume department on this specific point, in order to avoid any trouble with the finished picture. We cannot over-stress the importance of this caution." They especially urged Universal to be careful how it dressed Maria and that "extreme care" be taken in her kissing scene with Jon Hall, "as they are both attired in swimming attire." And as always, Breen warned the studio to avoid "gruesomeness."[15]

One interesting aspect of *Cobra Woman* that was never advertised by Universal or mentioned by the Hays Office was the fact that it was one of the rare South Seas movies where white people don't come in and cause all the problems that so horribly disrupt the native people's lives. Going back to MGM's *White Shadows in the South Seas* (1928), which made a star of another Latin actress, Raquel Torres from Mexico, white people's avarice always screwed things up. In that case it was exploitation of native pearl divers. In *Cobra Woman* there was a white missionary and a businessman on Harbor Island who were helping to arrange Tollea and Ramu's wedding. But Cobra Island was inhabited only by locals. They had a law that visitors were to be put to death. It was two local evildoers exploiting the island's spiritual beliefs to control the people and keep themselves in power. *South of Tahiti* and *White Savage* ran truer to form, as far as duplicitous white people were concerned.[16]

Cobra Woman

In *Cobra Woman* Tollea (Maria Montez) is set to be married to Ramu (Jon Hall), but she is abducted by the mute Hava (Lon Chaney Jr.) at the behest of her grandmother (Mary Nash), the queen of Cobra Island. She wants to bring her granddaughter back to the island to take the place of her twin sister, the evil high priestess Naja (Maria Montez). Ramu sets sail for Cobra Island to rescue Tollea accompanied by his friend Kado (Sabu). Ramu finds who he thinks is Tollea going for a swim in an island lake. It turns out to be the evil Naja. Naja finds herself attracted to Ramu but is incensed when she discovers Tollea is on the island. Ramu is captured by her guards and added to the group of island people who are to be sacrificed to quell the island's active volcano. Kado soon finds himself in captivity and tortured by the evil Martok, Naja's advisor who wants to take over Cobra Island, to tell him where Ramu went after escaping his captors.

Martok interrogates the queen as to Tollea's whereabouts, gets no answers, and kills her. As she is dying, she swears revenge. Ramu and Kado are captured by palace guards, causing Tollea to go to her sister and demand, as the first-born twin, her rightful place as high priestess. Naja is about to throw a spear at Tollea but loses her balance and falls to her death from a high castle window. Martok demands that Tollea perform the Cobra Dance as islanders are sacrificed to the volcano even though she is not immune to the bite of a cobra as her sister was. As she dances a huge fight breaks out. Hava kills Martok, which calms down the volcano. Ramu and Kado are sailing back to their home island when they discover Tollea has stowed away. The fade-out has Ramu and Tollea kissing while the monkey sews up a hole in Kado's shorts.

Cobra Woman would come to have a unique place in the Maria Montez universe. It was a favorite of pioneering underground filmmaker Kenneth Anger and director/actor Jack Smith, who starred in Ken Jacobs's *Blonde Cobra,* a takeoff on *Cobra Woman.* Virtually anyone who wanted to make fun of Maria and her accent repeats the "Giff me that Cobrah chwool" line she speaks when the bad sister is trying to take the powerful Cobra jewel from her good sister—even though the line is articulated perfectly coherently in the movie and Maria speaks with less of an accent in *Cobra Woman* than in any of the Neverland films. This was very important to her. She always saw her accent as an impediment to her career. She complained to Sheilah Graham that her director Robert Siodmak wanted her to make her accent thicker. He wanted her to say "every*sing*" instead of "every*thing*." She told the columnist, "It took me a long time to learn to say 'everything' and that's what I want to say. He say 'everysing' to make me sound quaint. But Bergman, she is not quaint. And I wish to be like Bergman."[17]

Montez herself used the movie much like Jack Benny used *The Horn Blows at Midnight.* When Erskine Johnson visited Universal during the filming Maria told him he came a day late. "Yesterday I had a fight with myself and threw myself out of a 19-story window." To her it became the prime example of her frustration with her Hollywood film career. She thought the movie was ridiculous, even calling it a "stinker" to a columnist. Considerable fun has been made of the minimal difference between the two sisters. The Universal trailer promised, "Montez—Queen of Technicolor—twice as lovely, twice as exciting," but Bosley Crowther in the *New York Times* noted that Maria played the dual role "without a trace of distinction between." The difference between the good and bad sister is there, but you do have to look. It is not as obvious as Joanne Woodward's shy, retiring housewife and raging slut in *Three Faces of Eve* (1957). Maria's performance is not unlike the four seasons in her new hometown of Los Angeles: present but subtle.[18]

The Montez-Hall-Sabu trio in their last film, *Cobra Woman.*

In fact, Maria is sweeter and plainer as the exiled sister in *Cobra Woman* than in any of her other films. While the bad sister is engaging in an orgiastic if slightly spasmodic dance as she condemns islanders to death in the volcano, the good sister watches with obvious horror at the ghastly proceedings. The differences were plainly there between the two sisters, but concentrating on the acting was missing the point. The movie was strictly meant to be wartime escapist entertainment. To that end there were two gorgeous women vying for control of the island, dozens of other beautiful sarong-clad women running about, a love story, a wildly athletic best friend, exotic native dances, a helpful chimp, good versus evil, a good queen willing to die for her people's deliverance, and an exploding volcano. All in glorious Technicolor. Pretty good for an average ticket price of 25 cents while the casualty lists constantly grew outside the theater.

One of the stories that plagued Maria's tenure at Universal occurred during the filming of *Cobra Woman.* Bathrooms were not in abundance when filming on the far reaches of the studio's extensive lot. Sometimes nature calls; other times it screams. Unwilling to make the long walk to the restroom, Montez used the floor of her dressing tent. The prop man had to clean it up, of course. In retaliation, he put some carbide powder on the floor, which would cause a small explosion when liquid came in contact with it. When she used the floor a second time, it exploded. Much to the amusement of those watching—and to everyone else at Universal when they heard the story—Maria came running out of the tent screaming, "They are trying to kill me!" Universal certainly was not MGM. No matter that Montez was one of the biggest moneymakers on the lot—respect and simple accommodations were not to be hers.[19]

Both *White Savage* and *Cobra Woman* had been announced as movies in preparation before *Arabian Nights* was even completed. With *Cobra Woman* ready to go before the cameras, Universal was openly projecting the trio into *Ali Baba and the Forty Thieves, Zorya*, which would become *Gypsy Wildcat,* and an untitled movie about Turkey that became the never-made *Stamboul. Cobra Woman* was the third film in a series and Universal wanted to keep the series as fresh as possible. The studio had to find the right fellow to helm the adventure. George Waggner was to produce the film and for his director he chose Robert Siodmak, whose early career was in Expressionist German films at that country's principal studio UFA. He had co-directed *People on Sunday* (1930) with Edgar G. Ulmer. That observational film of Berlin would feature several other filmmakers chased from Germany to Hollywood. The screenplay was by Billy Wilder from a story by Curt Siodmak; Fred Zinnemann was the cinematographer; and the co-producer was the Siodmaks' cousin Seymour Nebenzal, whose father paid for it.[20]

After making some films in France Robert Siodmak moved to America and eventually signed on with Universal. He brought his use of atmospheric lighting to *Son of Dracula* (1943), *Phantom Lady* (1944), and *Spiral Staircase* (1946). Keeping that same brilliant use of lighting, he would create two of the finest film noirs, *The Killers* (1946) and *Criss Cross* (1949).

On the face of it, Robert Siodmak would seem as odd a choice to direct *Cobra Woman* as Richard Brooks had been to write *White Savage*. But both of them were new to Universal, and like everyone else they had to be flexible with whatever assignments the studio gave them. Siodmak was happy to be at Universal. As a Jew, not only could he no longer work in the German film industry, his very life would have been in danger had he not escaped the country. So he began to prepare his trip to Neverland. *Cobra Woman* may not have been exactly his favorite example from his filmography but he did enjoy the experience. He was always known as an actor's director and got along without any blowups from Montez. He summed up his experience directing her. "She couldn't act from here to there, but she was a great personality and believed completely in her roles; if she was playing a princess you had to treat her like one all through lunch, but if she was a slave girl you could kick her around anyhow and she wouldn't object—method acting before its time, you might say."[21]

That all sounds very insightful and pithy, but the two times she was briefly a slave in *Arabian Nights* and *Sudan* she was as imperious as ever—and soon improved her status with the help of Jon Hall. One can only assume she espoused a willingness to play her part as best she could—but her naturally imperious nature informed most of her roles. This is a prime example of the minimal respect her studio afforded her. It is extremely unlikely she would have put up with being treated like a slave. She could be enough trouble when she was treated like a princess.

Universal continued its policy of filming part of the Neverland movies off the studio lot with *Cobra Woman*. The Los Angeles County Arboretum and Botanic Garden at the Baldwin Ranch in Arcadia would stand in for the lake where Naja takes a swim, only to be chased down by Ramu because he thinks she is his fiancée Tollea. It is one of the most iconic scenes in Maria's career. She is given her best chance to project the imperious character she did so well. Most of the movie finds her in fairly enclosed spaces. Here she gets to strut, head held high and wearing a sarong with gleaming silver accents, solitary and magnificent, across the lawn on the way to the pool, preceded by armed guards and followed several paces back by a legion of her ladies-in-waiting and more guards. She looks every inch the sort of evil high priestess who would happily feed her people into a volcano if it suited her.

It turned out the lake was not quite ready to represent Cobra Island. Director Robert Siodmak, art director Alexander Golitzen, and several landscape artists showed up prior to filming to check the place out. The first thing Golitzen decided was that they needed to skim the moss off the lake. The trees around the lake were not in bloom, so Siodmak ordered some magnolias to be moved in. The greensmen were ordered to cover the banks of the lake with carpet grass. Then there were the potted palms and tropical ferns that had to be added to the mix. Baldwin Lake in Arcadia looked like Cobra Island should look once the technicians had worked their Hollywood magic under the design of Alexander Golitzen.[22]

As it became increasingly evident that Montez was the chief drawing power of the Neverland movies, Universal sought out new ways to promote her exoticism and energy. The studio released a blurb originally prepared for the press book as *Cobra Woman* was coming onto screens across America as to how the actress introduced herself to her director. Siodmak was always presented by Universal as an experienced, in-charge European director who was unruffled by any situation—even when engulfed by Hurricane Maria. The blurb was perfect in that it made her exotic with her accented English, bursting with energy, personable in her own eccentric way, and about to be measured for the sarongs and robes that would pop the eyes out of the audience. The blurb describes her running into Siodmak's office, past his secretary and right up to her new director's desk. She introduced herself and told him that since he was a Leo the Lion her astrologer assured her they would make a terrific movie together. She apologized for being low on energy but promised him she would get some vitamin shots prior to the start of shooting. "When peecture start Montez weel be herself again. . . . You weel see the new Montez . . . full of pep . . . full of fire. We make heestory together." With that she blew him a kiss and went to the costuming department to be fitted for her island garb. The secretary watched her fly out of the office and could only conclude, "Giving vitamins to that is like turning on the electric fan when a hurricane is going on."[23]

It is not important whether these stories are true or not. The whole point of them was Universal's constant effort to portray Maria as an exotic, eccentric hot number who could promise the audience an enjoyable movie. In another studio release from the press book, Maria did more than just strut imperiously around the lake and kiss Jon Hall underwater. She also saved her studio the expense of having to find a replacement for the movie's trained macaw. Bird trainer Curly Twiford was standing with his macaw Peter on his shoulder as the arboretum set was being prepared. Being in such an environment, it seems, caused Peter to "go native." He left his Twiford perch and flew to the top of a nearby eucalyptus tree. All of his trainer's coaxing was for naught. Peter stayed in the tree. Three days later, all the whooping, throwing of small stones, and firing of an air rifle still had not brought Peter out of the

No one used photographs to further her career more determinedly than Maria. Here she poses for a visiting photog in her working clothes on the set of *Cobra Woman.*

tree. Montez may not have grown up wearing sarongs, but she was an island girl. She suggested finding a way to "turn the heat on him." Several prop men went to their trucks and brought back silver foil sun reflectors used to even the light on subjects when shooting. It worked. After fidgeting around a bit Peter headed back down and the filming could finally go on. All this seemed obvious to la Montez. As she explained to Robert Siodmak, "The way to catch a bird—or a man—is to turn up the heat."[24]

Reviews of *Cobra Woman* were even more diverse than usual. Predictably, the *New York Times* thought it was stupid and only simpletons would enjoy it. W. Ward Marsh in the *Cleveland Plain Dealer* thought it was nothing more than a serial in one chapter and the weakest of the four Neverland films. He even objected to the depiction of the locale. Inexplicably looking for reality, he complained that it all takes place "on a far-off tropical isle where there are no Japs today, no jungle fever ever, no mosquitoes at all." There was only one thing to recommend it. "Beautiful Technicolor makes *'Cobra Woman'* 20 times better than it really is." The *Showmen's Trade Review* opined the box office would rely solely on what moviegoers thought of the trio. The movie otherwise had little to offer. John Rosenfield in the *Dallas Morning News* agreed with Marsh that it was the nadir of the series, concluding, "If the *'Cobra Woman'* is part of Hollywood's escapist program, one must now find some way of escaping escape."[25]

The industry papers could usually be relied on to be positive about Maria's films because they were popular with audiences. *Daily Variety* thought it was "a super-fantastic melodrama," and Montez "is decidedly shapely and eye filling as a sarong-draped native girl, and dazzlingly gowned as the high priestess." The reviewer felt "she handled the dual assignment very well." The *Hollywood Reporter* noted the film's lush tropical locale and found it "entirely mythical escapist entertainment that was never intended to be taken seriously."[26]

Many smaller newspapers happily printed Universal's suggested review from the press book, which described the movie as "one of those glorified extravaganza epics with all sorts of romantic glamour, exotic costumes, fantastic scenes and magnificent photography." It also raved about its primary star: "Miss Montez has a certain camera appeal that makes her extremely popular in this type of movie." Lee Mortimer of the *New York Daily Mirror* agreed with the press book. He reasoned, "If you were a producer with a cast of thousands, a corny tale, a stage-set volcano island, several reels of Technicolor film and Miss Montez, what would you do? Probably what Universal did. Cast her in a double role. Undress her in both, as much as the law and Will Hays allow, and let nature take its course."[27]

Like Marsh in Cleveland, the *New Orleans Times-Picayune* wanted to find wartime relevance in the movie. Its reviewer went so far as to find that "popular rights" was the theme of *Cobra Woman.* Evil will lose in the end. "As a mercenary princess on a fictitious island, Miss Montez receives . . . just what she deserves and exactly what is about to happen to Hitler and Hirohito." It was extremely unusual for anyone to read actual war themes into any of the Neverland movies. But good did always triumph over evil, and that seemed to some to support the war effort while providing the audience with Technicolor escape.[28]

Things kept right on charging along in Montez world with the completion of *Cobra Woman.* On June 9 she appeared on the Eddie Cantor radio

The bad sister in *Cobra Woman* condemns islanders to the volcano.

show, once again good-naturedly providing living fodder for a comedian. A week later a much larger event in her world occurred when Sabu was formally instructed to report to the army for basic training on July 7. *Ali Baba* was being prepared to begin filming on June 28. Universal tried its hardest to keep Sabu out of the service until the filming could be completed. The army declined and the trio was broken up. It was up to Universal to rework the script to somehow replace one of its chief components. Turhan Bey was from the neutral nation of Turkey and not subject to the draft. His part in *Ali Baba* was considerably expanded. Bey, however, was an obvious adult with a definite air of seduction about him. Any part originally intended for the boyish Sabu had to be extensively rewritten.[29]

The new script by veteran screenwriter Edmund Hartmann was ready when filming of *Ali Baba and the Forty Thieves* started on the Universal lot on April 28, 1943. Clearly Hartmann took some inspiration from the 1940 Alexander Korda–produced *Thief of Bagdad,* which starred a very young Sabu. That film was full of genies and flying carpets. But producer Paul Malvern wanted his film aimed at the adult audience that had supported *Arabian Nights* and *White Savage* so strongly. Therefore, the relationship between Hall and Montez as well as the battle of good and evil were made key

On the Universal lot, "Andy Devine rides a modern magic carpet" with the help of Montez and Hall, according to the snipe.

to the script. The budget was set at a respectable $692,500 on a forty-two-day schedule with the studio's ace house director, Arthur Lubin, at the helm. He was fresh off the color hit *Phantom of the Opera.* After doing such a fine job on *Cobra Woman,* Universal's finest cinematographer, George Robinson, would film *Ali Baba* with Technicolor's W. Howard Greene running his company's complicated camera. They were so successful that Universal assured movie fans that the movie looked "Techni-Colossal." Richard Riedel was responsible for the all-important art direction on the film. As always, Vera West was hard at work on the pseudo-Arab garb required of the cast, with Indian saris and turbans put in the mix. All of them had to conform to the brilliant color that was the hallmark of a Technicolor fantasy.[30]

As was common to all the Neverland films with the exception of *Gypsy Wildcat,* parts of *Ali Baba* were filmed away from Universal City. The Thieves' cave and their wild riding was filmed at Red Rock Canyon National Park in the Mojave Desert. Longtime cowboy movie veteran Ray Taylor directed the second unit at Red Rock. This was really a cowboy segment with a bunch of guys in Arab costumes, so the choice of director was perfect. Additional desert scenery was photographed near where *Arabian Nights* was filmed at Kanab, Utah. The studio was not one to throw its money around; going off the lot was a mark of how important Universal thought the Neverland films to be. It had used the huge coiled cobra statue built for the high priestess's "altar" in *Cobra Woman* incessantly, the color cover photo featuring Maria and the cobra the studio arranged for the cover of *Pic* magazine on October 26, 1943, being a perfect example. Incidentally, Universal's Plexiglas globe logo, which had replaced the airplane circling the globe by the 1940s, does not introduce any of the studio's Technicolor films of the early 1940s. Universal was not willing to film a new one in color for the handful of Technicolor films that would be produced, so the films opened with color title cards stating "Universal Presents" instead.

Universal was always sure to publicize any wartime theme that could be gleaned from any of the Neverland films. Obviously, there were no Japanese on Maria's South Seas islands or Germans in the Arabian deserts. But the studio did find a theme it distributed through Ernest Foster of the United Press: the Good Neighbor Policy was alive and well in *Ali Baba.* Primarily, there was the Dominican Republic's Maria Montez, who "certainly would be the prize occupant of any harem." Just as many of Maria's cohorts in the South Seas had a Latin background, many of the harem roles in *Ali Baba* were performed by women with Spanish surnames. Estelita Zarco was born in El Paso, Texas, and moved to Hollywood when she was three. Paulita Arvizu was from Mexico City. Blanca Vischer was a Guatemalan who immigrated at twelve, graduated from Hollywood High School, and served as a Goldwyn Girl. Ramsay Ames, who played Maria's handmaiden Nalu, was of Spanish-English descent. She had been a Latin-style dancer and a singer in a rhumba band and was very new to films. She told Hedda Hopper that Maria helped her with her acting in *Ali Baba* and made certain she was not overwhelmed by the rest of the cast in her scenes. Montez was always chief among the pan-American contingent, and was always promoted by Universal as its "Latin-American good-will girl."[31]

The studio certainly liked to promote Maria as Hollywood spokeswoman for the Good Neighbor Policy, but it absolutely never passed up a chance to advertise Montez taking a bath. Soon after *Ali Baba* wrapped, Universal released a blurb originally published in the *Ali Baba* press book that perfectly summed up its view of the appeal of la Montez. In a suggestive "Where do we go from here?" piece, it is noted that in *Arabian Nights* she reduced the Dance of the Seven Veils to one veil. In *White Savage* Maria "wore a 'sheerong,'" a sarong so sheer you could see through it. In *Cobra Woman* her costume "was as tight as a snake's skin." So what's left for *Ali Baba?* "Well, for one scene she

For the shooting of *Ali Baba,* director Arthur Lubin "got into the water first to prove to his star that the swimming was fine" in the Pool of Midnight bathing scene.

slips out of a robe . . . and slides into a mosaic pool to take a bubble bath." And then, in a line that sums up the studio's approach to the Neverland films, Universal admits the bubble bath is "not strictly 13th century . . . but the effect is photogenic."[32]

Maria may have taken more baths on-screen than any other actress in the history of Hollywood. *Ali Baba* was special in this regard. First, she took a dip in the Pool of Midnight in a tight suit that displays a generous amount of cleavage when she stands up, and then takes a bath in the palace. Obviously, she was not really nude in the palace bathtub, however much the studio presented her as such. When she emerges from the bath all you see are her bare shoulders as one of the servant women blocks the camera's view by holding up a towel for the soon-to-be queen.

The lack of actual nudity certainly did not stop spectators flocking to the set. Montez tried to restrict the shooting of her bath scene to only the cast and crew. But 140 other people showed up. Arthur Lubin suggested she take a milk bath. His actress negated that suggestion most vocally. It had to be "a bubble bath or nothing." It took four hours to get the bubbles percolating properly and the water warm enough for la Montez. Sheilah Graham was present at the oasis. She noted that Maria instructed all of the men to turn their backs as she entered the bath. She slipped off her robe after Lubin called "Action" to reveal a skin-colored undergarment. Once the scene was shot and the still photos taken, Maria climbed out of the pool. The 140 onlookers had increased considerably. And they certainly were not turning their backs. Montez took a look at the mob and yelled, "Say, who's been selling tickets to this show!" Graham could only conclude, "What would Hollywood be without Miss Montez?"[33]

Sheilah Graham was not the only columnist invited to the palace by Universal. Maria's baths advertised not only the eroticism of the Neverland franchise but also the sexiness of the starring lady and chief attraction of the films. The studio let all the Hollywood writers know about the bath scene. Erskine Johnson was there. He noted, "Maria Montez will take a bubble bath in *'Ali Baba.'* Of course, there were no bubble baths in those days. But neither was there a Maria Montez." Frederick Othman was mostly concerned with all those "unchivalrous" fellows who showed up on the set. In spite of Maria's request that they turn around, many did not. Othman concluded, "The gentlemen were no gents."[34]

Universal put out its own blurb through United Press. The studio went much further into the spectacle of the water itself. The water was lavender colored to fit in with the Technicolor. Air hoses snaked into the water to create the bubbles. A fire engine was nearby to provide the steam. Eight bottles of shampoo and fifteen large packages of soap chips were not enough to produce the required effect so more were added. Maria protested the soap was too strong; it would burn her skin. The water still wasn't bubbling so Lubin ignored her and ordered more. Finally the water was hot enough and the bubbles were all over the place. The men were asked to turn around. Maria entered the bath. But there was a problem. Lubin called to her, "Maria! It's showing!" Alarmed, she cried, "What's showing?" "Your wedding ring," Lubin called back. She put her hand under the water. Perfect. Titillation but still a good girl.[35]

Two copies of the *Ali Baba* script were sent to the Hays Office on April 25, 1943. As usual, it responded in two days. Breen found the basic story fine, but did warn there was an "unacceptable amount of killings and some excessively gruesome details." As usual, female pulchritude was also brought into question. The censors wanted it made clear that Maria's oasis swim was not done in the nude. It had to be made evident she was wearing something before she entered the water. Then there were all those harem girls. The censors referenced "the numerous recent difficulties we have had with your studio relative to costumes and the unacceptable exposure of the persons of various actresses . . . [including] your lead and the various 'slave girls' and 'dancing girls.'" All of the problems were sufficiently overcome and *Ali Baba* received its certificate of approval.[36]

Ali Baba and the Forty Thieves

Hulagu Khan (Kurt Katch), leader of the Mongols, has conquered Baghdad. The caliph is organizing his army to retake the city while his young son Ali hides in the home of Prince Cassim (Frank Puglia), who turns out to be a traitor. He betrays the caliph, who is killed by the Mongols. Ali escapes and is wandering the desert when he accidentally finds the cave of the Forty Thieves. He uses their secret code, which he overheard as they left, to enter the cave. The Thieves return and their leader, Old Baba (Fortunio Bonanova), is impressed by the pluck of the boy. Ten years later young Ali (Jon Hall) is the leader of the Thieves, who are the main resistance to the rule of the Mongols. The Thieves hear of a Mongol caravan headed to Baghdad carrying Hulagu's fiancée and Cassim's daughter, Amara (Maria Montez). Ali rides to check out the caravan, meets Amara at the Pool of Midnight, and is arrested as he is talking to her.

Amara attempts to break her engagement to Khan, but her father forbids it. Ali recognizes Cassim and vows to kill him as a traitor. She is taken by the Thieves when they rescue Ali. Old Baba is killed in the fighting and his last wish is for Ali to regain his rightful place as caliph. Ali realizes Amara is the childhood friend to whom he pledged his love so long ago. He returns her to Baghdad, where Cassim tells her that Ali is the son of the caliph. Amara reveals that she loves Ali, but she is tricked into agreeing to marry Hulagu when Cassim is falsely threatened with torture. The Thieves sneak into the city, rescue Amara, and defeat the Mongols. Ali and Amara are united as Ali becomes the new caliph.

The trade papers were as enthusiastic about the Neverland franchise as ever. The *Hollywood Reporter* thought the two bathing scenes would help make "an 'Open Sesame' at the nation's box office." Both the *Motion Picture Daily* and *Daily Variety* found the movie a "worthy successor to '*Arabian Nights*.'" The latter was enthusiastic about Maria's contribution to the film: "Maria Montez is presented in costume and photography for every natural advantage to add to her following." Both of them lauded the direction of Arthur Lubin, the cinematography of George Robinson, and Paul Malvern's initial effort as producer.[37]

For once the *New York Times* was at least neutral about one of the Neverland movies, possibly because the reviewer was "A.W." and not the dyspeptic Bosley Crowther. A.W. found it exactly the kind of bofo ("great" or "exciting" in the slang of the era) take Universal would have on the Arabian Nights tales. If viewed "indulgently" by audience members, they ought to enjoy their night at the movies. Philip Scheuer in the *Los Angeles Times* was impressed by the Technicolor in *Ali Baba*'s "khans and robbers" take on the ancient tales. As for Maria, "Miss Montez is at her best while bathing in a pool." He complimented director Arthur Lubin on telling the story with the camera, "since no deathless prose may be heard issuing from anybody's lips."[38]

Reactions around the country varied. John Rosenfield in the *Dallas Morning News* did not care for the whole Neverland series. He was not impressed with "Maria Montez, Santo Domingo's gift to the cinema." Like most, he reduced her to her physicality, noting, "Her phizz and physique are first class but her unintelligible readings are godawful and not entirely a matter of accent." Edith Lindeman in the *Richmond (Virginia) Times Dispatch* noted that some reviewers have found parallels to the real war in the written dialogue. She thought this was a mistake. "Who listens to dialogue, anyway, when Maria Montez walks around with only a length of eggshell tulle between her and the Hays office?"[39]

The reviewer in the *New Orleans Times-Picayune* was one of those who perceived story angles in *Ali Baba* that might apply to the world situation. The problem was it appeared on a double bill with the equally Technicolored short *With the Marines at Tarawa,* which was directed by Louis Hayward using footage taken during the battle by Marine Corps photographers armed with Bell and Howell hand-cranked movie cameras. He lauded the production values and the rousing story pitting evil conquerors against defeated but still willing to fight citizens of *Ali Baba* but found, "It so happens that there is such an impact of blazing reality in the Marine film and in the army picture of the capture of Kwajalein which accompanies it, that Hollywood make-believe, no matter how sumptuous and eye-filling, seems pale and vaguely disturbing in comparison."[40]

It is easy to see how *Ali Baba* could be construed as mirroring wartime reality. A single card at the beginning of the movie informs the viewer that this is "Baghdad—in the days of the Mongol invasion." These invaders could be interpreted as Nazis. Once Ali shows up, the Thieves are transformed into freedom fighters in an occupied country, much like the French Resistance. Cassim could be seen as an Arabian example of a traitor selling out his country like the Norwegian politician Vidkun Quisling. Maria could be seen as

Ray Jones used cucoloris lighting to accentuate this studio portrait of Maria in *Ali Baba and the Forty Thieves.*

one of the brave women of the Resistance. She doesn't just stand around looking pretty; she opens the palace gate to let in more of the anti-Khan freedom fighters.

You could draw parallels to the war or just take the movie for the Technicolor fantasy it was meant to be. The reviewer in the *Seattle Daily Times* certainly did not mistake *Ali Baba* for anything else but Universal's successful attempt to let the audience "sink deep into a dream," particularly in the current income tax season. "When you watch this latest assembly of dream castles in '*Ali Baba and the Forty Thieves*,' . . . you live the life of a bon bon. Maria Montez is a gorgeous confection with little on her mind which carries you way past the long form into a land of fantastic splendor." In other words, it is pure escapism both from the world war and the onerous taxes being charged to pay for it. The country was thrilled to "sink" into Universal's latest dream. *Ali Baba* was so successful the studio gave producer Paul Malvern a bonus as pure reward. It was not part of his contract.[41]

There was a very clever device employed in the opening credits sequence. The credits are displayed on the wall above a pool. Oil jars above the wall

Jon Hall and Maria "read" the prop book created as the "title piece" for *Ali Baba.*

pour out liquid to dissolve the credits as the camera moves on to the next group. An introductory scene similar to that of *Arabian Nights* was shot but later deleted from the film. It presented a flute player in the Baghdad bazaar telling the background of the story. The framing scene that was used featured Ali and Amara as children committing themselves to each other by making a pledge sealed with their blood. It is referenced in a beautiful scene later in the movie when Ali is holding Amara at Cassim's house and, seeing Amara by the pool, realizes she is that same girl he pledged himself to so many years ago.

Ali Baba certainly gives Jon Hall his best role in the Neverland series. Many years later he gave his copy of the script to a friend, noting in the inscription, "This was the best one." Maria is featured in the press book and got top billing as usual, but it is far more Hall's movie than hers. They also seem more like true lovers rather than rescuer and rescuee after the climactic battle. The movie also gives Andy Devine a chance to be more than pure comic relief. Old Baba puts him in charge of protecting Ali. He has to do just that when Ali is knocked into a pool in the climactic sword fight in the battle to defeat the Mongols. Khan is about to stab him when Andy throws a sword at the murderous leader and kills him.[42]

Maria and Jean-Pierre Aumont first started seeing each other seriously in February 1943. He had been successful on the French stage and film industry prior to the outbreak of war with Germany and Italy. Aumont served in the French Third Mechanized Division when his country was invaded, being awarded the Croix de Guerre and Legion of Honor in the subsequent fighting. Following the German victory and occupation, he determined that France was no place to be Jewish and remain free and healthy. He left Vichy France to go to Portugal and on to the United States in late 1942. Aumont was in a play with Katharine Cornell and was soon signed by MGM. He went on to star in *Assignment in Brittany* (1943) and *Cross of Lorraine* (1943) before marrying Maria and joining the First Free French Army.

Like much in the life of Maria Montez, the story of how she and her future husband got together changed depending on the telling. What seems to be the truth was laid out in a *Photoplay* magazine with Maria's byline. She has them briefly meeting at a party in Los Angeles but no sparks flew. Maria felt Aumont was letting the woman he was with order him around and that was the last thing she wanted in a man. She saw him at the Brown Derby several weeks later and decided she had been too hasty. She told her companion Sir Charles Mendl that he must have a party and invite Aumont so they could meet properly. But she was soon off to New York for the premiere of *Arabian Nights.* On February 13 she saw him on the stairs of the 21 Club and, she wrote, "my heart leaped. The back and shoulders of a man looked so much like my fiancé, Claude [*sic*] Strickland, who had been killed in the war." The man, of course, was Aumont. He offered to light her cigarette and Maria "was suddenly excited." They saw each other every day for the two weeks they were in New York. She realized they were in love when the couple was on the train together on the way back to the West Coast.[43]

Elizabeth Russell described their meeting in slightly more romantic terms in her screenplay about Maria. She also has the meeting taking place at the New York premiere of *Arabian Nights.* Montez has been lying in bed in her hotel room, reluctant to go downstairs and take part in the festivities because she misses Claud Strickland so badly. A fellow from the Universal publicity department comes upstairs and takes her down to the party in the hotel's restaurant. This is where she sees Aumont for the first time. The publicity man introduces them. The key point of this part of the play is that Aumont looks very much like Strickland. Russell has Montez being convinced that the Frenchman was sent to her by St. Anthony, her patron saint. Later that night a box sent by the character based on Elizabeth Russell arrives from Los Angeles. It is the chain bracelet that Maria gave to Strickland as he was leaving New York to go back to England and the RAF. Because Aumont looks so much like her lost love, with the same stride, stature, and appearance, and because the bracelet arrives the same day she met him, Maria takes this as a sign that Strickland has released her. She is free to pursue her new love.[44]

Maria's niece Raina Paris pointed out that the story about the omens could be true as her aunt did very much believe in astrology and many other unseen things. She thought this was just part of growing up in the Dominican Republic when she did—her mother and all of her aunts had similar beliefs. Both Maria and Russell confirm the story of how closely Aumont resembled Strickland. Looking at photos of Claud Strickland in his RAF uniform and Jean-Pierre Aumont, it is hard to deny the resemblance. Plus, they were both cultured Europeans. Maria never had a prolonged romantic relationship with a North, South or Central American. Clearly, Aumont had plenty to recommend him on his own. Equally clearly, Claud Strickland had been very important to Maria Montez and the physical resemblance between the two men was part of the initial lure.[45]

Whatever the truth of the physical resemblance and psychic connection might be, Russell did use dramatic license as to where they met. But she did not exaggerate the immediate attraction. In the words of Jean-Pierre Aumont, "To say that between us it was love at first sight would be an understatement." He was completely smitten with both her physicality and her personality. He had seen *Arabian Nights* and "expected the same studied languor which she displayed on screen. Instead, I found her spontaneous, direct and childlike, warbling the tale of her nomadic life in an adorable Spanish accent." The curious thing is that after he gives this beautiful testimonial from his heart in his

Thirteen was Aumont's lucky number. Maria's astrology charts agreed, so the date was set for their wedding.

autobiography, he repeats all the phony Universal bio details of Montez's early life—the father as consul general of Spain, the convent in the Canary Islands, married for eighteen days to an Irishman, and then on a whirlwind trip to London, New York, and San Francisco, finally landing in Hollywood, "where her beauty and personality soon made her one of the most popular new stars." You wonder if he was just being loyal to her memory or if he never did know the true story. All he really cared about was the woman who was right there in front of him. And he found her endlessly charming and lovable.[46]

After returning to the West Coast by train, Aumont spent every evening he could at Maria's small house at 514 Walden Avenue in Beverly Hills. Their days were taken up by work at their respective studios. Maria was working on *Ali Baba and the Forty Thieves* at Universal while Aumont was filming *Cross of Lorraine* at MGM. They were rarely alone at Maria's house. He noted that the doors were always open and that an astrologer, a physical culture expert, a priest, a Chinese cook, and two Hungarian masseurs were constantly coming in and out. They did manage the occasional Hollywood-themed night out. They were photographed signing autographs at the premiere of *Flight for*

Freedom, dining at the Mocambo, entering and signing autographs at the Hollywood Canteen, and attending the huge celebration at the Hollywood Bowl for the drive to raise money for the building of the navy's prospective latest heavy cruiser, the USS *Los Angeles.*[47]

A photo of Jean-Pierre with his arm around Maria as he pointed to a calendar with July 13 circled was published around the country through International News Photos on July 9, 1943, with the caption, "Maria Montez and Jean Aumont apply for License!!" One of the things that often accompanied the photo was the Anglo-American fascination with the Latin American use of family names. Several times in her career, the press used her full name but never so often as when Maria married Jean-Pierre. *Photoplay*'s Cal York noted that now she would have to change her name from "Maria Gracia Garcia Van Dahl de Santos Silas y McFeeters [*sic*] to y Aumont." He also recorded his amazement that the couple would wed since Montez had "been much the play girl."[48]

The columnists were uncertain what to make of this whirlwind relationship and Maria's claim that she and Aumont would marry. Louella Parsons had no clue whether a marriage would happen before Jean-Pierre left to join the French army. "Your guess is as good as mine," she wrote. "And believe me, where the torrid Montez and her emotions are concerned it is just that, a guess." Her friend May Mann came to the moving-in ceremony for Montez's new studio bungalow on March 17. Jean-Pierre was there, and Maria introduced him as her intended. "He's mine," she told her friend. Both of them said they would marry soon and Mann found no reason to not believe them. Frederick Othman was at the same event but he was not so sure where the couple would end up.[49]

Jimmie Fidler was the most persistent of the scribes in his suspicions of Maria's motives, knowing full well her eager propensity for self-promotion and serial dating. Just before she met Aumont, he wrote, "Confidential Communiqué to: Maria Montez. Even if you fail to date every man in Hollywood be consoled, you've made a noble effort." The theme continued on March 23 when he wrote, "Silly notion: Maria Montez loving the same man in April that she adored in March." His April 4 column had a confidential communiqué to Maria: "Your current vows of undying love for Pierre Aumont are touching, but in view of your romantic record, I'll wait a few weeks before considering it a life-long passion." Five days later he thought the engagement announcement "has the aroma of pure publicity." Later in the month he wondered, "After so many publicity romances, why does Maria Montez expect columnists to believe her protests of undying devotion to Jean

Best man Charles Boyer kisses the bride while her husband kisses matron of honor Janine Crispin.

Pierre Aumont?" He gave his definitive answer to the marriage question one week later. He observed, "Maria Montez and her lasting love, Jean Pierre Aumont are un-lasting."[50]

Fidler seemed to be obsessed with whether or not the couple was really in love, but he was not the only columnist who had suspicions of there ever being Montez-Aumont nuptials based on the constant self-publicity campaign Maria had been relentlessly waging for the past three years. Typically, there was little effort to separate the created persona from the person who developed it. Cal York, *Photoplay*'s "Inside Stuff" columnist, wrote, "The amazing statements of French Aumont to the effect that Maria is an unselfish, misunderstood, self-sacrificing little woman has the town with mouths agape. They can't believe their ears." On May 21 Walter Winchell chimed in with the cynical observation that the couple would shortly announce the cancellation of "their planned merger—with attendant exploitation." On June 14 Louella Parsons announced, "There are those who do not believe they will ever wed." On June 23 Sheilah Graham assumed the relationship was no more than a publicity stunt and thought MGM would want to break up the

Montez-Aumont relationship because "they would like to link his name with one of their own unattached damsels—of which there are many."[51]

But the couple did get married on July 13, 1943—exactly five months after they first got together in New York. Thirteen was Aumont's lucky number. It was the date he wanted for their marriage. Maria had to consult her horoscope first. The stars were lined up properly so the Tuesday afternoon ceremony took place at 4:00 in the living room of Maria's Beverly Hills home. The ceremony was quite small, as all of the Gracia family was still in the Dominican Republic. Aumont wore a dark suit and Maria wore a simple white organdie dress with a short lace veil. Judge Cecil D. Holland, who had recently officiated at the wedding of Hedy Lamarr and John Loder, read their vows, while Charles Boyer served as best man and Janine Crispin as matron of honor. This was part of the European and North American tradition. In the Latin American tradition, there would have been a *padrino* and *padrina* to help plan and pay for the event as well give the couple advice. Either Montez wanted to embrace the tradition of her new country and/or her husband, or there simply were no Latin relatives around to assume the role. In any event she went with the northern European tradition prevalent in the United States.

Austrian count Degenhardt von Wurmbrand of the Steyersberg Castle south of Vienna entered with Maria on his arm to give her away. Her painter friend Frederick Sprague, who was in the US Navy painting portraits of naval leaders, played the Wedding March on the piano, in uniform. Alex Solomons, Aumont's father, was in attendance with the groom's stepmother. Jean-Pierre mother, Suzanne, had died in 1940 while he was in the French army for the first time. He placed a photo of her on the piano. Also at the wedding were Boyer's wife, Pat Paterson, Mr. and Mrs. Gene Kelly, Maria's wardrobe lady from the studio, Anne Fiedler, and her dress designer, Charmé Chadounne.

Adhering to tradition, the "old" thing Maria wore was her last remaining pair of nylon hose. "New" was the wedding dress by Charmé Chadounne, while "borrowed" was the Universal panty girdle made as a foundation for her *Ali Baba* costumes. "Blue" came from embroidered forget-me-nots on the white satin slippers that were a gift from Universal's costume designer, Vera West. Chicken-à-la-king was served for dinner. Wartime rationing was in effect, and Maria noted she used up all her meat points to get the chicken. Vegetables and citrus fruit came from her backyard victory garden. Universal sent the couple a silver service for twelve and Dominican leader Rafael Trujillo sent a cable to convey his wishes for their happiness.

A reception was held at the house for about fifty friends. Lieutenant Ronald Reagan, whom Maria had met on the excursion for the premiere of

The Sea Wolf, was photographed giving the bride a kiss. Elizabeth Russell caught the bridal bouquet of white roses and lilies of the valley. Actors Reginald Gardner and Simone Simon were there, as were Maria's producer on *Arabian Nights*, Walter Wanger, and her ever-loyal agent, Louis Shurr. Sir Charles and Lady Mendl (interior director Elsie de Wolfe) and Mr. and Mrs. Arthur Rubenstein were also in attendance.

This was a Hollywood wedding, so it was no surprise that seventeen newspaper and magazine photographers arrived to shoot the couple at 7:00 p.m. Among them were longtime Montez lensers like Gene Lester, Jack Albin, and Universal's Ed Estabrook. They had to fight for space with representatives from all the wire services. Fans were invited to take pictures of the couple as the two stood in the front entryway to the house. Several of the neighborhood kids got in on the act by running up to Maria to congratulate her. Of the magazines, *Movieland* covered the wedding most extensively. One of their photo spreads was of Maria kissing or being kissed by several of the guests. The photography and celebrating did not go late into the night. The bride, as well as several of the guests, had to be at the studio for makeup at 5:00 a.m. The groom did not have to report to MGM until 9:00 as he was only dubbing dialogue.[52]

One nontraditional aspect of the Montez-Aumont wedding was the lack of a honeymoon. Maria was about a third of the way through filming *Ali Baba and the Forty Thieves*, while Jean-Pierre was finishing *Assignment in Brittany*. Maria would be tied up with *Ali Baba* until September 1, while Aumont had only a week left before the completion of *Brittany*. So they started their married life in the house on Walden Avenue.

The newly married couple set off east once Maria had completed filming *Ali Baba*. Aumont's previous service and obvious good health assured he would have no problem being accepted into the Free French forces. His friend André Lichwitz was an officer in the First Army and wanted Jean-Pierre to be one too. To do this the former sergeant had to stop in Washington, DC, to take his officer's exam. He easily passed that but had less success with his second assignment. He had promised his friend Louis Jouvet to help him get clearance for his theater company to perform in the United States. The company had been all over Latin America after escaping German-occupied France, but in spite of Aumont's efforts it was not allowed into the States because the federal government could not clear all the members of the troupe.

Once the newlyweds arrived in New York, they took up residence at Maria's favorite New York address, the Sherry Netherland Hotel, and were able to spend time together until she had to return to Los Angeles to prepare for the filming of *Gypsy Wildcat.* They enjoyed the city, revisiting Club 21, where they had met, going window-shopping on Fifth Avenue, and taking a hansom cab ride through Central Park. She would also have to prepare her short foray into the middle of *Follow the Boys.* Career called Maria; renewed service to France called Jean-Pierre. He accompanied his wife to the train station for her trip back to Los Angeles. He noted, "She burst into tears behind the window glass of her coach. I didn't hold up that well, either." Aumont shipped out for North Africa on one of the mass-produced, always-crowded Liberty ships that served as an endless conduit of men and material from the United States to the war fronts. A month later he was officially assigned to the First Free French Army. On April 13, 1944, his unit left North Africa to be deployed for combat in Italy.[53]

As Jean-Pierre was waiting to catch a troopship to North Africa, Maria was back in Los Angeles starting the filming of what was finally called *Gypsy Wildcat.* The final title certainly fit better with the created Montez persona than the working titles of *Zorya* and *Gypsy Girl.* It was an effort to breathe more life into the Neverland fantasies that made Maria famous. This one took place in some vaguely eastern European country at an undetermined time when people still rode horses but, oddly, the women wore nylons and high heels. Universal assigned Roy William Neill to direct the film. Leading hard-boiled crime fiction author James M. Cain, another unexpected visitor to Neverland, worked on the script. Sabu was in the US Army Air Force, and Turhan Bey had been lent to MGM for *Dragon Seed.* Yugoslavian actor Peter Coe, who was much better known for his swimming pool and stage work than his film work, was added to the cast. He would play the poor boob whose love for Maria is unrequited and who has to die at the end. Leo Carrillo, scion of a very old Californio family who had played all sorts of ethnic characters, was the Gypsy leader in the film.[54]

James M. Cain was not thrilled when he was handed the script for *Gypsy Wildcat* for a rewrite. That much is clear. We should take the rest of the recollections of this famously acerbic writer with more than a grain of salt. He thought the thing "was simply weird." Striving mightily to separate himself from anything to do with the movie and to denigrate its star, he claimed that Maria looked vaguely familiar; she "must have checked hats someplace in Hollywood." He handed his finished work to producer George Waggner and when he went to his office to say good-bye he found Waggner rewriting Cain's rewrite. The writer thought he had made logical sense out of the mess he was handed. According to Cain's self-aggrandizing account, the producer agreed with him, but told him it was simply too literate.[55]

The exact language of Cain's description of his work on *Gypsy Wildcat* is suspicious, but his account does highlight a problem Universal had with Maria. Stacy Keach Sr., the dialogue director on *Ali Baba and the Forty Thieves,* remembered how much trouble Montez had with her lines and the delays in shooting it caused. Screenwriter Edward Hartmann had to simplify her character's dialogue. Waggner, who produced half of the six Neverland films, expressed the way the studio saw its star when he was said to have told Cain, "She couldn't play your dialogue. It has to be translated into the kind of baby talk she can handle. I'm pinching myself for the wonderful thing you've done with this bad dream I threw at you. Now I can put this thing in front of the camera." And so he did.[56]

Gypsy Wildcat presented the fewest problems for the Hays Office of all the Neverland pictures. It was submitted on September 3, 1943, with a request for a quick turnaround as Universal wanted to start production shortly and needed comments before mimeographing the script. One of the few complaints was over the snake eater. Breen noted that audiences generally "had a bad reaction" to snakes. It was suggested the fellow be changed to "a juggler or something." Breen also warned Universal that several local censorship boards would cut out the existing scenes of flogging, whipping, slugging, and branding. No complaints about Maria's clothes this time. She finally got what she had been asking for: her costumes completely covered her.[57]

Gypsy Wildcat

The film starts with a Gypsy fair. The tribal leader, Anube (Leo Carrillo), watches his son, Tonio (Peter Coe), play the violin for his main attraction at the Gypsy camp's shows for the local townspeople, the dancer Carla (Maria Montez). When she takes a break in the woods, she sees the local count being killed by an arrow as a stranger named Michael (Jon Hall) rides off. Michael shows up at the Gypsy camp just as Baron Tovar (Douglass Dumbrille) is accusing the tribe of killing the count. Michael defends the Gypsies and is arrested by the baron. He escapes and the Gypsies are taken to the count's castle. Carla finds Michael hiding near the castle and he kisses her passionately before leaving. Days later, when Tonio declares his love for Carla, she tells him she loves Michael.

Anube captures Michael and wants to turn him over to the count in order to free his people. Carla dresses him as a clown and the baron's troops do not recognize him when they search the caravan. Michael goes to the castle and informs the baron he is a messenger sent by the king to help the count and he knows it was the baron who killed him. He escapes yet again, is wounded, and is nursed back to health by Carla. The baron has recognized the necklace Carla always wears as identifying her as the daughter of Countess Orso and the rightful heir to the castle. The baron wants to marry her to keep control of the castle. Michael infiltrates the castle and is again caught. Carla agrees to marry the baron to save Michael's life and secure the release of her fellow Gypsies. There is a fight. The baron is about to kill Michael but Tonio intervenes and is himself killed. Carla takes control of the castle with Michael as is her birthright. The Gypsies are free to go their way.

Maria had to take a day off on November 23, 1943, in the midst of filming *Gypsy Wildcat* to shoot her very small part in Universal's contribution to the all-star extravaganzas that several studios produced to show their support for the war effort while featuring practically everyone on their lot. Paramount was the first with *Star Spangled Rhythm* (1942). Hope and Crosby are in it along with most of the rest of the studio's contract players. Warner Brothers came out with *Hollywood Canteen* in 1944. RKO and United Artists produced a New York counterpart, *Stagedoor Canteen* (1943). MGM did its part by producing *Thousands Cheer* (1943). Universal was not going to be left out. The studio's effort was called *Follow the Boys.* Released in 1944, it concerns the efforts of George Raft and Vera Zorina to reignite their failed marriage. The real points of the movie are to feature the deep list of contract players available to Universal producers and to illustrate how all of Hollywood supports the war effort. Among the featured acts are Donald O'Connor and Peggy Ryan jiving away, the Andrews Sisters, Jeanette MacDonald and Dinah Shore singing, Orson Welles doing magic tricks with Marlene Dietrich (because Columbia would not release his wife Rita Hayworth to do the part), and W. C. Fields performing his famous pool routine.

Maria's only part in the film is a brief segment in which George Raft introduces the idea of the Hollywood Victory Committee and its role in entertaining the troops. The committee, founded three days after the attack on Pearl Harbor, worked in conjunction with the Screen Actors Guild to allow actors not in the military to do their best to sell bonds and entertain troops all over the world. The committee also made sure that the stars it provided for particular venues had not played there recently. They wanted the boys to have variety. Montez has no dialogue but naturally sits front and center, with Andy Devine on her left and Robert Paige on her right. Nigel Bruce, Donald O'Connor, Peggy Ryan, and many other Universal stars are also present. The camera shoots Raft from the front as he speaks, then goes behind to

Hollywood Victory Committee scene in *Follow the Boys*—with Maria front and center.

shoot him in the foreground, showing the audience attentively listening in the background. Since she was sitting dead center in the crowd, Montez is in most of these shots.

After her day's work on *Follow the Boys* Maria headed back to the historically unclear (maybe the Middle Ages?) Neverland and *Gypsy Wildcat.* A note was planted in *Motion Picture* magazine reading, "Last time we lunched with Maria Montez she chatted excitedly about her role in *'Gypsy Wildcat,'* which gives her and her fans a respite from the sarong roles." Sarongs or not, the movie certainly fit the Neverland pattern. Once again Maria is royalty, put in great danger, and saved by Jon Hall. The movie may have been put in some vague, mythical country hundreds of years ago, but the story line is the same as the others in the series where Maria is an island princess or an Arabian princess. As usual, there was every effort to feature Montez's physicality. She wears far more clothes than usual, but much of the advertising for the film featured the dancing scene where Maria's dress is swirling up. In the actual movie it gets only slightly above her knees, but in the drawings to sell the film it is up around her waist, with the caption "Swaying Hips . . . Dancing

Ad for *Gypsy Wildcat*—the promise from Universal.

To Mad Adventure!!!" One of the most common set stills used to spark interest in *Gypsy Wildcat* showed Maria seated in costume pulling up her nylons. Leg art of the first dimension, but nylons in the Middle Ages? Pure historical accuracy was never the point in Maria's movies. Her legs always were.[58]

As usual with a Montez movie, the reviews were all over the place. True to form, Bosley Crowther in the *New York Times* thought it was moronic, advising viewers, "Set your brain at zero, if you decide to take it in." The

Gypsy Wildcat dance—the reality from Maria.

Seattle Daily Times was equally unenthusiastic. Their reviewer noted, "Candy kids, Maria Montez and Jon Hall have dipped deep into Universal's delicatessen to come up with a new concoction, '*Gypsy Wildcat*.'" Herbert Larson in the *Portland Oregonian* predicted, "The 10-year-olds will 'eat up' this cross-bow western" in a review he titled "Hall Wins Maria Again—Hero Outwits Nasty Villain."[59]

Columnists were more tolerant of this latest edition of the Montez-Hall team. Philip Scheuer of the *Los Angeles Times* enjoyed "the wriggly Miss Montez" and thought the movie was "a model of camera facility." But he was as baffled as everyone else as to where "this happy hunting ground is located." Scheuer's fellow *Times* film reviewer thought "'*Gypsy Wildcat*' gives Maria Montez a more picturesque and animated role even than usual." Sheilah Graham had written before about Maria's problem with her co-star. She took the opportunity to note, "Maria Montez who huffed and puffed and said she'd blow the Universal Studio house down if they teamed her again with Jon Hall is eating humble pie. . . . Maria is probably the least popular actress at Universal these days because of her silly tantrums." She gloated that they would also be paired in the future in *Queen of the Nile*. A month before this piece Graham had penned another column on how badly Maria wanted to be shut of Hall. She thought it was just one "beautiful torso" trying to dismiss another. She did quote a Universal executive who was sick of all the arguing. But, he wailed, perfectly summing up the studio's dilemma, "How can we fire a girl who made five million dollars for Universal last year?"[60]

The most enthusiastic review of any movie always comes from the press book prepared for it by the studio. The *San Diego Union* basically reproduced the Universal suggested review. Concerning "the tempestuous Maria Montez," it assured readers, "the role is one of the most alluring she has ever portrayed. . . . The Montez characterization of a wild Gypsy girl places her in the top ranks of movie stars."[61]

The official Hollywood publications were supportive as usual. *Variety* advised its readers, "'*Gypsy Wildcat*' is the latest in Universal's series of Technicolored Arabian Night cinematic dramas which, despite critical brush-off, have provided timely escapist entertainment for the customers, and solid profit to both distrib and theaters." It thought the star was "displayed to the best pin up advantage in eyeful and formful setups." The *Hollywood Reporter* thought it "a contender for high money honors," helped very much by "Maria Montez, a certain favorite by this time."[62]

Gypsy Wildcat may have been a slightly different take on the Montez-Hall teaming, but it was as popular as the other entries. On a budget of under $1 million, it realized a box office of over $2 million. As usual, Montez was the featured part of the movie to both reviewers and interviewers. One of the major things Universal wanted to push was the fact that the studio was finally acceding to Montez's constantly stated desire to shed the sarongs, desert wear, and bare feet for a film. Frederick Othman, columnist and United Press Hollywood correspondent, was set up with an interview with Maria. He called his piece "Maria Montez Gets to Wear Shoes, and She's Very Pleased about It." He reported that she was ecstatic to finally be wearing proper footwear in a picture. As Othman pointed out, "Miss Montez earned her employers several million dollars by not wearing shoes—and a few other things. Her costume usually consisted of body makeup, some sequins (solidly glued on) and as little gauze as the Hays office would permit." He noted with some dismay that she wore seven petticoats in her latest film. What seems like a positive to Maria is clearly a negative to everyone else. He asks the obvious question, "Miss Montez has beautiful legs and how are you going to give the cash customers a look when you're wearing seven petticoats?" Maria assured him, "I am now seeking ways to get around this difficulty." Getting into a carriage offered an opportunity. Her elegant countess dress could be bumped or

Maria takes another opportunity to show those legs in *Gypsy Wildcat.*

caught on the wagon. "When that happens," Maria observed, "there will be my legs, my legs on view."[63]

Clearly Othman felt Maria's appeal did not lay in heavy costumes, shoes, or thespian pyrotechnics. He wanted to see her legs. This certainly fit in with the desires of Universal, if not Maria. She liked the change of pace, calling all the clothes she wore in the movie "very unusual," even as she clearly understood the need to show off her legs. But she kept up the drumbeat for putting the Neverland movies behind her. She wanted to be in modern dramatic or comedic roles, as she told every interviewer who spoke to her. But she was under contract. Universal had her slated to play Cleopatra or at least a Cleopatra-like character in what the studio was calling *Queen of the Nile.* After several rewrites, it finally emerged as *Sudan,* and would be the last of the six Neverland films that made Maria Montez a star. Fittingly for the last in the series, Turhan Bey would get the girl, not Jon Hall.

6

Sudan

Sudan was scheduled to start shooting on the Universal lot on June 6, 1944. But prior to returning to the Technicolor desert, Maria had one other task to fulfill for her studio. Universal had paid attention to Montez's constant demands that she get the chance to appear mostly fully clothed in a modern black-and-white film; she finally got her wish. Sort of. She was top billed in a black-and-white musical the studio was calling *Hip, Hip Hooray* when it was submitted to the Hays Office on December 21, 1943. The censors had no particular problem with the script; though they did warn Universal "to be careful with the costuming of the chorus girls," hold the drinking scenes "to the absolute minimum," and not suggest nudity in a silhouette scene. For once there was no concern expressed over Maria's costumes. The movie was finally filmed as *Bowery to Broadway* from May 4 to July 1, 1944. Maria does not appear until the last of the three episodes in the film. But her part had to be filmed early since she had to report to *Sudan.* Typically, Maria was assigned an upper-class role, in this case in the character of a European vocal star.[1]

Bowery to Broadway seems more like a movie 20th Century Fox would make except it is in black and white. It tells the story of Irish American rivals starting in the beer garden theatrical productions of the Bowery in turn-of-the-twentieth-century New York. Avuncular Michael O'Rourke (Jack Oakie) is happy in the Bowery; sophisticated Dennis Dugan (Donald Cook) wants to move on to classier shows that would be featured on Broadway. In the slang of the time, O'Rourke was "shanty Irish" while Dugan was "lace curtain Irish." The film follows their rivalry through three episodes over the decades that take them, as the title suggests, from the low-rent Bowery to sparkling Broadway.

Marina (Maria Montez) does not appear until the third episode. She plays the sort of classy European entertainer Dennis wants to represent. Dennis brought her to Broadway and her first two musicals are hits. But then she insists Dennis star her in *Dark Autumn,* a drama that was a smash for her in Budapest. That drama and four subsequent ones all fail, which bankrupts Dugan. Marina leaves him. O'Rourke has not been doing well on his own, so he and Dugan decide to reunite and return to the Bowery. They produce a musical revue starring the daughter (Ann Blyth) of a song-and-dance team (Frank McHugh and Rosemary DeCamp) the two have been working with since their retirement from the vaudeville circuit. The show is a hit. Dugan thinks his agent P.J. (Leo Carrillo) put up the money for the show until O'Rourke takes Dugan up to a theater box to meet "our real angel. And I do mean angel." Marina turns as Dugan comes in. They embrace.

Bowery to Broadway seemed to be another effort to get every Universal performer except Deanna Durbin into one movie. Hoofers Donald O'Connor and Peggy Ryan have two numbers. They had to be filmed before the rest of the movie went before the cameras because O'Connor was due to enter the army. Space was also found for Universal contract players Turhan Bey, Leo Carrillo, Andy Devine, Louise Albritton, Susanna Foster, Evelyn Ankers, and Ann Blyth. Charles Lamont, one of the studio's most experienced directors, was at the helm. He had directed many of the studio's Youth Unit musical comedy films starring Donald O'Connor, Peggy Ryan, Gloria Jean, and Ann Blyth. He would go on to direct several of the wildly popular Abbott and Costello movies. The cinematographer was Charles Van Enger, who shot most of the silent Ernst Lubitsch Warner Brothers films and was assigned to every sort of movie Universal made in the 1940s.

Montez may have had her singing dubbed (once again by Martha Tilton) and dancing doubled, but she was top billed. At $25,000 for her four weeks on the set, she was paid more than any of the many contract players in the cast. Leo Carrillo received $15,000 for six weeks. Susanna Foster received $14,000 for five weeks and three days, while Rosemary DeCamp was paid $5,250 for seven weeks. Independent talent Jack Oakie topped them all with $75,000 for eight weeks. As always, Maria wound up being some sort of aristocrat in the movie. You wonder if the arc of Maria's character was a veiled insult by the studio. Marina is a major European star who is sick of the musicals that have proved so successful for her. She wants to do drama. She gets her wish and it's a disaster, very adversely affecting her career and her producer's pocketbook. Substitute Neverland movies for musicals and Universal for Dugan and you have the story of Montez's career as far as her studio was concerned.[2]

The press book for the film obviously did not set up Maria as headed for a fall. She was touted as one of the studio's biggest stars. In the prepared "review" of the movie Montez was listed first in the cast as she was in the ads. Her new look was lauded; she was "more glamorous than ever in modern dress." For all the noise Universal made in the press book about Maria finally playing a part in modern dress rather than a sarong or diaphanous desert

Maria may have finally got to wear modern clothes in *Bowery to Broadway*, but the most common photo released by Universal showed Maria in the one skimpy costume she wore in the film.

wear, the most common image of her released by John Joseph's publicity department featured the one sexy costume she wore. The scene was described in a blurb the studio released to the Associated Press. Montez enters the scene "without a sarong, but in a silver bra, scanty panties, and a long ostrich feather train." During the filming she wound up descending the stairs four times in this getup before everything finally went right. Except that when director Charles Lamont studied the playback he noticed Maria was singing the wrong song so her lips did not match the soundtrack. But he just shrugged and said, "Who cares? Who's going to be watching her mouth in this scene!" Universal always assumed the audience's attention was going to be on the stunning Montez body, not any acting she may be attempting.[3]

For all of Universal's concentration on the one scene in the movie where Maria displays her physique to its best advantage, it ignored the scene that demonstrated how much Maria had learned about acting in the past four years. She comes to Ann Blyth's birthday party in a modern dress and without a bit of imperiousness to try to convince O'Rourke to resume his partnership with Dugan, who is now broke. She has to admit that she was not enough to keep him happy. Friendship and their partnership can be as strong a bond as love for a woman. Dugan needs O'Rourke. This is certainly not a scene that would crop up in any of the Neverland movies. Maria took her part seriously. It is one of the best scenes of her Hollywood career and she wrings every ounce of poignancy out of it.

As usual, the trades were happy with the movie. The *Hollywood Reporter* found *Bowery to Broadway* "a musical mélange which pads a great deal of entertainment along its way" and described it as "cavalcadish in its coverage of thirty years of show business." *Variety* praised it as "a happy event, as much for the spectator as it will be for the theater exhibitor." Both lauded Maria's performance, with the *Reporter* finding it curious that Montez does not "arrive until the last reel or two, but carries on from there notably in a full-clad role quite different from her previous efforts."[4]

It is indicative of how big a star Montez was in the Universal firmament when so much was made of her wearing Vera West's modern dresses despite the short time she spent in the movie. Big-city newspapers took the topic very seriously. The *Pittsburgh Press* had its reviewer do a separate column titled "Maria Plays a Modern Girl," in which it is noted that the studio has "taken the sarong away from Maria Montez. . . . She plays a flesh and blood woman who is attractive in modern clothing." The reviewer fully realized the importance of this. "To Miss Montez's many fans, the news that she and the sarong had parted company was catastrophic. Letters came pouring into the Universal Studio objecting to the fact that the Montez curves were to be concealed beneath sixteen changes of modern clothing." But her fans should not worry. "The breathtaking Miss Montez is more breathtaking than ever in her first modern role."[5]

Small-town newspapers typically relied on the Universal press book to describe how Maria was clothed in *Bowery*. The *Bismarck (North Dakota)*

Tribune, Athens (Ohio) Messenger, and *Middletown (New York) Times-Herald* all noted, "They've taken the sarong away from Maria Montez, but you ought to see her now!" as she is both "curvaceous" and more "glamorous than ever in modern dress" playing a "ravishing Continental star."[6]

The syndicated columnists fell into line by commenting on the newly covered Montez. Walter Winchell lauds the "daring gowns which manage to cover everything without censoring anything." In September 1944 Erskine Johnson noted Maria had sixteen changes of costume, without "a sarong in the lot." Three months later he was having lunch with Montez and her three very excited sisters. But as always, "running true to form, Maria had to take time out to talk about Maria." Johnson listened to her take a new tack on her limited participation in the movie. She lamented how disappointed her fans would be since she is in *Bowery* for such a short time, but "eet ess the greatest dramatic performance Montez has ever givens. All the studios are now bombarding me weeth scripts." This last point had some truth to it. Independent producers like Edward Small, Seymour Nebenzal, and the King Brothers soon started to try to interest her in their proposed films.[7]

After completing her part in *Bowery to Broadway,* Maria had to report immediately to the set of *Sudan.* Universal had hedged its bets in the advertising for *Bowery.* The studio kept her happy by putting her in a more modern part but created many studio blurbs bemoaning how overdressed she was. Edwin Schallert of the *Los Angeles Times* was looking forward to the new movie as a return to type. He noted she "quit the exotic" in *Bowery* and—horrifyingly enough—she "wears lots of dresses and everything." Fortunately, she was off to make what was still being called *Queen of the Nile.* Even though she would not be playing Cleopatra, "her garb will outdo the famous voluptuary of the past." She would be back in skimpy clothes—where both Universal and Schallert felt she belonged. Meanwhile, producer Paul Malvern and director Jack Rawlins were off scouting locations in New Mexico.[8]

Three weeks prior to the start of filming, Maria was at the James Vigeveno Galleries in Westwood. The gallery specialized in paintings by Dutch and Flemish masters. Ernst Van Leyden, a contemporary Dutch painter trained in France and currently living in the wealthy Brentwood section of Los Angeles, created a series on famous refugees to America. Thomas Mann the German author was one. Maria Montez was, inaccurately, another. Ernst Leyden himself left Europe when the war threatened. It had cachet to be Dutch during the war years. He changed his last name to Van Leyden just to make sure people made the connection. The *Los Angeles Times* critic did not like the work. He

A Ray Jones portrait for *Sudan*.

thought the "suave charm of composition and color [Leyden] brought from France is gone." He was particularly disappointed in the portrait of Montez. "In real life, radiantly lovely, but here a bloodless manikin."[9]

Maria took that radiant loveliness back to Universal City prepared to become an Arabian princess once again. Most of *Sudan* was shot on the Universal back lot on standing sets dressed to look appropriately Sudanese or Egyptian, or at least sandy. A second unit was hard at work filming desert grandeur around

Gallup, New Mexico. Once again Babe DeFreest was doing the stunt work for Montez. She was such a talented rider and extras were so short by the third year of the war, Babe also played one of the Arab riders with an applied beard.[10]

It was clear Universal had high hopes for *Sudan. Daily Variety*'s anniversary issues were always crammed with ecstatic ads for upcoming movies placed by the production houses. In the eleventh annual issue in October 1944 the studio was effusive in its praise of the latest Neverland film. One of the ads from Universal had a cartoon of a woman entering the door of "Projection 3." She is saying, "Caught the 'rushes' of the previous day's shooting on '*Queen of the Nile*.' Never saw Maria Montez so lovely. . . . She's co-starred again with Jon Hall . . . and with the romantic hit of '*Dragon Seed*,' Turhan Bey! . . . It looks like the Technicolor topper to Universal's great parade of adventure spectacles."[11]

The Hays Office was back to the usual complaints after the easy time it had with *Gypsy Wildcat*. Maria had returned to her gauzy harem-type costumes and as always Universal was warned to watch the costumes of her and all the women and to be careful of the movements of the dancers. As was common, the censors wanted the studio to avoid "excessive gruesomeness" in the battle scenes. There was also a suggestion to contact the American Humane Society regarding the treatment of horses—especially if the film was to be released in England. They also wanted to substitute "beauty" for "sex" in the line "a queen who uses her sex to trap the unwary." All this was worked out and *Sudan* received its certificate on January 5, 1945.[12]

Sudan

Naila (Maria Montez) is an Egyptian princess who dances surreptitiously in the marketplace of the royal city of Kemis on the banks of the Nile. Her father is killed, according to Horadef (George Zucco), his chief counselor, by Herua (Turhan Bey), the leader of escaped slaves. Naila makes the mistake of telling Horadef that she plans to find Herua by going undercover as a peasant. He sends a band to capture her and sell her into slavery so he can become king. Naila escapes and meets two thieves, Merab (Jon Hall) and Nebka (Andy Devine). They are captured and about to be sold as slaves. Herua rescues them, takes them to his camp, and professes his love for Naila. While torn in her feelings, Naila nonetheless determines to arrest and prosecute Herua for her father's death when she returns to Kemis and assumes her rightful place on the throne. Herua pleads his innocence but, despite a broken heart, Naila condemns him.

Merab manages to help Herua escape, though he also loves Naila. He has taken Herua's place in prison, and when the guards find him, he claims he is the victim of black magic. Naila orders him released but soon joins him in prison after being taken captive by Horadef. While in their cells, Merab shows Naila the contents of Horadef's purse, which he has stolen. Naila recognizes her father's ring and realizes that Horadef killed her father, not Herua. Horadef puts Merab on the rack to get Naila to tell him where Herua's camp is. She tells him to save Merab, and then leads Horadef and his men to the camp. Herua lets her, at the head of the blackguards, through the pass on the way to his camp, and then orders his men to push tons of boulders on Horadef and his men. Herua's men defeat those who survive and Merab kills Horadef. Naila returns to her throne with Herua by her side while Merab and Nebka go back to being thieves.

Sudan is another typically convoluted story in which Maria is royalty, loved by several men, threatened with bodily harm, the victim of a duplicitous advisor to the ruler of the country, witnesses or participates in some final battle, and is finally saved by Jon Hall while various comic relief actors cavort through the proceedings. The one big difference in this finale of the Neverland series is that after Hall saves Maria, she goes off with Turhan Bey. This was unprecedented in the series of six. It's clear that Hall was no longer the beefcake wonder he had been, whereas Turhan Bey had become quite the heartthrob during the war years for his work at both Universal and MGM. He had a more European outlook, having lived in Vienna, than Jon Hall and recognized and appreciated Montez for what she was. He noted that she was "not only a star but a diva. . . . Maria was known to carry herself as a princess. She could not enter any kind of room without drawing attention to herself."

Universal brought out the A team for *Sudan.* Director John Rawlins had previous experience with Maria in *Raiders of the Desert* and *Bombay Clipper* before graduating to Walter Wanger's *Arabian Nights* and *Ladies Courageous.* Vera West designed the costumes; Jack Pierce was in charge of the makeup. The film was lensed once again by George Robinson and features some of the best Technicolor camerawork in the Neverland series. There are several horse chases over the dunes near Gallup, New Mexico. It certainly shows that Babe DeFreest, Maria's riding double, could really ride a horse. Maria rides more sedately in her close-ups, but is on horseback more than in any of the other Neverland movies. She was paired with a very experienced and gentle palomino named Captain. Producer Paul Malvern hired many locals to ride their horses madly over the dunes. In this world where Maria Montez, Jon Hall,

Aumont's father and stepmother visit Maria on the set of *Sudan* while Aumont is still overseas with the Free French army.

Andy Devine, and George Zucco were readily accepted as Arabs, Malvern could note, "A Navajo makes about as good an Egyptian as anybody we know."[13]

Maria's character is more harshly treated in this sixth outing of the Neverland series. She is branded with a large S on her forearm when captured as a slave, then chained to an overhead bar before the slave women are chained together as they are prepared to be moved. Maria never looked better in the series, but her accent was never thicker. It was as if she was so sick of these roles she just didn't care if she could be understood. She was also finally separated from Jon Hall as the curtain falls. This is ironic since, as always, Hall plays the hero who saves the day. He not only protects Maria when she escapes the slavers, he also saves the slave leader when he's about to be killed by Horadef the evil counselor. Despite all that, it is Turhan Bey who will rule beside the new queen Naila.

It did not help Hall's case that right in the middle of filming *Sudan* he wound up on the wrong end of a fight. It did not seriously affect the production, and Universal had no real control over him since he was under contract to Samuel Goldwyn, but the fight put Hall in a very bad light. On August 8 he attended a party at bandleader Tommy Dorsey's house. As usual, the stories vary as to what exactly happened, but the consensus is Hall was accused by Dorsey of embracing his wife, actress Pat Dane. The actor said this was all nonsense; they were just talking. Obviously, all concerned tried to minimize the incident, but Hall was disfigured for a time. What was not in dispute was the fact that in the "battle of the balcony," Hall was hit in the face with a weapon variously described as a knife, a broken bottle, or a clay pot. He wound up with a broken nose and cuts on his face. Director John Rawlins was forced to shoot around him as doctors worked to repair his nose and hide the damage. Right in the middle of making *Sudan* the male co-lead required an operation to reconnect the end of his nose. Frederick Othman celebrated Hall's return to *Sudan* by noting, "The end of his nose is sewn on almost as good as new." Studio executives thought makeup could cover the wounds sufficiently for the two days remaining to shoot his part in the movie.[14]

Maria completely put her foot down after *Sudan.* She adamantly refused to be put in any more brightly colored Neverland films where she was always surrounded by animals of one sort or another, and had to be rescued by Jon Hall. As good as they looked together on-screen, Arthur Lubin, her director on *White Savage* and *Ali Baba,* remembered they didn't get along all that well in general but their mutual animosity really came to the fore over who got the most close-ups. For at least two years Maria had been telling interviewers that she wanted another leading man. She was completely aware that the Neverland films, while making buckets of money, kept her in a box that did not allow her to expand her career. Once again, she had Dorothy Lamour as an example. The Paramount star had managed to largely put the sarong behind her thanks to the "Road" pictures with Crosby and Hope and the other dramatic fare Paramount finally started putting her in.[15]

Maria was particularly keen to do a film with family friend Charles Boyer. But she was willing to co-star with almost anyone, as long as she could get into modern clothing and away from Jon Hall and animals. When Universal demanded that she star in *Frontier Gal,* yet another costumer where horses would be all over the set, she flat refused. She hated the script and everything else about the movie. Montez told the studio's leaders she would do only a contemporary dramatic or comedic film. Maria felt she did good work in *Bowery to Broadway* and proved her comedic ability on the many radio programs she had done.

It is interesting to note the various ways Maria voiced her increasingly adamantine statements about changing her career in spite of Universal's intransigence. She complained to interviewers, constantly petitioned her studio, and paid attention to other actors fighting the same fight. Shortly before Montez started *Bowery to Broadway* and with *Sudan* set to go, she read of Olivia de Havilland's victory over Warners. The actress had claimed the right to extend her contract beyond its seven years since she had spent six months on suspension for refusing parts she thought beneath her talent. She sued the film company and won. It was noted at the time as the "freeing of slaves" from the onerous contracts and practices of the studios. Jack Warner, never a live and let live guy, threatened to ban de Havilland from all the studios. When Sheilah Graham asked her if she got lots of thanks from Hollywood contract players, Olivia said, "No one, but this was very touching—Maria Montez, whom I didn't know, sent me a bouquet of flowers."[16]

The unhappy actress had very straightforwardly expressed her feelings about both *Sudan* and the desire to change her career in an interview with Frederick Othman for his column. He starts out by noting, "The subject today is curves. Beautiful, symmetrical curves." Maria could not argue. "There is something about me the public likes. . . . It may be my legs . . . it may be my eyes, but it is something." She was upset that her latest movie was no different from the others in the series. "I play in this one like I play in all of them, a strip tease," she told the columnist. "That is the trouble. What is the use of being a great actress if the people never look above your neck?" As for her place at Universal, she noted, "I am a very unhappy girl. This is the last picture of this type I am going to do. I have given them plenty of notice. I want to do a dramatic picture. I want to play with Boyer or Gable or Cooper." Then, in a perfect summary of her whole approach to her career, Maria said, "I want to learn something. I want to get ahead. I will get ahead. Even if I break my back I will get ahead."[17]

Of course, the photo accompanying the column was of Maria in a two-piece sunsuit showing off her legs to great advantage. Maria could complain all she wanted about not being taken seriously as an actress, and columnists would write about it—while still panting as Othman did over her "beautiful, symmetrical curves." Newspapers would print it while the editors found a good sexy picture of her to illustrate the column. This fixation on her legs and general sexuality, initially very much encouraged by Montez herself, followed her throughout her career in Hollywood. She certainly brought it on herself with her outrageous acts and statements when she was originally fighting for recognition. The problem is that it is extremely difficult to get out from under that in your later career. Getting anyone to take her seriously as an actress was an uphill slog. But a determined Montez was a force to be reckoned with.

The new serious Maria in a 1945 Ray Jones photo.

The reviews of *Sudan* were akin to Othman's column. They largely concentrated on how Montez looked in the role. As usual, the Hollywood newspapers lauded both Maria and the film. The *Hollywood Reporter* found *Sudan* "a first-rate Western story, done up in a toga." As for the star, "Maria Montez glamorizes the princess role with the sultry finesse at which she is singularly adroit." *Variety* thought it was part of "the winning tradition of these films which are box office bonanzas. . . . The stellar combination of Maria Montez,

Jon Hall and Turhan Bey, already thoroughly established in the public's esteem, soars to loftier artistic heights in *'Sudan'* with Montez especially turning in a performance that is certain to increase her already large following. Slimmer, more beautiful, and, above all, now a polished actress, la Montez in this one has fastened her grip onto screen stardom beyond any question of a doubt." The *Motion Picture Daily* thought *Sudan* was the best film in the series since "*'Arabian Nights'* started the studio upon this profitable vein of product."[18]

At least one reviewer cared little what the movie was about or who else was in it besides Maria. He understood that it was necessary to do the Neverland series in color and *Sudan* was no exception. But Jake Rachman of the *Omaha World Herald* wondered if sound was necessary for the movie. The whole point of *Sudan* was to show off "the Latin lady with the perfect dimensions." And since you "spend 90 per cent of your time just looking at her it would not be impossible to get through a picture with only a few subtitles and no sound." The story is okay, the music is rousing, and the Technicolor is beautiful. But more important, "as we hinted, Miss Montez is the screen's No. 1 eyeful."[19]

Bosley Crowther, ever acerbic, found *Sudan* dumb beyond measure, as "Maria Montez saunters [through it] with the regality of an usherette." More negativity was aimed at *Sudan* from various critics. That was to be expected. But what was dangerous, and what fed right into Montez's own feelings, is that many of these reviews commented on how stale the whole Neverland enterprise had become. When Edwin Schallert in the *Los Angeles Times* first heard about the story line of *Queen of the Nile* he wrote, "This has the air of being one of those last gasps in a series, when the scenarists have encountered brain fog more or less complete. I think the series—more properly the spasm—started with *'Arabian Nights'* some two years ago but it has rather consistently deteriorated since then." Jimmie Fidler agreed. He observed that Montez lost her argument with Universal over starring in a light comedy. Instead she will be in *Queen of the Nile,* which "sounds familiar."[20]

Film Bulletin called its section summing up the reviews of the New York newspapers—the *Times, World-Telegram, Herald Tribune,* and *Post*—on the movie " *'Sudan'* Just Another Montez-Hall Color Fairy Tale." The *Herald Tribune* in particular thought this was the same old Maria. "The formula for her fantastic escapades remains unchanged. . . . She is still the reigning queen of a mythical throne; she continues to have wicked chancellor trouble, and she is again rescued by Jon Hall as a benevolent vagabond." And, as always, she is "thinly clad." No matter how good "Maria looks in Technicolor, *Sudan,* like other Montez-Hall palace dramas, "is hardly worth the actor's while." Fairfax Nisbet in the *Dallas Morning News* admired Maria's "lush contours," but the movie, in its Technicolor splendor, could best "be seen and not heard." It is just another movie in the chain. *Photoplay* magazine's damning review succinctly summed up *Sudan* and agreed with all of Maria's worst fears by noting, "Pardon me, haven't we met before, little picture?"[21]

Despite the many disappointing reviews, *Sudan* looked magnificent in Technicolor and was the typical escapist fare all the Neverland movies were. Like the other five films in the series, it made a significant profit for Universal and the studio was as set on continuing the fantastical stories as Maria was dedicated to escaping them. The movie had a very impressive opening in Los Angeles, making $50,000 in four theaters its opening weekend. This was in spite of the city's theaters closing in honor of President Roosevelt's funeral procession in Washington on Saturday, April 14, following his death at Warm Springs, Georgia, on Thursday.[22]

With the filming of *Sudan* winding down in late August 1944 and nothing else scheduled for Montez until the disputed *Frontier Gal* after the new year, Maria wrote constantly to Jean-Pierre overseas, enjoyed friends, did studio assignments, was featured in fan magazines, and performed on several radio shows. One of the happy changes in Maria's life at this time was the arrival of three of her sisters, Lucita, Adita, and Consuelo. The stated reason for their coming to the United States was to finish their education. Maria's niece Raina Paris said the real reason was that Maria yearned to be with her family and wanted to give her sisters the opportunity for a fuller life than they would have had in the Dominican Republic. Elizabeth Russell repeatedly commented in her screenplay about her friend that one of the reasons her father left her $20,000 and why she was constantly badgering Universal to raise her salary was so that she could establish herself in the United States and bring her brothers and sisters north so they would not be in a country totally dominated by Rafael Trujillo. The sisters arrived in Philadelphia in September 1944 to study English. After a few weeks Maria arranged for them to take a train out to the West Coast. They all arrived in Pasadena on October 28 to pose for Universal's chief off-lot photographer, Ed Estabrook, at the Pasadena train station. Hollywood folks would often get off the train there to dodge the crowds and the newspeople who were inevitably waiting around Union Station in downtown Los Angeles.[23]

The sisters lived with Maria at her Beverly Hills home and listened to innumerable stories about the glories of Jean-Pierre, worked on their English, posed for Ray Jones at the Universal portrait studio, and generally enjoyed being in Los Angeles. Maria took her role as big sister seriously and tried to pass on her life lessons to her sisters. She told them to "make women friends. . . . This is very important. Important as never before." Maria knew they would go

Ed Estabrook photo of the Gracia sisters at home.

out with men, but they had to be careful. "Never, I say to them, beetling my brows and baring my teeth . . . never believe more than a tenth—and that with reservations—of what a Wolf says to you. Expose yourself to the yachts and apartments and blandishments of the Wolf-Pack, if you wish, for all experience is good, even when it is bad. But—learn how not to be interested in etchings!"

Some of the advice she gave her sisters seems to have come out of Maria's own hard-learned lessons. She told them, "Do not be phonies. . . . If you change your personalities, you will not be Adita, Consuelo and Lucita. You will be three other people, and that is not good." She stressed the work ethic. "There is nothing I want that I don't get. But I am willing to work for it." Then the woman who was willing to completely abandon the life she knew to pursue a dream warned them, "Do not forget that a disappointment is merely a puncture in the tire of hope, and learn to like loneliness. It is good to be lonely—and to be friends with yourself." That loneliness disappeared when she met "the divine . . . scintillating . . . glorious" Jean-Pierre and returned when he left for the war.[24]

Maria made it evident how happy she was to be united with her sisters in a bylined article for *Photoplay* she called "My Sisters and I." This is not the Queen of Technicolor writing. It is the oldest sister who longed for the large family she grew up with. "It is so wonderful," she starts. "We are so crazy. We are so happy. This is a dream I have had for a long time—having my sisters with me." She notes her mother is against careers for her daughters but Maria wanted to give them a chance at the life she was experiencing. She desperately missed her husband who was overseas fighting in the war. With her sisters around her, "Now I am not so lonely, and Jean Pierre must feel good to know I have some of my family with me."[25]

One of the key lessons she tried to impart to her sisters was the necessity of losing their accents. Maria had experienced her own accent as nothing but an impediment. She believed, "You can never rise to sustained greatness if you have an accent because you are limited." McClelland Barclay had exclaimed that she was the perfect cosmopolitan woman because her face was without nationality. To become the great actress she wanted to be she was determined to lose her pronounced accent. "A Russian role with a Spanish accent—it would never work." Whether studying with language expert Dr. Simon Mitchneck or welcoming her sisters to their new home, expanding her career was never far from Montez's mind.[26]

Maria's sisters certainly became part of the Montez publicity engine. Universal's Ed Estabrook was sent out to cover the four sisters' visit to Hollywood Farmers' Market as they looked at all the unique wares at the various stalls and returned to their car with a cart full of cut flowers. Estabrook also headed over to Casa Montez to shoot the sisters singing at the piano and dancing in the living room. This was a new presentation of Maria. This was not the blazing commissary actress in low-cut dresses who had garnered so much initial attention. This was a far more relaxed, family-oriented Maria, happy to be running around with her sisters.

This same homespun Maria appeared in a Louella Parsons column at this time. Gone was the blustering, the endless self-promotion, the proclamations concerning her devastating beauty. Parsons did note, "I must admit I am always fascinated with the Montez girl. There's never a dull moment when you talk to her. Her life as she tells it is far more romantic than any fiction." What Maria wanted to tell the columnist is that she was going to have a baby. When Jean-Pierre returned, of course. She had not told Universal about this yet and told Parsons she would take only a year off when the time came. Knee deep in sisters and planning to have a baby as soon as her husband returned from the war. The commissary actress had served her purpose and was gone. Montez wanted to be taken seriously.[27]

Maria rarely went out to nightclubs with her husband away, but she kept up the round of parties she had always enjoyed. They were just more sub-

The Universal snipe noted the "Montez sisters haven't all been together since they were little 'muchchas' in their native Dominican Republic." The studio sent Ed Estabrook out to record them shopping at L.A.'s famous Farmers' Market.

dued, if more cosmopolitan due to the war. On June 13, during the filming of *Sudan*, she went to party at the house of her close friend the designer Elsie de Wolfe. It was quite an affair, with over fifty top stars attending, including Judy Garland, Mary Pickford, Joan Fontaine, and her sister Olivia de Havilland. A week after that she was dining with the American-born son of Alexander, prince of Thurn und Taxis, the director Alexis Thurn-Taxis, and his wife Lillie Messinger. For several years after his very eventful experiences in World War I he had produced Broadway plays and directed low-budget movies under the more American-sounding name Cliff Wheeler. By the 1940s he had returned to his original name and was back at work on films. Three weeks later Maria was with her friend Joan Fontaine once again at the Beverly Hills Hotel Palm Room for a fashion show featuring the Lilly Dache hats they both loved.[28]

On September 9 Maria was at Elsa Maxwell's formal dinner party celebrating the liberation of Paris along with Orson Welles and his wife, Rita Hayworth, Cary Grant, Greer Garson, and dozens of other celebrities. Maxwell was the most famous party giver of the era, and the doings at a rented Beverly Hills house were covered by *Life* magazine. Montez had been at Universal City on August 23 when the official announcement of the freeing of Paris set off celebrations all over the lot. She joined Ann Codee and a group of French players on the set of *The Mummy's Curse* in the singing of "La Marseillaise," the French national anthem. Besides the parties, Montez was at the premieres of *Wilson* at the Cathay Circle Theater on August 10 with Charles Boyer and his wife, and *Dragon Seed* at the Egyptian Theater on the 19th to support Turhan Bey and to raise money for the War Chest and United China Relief.[29]

The parties and premieres allowed Montez to spend time with friends and relax from her filming schedule, but there was always an element of being on the job as the press inevitably covered stellar parties and premieres. She also remained busy doing the work of a star for herself and her studio. On October 31 she was photographed at a thank-you party for the postmaster general at the Hollywood Post Office. A stamp had been issued to commemorate the fiftieth anniversary of motion pictures. Fittingly, it illustrated a group of soldiers watching a movie projected on a sheet in a jungle camp. Mary Pickford gave the address while Ilona Massey sung the national anthem. On December 14 she was nominated for the Golden Apple Award given by the Hollywood Women's Press Club to the most and least cooperative stars. She and Lucille Ball lost out to Betty Hutton in the most cooperative woman's category. The same day Philip Scheuer's column in the *Los Angeles Times* noted that many current stars were new to the audiences opening up in France following the June liberation of Paris. Scheuer pointed out that in 1940 Gene Tierney was still on the stage, Maria Montez "was still to wriggle" into Hollywood, Rita Hayworth "was an obscure second lead in B pictures," Alexis Smith was just leaving Los Angeles City College, and Betty Grable had only been seen in "one collegiate musical after another."[30]

While she was engaged in the social whirl after *Sudan* finished filming, Maria immediately renewed the drumbeat for changing her career and image. Herald Heffernan, the Hollywood columnist for the North American Newspaper Alliance (NANA), started his August 29 column by comparing Maria to Dorothy Lamour. Both of them grew tired of the limited roles available to the wearers of the sarong. Back in 1942, when she was thrilled to be more than set decoration, Montez had said, "Let the other actresses grab those Academy Awards. Montez will be happy so long as the boys on Main Street yell when she comes on the screen." But this was late 1944, and she now wanted parts that did more than show off her stunning physique. Heffernan also covered Universal's response to the pleas from its contract player. He observed, "Universal isn't the studio to tamper with art once it has a box-office bird in the hand. Said an official of the studio, 'When Maria quits showing that bare skin, she'd better look to the box office.'" The writer had heard that Universal was preparing a comedy for her, but was hedging its bets by ginning up a jungle story "that will show plenty of epidermis."[31]

All this prepared the scene for the fight over *Frontier Gal.* Universal had been setting the stage for Montez starring in a western as far back as November 1943, when Inga Arvad noted in her "Gossip in Hollywood" column that Maria's next picture was to be a western. This perplexed her. "La Montez with a gun in each hand—one would think she needed no such props." *Motion Picture Daily* mentioned it two days later. The drumbeat continued the following month when an item was released to *Daily Variety* referring to the screenplay for a western to star Maria and Jon Hall. It continued in January when Glenn Pullen, writing in the *Cleveland Plain Dealer* while Maria was in town on a bond tour, reported that she would leave the jungle for the Wild West. Universal was still looking for a title. Pullen suggested "Prairie Fire."[32]

The Arabian movies Montez had been starring in were often described as "easterns"—westerns with a lot of sand, skimpy clothes on the women, and beards on the men. *Frontier Gal* was an actual western. Small town, big saloon, bad guy, territorial prison, gunfight, all horses, no camels. Jon Hall was originally set to play the drifter who falls in love and fathers a child with the saloon owner before he is arrested and sent to prison for five years. When he returns there is a fight between him and the bad guy because they are both in love with the saloon owner. Needless to say, Hall is victorious.

This was basically the plot line of every one of the Neverland movies and Maria was having nothing to do with it. But Universal was no more listening to her than Warner Brothers listened to Olivia de Havilland when she complained about the vapid roles she was constantly given in her early career. It agreed wholeheartedly with Edwin Schallert of the *Times,* who wrote that the Montez everyone wanted to see was dressed in something clinging and revealing. How they planned to do this in a western was not clear. Presumably it would involve dancing of some sort. Perhaps a bath. Since her contract made it clear she had to work in any film the studio assigned her, when she refused *Frontier Gal* Maria was put on suspension.

Yvonne De Carlo took the suspended Montez's place and the script was altered, turning the "gal" from a Mexican to a European. This worked out for the studio in the dance scenes because there was no need to double her since De Carlo had been a professional showgirl at the Florentine Gardens and Earl Carroll's. It turned out that Montez would not have had to act yet again with Jon Hall had she accepted the role. He was increasingly on the outs with Universal. As he was a noncontract player, the studio had no need to keep him busy. Rod Cameron was brought in to be the drifter/lover. Even so, Maria would not be moved in her refusal to film *Frontier Gal* and her suspension without pay by Universal went into effect in April 1945 when filming started. Legally, this was completely within the studio's rights as contract players had no right of rejection over the movie the studio picked out for them.[33]

There is one aspect of *Frontier Gal* as released that is particularly hard to imagine Maria filming. At the end of the movie Rod Cameron gives the hard-headed, independent Yvonne De Carlo a good spanking. As was the case with Maureen O'Hara and John Wayne in *The Quiet Man* and *McClintock,* this, of course, makes her love the spanker all the more. It is difficult to imagine Maria Montez over any man's knee being spanked and subsequently meekly submitting to him. Her whole persona had become that of the woman who tamed "Holly-wolves" and anyone else who caused her problems. She was always pictured as imperious, and even if she did require saving from the bad guy who had fallen for her, she never seemed to bend completely to the will of her savior. This could have been one of the many reasons she so adamantly refused to do the picture.

While Maria was criticizing *Sudan* and aggressively voicing her displeasure over *Frontier Gal,* the American military and government were gearing up for the inevitable invasion of the Japanese home islands. It was predicted to be a bloodbath. The overall plan for the final battles of the war was called "Downfall." The timetable set for the invasion of the southern island of Kyushu was December 1, 1945. The northern island of Honshu would be hit on March 1, 1946. The Japanese had started using kamikaze aircraft during the naval battle for Leyte Gulf in November 1944. The battle for Iwo Jima in February and March 1945 saw more suicide attacks by the Japanese and some of the bloodiest land warfare in the Pacific theater. It was even worse on Okinawa from May to June. The closer the fighting came to the home islands, the more fanatical the defense became. Allied intelligence was aware that the Japanese government had been stockpiling armaments, aircraft, and troops all over the core islands of the Japanese chain. Civilians were being armed and trained in defensive combat. No matter how obviously the war was irretrievably lost, the Japanese government seemed committed to a fight to the death.

General Charles Willoughby, Douglas MacArthur's chief of intelligence, estimated that American casualties would be 1 million men if land invasions of Kyushu and Honshu were carried out. So many Purple Heart medals, awarded for being wounded or killed in combat, were produced and stockpiled for the assumed casualties that they were still being given out in the twenty-first century. The atomic bombs dropped on Hiroshima and Nagasaki ended the war and negated the need for a direct invasion of the home islands. The Purple Hearts waited in military warehouses all over the world to be awarded to wounded or killed soldiers in the fighting in Korea, Vietnam, Grenada, and the Middle East. Thousands more of them remain in storage seventy-five years and several wars later.[34]

Part of the fallout from this fear of enormous casualties was a marked escalation of the number of men drafted. All of this had an impact on Montez World. The army had already called in Jon Hall twice for a physical examination. He was rejected both times. On May 8, 1945, he was called in for a third time and was finally drafted. He reported to Fort MacArthur near San Pedro and was posted to Fort Ord near Monterey for training. He almost immediately went into the hospital and was treated for gallstones for the majority of his ten weeks in the army. Hall was discharged for medical reasons on October 15, 1945.[35]

Turhan Bey was also called up in the huge drafts of 1945. He had been technically neutral as a Turkish citizen until Turkey declared war on the Axis in February 1945. Like Hall he was drafted in May 1945, but unlike Hall he had no physical problems. He was sent to Camp Roberts near San Miguel, California, for basic training. After basic he was assigned as an entertainment specialist. He was sent overseas to Guam and Japan to arrange shows for the occupying troops. Bey was honorably discharged in October 1946.[36]

The surprisingly successful quartet of Maria, Jon Hall, Sabu, and eventually Turhan Bey that Universal put together for the extremely popular Neverland movies was no more. Three-fourths of it had gone to war. Maria was by herself now and felt she had the strongest position she would ever have for extricating herself from the sort of skimpy-costume movies she desperately wanted to put behind her. *Frontier Gal* was no more than a western wrinkle on the same old persona, just as *Gypsy Wildcat* had been a Gypsy take on it. As 1944 merged into 1945, Maria found herself in a complicated career position she herself created. She had issued a direct challenge to Universal and she was not backing down.

Maria did have one big event to look forward to while the arguments with Universal continued. Jean-Pierre was finally coming home after eighteen months overseas with the Free French Army. This caused her to drop anything else that was going on in her life and take a train to New York. With the war coming to a close in Europe and her husband coming home, Maria's extensive home front war activities were also coming to an end. Like many Hollywood personalities, she had sold bonds, entertained troops, visited military camps and canteens all over the country, and done whatever she could to be an ambassador of the Good Neighbor Policy. Maria may not have had a singing or dancing act to bring to military bases to entertain the men. But she did have herself—and that she was willing to spread around.

7

Maria on the Home Front

By the middle of 1945 the entire co-starring group in the Neverland series was in one branch of the military or other. Jon Hall and Turhan Bey were stateside in the army. Sabu was in the Southwest Pacific in the Thirteenth Army Air Force as a tail gunner in a B-24 flying out of Morotai northwest of New Guinea. He would complete forty-two combat missions. Even Peter Coe, Maria's co-star in *Gypsy Wildcat,* would serve three months in the Marine Corps before being discharged for being physically unfit. Her lover and presumed fiancé, Royal Air Force flight lieutenant Claud Strickland, had been killed in action over Belgium. Her husband, Jean-Pierre Aumont, was overseas in the Free French Army. He would be wounded twice after having served in a tank unit in the initial battle for France. Her portraitist and friend Frederick Sprague, who also played piano at her wedding, went into the US Navy. McClelland Barclay, who labeled her "the perfect cosmopolitan woman" and paid for her one modeling assignment in New York, died in the South Pacific on July 18, 1943, when his ship, the *LST 342,* was torpedoed by a Japanese submarine in the Solomon Islands. Her native country declared war on Japan and Germany and supported the Allied war effort with its agricultural products. No matter how much she liked living in the fantasy world she created in her own head, there was nothing abstract about World War II to Maria Montez.[1]

If you were a Hollywood star during World War II, particularly a female Hollywood star (unless you were Greta Garbo), it was presupposed you would support the war effort and the military waging it with your presence and participation. The Hollywood Victory Committee was founded December 10, 1941, with the task to create and organize personal appearances by film stars. The committee was "was formed as a means of coordinating the requests for 'free talent' and as a means of offering protection to the actors, the studios and the radio networks in Hollywood, so far as authentication of requests is concerned, and so far as an accurate check as to the officialdom of the sources of request for 'free talent.'" The United Services

Maria and Irene Dunne with French servicemen at the Hollywood Canteen, 1943. (Courtesy of the Academy of Motion Picture Arts and Sciences.)

Organization (USO) was a separate, government entity created by presidential order on February 4, 1941. It not only set up rest and recreation centers for the military all over the world, it sent troops of entertainers, famous and not, to every part of the United States and the extended war zones.[2]

The film industry's biggest contribution to soldiers on local leave was the Hollywood Canteen. It opened on October 3, 1942, and was built by studio technicians, run by Bette Davis and John Garfield, and its financing was arranged by Jules Stein, president of the Music Corporation of America. Stars from all the studios could be found cooking in the kitchen, serving food and drinks to servicemen, performing on the canteen's stage, signing endless autographs, writing letters for soldiers, dancing their feet off, and just talking to guys. Many women working for the studios served as hostesses after a hard day's labor on the lots. Many Hollywood women also went overseas on tour, most famously the Four Jills in a Jeep—Kay Francis, Carole Landis, Martha Raye, and Mitzi Mayfair. They were the subject of a best-selling book by Carole Landis and a subsequent 20th Century Fox movie. Bob Hope was the most famous wartime performer, but Frances Langford was with him wherever he went and frequently visited military hospitals to bring a bit of home to the wounded men. Jack Benny and Gary Cooper, among others, headlined overseas tours. Carole Landis and Ann Sheridan performed in both the European and China-Burma-India theaters of war. For their part, the studios worked with the federal government's Office of War Information to turn out product that would support the ideals of the war effort.[3]

Montez was certainly never a star on the level of Bette Davis, and her immigrant status made it difficult to go overseas to entertain the troops. Plus, she had no act. She could not sing like Frances Langford or dance like Mitzi Mayfair. But she was determined to play a part in the war effort. Maria certainly wasted no time in this endeavor. She had Christmas Eve dinner with the cadets at the Merchant Marine School in San Pedro seventeen days after the bombing of Pearl Harbor. Three months later she was presenting one of the seven bottles that had been thrown into the Pacific to judge the directions of local currents to the navy's hydrographic office. They created charts from this information aimed at aiding persons from torpedoed vessels to reach land.[4]

This set the tenor for the actress's wartime activities, most of which were of a personal, one-on-one nature. She welcomed military visitors to her sets at Universal, spent time at the Hollywood Canteen as well as the Stage Door and Merchant Sailors Canteens in New York and the National Press Club Canteen in Washington, DC. She worked with the Hollywood Victory Committee in its bond tours of stateside military bases and visited camps whenever she was filming near one or on quick weekend trips to those in the Los Angeles area. And she most certainly was an enthusiastic part of the Pin Up Industrial Complex that made sure military members all over the world had images of spectacular women to remind them of home. Maria may never have become an American citizen like her friend Sabu, but she was thoroughly invested in supporting the Allied war effort in any way she could. One of the instrumental factors in bringing Maria to Hollywood in the first place was the industry's support of the United States' Good Neighbor Policy toward Latin America. Montez never forgot that. The Dominican Republic was one of the Allied nations from the beginning of US involvement in the war. While the small country did not send troops to the fighting fronts, its merchant marine paid the price in the submarine warfare brought to the Caribbean Sea by the Germans; four Dominican ships were sunk, resulting in the death of twenty-seven sailors.[5]

The Dominican government was certainly aware of the publicity benefits that could be accrued by the Hollywood stardom of one of its citizens. Interest in the positive effects Montez could bring to the Dominican was ratcheted up

Maria receives the Order of Trujillo and the Juan Pablo Duarte Order of Merit from Flor Trujillo and is declared "a Latin American ambassador of good will" in the East Gold Room of the Ambassador Hotel, October 24, 1943.

by her success in *Arabian Nights.* President Rafael Trujillo first contacted her at the end of August 1943 to tell her that he had nominated her to the Dominican Congress for the two highest decorations the republic could award. The Congress approved, and on October 20 the president sent his daughter, Flor Trujillo, who served as first secretary of the Dominican embassy in Washington, DC, to Los Angeles to decorate Maria Montez. The two had been acquainted since meeting in Santo Domingo when Maria was married to William MacFeeters. Flor, noted by the *Los Angeles Times* as the only Latin American female diplomat in the United States, used the moment to declare her country's dedication to the Allied cause. She also announced a change Maria subscribed to wholeheartedly: "Latin American women are modeling after their sisters in arms in the United States in their efforts at gaining freedom of thought and action and overcoming the old Spanish tradition which keeps the gentler sex in subjugation."[6]

The decorations awarded by the Dominican Republic were the Order of Juan Pablo Duarte, named for the man most identified with separating the Dominican Republic from Haiti to become an independent state, and the Order of Trujillo, named for the current head of government. The medals were awarded to both military personnel and civilians. Montez was awarded both medals in the grade of officer, which was intended for professors and heads of schools, officers of colonel status and above, and civilians of importance. The actress's niece Raina Paris speculated, "I think it was about recognizing that she had become this important person in the world, and for recognizing her service to the country as a sort of ambassador from the Dominican Republic." She also noted that her mother Teresita and all her aunts opposed the Trujillo government.[7]

The postal telegrams sent to all of the local publications in Los Angeles alerting reporters to the event at the East Gold Room of the Ambassador Hotel were dispatched at the behest of Jose Aybar, Dominican consul general for the western United States, by Ismael Aviles, Dominican consul of Los Angeles. Aybar hosted the October 20, 1943, reception, but Flor Trujillo bestowed the medals on Maria in front of over two hundred guests. In his speech, Aybar declared the actress an ambassador of goodwill in the war effort. "In paying you this homage, President Trujillo has had in mind that you have always been an influential citizen in the promotion of an ever-closer cultural understanding between the Dominican Republic and the United States."[8]

Montez did serve as a representative of her country in articles such as "Foods of Our Allies" in *Modern Screen,* where she spoke of the physical beauty of her homeland and its romantic nature. Maria goes on to describe the chicken and rice or red beans feasts that were her favorite, topped off by *quesillo de pina* (pineapple cheese), a rich pineapple custard dessert. The medal ceremony was sufficiently publicized that it wound up in Feg Murray's nationally published Sunday supplement cartoon "Seein' Stars." Trujillo certainly got the publicity he wanted. But it should be noted that although she wrote her mother frequently, Maria never stepped foot in the Dominican

Republic once she left it in 1939 and she arranged for three of her sisters to immigrate to the United States in October 1944. The youngest sister, Teresita, and her youngest brother, Jaime, followed eventually. At least in her publicity she still made it evident she had an interest in her home country. In May 1944 the *Silver Screen* issue that had Maria on the cover also had a note that she was currently reading up on the history of the Dominican Republic for the basis of a novel she planned to write.[9]

The medals were not Montez's only foray into being an ambassador for the Good Neighbor Policy. She waged a career-long battle against her marked accent because she realized it kept her from being considered for numerous parts. She certainly did not try to change her accent because she wanted to separate herself from her Latin roots or was in any way ashamed of them. She used her native Spanish to record transcribed radio programs as part of "Hollywood Visits America" in 1943. It was a series sent to South America for general broadcast under the direction of the radio division of the Inter-American Affairs Committee. For the same group she participated in *Caravan of Questions,* a Spanish-language program meant to help Latin Americans learn more about the United States. On April 14, 1943, she was part of a Hollywood Victory Committee contingent that included Leo Carrillo, Gloria Jean, Walt Disney, Desi Arnaz, and Carmen Miranda's Bando da Lua at the Pan American Day celebration at Los Angeles City Hall. Over ten thousand people attended the flag-draped celebration, which was presented live on radio. The previous year she had traveled to Corpus Christi, Texas, with Desi Arnaz to participate in that city's Pan American Day celebration. A month after returning from Texas she was in Sacramento addressing a Spanish-speaking regiment of the California State Guard. Calling her "an ambassador of goodwill" may have been just a part of the awards ceremony, but Maria Montez took it seriously. She spoke out for better relations between the three Americas whenever the opportunity arose.[10]

Typically, when she was between movies, Montez headed off on a tour to publicize her most recently released film and to sell bonds. Her first chance to do so was the six weeks she had between the early September wrap of *Arabian Nights* and the October 31, 1942, start of filming for *White Savage.* Maria was part of a major bond show at San Francisco's Civic Auditorium on Wednesday, September 30. Cliff Work, general manager of Universal Studios and a former San Franciscan, helped set up the event and provided the star power. The studio sent the entire Montez-Hall-Sabu trio. Maria, the *San Francisco Chronicle* wrote, "admits she is the most beautiful woman she ever saw." Lupe Vélez, Leon Errol, Chester Morris, Dick Foran, and Sophie Tucker, "last of the red-hot mamas," were also scheduled to appear. Several local dancing and singing acts rounded out the evening's entertainment. The arriving stars would be taken to the Palace Hotel from the train station in the morning and returned to the hotel after the show to spend the night. At 7:45 p.m. a military procession marched the stars to the auditorium, where the national anthem was sung. Entrance was a $5 war stamp for orchestra seats, with balcony seats going for a $1 war stamp. Special sections were reserved for buyers of $1,000 and $500 war bonds. The tickets were available at all motion picture theater box offices, banks, and stores.

Besides the entrance price, money was raised by auctioning $4,000 worth of items donated by local businesses and civic groups; payment for these had to be by war bonds. Among the items offered were a painting of Brigadier General Jimmy Doolittle, who led the raid on Tokyo in April 1942, and a wood carving of General Douglas MacArthur executed by inmates at San Quentin prison and donated by its warden. Mayor Angelo Rossi provided a symbolic key to the city. Charles S. Howard donated a silver embossed shoe from his famous racehorse Seabiscuit. Also available for bids was a piece of the destroyer USS *Shaw* that exploded at Pearl Harbor. Two champagne bars were operating at the theater, with all proceeds going to the organizers of the rally. When ticket sales and proceeds from the auction were tallied up, the evening realized $1,250,000 worth of war bonds and stamps. The American Women's Voluntary Services, the sponsors of the event, collected it and turned it over to the federal government.[11]

As usual at her formal wartime bond show appearances, Maria gave a studio-prepared speech urging the audience to buy bonds and later answered questions from the audience or spoke to selected soldiers on-stage. On the way back to Los Angeles she dropped in at several of the military bases stretched out along US Highway 101 connecting San Diego with Los Angeles and San Francisco. In these informal visits, she would have dinner with the men or speak and dance at one of the off-duty clubs on the base. In general, she and whoever accompanied her were welcomed by officers but spent most of their time with enlisted men. In this she copied the plan of the Hollywood Canteen, which allowed officers only in a small, restricted area of the club to watch the performers and see hundreds of enlisted personnel dancing, eating sandwiches, and getting autographs. All Maria could offer on these visits was herself and her dedication to America's troops.

Maria's next filming break was between the early January 1943 completion of *White Savage* and the April 19 start date of *Cobra Woman.* This time she headed for the East Coast both to promote her latest released film and to entertain the troops. Her first stop was Boston. She was the headliner of a

Universal extravaganza celebrating the release of *Arabian Nights* at the RKO Keith Memorial Theater. As with the November 19, 1941, premiere of *"Keep 'Em Flying"* in Detroit, Universal wanted to get as much of the studio's star power as possible to kick off one of its biggest films. Jon Hall was a contract player with Samuel Goldwyn and rarely promoted his Universal films. Sabu was with the studio so he accompanied fellow Universalites Nigel Bruce, Dick Foran, Donald O'Connor, Peggy Ryan, and Gloria Jean to Boston. Montez got along fine with all the men, but young Gloria Jean remembered being a little afraid of her. Maria had lots of ideas about makeup for the fifteen-year-old—ideas Gloria thought were too much and her mother absolutely nixed. Gloria Jean had never met anyone quite like Maria and simply did not know what to make of her. The audiences always enjoyed her but she was never a close part of the group. Gloria thought she was "conceited" and did not feel comfortable around her. She was very temperamental: "I never knew how she's gonna be." She much preferred the easygoing Donald O'Connor and Sabu. Montez did engage with the others when it came to the nightly singing of "God Bless America" and was obviously popular with the audiences. It did strike Gloria how much less severe Maria's accent seemed to be when she was talking to people and not being filmed.[12]

The "Hollywood Special" arrived at Boston's South Station on January 20 on a blacked-out train. It was not for fear of German air attack; it was due to a power failure that put out the lights all the way from Worcester. After spending the afternoon at the hotel, the troupe headed over to the Keith Theater, where they were to take the stage at 9:00 p.m. and perform a show prepared back at Universal especially for the occasion. Originally the movie was going to be shown only once, after the stage show, but demand for tickets was so great that another showing was prepared for 6:00 p.m.

The Universal players were staying in Boston after the preview to appear at the annual Greater Boston United War Fund rally at the Boston Garden to regale the audience "with glamour, song, dancing and gaga." Maria posed for a photograph for the *Boston Traveler* holding a red feather, the symbol of the War Fund, over a poster with the slogan of the event, "Give Enough, Soon Enough!" The red feathers and the posters would be displayed in store windows all over the city. The goal of the campaign was to raise $7,800,000 by February 10 for Boston's war and home front services. The money would be raised at special events and by forty thousand volunteer solicitors. The Boston Garden extravaganza would feature not only the Universal contingent but also Robert Young, Laraine Day, Lynn Bari, and Raymond Massey, who was currently a major in the army of his native Canada. Joining at the last minute

Maria in uniform on an M3 "General Lee" light tank at Fort Knox, Kentucky. The snipe reads: "A luscious Latin, Miss Montez is what the soldier boys ordered in the way of a special visitor to their camps. . . . Asked if she enjoyed her ride, the star rubbed herself and said dubiously, 'I tank so!'"

were four army air force fliers, including Lieutenant Hank Potter, Jimmy Doolittle's navigator on the Tokyo raid. Governor Leverett Saltonstall and Mayor Maurice Tobin would start off the festivities with Nigel Bruce, Robert Young, and Donald O'Connor serving as masters of ceremonies.[13]

After Boston, Montez joined Eddie Foy Jr. for a USO tour of southern and midwestern army bases at the behest of the Hollywood Victory Committee. The committee often sent out large groups all at once. Montez and Foy were only one part of a many-faceted tour the committee was calling "Hollywood on Parade." Foy was a Broadway veteran and had an act. He was hot at the time because he had just portrayed his father, vaudeville and stage star Eddie Foy Sr., in what would be an Academy Award nominee for Best Picture, *Yankee Doodle Dandy*.

They opened their tour at Camp Tyson in Paris, Tennessee, and moved on to Camp Forrest near Nashville, Tennessee; Fort Knox near Louisville, Kentucky; Camp Atterbury near Columbus, Indiana; Chanute Air Field in Champaign, Illinois; and Camp Grant near Rockford, Illinois. The most publicized of the stops was at Fort Knox, the headquarters of the army's armored force where tens of thousands of tank crews, maintenance, and communication troops were trained during the war. It was also the depository of the federal government's gold bullion holdings as well as where the key documents of American history, including the Declaration of Independence, the Bill of Rights, the Constitution, and the Gettysburg Address, were stored for safety until after the successful D-Day invasion of France.[14]

Maria was willing to do most anything for publicity and to appeal to the soldiers. Two often-reproduced photos emerged from the visit to Fort Knox. In the first she donned a tanker's uniform, jacket, boots, gloves, and helmet and posed on the turret of an M3 light tank with the tank's cannon between her legs. As the Universal snipe on the back of the photo pointed out, "There's a lot of 'fire' power in this picture!" (*Snipe* is the term for the studio's or publication's description of a photo, attached to the back of the print.) The second photo resulted from a fall Montez took on the base. She was photographed in a dress on a tank having her knee patched up. When the photo of the camp doctor administering to Maria's shapely limb ran in the *Emmetsburg (Iowa) Reporter,* the copy editor captioned it "Nice work if you can get it."[15]

On the way to Camp Atterbury, Maria and Foy stopped in Indianapolis to attend a dinner and reception put on by Universal at the Hotel Lincoln. Maria always made it a point to meet exhibitors whenever she was touring for one of her films or for bond sales. She was introduced to the local theater owners and the press in Indianapolis and was a big hit. The exhibitors told *Showmen's Trade Review,* "The charming Maria Montez, Universal star . . . is the best 'salesman' Universal has ever sent on the road." The duo left Indianapolis the next day to get to the scheduled evening performance at Camp Atterbury, which provided combat training for various army units.[16]

Maria was back at Universal early in April 1943 for the pre-production tasks necessary to start filming *Cobra Woman.* Like all of Montez's films, most of this one would be shot at Universal City, with standing sets made up to look like whatever part of Neverland was called for. But the six key movies of her career were A pictures and made so much money for the studio that the producers of them could convince the accountants on the lot to let the company go on location. This was the case with *Cobra Woman.* The scenes where Jon Hall mistakes the bad sister for the good sister as she goes for a swim was shot at Baldwin Lake at the Los Angeles County Arboretum and Botanic Garden near Arcadia, California.[17]

The other big attraction in Arcadia is the Santa Anita Park racetrack. It had quite the varied career during the war as horse racing was put on hold for

Sam Kaufman, who had retired from Universal's makeup department in 1939, returned during the war due to the labor shortage all the studios were experiencing. Here he is touching up Maria's makeup on the set of *Cobra Woman.*

the duration. It was first used as an assembly center for Japanese Americans, who were brought there on Pacific Electric train cars from the defunct Santa Fe Le Dome train station in Los Angeles in one of its last uses as a depot. By March 1942 over nineteen thousand people were living in the hastily built barracks at the former racetrack. From Santa Anita the internees were sent to relocation camps all over the western United States.[18]

By September all of the prisoners had been relocated. Santa Anita was then turned over to the army and was remade into a training camp for over twenty thousand ordnance troops. Eventually over one hundred thousand men would train there. Every night after filming scenes at Baldwin Lake Maria went to the base to visit the soldiers. There was no formal show. She just spent time with the men, talking, eating, and dancing with them to a jukebox.[19]

The most concentrated bond selling took place during the eight war loan drives overseen by the War Finance Committee. But bonds were certainly advertised and sold between the huge official drives. The film industry's War Activities Committee helmed such an event between the second and third war loan drives. Virtually every movie theater in the country showed a specially prepared newsreel that involved members of the Hollywood community with a survivor of the Jimmy Doolittle raid on Japan in April 1942. Captain Ted Lawson was the pilot of a B-25 dubbed the "Ruptured Duck." With the exception of Doolittle, Lawson was the best known of the raiders. He wrote the Random House best seller *Thirty Seconds over Tokyo,* which was initially serialized in six issues of *Collier's* magazine in May and June 1943 and filmed by MGM in 1944.

Lawson was featured in the War Activities Committee newsreel released in July 1943 as part of a campaign to sell $130,000,000 in war bonds and stamps to build an aircraft carrier to be christened the "Shangri-la" and other ships. This was the mystical country featured in James Hilton's novel and the subsequent film *Lost Horizon* (1937) that President Roosevelt claimed was where the Doolittle Raiders had taken off. Lawson is shown purchasing war stamps from Hedy Lamarr, Maria Montez, Lynn Bari, and Susan Hayward. Universal released a publicity blurb to show its star was no passive bystander. As the pilot was showing the route of the flight to Tokyo on a globe, Maria licked one of the stamps and put it over Japan. "'There,' exclaimed the fiery Latin American, 'that is how war stamps will obliterate Japan.'"[20]

Maria Montez married Jean-Pierre Aumont on July 13, 1943, just as her newsreel with Ted Lawson was starting to show up in theaters. She was back at Universal City and in the middle of filming *Ali Baba and the Forty Thieves.* Their nuptials were strictly a wartime affair. They had only met five months before, but Aumont's desire to rejoin the French army was their constant companion. After serving in the disastrous first campaign against the German and Italians he had no desire to sit out the rest of the war making movies in Hollywood. Aumont originally wanted to put the wedding off until he returned from the war, but like so many couples of that time they decided to marry before they were split for who knows how long while the husband did his military service.

The ceremony was a simple one, with both the vows and reception held at Maria's house, where the guests feasted on food that was based on how many points were available on the couple's coupons in their war rations books. There was no honeymoon because they were both finishing films and Aumont was to leave to join the Free French forces in New York as soon as his work was completed. Maria would not see her husband for the next eighteen months, after he trained in North Africa and fought in Italy and France. Cal York noted in his column "Inside Stuff" that Jean-Pierre would wear his wedding ring "into the world conflict." Jimmie Fidler, who never believed the Montez-Aumont relationship would amount to anything, did not exactly apologize for his skepticism. But he did note, "How confusing to read publicity blurbs about Maria Montez' matrimonial bliss instead of her new romances."[21]

Maria's marriage was very much part of her publicized wartime activities. It both made her one war wife out of millions while emphasizing her exotic status, as she was married to someone in the Free French army rather than the American military. Universal made sure to release photos of Maria tending her victory garden and backyard citrus trees. The studio also facilitated Maria taking part in a *Photoplay* symposium called "I Put out That Torch." Maria counseled readers not to let the flame of worry infect your friendships. "When I didn't hear from Jean, I walked the floor nights. I haunted the mailbox. I trembled when the phone rang. But I did all this alone. If friends were around, I made wisecracks; I was flippant. Just because I was unhappy and worried to the point of desperation was no reason why they should worry too." In another piece, signed off on by Magda Maskel, through whose Universal office all magazine articles were approved, Maria wrote an article, with the help of May Mann, called "War Time Wives" in which she told wives to keep all the promises they had made their husbands and never give them reason to be jealous or worried, write often, help out the home front war effort however they could, and be good humored and not feel sorry for themselves. She realizes how hard it is to think of one's husband and not know his whereabouts or if he is safe. But, like Maria, they are not alone in their worry. "I think of the millions of women all over the world who have the same thought and feeling."[22]

In the July 1944 issue of *Screen Stars* magazine Maria included her war work in an article she called "My Most Thrilling Moments." Her first Catholic Holy Communion in Barahona was one. Seeing her name on the marquee of Grauman's Chinese Theater was another. So was receiving the two Dominican medals, being declared a goodwill ambassador, and her numerous war bond tours. But right at the top of the list was meeting Eleanor and Franklin Roosevelt at the White House. "I was so thrilled and proud," she wrote, "to have had the great privilege of being in [the White House] and living in America."[23]

She expressed that same thrill in the note she sent Eleanor Roosevelt accepting her invitation. Most of the other notes were straight acceptance. Maria wrote,

> Dear Mrs. Roosevelt,
>
> It is with great pleasure that I accept your very kind invitation to luncheon at the White House. It is a privilege (sp.) I shall always cherish.
>
> Sincerely,
> Maria Montez[24]

Maria was due for lunch at the White House and the Washington, DC, balls on the weekend of January 28, 1944. Before she headed to the president's birthday celebration Maria had agreed to be part of another of the war bond tours she was so proud of. The Hollywood Victory Committee planned to send out several teams of stars to participate in the fourth war loan campaign at the request of the Treasury Department. Maria was free to participate because she had completed *Gypsy Wildcat* on December 16, 1943, and was not scheduled to begin her part of the filming of *Bowery to Broadway* until May 15, 1944. The major war loan drives were huge moneymakers for the federal government, faced with the staggering costs of war. Montez headed to Cleveland with MGM's suave leading man Lee Bowman. The Victory Committee termed the fifty-four actors sent out all over the country "Bondbardiers."[25]

Cleveland's quota in the drive was $672,000,000, with the bulk of that coming from major investors and corporations. The quota on E bonds to individuals was $174,000,000. The acting duo was in the Great Lakes city from January 17 to January 26, 1944. The *Plain Dealer* reported, "They are here to do what they can for America and the war." To that end they did numerous interviews with the local press, spoke to the assembled workers at the Thompson Aircraft Products Company on January 18 and with workers at the Ravenna Ordnance Plant, Cleveland Chain Company, and Jack and Heintz Company (manufacturer of a variety of aircraft parts and instruments) on the 24th. In between they visited the American Stove Company, the massive Westinghouse plant, and other smaller shops.

Maria, beamed in from Hollywood by the Hollywood Victory Committee, at the Westinghouse factory in Mansfield, Ohio, 1944.

They were interviewed on local radio shows such as Jean Law's morning program at WJW and *Mutual Goes Calling,* where they spoke with Cleveland-area native and Marine Corps combat correspondent of the fighting on Tarawa, Staff Sergeant Peter Zurlinden, and urged all listeners, both at home and in the studio audience, to buy bonds. Montez and Bowman also starred in a noontime parade sponsored by the Retail Merchants Board that drew twenty thousand spectators to elegant Euclid Avenue on January 20. Besides the two Hollywood stars, a major attraction at the parade was the big guns from the Erie Proving Grounds and mobile equipment from the White Motor Company and the Cleveland Tractor Company.

Maria's view of the properness of things was captured perfectly in one of the photographs taken on the tour of the Westinghouse factory in Mansfield, Ohio. One of the many things the company was producing for the government was binoculars. Maria stands next to the very serious-looking plant manager in his business suit and vest, and his secretary, wearing a very sensible work jumper. Maria holds the binoculars up to her eyes, her hair perfectly coiffed, a Lilly Dache hat on her head, swathed in the magnificent full-length mink coat she got Universal to pay for around her. They are all three in front of a wall of classical industrial windows strengthened by wire running through the glass. Maria looks like she was beamed in directly from Hollywood. She may have been touring a huge wartime factory, hanging with the manager, talking to the workers, and in general showing her support for the war effort, but Maria Montez was dedicated to being a movie star and was absolutely determined to look the part no matter where she was or what she was doing. As Jimmie Fidler observed, "Maria Montez looks like you'd imagine a movie actress should look off-screen." She certainly did at Westinghouse.[26]

Montez and Lee Bowman avidly sold bonds and spoke to fans and war workers for the entire ten days they spent in the Cleveland area. They also did several interviews with local reporters. Glenn Pullen of the *Cleveland Plain Dealer* noted happily that "Hollywood's curvaceous Maria Montez" was in town supporting the fourth war loan drive and mentioned where she would be visiting. W. Ward Marsh also interviewed her for the *Plain Dealer.* He noted she preferred to talk about Jean-Pierre Aumont and the letter of commendation he received from General de Gaulle rather than her latest work in *Ali Baba and the Forty Thieves,* which she said was mostly Jon Hall's film. Marsh could not believe that. "If the red-headed, hazel-eyed Montez has anything more than usual to do with it, *'Ali Baba'* cannot miss. And while she confesses that it is more Hall's picture than hers, it is difficult to see how the camera could keep its lens away from her." He noted how well she photographed in black and white for "the little bond drive picture" (*One for the Boys*) she did recently. Maria told him she hoped to make more black-and-white movies when she returned to Hollywood. Marsh did criticize her speeches given in Cleveland as "over-scripted." She responded that she wanted to discard them and just talk to the workers in the defense plants in her own way. The writer concluded, "She seems to be the most nearly 'natural' for the camera of any stars who have visited here." And as icing on the cake, "she can walk magnificently."[27]

Maria next took that magnificent walk to Washington, DC, and the celebration of President Franklin D. Roosevelt's sixty-second birthday. On January 23 the Associated Press sent out a blurb to all its contracted newspapers stating that Lucille Ball, Brian Donlevy, Jinx Falkenburg, John Garfield, Maria Montez, Walter Pidgeon, Red Skelton, and pianist-conductor José Iturbi would participate in President Roosevelt's birthday celebrations on behalf of the National Foundation for Infantile Paralysis in Washington on Friday and Saturday. The contingent "would also appear at the presidential dinner Friday night and at birthday balls in the various Washington hotels

The "good neighbor" with Eleanor Roosevelt in Washington, DC, January 28, 1944.

Saturday night." The celebrities were eventually joined by Joan Fontaine, Brian Aherne, Virginia Field, Sir Cedric Hardwicke, Guy Lombardo, Mary Martin, Ida Lupino, Louis Prima, and Lieutenant Charles (Buddy) Rogers, whose wife, Mary Pickford, was also there and sat to the right of President Roosevelt.

Maria would wear the medals awarded her by the Dominican government to the presidential balls celebrating Franklin D. Roosevelt's birthday on January 30, 1944, savoring her role as a good neighbor ambassador. Balls to both celebrate FDR's birthday and to raise money to fight polio had been held all over the country since 1934, the celebrations expanding over the years. By 1944 the hundreds of parties held all over the country had been joined by a huge celebration in Washington, DC. The president created the National Foundation for Infantile Paralysis in 1938 not only to support the work being done to fight polio and its consequences at its facility in Warm Springs, Georgia, but to help victims of polio all over the country and try to find a cure. Hollywood stars brought attention to the balls and were instrumental in raising money for what came to be called the March of Dimes.

This was certainly a watershed moment for the immigrant who had risen in three and a half years from unknown screen candy to a star lunching with the president and first lady as a representative of Hollywood and the Good Neighbor Policy. A star among other stars, all popular enough with fans to help raise hundreds of thousands of dollars at several balls for the fight against polio. They clearly were very successful. *Variety* reported that this, the eleventh of the birthday balls, was the "biggest grosser ever."[28]

Maria's was one of the five star photos published in the forty-two-page official program, *The President's Birthday Ball, 1944*. There were also full-page pictures of the president and first lady, a photo of the president with two children suffering from polio, and a picture of seven children featuring the logo "Because you dance, we may walk." An events calendar was also published. On the evening of Friday, January 28, 1944, a reception and dinner at the Mayflower Hotel was scheduled, followed by midnight shows with the Hollywood stars at Loew's Capitol, Warner Brothers' Earle, and Lichtman's Howard Theaters. This would be followed on Saturday by the birthday dinner dance at the Shoreham Hotel, with other dances held at the Mayflower, Statler, Wardman Park, Washington, and Willard hotels and the colonnade of the Lincoln Memorial.[29]

As noted above, Maria's visit to the White House would be key in her "Most Thrilling Moments" piece she wrote for *Screen Stars* magazine. She wrote that she had been in the United States for such a short time at that point and then "had the great honor to be received . . . by the President of the United States and Mrs. Roosevelt. I was pleasantly surprised that the President should know who I was. . . . He congratulated me on receiving the decorations from my country. To think that the President of the United States of America would know me as an individual was a very great thrill." This is Montez minus all the bravado she generally showered on the press. She had already achieved the successes of seeing her name blazing on a marquee as the star of a major movie. But spending time with the president and first lady was undoubtedly more than even Maria had dreamed of. It is one of the great stories of an immigrant made good, and she understood and reveled in it. Hedda Hopper wrote that Maria was "aglow" from her bond tour and White House visit when she returned to Los Angeles.[30]

Following the president's birthday balls and dinner, several of the stars stayed in Washington on February 1 to appear at the servicemen's canteen operated by the National Press Club to entertain the soldiers and sailors. *Los Angeles Times* columnist Bill Henry reported that "noisy applause, whistling, and such remarks as 'Whacha doin' tonight?'" greeted "willowy Jinx Falkenburg,

According to the snipe: "Maria Montez, Universal star, dances with the merchant sailors at the United Seaman's Service Canteen," June 1943.

carrot-topped Lucille Ball and exotic Maria Montez." They were joined by Walter Pidgeon, John Garfield, and Brian Donlevy. All of them spoke to the crowd and signed autographs. Red Skelton then came on to do his full show. When Montez was introduced to the military audience, she was greeted by a roomful of two-toned wolf whistles. Ever the good neighbor, she instructed the men, "In my country, whistling at a lady is a mark of disrespect." A hushed silence fell on the crowded room. "But," she added, "I am not in my country."

The resounding whistles nearly raised the roof of the canteen. The soldiers immediately dubbed her "the girl of the whistle stop."[31]

Maria and the other women spent the night talking and dancing with eager military men. It was the perfect capper to a very successful weekend in Washington. The stars all played their part in making this birthday ball the most successful yet. In an article for *Variety* Andy Kelly described Maria's presence at the presidential balls. "Maria Montez, titan haired charmer from the Dominican Republic, vied with Joan Fontaine for the beauty honors. This was not the Montez of a hundred nightclub appearances. As befitted the occasion, this was a sleekly elegant Montez. The Universal star was garbed in simple and quiet black. Her only ornaments, two highest honors conferred on her by the Dominican government, pinned on her shoulder."[32]

Three days later Maria was among friends and admirers. She was a guest at the fifteenth annual dance held by the Press Photographers Association at the Waldorf Astoria Hotel in New York City. The profits from the evening were donated to the American Theater Wing War Service, which operated the Stage Door Canteens. Montez had spent many evenings at the Hollywood Canteen and went to its New York counterpart after the photographers dance.[33]

What was being called *Queen of the Nile* but would be released as *Sudan* was not scheduled to start filming until June 6, 1944. Before she was to report to the Technicolor desert again, Maria was scheduled to play a part in the third act of a black-and-white musical that would be released as *From Bowery to Broadway.* But when she returned to Los Angeles from the war loan bond drive and her visit to the White House in February, she found Universal lustily publicizing the western it was preparing for her and Jon Hall. The studio's idea was clearly to continue to shake up the Neverland fantasies with other locales besides the South Seas and Arabia, as they had done with *Gypsy Wildcat. Variety* reported that Maria Montez, "that hot breeze from the tropics," would star in what the studio was calling "a super-Western to be made in Technicolor." A week later it was reported that Malcolm Stuart Boylan had been rehired by the studio to work on the script on this as yet unnamed western. Universal clearly had not lost faith in the continuing popularity of the Neverland fantasies as the war was reaching its most lethal phase.[34]

But Maria was not just sitting around waiting for her studio to start filming her next movie. Soon after her return to Los Angeles she was scheduled to present the ten thousandth movie program given to the army on February 24. The commander of the Army Service Forces, General Brehon Somervell, accepted the film. A week later, on March 2, Montez attended the pared-down wartime sixteenth annual Academy Awards at Grauman's Chinese Theater on

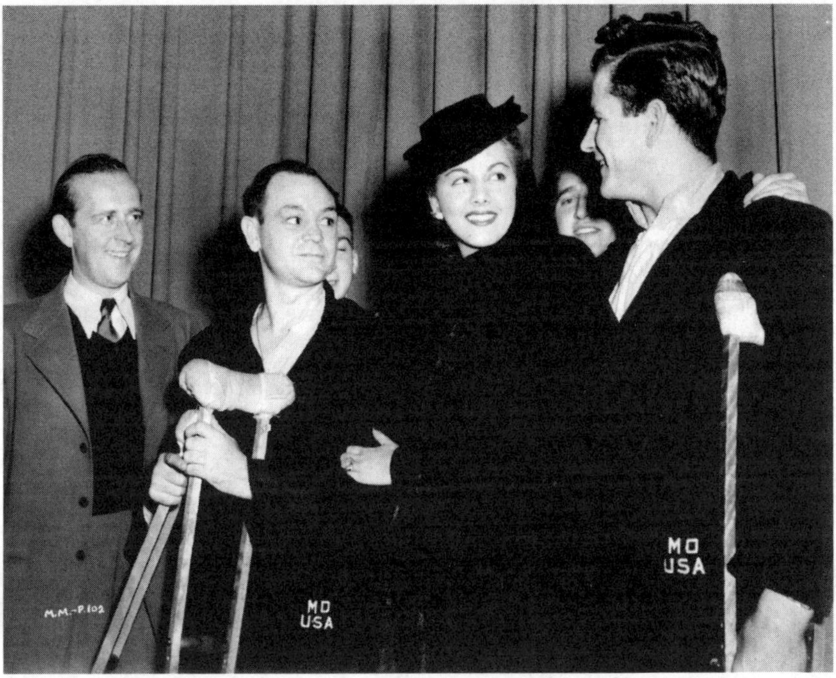

Maria, described in the snipe as a "Latin-American beauty of the films" visits men at the hospital at Fort Knox, Kentucky. Eddie Foy Jr. is left of Maria.

Hollywood Boulevard. Bleachers were set up for fans at the entrance and there were lots of photographers to capture the arriving stars. Jack Benny was master of ceremonies while Kay Kyser's band played in front of ten tiers of seats that had been set up behind the stage for two hundred servicemen from all branches. One of the highlights of the night was the presentation of the motion picture industry's service flag with its 78,808 stars representing members of the business in one of the branches of the military.[35]

At the beginning of April 1944, the Hollywood Victory Committee answered a War Department request for entertainment at army and navy general hospitals throughout the country. Some 430 players, including dancers and hostesses, made voluntary appearances at 188 dates throughout the country. With the Technicolor western still in the discussion phase and two months remaining before the scheduled start of *Queen of the Nile,* Maria was available to participate in the hospital tour. She and her matron of honor, French actress Janine Crispin (who replaced the originally scheduled Lois Collier of Universal), played in several of the fifty-four night and weekend camp shows that were held at numerous military facilities between San Diego and San Francisco. She was back in Los Angeles in time to appear on the *Mail Call* radio show set up by the Hollywood Victory Committee for the Armed Forces Radio Service recorded in Los Angeles. Bob Hope and Dinah Shore served as masters of ceremonies for the May 30 show, which was dedicated to soldiers from Georgia. Maria did a comic bit with Hope in which she came ashore on Fly Island looking for a husband; Hope played Robinson Crusoe and Eddie "Rochester" Anderson was Friday. The most prolonged laugh came when Hope offers to take her sarong and hang it up to dry. After Maria assures him she has two more under it and plugs *Cobra Woman,* cannibals come ashore and Hope and Rochester run off. Two days later she was at Universal City for the first day of filming on *Queen of the Nile.*[36]

The Hollywood Victory Committee was responsible for ensuring the stars' presence as entertainers for military audiences all over the United States and the rest of the world. Closer to home, the whole industry got together to create the Hollywood Canteen. Bette Davis, John Garfield, and Jules Stein were the principals in getting the canteen in gear. But once the former livery stable and nightclub called the Old Barn had been secured on Cahuenga Boulevard just south of Sunset Boulevard in Hollywood, designers and crafts people from all of the studios pitched in to make the place as homey as possible for the soldiers and to function as a club for its hundreds of daily visitors starting on October 3, 1942. Actors and actresses as well as volunteer hostesses were in the canteen every night. They did everything they could to make all the visiting military of both the United States and its Allies feel welcome and give them something to write home about.[37]

Virtually every star and starlet in Hollywood spent some time at the canteen. James Hilton, one of the foremost novelists of the day, whose books inevitably wound up as blockbuster movies, wrote a piece for *Photoplay* about the canteen and the international nature of those who were "among the most frequent visitors and most tireless of all canteen workers." Besides southerner Kay Kyser, who brought his band every week, these included "Bette Davis (New Englander), Marlene Dietrich (once German), Hedy Lamarr (once Austrian), The Basil Rathbones (British), Ingrid Bergman (Swedish), Charles Boyer (French), and Maria Montez (a Good Neighbor)."[38]

On other nights Montez would visit one of the innumerable military training bases that had popped up all around Los Angeles to take advantage of the yearlong sunshine. One of them was the Polaris Flight Academy at Lancaster. It was a private training field that initially began training Royal Air Force pilots and added army air force personnel after Pearl Harbor. One of the men who served there was English actor Martyn Green of the D'Oyly

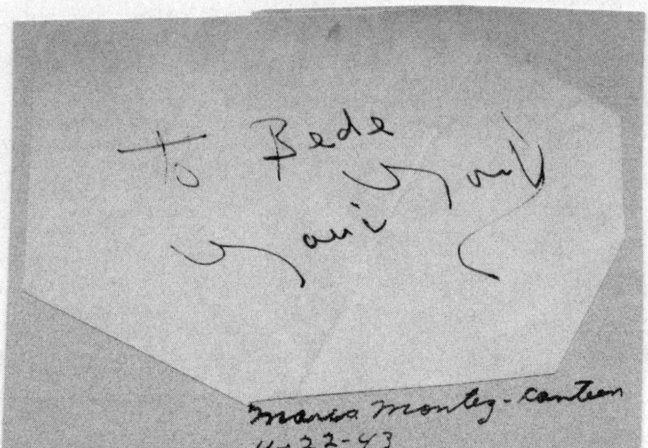

Maria at the stage entrance to the rear of the Hollywood Canteen, where fans would hang around to get autographs.

Carte Opera Company. In a 1954 interview for an appearance at the Hollywood Bowl, he fondly remembered his wartime service at Polaris. One of his favorite memories was the night a cadet arrived with a beautiful Latin woman at a cadets' dance. "She turned out to be that rare and charming person, Maria Montez." As usual at her military visits, she danced, talked, charmed, and created memories for scores of soldiers.[39]

Universal Studios saw a huge surge in revenue during World War II, with Abbott and Costello among the biggest moneymakers in Hollywood. But Maria Montez was also a key contributor to Universal's prosperity. She was a major star on the lot and the studio acted accordingly. During the war the publicity department distributed numerous items to demonstrate her contribution to the war effort and support of the military. One of them was called "Maria Montez Pin-up Nominations," a collection of names various military groups gave to her. They included "Sarong Queen," suggested by the men in sickbay at Fort Trumbull Coast Guard Station in New London, Connecticut. To the crew of a B-26 medium bomber in the South Pacific named the Montez Marauder, she was "the most desirable girl to have a 10,000-foot jump with in a parachute." Reflecting its military occupation, the Maintenance Battalion of the Twentieth Armored Division, Camp Campbell, Kentucky, declared Maria "Miss Maintainer of Morale." To the headquarters personnel of the Forty-Seventh Infantry Regiment in Morocco, she was "the real pin-up girl for us G.I.s here in Africa."[40]

All these names soldiers dreamed up for Maria and Universal distributed played their part in an article for a Sunday supplement written by Dee Lowrance, "Leave Us Phrase It." The author runs down several of the names granted to pin ups such as Betty Hutton, Veronica Lake, Dorothy Lamour, and Esther Williams. When he gets to Maria and Deanna Durbin, he notes, "At least the boys, and the press agents, keep the titles somewhat in character when they are passing them out." The far more staid Durbin was given names like "Queen of the Barracks," "The Girl We'd Like to Come Home To," "Guardian Angel," and "Ideal Hostess." Lowrance noted that Montez is "much more vital" with her "sultry personality" than Durbin. Among the names mentioned for Maria were "Morale bracer" and "Dynamite Damsel."[41]

In line with all this nicknaming was another blurb Universal sent out through the United Press. In it the studio noted that a group of deep-water sailors had taken to referring to Montez as their "favorite among tape-up girls." The sailors declared, "There's no place to stick pins on a battleship. So, we just use tape." According to the United Press, "1,600 sailors requested the Latin actress to send them pictures in poses which will 'keep the chill out of cold bulkheads.'" A sultry photo of Maria with two sailors demonstrating how to use tape to attach a photo of her to a bulkhead often accompanied the blurb.[42]

Maria had relied on photographs throughout her career. So it should be no surprise that she enthusiastically played her part in the Pin Up Industrial Complex that thrived throughout the war. The complex was centered in New York and Los Angeles with some help from Chicago. New York and Chicago's chief contributions were showgirls and the occasional ecdysiast from their numerous nightclubs and burlesque houses. Print material in the form of magazines like *Film Fun* and *Laff* or the drawings of Alberto Vargas, George Petty, Gil Elvgren, and Zoe Mozert originated from New York. From Los Angeles came a seemingly endless supply of photographs of Hollywood actresses. Both ingénues desperate to get some attention and established stars wanting to keep their desirability edge.[43]

Ted Gill wrote a piece for the Associated Press about the effect the need for "leg art" had on Hollywood's part of the vast and always hungry Pin Up Industrial Complex. "Comes a war, and sedate young ladies of the silver screen, who went into acting for art's sake and never would think of displaying a trim, dainty ankle or a bare shoulder, now are going in for leg art." Marjorie Lord at Universal was a perfect example of this. She had stage experience and looked forward to acting on the screen. Instead, she found herself in Ray Jones's studio posing in a tight dress looking glamorous and in a bra top sunsuit looking delectable. Eventually she was in a streetcar conductor's uniform to demonstrate that the Los Angeles Railway was now accepting female conductors.[44]

All of the studios' mail departments were flooded with requests for photos of their favorite pin up girls dressed as briefly as possible. Actresses who had never before gone in for pin up type photos agreed to join the complex. Sheliah Graham addressed the phenomenon in a 1943 column: "Even the more sedate celluloid queens like Greer Garson and Barbara Stanwyck are pitting their pretty underpinnings against those of Betty Grable, Maria Montez and Judy Garland." Olivia de Havilland and even Jean Arthur were willing to sign up with the complex. They played their part "in pictures showing girls with attractive curves posing in bathing suits, play togs and other eye-catching costumes." The new motto had become 'If it's cheese cake the boys want, they'll get it.'"[45]

Dinah Shore introduced Maria on *Mail Call* as "that lovely young star and one of your favorite pin up girls." Letters or V-mails requesting photos would be sent to Universal City or Universal Studios from military bases all over the United States; the European theater, with a specific army post office

Esquire's Date Book for 1943 featured cartoons, cocktail mixes, short articles, twenty-one George Hurrell pin ups, and la Montez on the cover, perfectly lit.

Maria in a classic pin up pose, arms raised to lift and separate.

number, care of the postmaster, New York; and the Pacific and China-Burma-India theaters, care of the postmaster, San Francisco. Letters from the navy, coast guard, and marines would be addressed from the Fleet Post Office in the same two cities. A common one was sent to Maria from a lieutenant on Guadalcanal requesting a signed photo for his Officers' Quarters and telling her how they were all "sweating out" the promised arrival of *Ali Baba and the Forty Thieves.* Another request came from a fireman first class who just returned to the submarine base at New London, Connecticut, after ten months at sea. A coast guard machinist mate writing from the USO in Milwaukee, who proclaimed himself one of Maria's "most ardent fans," asked for a photo to "pin up in my locker." Other requests came from a private in the medical section at Fort Douglas, Utah, a corporal in New Guinea, and civilians in New Zealand. All wanting photos. Signed if possible. All telling her how much they enjoyed her movies. This was common for wartime female stars, but Maria kept Universal's mailroom very busy.[46]

Popular magazines joined in the pin up tsunami. *Screen Guide* celebrated the military's favorite pin ups in an article called "The 'most' Girls of Hollywood!" The first two-page spread featured Hedy Lamarr, Betty Grable, Betty Hutton, Belita, and Maria—who was known to various parts of the military as the "sarong siren," the "Real Pin Up Girl of Africa," and as the "Battalion Queen" of the navy's flight school at Dartmouth. The second spread included Merle Oberon, Ann Sheridan, Paulette Goddard, Dorothy Lamour, "latecomer" Jean Arthur, and the "Almost" girl Shirley Temple. *Eyeful* magazine promised "gals, gags, giggles." It ran a piece called "Whee! Whee! Maria" in 1944 that consisted of pin ups taken earlier in her career. In one she is in a bathing suit, in another picture, taken from below, she wears a white bra top and holds her arms up, and another features her in a sarong from *White Savage.* The article assures its readers that this "Latin lovely of Universal Pictures is a jungle sigh-ren, who knows the way of all flash."[47]

The pin up phenomenon was being recognized all over the country. The *Hartford Courant* described the pin ups as "the lovelies whose likenesses our boys in service, wherever they may be located, insist upon putting up somewhere near them to feast their eyes upon during lonely, nostalgic moments." Many of the soldiers had photos on their walls or lockers of girlfriends or wives. But when they wanted true pin ups they turned to "the cinema capital and here are a few reasons why"—the article was illustrated with photos of Montez, Dona Drake, Betty Grable, Martha O'Driscoll, and Pat Morison. Maria's photo features her in a sarong from *White Savage.* In New York City, Irving Klaw, who would become famous in the 1950s for his photos and movies of Bettie Page, was doing excellent business at his Movie Star News photo store in New York. In a 1944 article about him he observed, "The race for Pin-Up Girl of tomorrow comes down to Maria Montez and Susan Peters." Not surprisingly, he found the best customers for his photos were GIs. The De Luxe Photo Service, which offered "Photos of Your Favorite Stars" in many fan magazines and men's magazines, obviously reached the same conclusion. Its ads featured a Ray Jones photo of Montez in *Ali Baba and the Forty Thieves* as an example of its wares.[48]

Frederick Othman always saw the sharp mind behind Maria's boisterous presentation. In a column he titled "Maria Montez Wonders," he has her trying to figure out why, when 10,000 soldiers write for her photograph 9,999 of them want her in as few clothes as possible. She claimed she just could not understand it. She was in the midst of filming *Arabian Nights* when Othman interviewed her, and at the moment she was "wearing as little as the law (and the Hays office) allows." She opined that the soldiers "must be sculptors at heart. Else why would they want pictures of me without clothes?" On the set, Othman "just stood there, dumb-like, looking at the proceedings which were as torrid as they were Technicolored." He assumed Maria went back to "her assistant dancing beauties, almost certainly thinking how easy it was to get these columnists to write what she wanted."[49]

So ubiquitous and popular had the products of the Pin Up Industrial Complex become that the Hollywood USO Canteen on Hollywood Boulevard held the "World's First Pin Up Exhibition" on December 4, 1944. There were dozens of eleven-by-fourteen-inch and eight-by-ten-inch matted photographs on display. Jane Russell, Toni Seven, and Martha Tilton were on hand to sign their own photos. The ultimate show of acceptance of the pin up came from the foremost arbiter of all things excellent in filmdom, the Academy of Motion Picture Arts and Sciences, which held Hollywood studios still photography exhibits in 1941, 1942, 1943, and 1947. Contributing photographers had to work for one of the studios. Medallions with a relief of the Oscar statue were awarded to the top two winners in each of the sections. A pin up category was added to the original eight categories for the 1943 exhibit. Universal's Ray Jones won for his photo of Ramsay Ames in a two-piece bathing suit leaning on a rattan matt.[50]

Jones did scores of pin ups of Montez but very rarely placed her in a bathing suit. Generally, they were glamour shots in a very clinging dress without a bra or a portrait in a sarong or desert veils to help sell a particular movie. These photos had enormous distribution. One of them was used when Montez was "pin-up girl no. 8" in *Movies* magazine's pin up feature, which ran in successive issues starting in late 1942. Her measurements and three more enticing photos were on the back of the pin up page. (Betty Grable was number 9.) Maria was the pin up in *Motion Picture* magazine's December 1943 issue in a dark dress that tied behind her neck and showed off her breasts. Jones's pictures of Maria from that same session were published as the pin up of the week in *Yank, the Army Weekly* magazine on November 29, 1942. The same photo was in *Stars and Stripes,* another army publication, two weeks later.[51]

Two of the most popular parts of *Yank* were the beloved comic strip "Sad Sack" by Sergeant George Baker and the weekly pin up in the back of the magazine. In some lunatic frenzy of puritanical zeal, the editors were initially prohibited from publishing pin ups. That policy was soon rethought and *Yank* pin up pages got tacked up on walls all over the world. *Life* ran an article on the phenomenon and published four of the favorite pin ups from *Yank*: Elyse Knox, Dusty Anderson, Doris Merrick, and "luscious" Maria Montez. Given the popularity of Montez's pin ups in *Yank*, it figured that when Sergeant Leo Hofeller, *Yank*'s picture editor, and Yeoman Third Class Allen Churchill, its naval representative, did a separate one-shot magazine called *Pin Me Up: A Book Full of Pin-up Girls*, Maria was there in the same dark dress with a tight top, plunging neckline, no bra, and a wonderfully sensual expression.[52]

Yank was the most popular and widely distributed military publication of World War II, but it certainly was not the only one. Many of the others featured pin ups as well. *Brief* was the official publication of the Seventh Army Air Force in the South Pacific. Maria was the pin up for its August 29, 1944, issue. The photo showed her from the waist up, wearing a negligee. The caption noted, "She poses here with claws well sheathed and velvet purr silent." The *Caribbean Breeze* was the magazine of the Sixth Army Air Force in the Caribbean Sea area. The July 1944 issue features Montez lying on a bed with her arms above her head with what the *Breeze* called "slinky sinuosity." Maria graced the pages of military publications all over the world in pin ups that found their way to innumerable barracks walls.[53]

Montez appeared in many other pin up photos in civilian publications that generally found their way onto military bases as well as to homes all over America. The most famous of these publications was *Esquire* magazine. Founded in 1933, the magazine originally concentrated on men's apparel and articles by some of the leading writers of the day. By the late 1930s Alberto Vargas was drawing his "Varga Girl" while George Hurrell was photographing his "Hurrell Girl" for the magazine. By now it was perceived as the leading men's magazine. When *Esquire* published a Hurrell pin up–filled pocket diary for 1943 Maria was on the cover in a stunningly clinging purple dress that was expressly cut to show off her breasts. That same year she was in the thirteenth series of Hurrell's Esky Card sets published by the magazine. Maria is in a black dress with a deeply scooped bodice in her postcard-size portrait. In 1944 she was Hurrell's full-page, full-color pin up in a red and white sarong and bare feet. The accompanying blurb spoke of the medals awarded her by the Dominican Republic. To the writer they meant, "Montez makes the Good Neighbor Policy a pleasure."[54]

George Hurrell took this 1942 portrait of Maria. At his private portrait studio in Hollywood, he was completely free of the restrictions imposed on film studio photographers.

Hurrell already had a history with Montez. In 1941 he took what were probably the most sensuous photographs of her film career at his studio on Sunset Boulevard. Official Universal portraits would never look this overtly sexual. Most movie magazines and newspapers would not have published them. The photo, from the series Hurrell would use in exhibits, has Maria lying on the floor, wrapped seductively in a leopard skin negligee, staring right at the camera with the most sensuous expression you could achieve on film and the fullest cleavage the law would allow, with the negligee pulled to the side exposing her thigh. Her hands are on either side of the unbuttoned opening in the brief covering. Whether she is holding it closed or about to pull it open is up to the viewer's imagination. A slightly less crazily sensual photo from this session was one of nine full-page pictures used by *Motion Picture* magazine for an illustrated article on Hurrell in its March 1942 "All Glamour Issue."[55]

Maria was always a favorite of Hurrell. He had served with the First Motion Picture Unit of the army air forces at Camp Roach in Culver City from 1942 to 1943 and was back at his studio at 333 Rodeo Drive in Beverly

Hills in August 1945 when the Associated Press's fashion editor, Dorothy Roe, approached him for an article. She was interested in the question "Has ideal U.S. beauty curves or elegance?" She asked Hurrell and fashion designer Stella Brownie their opinions. Not surprisingly, Brownie, who specialized in designing dinner dresses and evening ensembles for the FoxBrownie Company, favored tall, slim models with slender hips who exuded "charm," on whom the dresses would just hang. George Hurrell, the leading portrait photographer in Hollywood, stressed "glamour" and the necessity of "bumps." Meaning hips and breasts. Roe asked the photographer to pick his favorite women to shoot as pin ups. He went by hair color in his response. Jane Russell was his premier brunette, Veronica Lake his preferred blonde, and Maria Montez his favorite redhead.[56]

Photos of Maria showed up all through the Pin Up Industrial Complex. An article in *McCall's* that concerned how she retained her vitality in the face of all her commitments featured six pin up photos on the first page. She was a favorite of *Pic* magazine, which was an essential source of photos for all branches of the military. *Pic* was oversize, like *Life*, and photographer Bob Wallace was there to specialize in pin ups of Hollywood actresses. In Maria's October 28, 1941, cover she is wearing a clinging green dress with her full, braless chest on spectacular display. Maria was back on the cover on July 21, 1942, in a blue dress with a tight bodice. The squib describing the cover photo labels her "possibly the most beautiful girl in Hollywood." The illustrations on the inside try to prove the point. One of the sexiest of all Montez photos is a Bob Wallace pic that shows her lying nude on her stomach in bed in a right-side shot from the small of her back to her smiling face. The three photos on the opposite page by Ray Jones, who had to please the Hays Office, were more subdued.[57]

A year and a half later she was back on the cover of *Pic* in her two-piece *Cobra Woman* costume posing with the huge cobra statue created by Universal. She is a pin up in one of the last magazine issues published before the end of the European war. In one of *Pic*'s overseas editions for the armed forces all of the ads have been removed, replaced by pin ups. One of them is a photo of Maria in her sarong from *South of Tahiti*. Later in the issue is an article about *Sudan* featuring a one-third-page photo of her in "the fetching wardrobe" for the movie. She would be equally embraced in other wartime publications such as *War Laffs: Fun for Fighting Men* and in photo-oriented general magazines such as *See*.

Universal Studios had released a sheet to newspapers and magazines extolling its contract player Maria Montez as a soldiers' favorite and an active

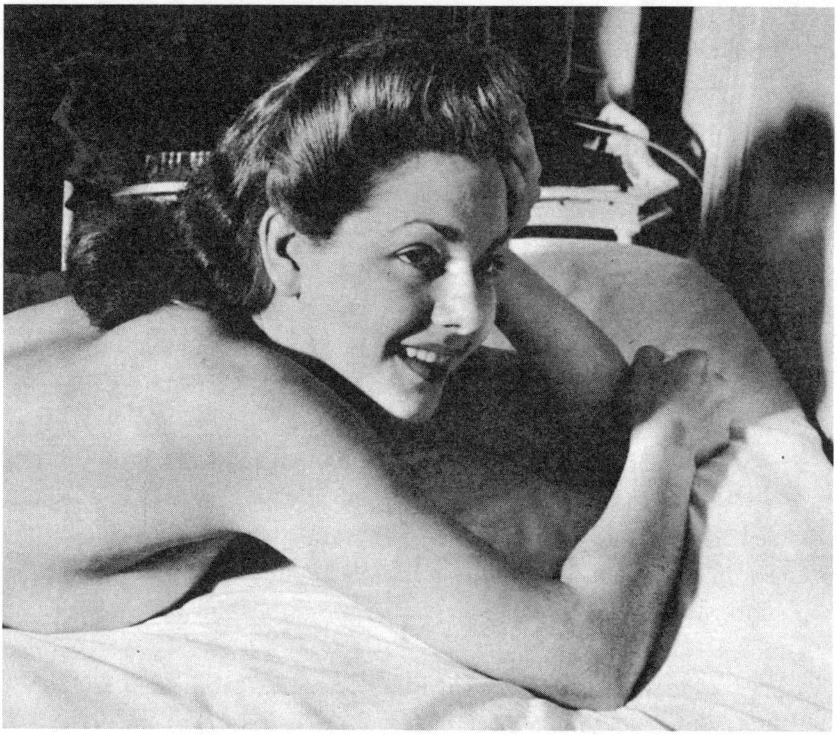

Bob Wallace photo for *Pic,* July 21, 1942.

participant in the home front war effort. Naturally the studio had to back up its boast, so Universal released a steady stream of stills of Maria doing her part. She had great legs and the studio rarely passed up a chance to put them on display. Since silk was being used to make parachutes during the war, not women's hose, several makeup companies developed a cream to apply to the legs to make it look like a woman was wearing nylons. The more ambitious user drew a black mark up her legs to reproduce a seam. In 1942 several of Hollywood's actresses posed for photos showing how to apply the makeup. Montez did at least two of them for Miner's Liquid Make Up, whose motto was "Pour Yourself a Pair of Stockings." The photos show a bent-over Montez with her dress up over her knee happily making up her legs.[58]

Ray Jones took Maria into the portrait gallery in mid-1942 to do a series of her dressed in work clothes, designed by the Sterling Company, aimed at female war workers. The snipe on the back notes that Montez is stepping out of her glamorous roles "to demonstrate the chic styling of her 'Miss Yank' defense work costume." So popular was this series of photos it was used to illustrate an essay by Dee Lowrance for the October 11, 1942, Sunday supplements in newspapers around the country called "Factory Girls Balk at Cast-off Overalls." He explained, "Girls are ready and eager to take the places of their soldier-brothers, sweethearts and husbands in America's war industries. But they darned well resent having to do so enveloped in the overalls the boys left behind them." The three photos feature Montez in a jumper and two models of overalls for factory and aircraft workers.[59]

Universal also released a 1942 photograph of her demonstrating the use of cotton in clothing "both practical and appealing" and 1943 images of her modeling dresses that demonstrate the designer's ability to stay within the strict governmental regulations on the use of materials in wartime. These photos were preceded by an odd photo pushing "bells for belles . . . the latest trick for getting around in the blackout." They appeared early in the war when the West Coast still feared Japanese bombers. The small detachable bells were placed under the instep of a high-heeled shoe when the sirens sounded. They would ring and therefore warn other pedestrians of your presence in a blackout. The photo gave Maria another chance to support the war effort while showing off her legs in her pre–*Arabian Nights* clawing-for-attention period.[60]

Like all the studios, Universal invited soldiers and sailors to the lot to see how films were made and to meet the players. Needless to say, one of the several studio stills men was always handy with his Speed Graphic camera to capture the scene. Maria was photographed on the set of *Ali Baba* with two members of the Women's Auxiliary Ferrying Squadron, which delivered airplanes from the factory to air bases. Marine Corps gunnery sergeant Victor Maghakian and Lieutenant W. S. LeFrançois, who both won the Navy Cross on Makin Island with Carlson's Raiders, presented her with "a Jap bullet brought back from the raid." Army sergeant Clark Rhoden brought her a swastika flag from the Munich beer hall where Hitler founded the Nazi Party. As Universal's proclaimed international ambassador of goodwill, she was photographed often with members of Allied services who were visiting Universal—members of the Free French air force, Britain's Royal Air Force, the Royal Australian Air Force, and the Chinese Air Force were all subject to Universal photo releases when they visited Maria at Universal City.[61]

All these visiting soldiers were mixed in with the US Army Signal Corps photographers who did part of their training at Universal as well as several other studios. The classes were held at Ray Jones's still photography department. Army photographers were given free rein to roam all over the Universal lot. Many of them found themselves around the set of *Arabian Nights.* There was a lot to shoot there. Harem girls, guys on horseback, various colored

At Universal City, Sergeant Victor "Transport" Maghakian and Lieutenant W. S. LeFrançois present Maria with "a Jap bullet."

sands, a huge fur-lined bathtub and, of course, la Montez in her Arabian finery. The Signal Corps photogs must have loved it. What an outstanding way to train.[62]

Universal issued several wartime photos that had a light touch. Certainly, one of the oddest is of Maria and Sabu sitting on the back of "his favorite elephant, Bonnie," while she picks up scrap with her trunk. They are "participating" in the collection of scrap iron for one of the many salvage drives carried out by the government during the war. The snipe, of course, noted that all three of them appear in *Arabian Nights.* Sabu looks right at home. Maria is making the best of it. Dressed in the same clothes, the duo is shown in another photo pitchforking some straw to feed the gnu that appeared in the film.[63]

Whatever animosity existed between Maria and Universal, she often appeared in pieces helping to push the studio's involvement in the war effort. Soon after Pearl Harbor, Montez was photographed sitting with Gloria Jean in a truck full of office equipment for the Office of War Information. The description of the photo explained they "led" the campaign to collect surplus typewriters around Universal to donate to the armed forces. In another

According to the snipe: "Sabu, former jungle boy, brought his favorite elephant, Bonnie, to Universal Studios to aid in the collection of scrap iron for Uncle Sam's salvage drive. Bonnie rounded up better than 50 tons of junk. Maria Montez, as shown here, went along for the ride and helped direct the operations from aboard the pachyderm."

series, the Office of War Information celebrated Linda Darnell's efforts in a similar vein at 20th Century Fox. Maria's photo was the largest in a *Collier*'s article on how Universal's players got to the lot in the face of gas rationing. She was shown in full color astride a scooter. The studio received a concurrent burst of publicity along with it star on her bond trips. Universal released photos of Maria on a tank at Fort Knox and in various Cleveland war plants, and also of her receiving a replica of an armor-piercing shot manufactured at the Westinghouse plant in Mansfield, Ohio.

The news services released photos of Maria and Jean-Pierre Aumont at the June 30, 1943, Hollywood Bowl rally to raise money to build the heavy cruiser USS *Los Angeles.* American battleships were named after the country's states, heavy cruisers for American cities. Bonds were sold in cities all over the country to earn the naming rights. But it was the effort to pay for the *Los Angeles* with the help of movie stars that garnered an article in *Movieland* magazine. Los Angeles needed to raise $40 million to build the cruiser. Twice that was eventually raised, paying not only for the cruiser but also four destroyers.[64]

Not all Montez's wartime photos were created by Universal. There was always a photographer on hand every time she showed up anywhere official. Whether it was her numerous appearances at the Hollywood Canteen or dancing with an obviously overjoyed merchant sailor at the United Seaman's Service Canteen in New York, someone was there with a camera. Same thing when she posed with a bevy of bathing-suited young women as a judge at a beauty contest at the Victory House in downtown Los Angeles's Pershing Square on the Fourth of July, 1942. Universal got more mileage out of this when the four top placers showed up in their bathing suits the next day on the set of *Arabian Nights.* The Wide World–distributed photo elevated the four women to "candidates for movie roles." One of them actually appeared in the film as a harem girl.[65]

The civilians on the American home front did not directly fight the Axis enemy in the European, Pacific, or China-Burma-India theaters of war. That was up to the military. Those men and the few women with them were actively engaged with the enemy. The unconditional surrender of the Axis was their country's stated, unequivocal goal. But it could never have been achieved without the help of the home front. The emotional support the troops so desperately needed, the ammunition, weapons, airplanes, and ships with which they fought, the food that sustained them, the hospitals that tried to put them back together after physical or mental wounds—all this was paid for and produced by the home front. The United States was the Arsenal of Democracy not only for its own armed forces but also for all its Allies. Hollywood, like every other American industry, played its part in this battle of the home front.

The studios made the movies that entertained not only audiences in the United States but soldiers sitting in jungles and ruined European towns, sailors on ships all over the world, and airmen who had to listen to their dialogue over the noise of airplanes being prepared for the next day's mission. Thanks to the work of the Hollywood Victory Committee, entertainers were dispatched to every corner of the United States and to the three war fronts. Stars were given a special place in American lives and were expected to get off of the sound stages and directly support the war effort. Maria Montez did just that, as a representative of both Latin America and the United States. The best things she could give all those GIs and bond buyers were her presence and her interest. She could not sing or dance to entertain them. She could only look great and be her effervescent self. Certainly, many of the large organized bond drives she took part in helped her in publicizing her career. But on scores of occasions, she simply went out to a nearby base to spend some time with soldiers or sailors. No cameras around. No Universal flacks. Just Maria doing her part to support the massive war effort and all those soldiers involved in it. Her former fiancé was dead in Belgium, her husband was fighting in Europe, her friend Sabu was flying missions in the South Pacific, and she was a Hollywood star and dedicated good neighbor. Maria was involved in the war and it was important to her to do her part.

8

Suspended

Like so many things in Maria Montez's life, the homecoming of her husband was not run-of-the-mill. For the past eighteen months Jean-Pierre Aumont had been fighting in the Italian and French campaigns with the First Free French Division. Wounded twice, in November 1944 he was ordered to Paris to stage plays at the Ambassadeurs theater for soldiers on leave as he recuperated. He was back with the division by February and still with it when it was finally pulled out of the line on March 7. Aumont was separated from his division in April 1945, when he was sent to the United States with orders to set up exhibits on the participation of the French army in the battle for Europe, first in New York City and then in San Francisco, as part of the initial United Nations Conference. Aumont alerted his wife of his impending arrival and she set off for New York as soon as possible. Columnist Hedda Hopper, who always favored Montez, was also alerted. She wrote of Maria, "Wives don't wait anymore. That's the reason Maria Montez is in New York to meet Pierre Aumont."[1]

Maria had done all the things wives all over the country did. She wrote faithfully to her husband and eagerly awaited the daily mail hoping for letters from him. It is only speculation, or the odd mention in a column, that gives any idea of what the letters were like. Typically, wartime letters were encouraged by the military to be upbeat on each side. Civilians shouldn't complain a lot about food shortages or the long hours they were working in defense plants. Soldiers should not write about the horror that surrounded them every day. One letter from Aumont spoke of his panic when he met Marlene Dietrich in Italy and she told him Maria was getting a divorce. "My Maria?!" gasped Jean-Pierre. No, said Dietrich, her daughter Maria.[2]

Aumont had confidence in his wife's fidelity while he was overseas. He told Louella Parsons, "When I married Maria Montez people said it would not last, but I know my girl. She waited for me and carried herself with dignity. All the time I was gone. I am very proud of her." And although she went to parties with friends and occasionally to nightclubs, she was not the old Montez intent on being seen with every available man in Hollywood. No more comments on taming Holly-wolves. She was a married woman and a wartime wife. Maria wanted badly to change the perception of her original publicity to bring out the serious nature that always underlay all the craziness. When Walter Winchell wrote in his March 17, 1944, column, under the subheading "Memos of a Midnighter," "Maria Montez' latest is *Esquire*'s and Warner's photographer H. Waxman," she was livid. She had no "latest" and Henry Waxman was only a photographer she knew from her work with *Esquire* magazine. On April 11 Winchell wrote one of his very rare retractions. "Maria Montez got a bum break when an item blended her with a reporter on the coast. She hasn't had a date with any male pal since her groom went overseas."[3]

Bob Thomas wrote a column about a wartime "date" with Maria that was arranged and paid for by Universal. Making it a letter to Jean-Pierre, he noted, "She has been a homebody since you left to fight for France." He did observe that she looked luscious in her gown as the studio limo took them first to Romanoff's and then on to the Trocadero, where they met with "the Latin Colony," including Carmen Miranda, band leader Xavier Cugat, and actor Arturo de Cordova, who had appeared in a dozen Hollywood films and over a hundred Mexican films. Since the table talk, even from Miranda, was in very rapid Spanish, he understood little. Then when he asked Maria to dance she told him she had promised her husband she would dance only the rhumba while he was gone. No close dancing. He kissed her cheek at her door and she went into the house. Thomas summed up, "You're a lucky man, Jean." At least he got a column out of the evening.[4]

Gladys Hall was a contributor to many Hollywood magazines and Maria's friend. She wrote a wonderful tribute article to Montez in 1944 she called "I Thought, 'How Remarkable She Is'" for *Silver Screen*. Hall noted Maria had arrived in Hollywood only four years ago. "Her really epic beauty of face and figure, plus a warm, outgiving nature, spontaneity, wit and intelligence completely won public, press and colleagues—who gave her stardom." She made her marriage to Jean-Pierre Aumont, who had to depart for overseas, "by her ardor and singleness of devotion, a thing of dignity, tenderness and genuine beauty." No wartime scandal had attached to her name. "Exotic as she is, and desirable, alone as she has been for so long, life-loving and of a tumultuous vitality, wolf-bait as she ever was, neither breath of gossip or breath of wolf has touched Maria Africa de Santos Silas Aumont."[5]

Montez was a bona fide movie star by this time and nothing in her life happened without press notices, generated by Maria herself as well as Universal. After telling Hedda Hopper she was headed to New York to meet

Maria and Aumont, the latter just back from overseas, at the Sherry Netherland Hotel, New York.

Jean-Pierre, Maria shared her feelings about reuniting with her husband with her friend Gladys Hall for an article in *Photoplay.* The need to garner publicity out of this most private of occasions may have marked her status as a Hollywood star, but her emotions were soon to be shared by hundreds of thousands of other American women.

As Maria explained to Gladys Hall concerning her reunion with her husband, she waited in a New York hotel room not as the Queen of Technicolor, but as just another war bride. Remembering the four-day train trip from the coast, Montez reflected the thoughts common to women from one end of the United States to the other in 1945. "All the time on the train, I am worried. All the way I keep thinking, am I going to love him as I think I love him? Will he be the same? Will it be between us, after eighteen months, will it be the same? Like wheels inside my head the thoughts go until I think I am crazy. . . . [Then] I begin to worry whether he will love me as he did."[6]

Finally, after an anxious week, Alexandre de Manziarly, head of the French Military Mission, called to say Aumont had arrived and would be with her in two hours. Maria dressed in the clothes he liked, wore his favorite perfume, worried that she had become too skinny. When Aumont arrived at the hotel he found the desk clerk was prohibited from giving out guests' room numbers. So he called from the lobby. "This is the moment I have waited for," he thought. "I shall hear her voice again at last, hear her first greeting." When Maria received Aumont's call she could not sit still. "When I heard his voice, knew he was here . . . I could not, of course, delay the first sight of him by waiting inside the door. I rushed out into the corridor. . . . What happened after that is a story of those hours that make you know the kingdom of heaven is [touching her heart] here. I have now wings in my feet, wings in my brain, wings in my heart." She also had photographers waiting to be called to their room.[7]

It was not just photographers who were alerted to the Aumonts' happy reunion. *Silver Screen* magazine published two items about the happy couple. Bee Bangs's "Hollywood Earful" had a photo of Maria and Aumont in his uniform at the Mocambo in New York and there was another pic of the couple with Betty Hutton at a party for Bebe Daniels and Ben Lyon in "Topics for Gossip." The columnists announced the happy event to all of America. Harrison Carroll wrote that Maria was not sure if she could get a space on a train going east to meet her husband. She claimed not to care about a seat: "I'll ride in the baggage car if I have to." Louella Parsons found Montez very happy now that her husband had returned. She wrote, "Maria Montez is the happiest and most excited girl in ten states. She actually beams on her husband." Based on all this obvious joy coming from the couple, Sheilah Graham wrote, "There are lots of red faces in Hollywood because of the apparent success of the Maria Montez-Jean Pierre Aumont marriage." She noted that several people had tried to break them up, certain the marriage would never work. Sheilah was happy to report they were wrong.[8]

Her husband being back and in one piece was an answer to a prayer Montez prepared for *Photoplay* magazine. The editors asked Maria, Alan Ladd, Lionel Barrymore, John Garfield, and Olivia de Havilland to submit their hopes for the future in an article published as the war in Europe was coming to an end, "My Easter Prayer." Montez's contribution was right from the heart.

> My Easter prayer is one I have made a thousand times since my husband went overseas to the battlefronts and the war became a hauntingly terrible personal thing.
>
> I pray little prayers each day for the war to end soon with victory in our hands.
>
> I pray my husband will be unharmed.
>
> I pray all the men who have left their homes for the loneliness and danger and suffering that war brings to them, in a measure that we—the safe ones—can never understand, will come back safe and soon.
>
> I pray there will be peace and freedom in the world.
>
> I pray for happiness as a possession shared.
>
> I pray for little things important only to me and for the things which make life good for all of us.[9]

The Aumonts spent two weeks in New York as Jean-Pierre finished arranging his exhibit. They paid a happy visit to the 21 Club where they first got together in 1943. Needless to say, they were photographed wherever they went. Still in service and wearing his uniform, Aumont joined his wife on a train bound for Los Angeles where he would prepare the exhibition on the Free French forces for the opening meetings of the United Nations in San Francisco. Waiting to greet the arriving couple were Maria's three sisters Adita, Consuelo, and Lucita. They had been living with her for the past several months and the ever-effusive Maria kept describing the brother-in-law her sisters had never met as a "Greek god." Jean-Pierre recalled them looking a little alarmed as they welcomed "the wan and peaked specimen of a soldier I had become—speechless with disappointment and disbelief, my three sisters-in-law attempted a half-hearted curtsy." Then they all piled into the car and went home to Beverly Hills.[10]

There was a problem in Chicago on the way to Los Angeles. Montez never traveled without a variety of changes of clothes and many hats. Her husband was still wearing his uniform and had everything else in a duffel bag that could be slung over his shoulder. But Maria had twenty-one pieces of luggage. This flew in the face of the governmental edict to wartime train travelers to travel light since the trains were all so packed. Besides having far too many bags, it wound up that two of the pieces were missing—those that

Maria and Jean-Pierre arrive home on the Union Pacific's *City of Los Angeles.*

contained her beloved Lilly Dache hats. Maria was vocal in her anger over her missing bags. "Every time I go to Chicago somebody has steal something," she told anyone who would listen—including a reporter from the *Chicago Sun.* She then proceeded to bang the side of the baggage car with her clenched fist. "I will not move until they come back. I will sue somebody. I will cry!"[11]

Chicago's trainmen were not amused by her ranting and with the wholehearted support of the *Sun* in its front-page coverage on April 10, 1945, declared her banned from taking trains through the city. This was big news in the Chicago newspapers and also made *Daily Variety.* Obviously Universal did not welcome this ban—not only did it make her look foolish and narcissistic for dragging all that luggage to and from New York, far worse, it made her look unpatriotic for ignoring the government's edict on what passengers could take on a train. Universal found a partial solution to the problem by having the head of the studio's Chicago branch film exchange, Ben Katz, purchase eight small ads on the bottom of the front page of the *Chicago Sun* for the April 12 edition. Taking out the ads worked. The *Sun* backed off its campaign against Montez, the railroad lifted its ban on her, and the whole megillah evaporated. The fact that President Roosevelt died in Warm Springs, Georgia, two days after Maria's meltdown certainly helped quash the story in Chicago.[12]

Maria's place in the Hollywood firmament was evident when *Movies* magazine ran a piece called "Home to Hollywood" about servicemen returning from their war service in combat zones to try to restart their film careers. The long article describes both the overseas experiences and return of Clark Gable, Robert Montgomery, John Carroll, Louis Hayward, Craig Reynolds, Frank Reynolds, and John Houston. Several inset black-and-white photos accompany the seven-page article. But the only large color photos, and the only ones with a woman in them, are the two pictures of Maria and Jean-Pierre in their New York hotel room, embracing, with Aumont still in his uniform. His war service was summed up as were the others mentioned, but he is also quoted as being ecstatic to be back "with Maria again." Maria is the only woman quoted. She said, "I haven't asked any questions. I've just looked and looked at him." Montez's dual roles as both just another woman welcoming her man home and an exotic are perfectly demonstrated by the *Movies* article. She is married to the only soldier in the article who was not in the US military.[13]

As she and Aumont were driving home from the Pasadena train station, Maria was being confronted by a whole series of life-altering challenges. The good news was that her husband, who had barely survived the jeep wreck that killed the commander of the First Free French Division, General Diego Brosset, had returned in one piece with a job at MGM waiting for him. The studio certainly recognized the publicity power of his service. In its 1944 biography his occupation was listed as "actor, soldier." The bad news was virtually everything else. As things stood in April 1945, Universal had no choice but to suspend production on anything that might have been dreamed up for Maria and the rest of her colleagues in the "eastern" films. The films remained very successful, but the entire male contingent of the team was in the service. Montez hated *Frontier Gal,* the proposed movie Universal had been advertising her supposed involvement in for over a year. She refused to be in it,

The Thanksgiving of 1945 must have been one of the most heartfelt in the long history of the holiday. With a Blue Star service banner in the background, Jean-Pierre, in his dress uniform, enjoys the traditional turkey. The snipe reads: "A Movie Star Counts Her Blessings"—and there were many. Maria's husband is home, they are celebrating their first Thanksgiving in three years, she is pregnant, and she has almost finished shooting *Tangier.*

demanding instead to be put in a modern drama or comedy. She wanted a role that would require her to be an actress, not just an underdressed Technicolor fantasy—and she definitely wanted to avoid dealing with Jon Hall or animals of any sort. This was a huge risk on her part. Not only was she turning her back on the type of films that had made her a star, she was adamant about changing the audience's perception of her and proving she had the acting skills her critics always questioned. Even more important, she was insisting it was her choice entirely, not Universal's.

Film studios rarely wanted to change what they perceived as a winning formula just because the actor engaged in the formula got sick of it and wanted to explore other possibilities. They were convinced that a key part of their job was to find their actors a type that the audience could embrace and would accept seeing them in over and over again. From Mary Pickford wanting to cut her blonde ringlets and play adult roles to Dorothy Lamour taking it upon herself to cut her waist-length hair to get out of sarong roles, nothing was more aggravating to a studio than when someone it had groomed into stardom wanted to upset the gravy train by demanding to play a part outside of an established persona. Not only did it threaten to overturn a pattern that worked and made money, it meant that the star had become "difficult."

Universal was completely dedicated to making more of the same if a team worked out. In the late 1930s and '40s Andy Devine and Richard Arlen made fourteen low-budget Aces of Action movies, changing only the character names and the action's locale. In the same period Boris Karloff, Bela Lugosi, and Lon Chaney Jr. played variations on Frankenstein's monster, Dracula, and the wolf man. By the 1940s Abbott and Costello were kings of the lot and completely ensconced in their screen personas no matter what the movie was about. Basil Rathbone and Nigel Bruce did Sherlock Holmes movies that changed little except for updating the duo into World War II. Once Maria clicked in *Arabian Nights* there was little hope the studio would be interested in letting her try new things. Plus, it was clear Universal had no confidence Montez could carry a modern film without the large surrounding cast she had in *Bowery to Broadway,* and the studio had no desire to star her in anything other than variations on the Neverland fantasies that had proved so popular.[14]

The problem was Maria had read the *Frontier Gal* script, in which she was slated to play (in Technicolor) the owner of several saloons, with two men once again fighting for her affections and the addition of a five-year-old child to boot. She was adamantine in her refusal to play the part. This was a breach of her contract, which granted Universal executives the authority to assign her to whatever project they saw fit. The studio had put money into preparing the public to see Maria in western garb instead of a sarong or diaphanous Arab getup. Suspension notwithstanding, her refusal to play the saloonkeeper made perfect sense to Maria. "I am proud of who I am. I play proud characters, and I cannot play women who are pushed or laughed at."[15]

The frame of mind that led to Maria's rejection of *Frontier Gal* and acceptance of a suspension was perfectly captured in mid-1945 when Pete Martin interviewed her for an article in the *Saturday Evening Post.* She was already expressing her refusal to continue to appear in the fantasy pictures that had been her staple. Martin quotes her as saying, "That '*Cobra Woman*' was a steenker. I never like my peectures. I have quit one hundred and forty-eight times." Like so many other interviewers, Martin indulged himself in poking fun at Maria's accent. But her intent is perfectly clear. She wants both to change her flighty commissary actress persona and to tackle more serious roles. Whatever critics may have thought of her, Montez clearly took herself seriously as an actress and had no illusions about the quality of the films that made her famous or the limitations of her chief co-star. She told Martin she refers to her Universal leading men as "my leetle people." She would "rather play third feedle to Boyer than first feedle to one of them. I have nothing against Jon Hall. I have a deep, warm feeling for heem, but I don't want to make another film with heem."[16]

While Maria is stating her declaration of seriousness, Martin portrays her companion from the Universal publicity department, Maggy Maskel, as practically writhing in agony as Maria goes off script to say what she really thinks about her movies. Maskel had soldiered on in the publicity wars for several studios. Her lasting contribution to Hollywood lore came from her earlier stint with Columbia when she loaned Rita Hayworth a black lace nightgown her mother had made to help Bob Landry of *Life* magazine create World War II's second most famous pin up. Now she was the head of magazine interviews for Universal and was just not used to having one of her charges go rogue and spritz on passionately and at great length about how lousy her movies were.

But clearly what was on Maria's mind was changing the direction of her career. "Every time I begin to emote, I look up and there is a horse—stealing my scene," she tells Martin. However uncomfortable all this talk makes Maskel, the writer sides with Maria, concluding, "It would be interesting to see what Montez could do with a role different from the How-dare-you-spik-to-me-zat-way-do-you-not-know-I-am-the-Queen-of-Egypt parts that have been her portion. She might fall flat on her determined puss while trying it, but at least the role would know it had been given a wrestle."[17]

All of the crazy early behavior had done its job. She was given the lead in *Arabian Nights* and became a bona fide star with the Neverland series. The commissary performances, the endless nightclub entrances and constant dating, the harping on how beautiful she was, and the scooping necklines sure to attract photographers' attention had worked. She had been noticed, she was successful, and by 1945 she felt she did not need such tactics anymore. Now that she had become, in publicist Henry Rogers's words, "important," she could finally quit having to be "the exception." She told columnist Erskine Johnson, "When I first came to Hollywood three years ago I realized that Hollywood loves a phony. It was crazy, but it was all right with me. Now look at me. I'm a star, and I'm still in one piece."[18]

For at least the past year her constant theme in interviews had been that she wanted parts that did more than show off her body, parts that had dramatic depth, parts in movies where there were no horses or exploding volcanoes—or bathtubs. For the past two years Maria's public persona had been that of a wartime wife loyally writing to her husband, a constant presence at military bases all over the country supporting the war effort, and an ambassador of goodwill with Latin America. She felt she had shown Universal that she could handle a modern, dramatic part in *Bowery to Broadway.* She simply was not going backward by appearing in *Frontier Gal.* For once, she was supported by Jimmie Fidler. Sort of. He wrote he was "staggered" that Maria took a suspension rather than play in *Frontier Gal.* He reasoned, "Considering the roles which Miss Montez has enacted, presumably with no objection, any part capable of stirring her resentment really must be bad!"[19]

The desire to move on from a firmly established persona was not the exclusive problem of Maria Montez. When Edmund O'Brien was a leading man early in his career he played the energetic, dedicated good guy over and over again. He observed, "The funny thing about Hollywood is that they are interested in having you do one thing and do it well, and do it ever after. That's the sad thing about being a leading man—while the rewards may be great in fame and finances, it becomes monotonous for an actor. I think that's why some of the people who are continually playing themselves are not happy." Maria fit that profile perfectly and was determined to move on with her career.[20]

The Aumonts and the Montez sisters—soon to be joined by French journalist Jean Roy—moved into a new, much larger house at 1100 Tower Road in Beverly Hills just as Maria was suspended. Higher house payments joined the numerous career problems facing her, only some of which she was aware of. But it did give Montez a new wrinkle for publicity. Several articles would appear about the happy insanity of the multilingual Montez-Aumont homestead. The three sisters, the masseur, Maria's language coach, the ever-serene Aumont, Maria's astrologer, and various servants all roamed about the place holding conversations in several languages. They would eventually be joined by Maria's youngest brother, Jaime, who as Jaime Garcia would have a small part in *City across the River* (1949) before serving in the army during the Korean War. Hedda Hopper, for one, thoroughly enjoyed her time spent in the house, which she said was ruled by "Maria's effervescence."[21]

Walter Wanger searched the country for "The Most Beautiful Girl in the World" and found Yvonne De Carlo right on the Universal lot to play the dancer in *Salome, Where She Danced.*

No matter how happy Maria's house might have been, she was dealing with a tough adversary in Universal. Like their chief rival for national entertainment attention, major league baseball, all studios were constantly in the process of grooming newcomers to take their stars' place when they inevitably stumbled, got older, or became difficult. Edwin Schallert in the *Los Angeles*

Times saw what Universal's intentions were. He titled his June 1945 article discussing the career of Universal's latest hire, "Yvonne De Carlo Stands out Again as 'Threat Girl.'" She was clearly being groomed to replace Maria, much as she had been used earlier by Paramount to get Dorothy Lamour back into a sarong. But worse than that, the new management at Universal was determined to change the studio's character. Studio heads Nathan Blumberg and Cliff Work envisioned an output of largely A pictures, jettisoning the serials, westerns, horror movies, and fantasies the studio was known for. They and the other studio heads saw no place for Maria Montez in this future.[22]

Acquanetta may not have worked out as a challenge to Montez two years before, but Yvonne De Carlo presented a much greater threat. She had the requisite "exotic" looks to play Maria's roles, thanks to a combination of Sicilian, Scottish, and English genes. But several things set her apart from Montez. She was born in Vancouver, British Columbia, and spoke what to US ears was the unaccented English typical of western Canada. Plus, she had been a professional showgirl at the Florentine Gardens and Earl Carroll nightclubs in Hollywood. She was well enough known from her dancing and singing in these major clubs to appear on the cover of risqué *Laff* magazine in full color in her underwear with the title "Yvonne DeCarlo, Popular West Coast Showgirl" and be featured a year later in the same magazine in an article about the Florentine Gardens. Adding De Carlo to Montez as contract players caused reviewer Jake Rachman to write that this gave Universal "two of the most notable Technicolor torso tossers under contract" and "a corner on anatomical movies."[23]

De Carlo always wanted to make movies. She began dancing at Nils T. Granland's Florentine Gardens in 1940. She briefly moved on to the ultimate showgirl venue in Los Angeles, the Earl Carroll Theater. She was fired from there because she violated Carroll's long-standing rule against his showgirls freelancing outside the theater without permission. In her case she took a small part in a film. She went back to the Florentine Gardens but finally signed a contract with six-month options at Paramount in March 1942. The studio used her almost exclusively as a threat to Dorothy Lamour, who was balking at ever wearing another sarong. Seeing the situation for what it was, Lamour returned to the fold by playing island girls in *Beyond the Blue Horizon* (1942) and *Rainbow Island* (1944). But after two years at Paramount De Carlo never moved much beyond being scenery dressing in several movies and the subject of pin up photos. Paramount did not pick up her option in 1944, telling her that they believed exotic types were passé.[24]

Following rejections by MGM and Warner Brothers, Universal expressed some interest and she went to the studio for an interview with the head of casting, Bob Speers. De Carlo happened to be sitting in the waiting room of his office when independent producer Walter Wanger came by. She looked a lot like Joan Bennett, the producer's wife. A screen test was arranged and De Carlo was subsequently signed by Universal. But there was a war on. The story released by the studio was that her position was secured by a letter from twenty-one Royal Canadian Air Force bombardier students lauding their favorite pin up. Acceding to the request of an ally's servicemen was a way better story than she looked like a guy's wife.[25]

Wanger was preparing a new film based on a nineteenth-century Viennese dancer/spy who eventually comes to the American West called *Salome, Where She Danced.* The odd name of the film came from the small Arizona town of Drinkman's Wells changing its name to Salome to reflect the positive effect the dancer had in reforming its lawlessness. The role called for someone who would constantly have men falling in love with her, and Wanger was determined to find a new face to fit the bill. He was quite well known for vocally stressing the need for quality films that had something to say. But he came to Universal to make popular films, not great art. *Arabian Nights* had been a blockbuster and made a star of Maria Montez. Now Wanger had dreamed up the publicity idea of searching for what he called "the Most Beautiful Girl in the World" to star in his latest film. John Joseph and the Universal publicity department went to work to fulfill Wanger's quest. Russell Birdwell had garnered considerable publicity for *Gone with the Wind* by ostentatiously searching everywhere for an actress to play Scarlett O'Hara. With the same objective in mind, Universal claimed to be scouring the country for a fresh beautiful face to play the lead in *Salome.*[26]

Charles Huy of the publicity department sent out a letter in May 1944 to Universal offices all over the country enlisting them in what he insisted was a "search," not a "contest." They were instructed to use "indirect plantings" (bits submitted by third parties as gossip rather than direct handouts from the studio) in major newspaper columns that Walter Wanger was looking for "the Most Beautiful Girl" to play Salome. Then, through local newspaper contacts they were to enlist members of the public in the effort by encouraging them to send clips and photos of local girls to be considered. National radio shows like Tom Breneman's *Breakfast at Sardi's* (which became *Breakfast in Hollywood* in mid-1945) could be utilized to put out word of the great search. The film exchange managers in each region were urged to enlist leading local photographers in submitting pictures of their favorite models. The military could play a part by submitting the names of favorite USO hostesses. The whole campaign was to be carried out in three phases. First, undertake the search for "the Most Beautiful Girl in the World"; second, build her up once found; and third, promote *Salome, Where She Danced.* [27]

Ray Jones was kept busy in the Universal portrait studio taking pictures of all sorts of would-be actresses as part of the publicity campaign. The most heavily publicized of the "finds" was Ina Owenbey, who had been noticed by a Universal publicity man running an elevator at the *Los Angeles Times.* Not only was she beautiful, she worked for one of the best publicity sources on the West Coast. So, with complete coverage by the *Times,* she was brought to the Universal portrait studio, made up by Jack Pierce, dressed by Vera West, and coiffed by Buddy King. Besides going home with several Ray Jones photographs, Owenbey did win a small part in the film as an extra.[28]

Yvonne De Carlo had better luck. Wanger immediately liked what he saw and Universal signed her to a standard contract for $150 a week with options at the end of the first year. She certainly did not have to start a De Carlo for Stardom Club. She won the role of Salome, and one of the largest buildups in Hollywood history was kicked into gear by Universal. The publicity department played "the Most Beautiful Woman" angle for all it was worth, with stories on the theme planted in any newspaper or magazine that would print them. Ray Jones was, of course, enlisted in the campaign. He took photographs of De Carlo with her hair up in evening gowns, with her hair down in sports fashions, in dance poses in her Salome costume, and scores of pictures of her arresting physicality in the most revealing bathing suits the censors would allow. A common descriptive snipe attached to the back of one of these photos read: "Salome: Yvonne De Carlo. Here she is . . . 'the Most Beautiful Girl in the World' as far as Universal film producer Walter Wanger is concerned. The 20-year old Vancouver, B.C. beauty was supposedly selected out of 20,000 girls considered by Walter Wanger for the starring role in '*Salome, Where She Danced*' after a nationwide search." On the film's opening weekend, Universal created an ad for *Salome* that showed De Carlo in her bare-midriff dancing costume with the legend, "One out of twenty thousand" blazing across the top of the ad.[29]

The critics savaged *Salome, Where She Danced,* expressing open incredulity that the producer of classics like *Stagecoach* (1939) and *The Long Voyage Home* (1940) could have had anything to do with what came to be called "Wanger—Where He Flopped." But the fans loved both the movie and its star. De Carlo had arrived. Photographs continued to flow out of the Universal portrait gallery and the new star was profiled by the fan magazines. Michael Sheridan dubbed her "Venus De Carlo" when he told her tale in *Motion Picture* magazine. She was multitalented, looked exotically delectable and, after being largely ignored by Paramount for two years, was thrilled to star in anything Universal put before her. "The studio knew I would play opposite Rin Tin Tin if they told me to, and I would gladly agree to be the mother of the seven dwarfs," she remembered of that time. De Carlo was equally well received as an exotic in *Song of Scheherazade* and *Slave Girl* in 1947.[30]

But one of the things that hammered the nails irretrievably into Maria's coffin at Universal was how successfully De Carlo played in modern film noir movies. Former newspaperman and Warner Brothers producer Mark Hellinger came to Universal in 1946 to film *The Killers.* The following year he used Yvonne in *Brute Force,* where she effectively played the Italian girlfriend of prisoner Howard Duff and the reason he is in jail. Hellinger promised her the female lead in *Criss Cross* a year later. He died in December 1947, but the new producer, Michael Kraike, honored the commitment; De Carlo played the former wife of armored car driver Burt Lancaster and current wife and gangster's moll to Dan Duryea. She is the catalyst for Lancaster's good-guy character to propose and carry out an armed robbery that goes completely wrong, leading to his eventual death. The first time Lancaster sees his ex-wife De Carlo after returning to Los Angeles in *Criss Cross,* this most *fatale* of film noir's *femmes* is dancing in a nightclub with Tony Curtis in his film debut. Not a word passes between the partners, but the screen is soaked with sexual tension as they move in each other's arms. No matter how nice he is to his mother and younger brother, in the film noir universe Burt Lancaster is clearly doomed by loving such a woman. This was simply not the sort of scene or part that Montez was capable of carrying off at that time.

The prevailing wisdom in Hollywood was that Maria had made a horrible error by accepting suspension. Hedda Hopper fastened on how badly she lost out by not wearing the gorgeous gowns Travis Banton designed for *Frontier Gal.* Charles Samuels summed up the longer view in *Motion Picture.* He recognized De Carlo's talent and the threat it represented to Maria. "As the months of her idleness passed, it seemed to Hollywood that Montez had made the mistake of her life. Yvonne De Carlo, who had replaced her, was being given the biggest publicity in the history of Universal. And Miss De Carlo was a type eminently suited to play the seductive roles that had always been Maria's specialty." Associated Press news features writer Rosalind Shaffer pointed out another factor in De Carlo's favor. Unlike la Montez, "Yvonne shows no signs of temperament."[31]

Samuels was hardly the only Hollywood scribe to see what was happening. *Los Angeles Times* Hollywood columnist Edwin Schallert wrote that because she replaced Maria in *Frontier Gal,* De Carlo became "the 'beeg' threat at the moment in the screen life of Maria Montez." Still, when Schallert met Maria at Jinx Falkenburg's party in mid-June, a week after the column appeared, she was unfazed by all the negative assessments of her decision to go on suspension. She told him she was returning to work at Universal in *Tangier* and would no longer appear in the romantic fantasies that had made her career. She realized *Sudan* was a major moneymaker like the five other Neverland films, but noted that many of the reviews observed that the style was getting stale. For all of her flash, Montez had a crystal vision of what she wanted from Hollywood. With an insight typical of how she judged her career and how much attention she paid to reviews, Maria told Schallert, "I want to quit these films when they are at the peak, not on the downbeat. It isn't only that the pictures are all the same, but the stories are one just like the other."[32]

Yvonne De Carlo did become the reigning exotic at Universal. She had never been in the same room with Montez until she was filming *Song of Scheherazade* with Jean-Pierre Aumont in late 1946. De Carlo's foreboding at the thought of finally meeting her "rival" was typical of the expectations most of Hollywood had of Montez—volcanic behavior was anticipated. De Carlo recalled being a bit nervous when she first met Maria, having heard she was a "human buzz saw." What she did not know was that Maria no longer cared what sort of threat her rival might be. As much as columnists like Sheilah Graham wanted to gin up a feud between the two, it just did not work. After kissing Jean-Pierre, Maria came toward De Carlo, who thought, "Oh boy, this was it—the big shootout at the old corral." To her surprise, Montez "couldn't have been more pleasant." Despite the public's false perception that the two were dire enemies fighting over the same parts, she and Yvonne wound up being quite friendly. De Carlo noted, "I learned that Maria Montez was not to be judged by ordinary standards. She inhabited a self-designed world in which she was royalty, and this was something she sincerely believed. She told me she had lived as royalty in the Mayan period of history and showed me a scarf that she said came from that life. Who was I to argue? I listened, nodded, and silently marveled at the quality of cloth that could survive so many centuries."[33]

This fantastical story about the Mayan cloth notwithstanding, Maria expressed her friendship and level-headed understanding of how Hollywood worked to De Carlo a couple of weeks later, when the two had lunch with Pat DiCicco, a sort of agent, man about Hollywood, and probable gangster. At the time Yvonne was secretly dating Howard Hughes and felt he was the love of her life. Both Maria and DiCicco knew all about the relationship and warned her that Hughes had women stashed all over Hollywood; trusting him was out of the question and she certainly should not give him her heart. De Carlo knew only about the women who had been in Hughes's life previously. This new information was unsettling to her. She was very grateful for the inside information given to her by a friend who had a far broader understanding of Hollywood.[34]

Although Yvonne De Carlo may have been presented to American audiences as exotic, she was from British Columbia and spoke unaccented English. With the end of the war and the evaporation of the Good Neighbor Policy with Latin America, Hispanic stars' lights began blinking out in all of the studios. Even Carmen Miranda, the biggest of the Latin stars and the highest-paid woman in the United States in 1944, found parts scarce after the war. She played numerous nightclub dates and several television shows, but Miranda, who made eight major films between 1940 and 1944, made only five movies in the decade between the end of the war and her premature death from a heart attack in 1955 at forty-six.[35]

But there was another, far more serious problem between Maria and her studio than an actress wanting to change her image or the success of Yvonne De Carlo. As the war was ending, Universal was once again intent on reinventing itself. The management team of Nathan Blumberg as studio president in New York and Cliff Work as production chief in Los Angeles took over Universal in 1938. By 1939 they had the money-losing studio back in the black for the first time since 1932. The war years proved to be boom times for Universal. The studio netted profits of $2.8 million in 1942, $3.8 million in 1943, $3.4 million in 1944, and $4 million in 1945 ($14.1 million in 2021 dollars). The studio advertised, "Universal Pictures Company, Inc. today is in the strongest financial condition in its history."[36]

This sufficiently whetted the management's appetite to do battle with the major majors once the war ended. Blumberg and Work planned to resurrect Carl Laemmle Jr.'s plan from the early 1930s and start making A-list, quality films again and phase out as much as possible all movies under seventy minutes, including the serials, westerns, and team-oriented series that had proved such a money-winning combination during the war. The five major major studios had been doing fewer B movies ever since the 1948 consent decree that resulted from the *United States v. Paramount Pictures* antitrust case, which barred the blind selling of features to theaters and limited block booking to five pictures. Blind selling referred to the practice of selling undisclosed movies to theaters and theater chains, forcing the venues to block-book these films along with the more popular A pictures.

Since the studios could no longer lump in their weaker films with their better ones, they quit making as many B pictures. Besides the Justice Department's successful lawsuit to end block booking, pursued under the provisions of the Sherman Anti-Trust Act, television, available for free and in one's home, was beginning to threaten the studio's profits and further weaken the need for B pictures. Blumberg and Work were convinced that by concentrating on A pictures they could successfully compete for the screen space that was opening up thanks to fewer B pictures being produced.[37]

Just as Universal was mulling over a possible future of concentrating on quality films, William Goetz, vice president in charge of studio operations at 20th Century Fox and son-in-law to MGM's Louis B. Mayer, joined with Leo Spitz, an associate producer at RKO, to lead a group of independent producers in organizing International Pictures in 1943. The stated aim of the new company was to make only A-list movies. Its films, such as *Casanova Brown* (1944) and *Along Came Jones* (1945), were excellent but did not deliver enough box office to allow International to expand. The new studio felt this was possible only if it merged with a larger studio. Its initial deal with England's Rank Productions fell through and Goetz and Spitz turned to Universal. The lure of the merger to International was to give it a permanent distributing outlet, reliable studio space, and participation in cost savings available only to an integrated producer-distributor. The benefit to Universal was the chance to tie in with a quality producing team that would help attract other independent producers to the studio and ensure the kind of A-list pictures the studio wanted to make.

Under the new system Nathan Blumberg and J. Cheever Cowdin would continue to run distribution and business affairs from New York, while Leo Spitz and William Goetz supervised production in Los Angeles. Cliff Work was demoted to "senior studio executive." On July 30, 1946, the studio officially became Universal-International (U-I) and was faced with how to rearrange the studio to fit the new ideal. One of its problems was what to do with Montez.[38]

Whatever problems U-I might have had regarding Maria's future in movies, she certainly was successful in the sideline activities integral to any star's career in the 1940s. She had numerous appearances on radio shows and in advertisements. Not only were both mediums a boon to the individual star financially and in publicizing his or her name, the studio got a cut of the profits, the recognition of its actor as a "Universal star," and free advertising of the star's current film.

Montez had been plastered all over the fan magazines since 1941 but was not featured on the radio or in major advertisements until she hit it big in *Arabian Nights.* Maria was particularly popular with advertisers. *Arabian*

Nights led directly to a "perfume enhancement" of the same name and half-page ads for Max Factor makeup. The film was also mentioned in the ad she did for Regent, "the milder, better tasting cigarette." It asked if you were a Diana Barrymore, Robert Cummings, or Maria Montez type. If you were Maria's type, you would want the company's "King Size" cigarette because it "means a smoke that's over 20% longer." While Ray Jones rarely posed Maria in the studio with a cigarette, she was generally photographed in nightclubs with a cigarette in her hand.

By the end of the war, Montez had been featured in major ad campaigns for Royal Crown cola, Pepsi-Cola, Lux soap, Jergens lotion, Max Factor makeup, Woodbury powder, Deltah pearls, Yammi yogurt, Hollywood bread, Ry-Krisp crackers, "Flare-Top All Cake Ice Cream Cones," and General Electric radios. She continued to be in high demand right through *Siren of Atlantis*. In 1945 Woodbury choose Maria to help launch its new facial makeup product, "film finish powder." Sunway Fruit sought to do the same for its new dehydrated fruit drink called "Freshie" and to retain her help in pushing its "Dari Rich Chocolate Syrup." Dixie Cup wanted to keep her image on its drink cups, while Royal Crown cola planned to create a third generation of ads with her. By the end of the war Maria was featured driving a Los Angeles–manufactured three-wheeled car with a plastic body and a fifty-eight-horsepower aircraft engine guaranteed to get forty miles to a gallon of gas.[39]

Serta, a mattress company, was another concern that had already featured Maria in ads and in early 1945 was eager to repeat. It assured the studio the ad "will be in absolutely good taste," featuring neither a mattress nor a bedroom. Reflecting the growing disaffection of the studio toward her, Universal's exploitation director Harry Ormiston actually expressed surprise in a February 19, 1945, memo that "the Serta boys still want to continue to plug Maria Montez." While he approved the ad campaign, he refused to send the three thousand photographs of her Serta wanted to distribute in its stores, and advised the company to obtain what it could from local theaters. This is in stark contrast to the studio's eager campaign in 1943 to publicize Montez and *Arabian Nights*. Universal was only too happy then to send out several hundred photos of Maria requested by the medical detachment of the 108th Infantry Regiment.

Montez agreed to the use of her image in the Serta ad and, ever the opportunist, she tried to wangle some free mattresses out of the deal. After all, her three sisters were now living with her. She asked for one full-size and three twin-size mattresses and box springs. Howard Mayer, Serta's advertising agent, responded that the company would like to comply, but the war had caused a critical shortage of the material from which the mattresses were constructed. But Maria was nothing if not persistent—and by the summer she had her mattresses. In August 1945 owner Leo Simon wrote to the actress in hopes that she would personally respond as to how comfortable she found her new bedding. Explaining the need to discontinue the use of inner spring coils due to the shortage of high-grade steel because of wartime needs, he hoped she would still enjoy the mattresses sent her way and write and tell the company what she thought of the product. It is indicative of how happy he was in having Maria advertise his product, and possibly how enamored he was of her, that Simon personally wrote to assure the actress, "This information is not wanted for publicity use, but simply for our own knowledge and study."[40]

Universal's reaction to Royal Crown cola's proposed third generation of advertisements with Montez was the perfect summation of her precarious position with the studio after *Sudan* wrapped and they argued over *Frontier Gal.* In January 1945 Royal Crown approached the studio about making a new set of ads with Maria. Harry Ormiston in Universal's publicity department wanted to accept the offer and pointed out to Universal management that it should demand a high fee because "after all, Montez is a top box office name." When writing back to Royal Crown, Ormiston, in perfect summation of the studio's view of its star, urged the company to make the ad "as sexy as possible." He also used the occasion to point out the "disconcerting" problem that *Sudan* would not be released until March 1945 with no other Montez features to follow for months. A proposed ad in the May issue of *Good Housekeeping* would not help Universal much. He noted that *Salome* would be released on April 20 starring their new find, Yvonne De Carlo. He thought she might be perfect for a Royal Crown campaign and volunteered to send along "a few pictures" of Yvonne so the advertiser "would know what she looks like."[41]

As the battle continued over *Frontier Gal,* not only did advertisers continue to clamor for Maria's services, she was offered the best radio part of her career for the *Old Gold Comedy Theater.* Radio was at its apex as an entertainment medium in the mid-1940s and featured several programs great and small that helped publicize Hollywood. It was a vital part of any actor's career and the studios were always trying to get their players on one of the shows. Since Maria could not sing and as yet none of her movies had been dramatized on radio, she mostly appeared as herself or slight variations of her established persona, starting with the Cresta Blanca and Bob Hope shows in February and March 1943.

Montez continued portraying the sexy persona she and Universal had created for her in a number of other radio shows. She again played herself on

Maria was a guest on numerous radio shows. Here she is with Ed Gardner, the tavern manager on *Duffy's Tavern,* who also believes it pays to show a little leg. (Courtesy of the Wisconsin Historical Society.)

the *Jack Carson Show* on November 10, 1943, receiving $1,000 ($15,000 in 2021) for her appearance after a day of rehearsal. Eight months later she was volunteering her time on the Armed Forces Radio Show *Mail Call.* Announcer Bob Hope did a South Seas island skit with her, aided by Eddie (Rochester) Anderson and the man of a thousand voices, Mel Blanc. She joined Milton Berle on his *Let Yourself Go* program on October 3, 1944, and one month later she again guested as herself on *Duffy's Tavern.* The show was required to mention at least once that she was a Universal player and was appearing in *Bowery to Broadway,* and her price escalated to $1,250.

Three days after attending the seventeenth annual Academy Awards at Grauman's Chinese Theater on March 15, 1945, Maria was in a skit called "Magic Carpet Cannibals" on the *Charlie McCarthy Show* aired from Williams Field at Chandler, Arizona, southeast of Phoenix. Maria's film mate from *That Night in Rio* was the announcer. Don Ameche introduced her as "the very charming and exotic Maria Montez." The bit with Charlie not only played off of Montez's roles in the Universal easterns, it also allowed McCarthy to happily pant over her as they flew over Williams Field on a flying carpet. Ameche was relegated to being the tail gunner on the carpet. Charlie had Maria right up front as the co-pilot. The biggest laugh in the show came when Ameche asked if they had a de-icer on the carpet. Charlie replies, "Yes, she's sittin' right beside me." The lines given to Maria are to set up Charlie. She says, "Charlie, you're so kind, so clever, so sweet." He responds, "You're so [pants three times]." The carpet finally crashes and the trio must confront the cannibal chief. Ameche, a Kenosha, Wisconsin, native whose father was born in Italy, starts slowly talking to the chief in American-accented Italian. Maria lets loose a machine-gun barrage of Spanish that could only come from a native speaker. The chief looks at them and asks if anyone around here speaks English. Not Shakespeare, but the military crowd ate it up.[42]

While *Frontier Gal* was being filmed without Maria, she had signed on for her one leading part on an episodic radio program. She was booked to star on the May 13, 1945, show of Harold Lloyd's *Old Gold Comedy Theater.* The radio play was to be a half-hour rendition of the 1934 movie *She Loves Me Not.* Maria played a cabaret dancer (whose name was changed to Dolores Lopez from the original Curly Flagg to explain her accent). The story line had Maria hiding out in a Princeton University dorm room with two male students (co-stars Tom Drake and Freddie Bartholomew) after witnessing a murder. The killer pursued her, while the two Princeton students were as befuddled by her presence as the real-life Harvard freshmen had been four years earlier. On top of this, the father of one of the students owned a movie studio that the dancer was desperate to get into. It all came out right in the end, of course, with the crook arrested and Maria meeting the studio head.

Montez played her part well and was quite funny. She did sometimes talk too fast, but she was generally understandable and the audience laughs came in all the right places. As in her films, Maria was imperious, dominating every scene she was in. The strength of her personality registered well on the radio, but the limitation imposed by her accent was an even more obvious problem. Maria had been studying with Russian-born English-language coach Dr. Simon Mitchneck since early in 1944. But clearly there was still work to be done.[43]

The *Old Gold* program did little to further Maria's high ambitions. It did not lead to more character work on episodic radio programs or change the static view of her held by Universal and the rest of Hollywood. Even sadder in the face of Maria's often-stated desire to be appreciated for her acting was her nonappearance on the March 21, 1947, *Hollywood Tour* show. Rod Cameron was not only pushing their movie *Pirates of Monterey,* he gushed away about Yvonne De Carlo and their recently completed *Salome, Where She Danced.* In what was largely the story of her Hollywood career, Maria was reduced to a simple object of lust. A dialogue between Cameron and Cal York, host and *Photoplay* gossip columnist, went out over the airwaves:

> CAMERON: Take Maria Montez for example . . .
> YORK: I'd love to . . .
> CAMERON: Well, I got the gun-smuggler role . . .
> YORK: I'd like to smuggle up to Maria myself.
> CAMERON: The word, Cal, is snuggle.
> YORK: You say your lines and I'll say mine.

This bit of dialogue was sent to Universal for its approval since it was one of their stars being discussed. The studio gave it.[44]

The radio work came along at just the right time. Montez had little to do at Universal after the late August 1944 completion of *Sudan.* The studio kept pitching *Frontier Gal* to her and she kept rejecting it. Since her own studio was so reluctant to find a modern dramatic role for her, she looked elsewhere. She contacted Warner Brothers producer Jerry Wald who, she heard, was interested in adopting James M. Cain's 1937 novel *Serenade.* It would certainly be an uphill struggle given that the chief female protagonist was a Mexican prostitute. It seems an odd choice for Maria, but she was determined to find a dramatic role. Plus, as with her previous effort to land the part of Dona Sol in *Blood and Sand,* her accent would fit the role. This didn't work out. Warner Brothers would eventually film *Serenade* in 1956 with producer Henry Blanke. The female character had become a bullfighter's daughter, played by Sarita Montiel.[45]

In June 1945, a few weeks before Maria's work on the *Old Gold Comedy Theater,* Universal suspended her. She was taking a big chance but her formidable mind was made up. Maria had congratulated Olivia de Havilland on her successful 1944 lawsuit against Warner Brothers, which prohibited the studios from attaching the time an actor was suspended to the time on his or her contract. She was soon to take advantage of that new freedom. Maria had a new house, three sisters living with her, and a husband just back from overseas duty. Tough time to have your source of income dry up. But the single-minded determination that drove her from the Dominican to New York and on to Hollywood burned as brightly as ever now that she was a bona fide movie star. She kept telling interviewers that she wanted to be in a movie where she could prove herself as a dramatic actress. If doing that called for a suspension, then Maria would be suspended. So Maria's paychecks from her studio ceased. *Frontier Gal* would go on without her.

Meanwhile, as Maria's agent Louis Shurr argued with Universal and its lawyers, she kept in touch with the columnists as always, pleading her case for a serious part. Toward the end of June, Montez used some of her suspension time to meet with columnist Erskine Johnson at her home on Tower Road. Her discussion with Johnson certainly could not have endeared her to Universal as she continued the themes she had expressed to Pete Martin several months earlier. She thought the recently drafted Jon Hall was luckier than she since "the Army liberated him from Universal." She continued on her well-established theme that the studio would not let her branch out. She claimed Universal refused her request to buy the rights for the Ben Ames Williams novel *The Strange Woman* for just this reason. It is the story of a charming but heartless woman who uses her beauty and allure to manipulate the men in the story, which is set in Bangor, Maine, from the 1820s to the Civil War. It was exactly the kind of movie Montez now wanted to do. "I've spent five years doing the same story over and over again," she told Johnson. "It's such a bore. The only cost of my scripts has been what they have to pay the stenographers to re-type the last one with new character names." Maria flatly told the columnist she would remain on suspension until her studio offered her a dramatic role.[46]

Since she had some free time and a husband back from the war, Maria and Aumont managed to get away to San Francisco for a pleasure trip for several days after his final demobilization from the French army in June. Since she wasn't going to the lot, Montez also had the chance to help her friend May Mann, columnist and author, plan her August 26 wedding to concert singer and wartime aviation executive Alfred Leon. It was a true Hollywood event. Not only were Maria Montez and MGM's Kay Williams the bridesmaids, Joe E. Brown gave away the bride and the ceremony, with 250 guests, took place in the garden of Rudolf Valentino's former home Falcon Lair. The property had been owned by wealthy South American man-about-town Juan Romero, who sold it to actress Ann Harding because he got tired of being constantly referred to as the man living in Valentino's house. But he sold it with the stipulation that he would not have to move out until September 1 so his friend May Mann could marry there as he promised her.[47]

Besides the dedicated work of Louis Shurr, who kept reminding Universal executives of how successful his client's films had been, the studio must have got a bit of a shock when it started getting so many calls and letters supporting Maria from theater owners and film distributors all over the country who wanted a new movie from her and urged the end of her suspension. Her hard work in maintaining contact with those who actually brought the Hollywood product to movie fans paid off when she had to plead her case to Universal to change her contract to reflect her desire for modern roles. Despite Universal leadership's anger with the star, exhibitors and advertisers had nothing but positive relations with Montez. Maria never felt like she had to fight advertisers for respect the way she did the rulers of Universal. Advertisers and especially theater owners made it evident they wanted and valued her services.[48]

Louella Parsons thought Maria would be making up with Universal soon. She was right. It took a three-month suspension, but she got what she asked for. The new contract she signed in September 1945 reimbursed Montez for lost pay and gave her more money per week, top billing in any movie in which she appeared, approval of leading men and directors, and the power to accept or reject parts. Universal had no choice but to comply with its star's demands to give "a wrestle" to a modern dramatic role. *Tangier* would be her big chance. The studio's publicity department set about preparing the public to expect a new Montez in the picture. One of the first press releases issued on the movie promised, "Maria Montez gets the first modern dramatic role of her career in Universal's '*Tangier*' in which she portrays a Spanish girl who conducts a six-year death hunt for her hated enemy. Studio officials say the picture will end the 'color fantasies' that Maria has made for the past five years."[49]

Montez was ready and eager to get back to work once her suspension was ended by the new contract. She finally had a movie more to her liking. *Tangier* was meant to be a vaguely film noirish postwar intrigue type of movie. It would be a modern story with Maria being dressed by Travis Banton. Charles Boyer was nowhere to be seen, but neither were Jon Hall or any horses, camels, or jungle cats. But it wouldn't be Montez if there were no complications. The big experiment started filming on September 24, 1945, after final script approval had been won from the Hays Office. The censors had made sure the

Maria in a Travis Banton gown with dancing partner Kent Taylor in *Tangier.*

early torture scenes with "excessive brutality and gruesomeness" were deleted. The dancers were officially warned about not executing "unacceptable bumps or forward motions of their bodies." Maria's various on-screen clothes changes were to be "handled with care" behind a large screen. As usual, Maria's breasts were a concern. When the German agent struggles with her to retrieve the diamond she had placed in her cleavage Breen demanded it be handled "with the greatest possible care to avoid any offensiveness."[50]

Tangier

There are obvious echoes of *Casablanca* in the opening scenes of *Tangier.* The camera zooms in on a map of North Africa at the Straits of Gibraltar to find the city of Tangier. It then moves from the busy streets to the lobby of the Ritz Hotel. While a sinister German checks in downstairs, upstairs disgraced American journalist Paul Kenyon (Robert Paige) tries to get hotel gadabout Pepe (Sabu) to introduce him to the popular dancer Rita (Maria Montez). Later, Rita is on-stage engaged in a hot dance with her partner, Ramon (Kent Taylor). She slips off-stage to be replaced by Dolores (Louise Allbritton), who is wearing a wig and the same dress as Rita. This subterfuge allows Rita to sneak into the room of a recently arrived German to search for papers linking him to the elusive Spanish Fascist Balizar. She finds a large diamond and hides it in her cleavage. The German returns, they struggle, and Ramon kills him with a knife. The couple goes downstairs to finish the dance routine.

It turns out Rita was not there to steal anything. She was looking for information. She suspected the man who rented the room had ties to Balizar, who tortured and murdered her father and two brothers in Fascist Spain. She took the diamond hoping it would ensure contact with Balizar. Meanwhile, she has to deal with Colonel Artiego (Preston Foster), the local police chief, Paul Kenyon, and Ramon—all of whom are in love with her. Amid much dancing and even more pursuing, Rita keeps looking for the elusive Balizar. Finally, an agent from the Allied Commission for the Recovery of Nazi Loot, whom the conspirators wrongly thought was the murderous Fascist they sought, informs them that Colonel Artiego is really Balizar, who wants the diamonds to escape Tangier. Ramon attacks Artiego and is shot. Dolores says she knows where the diamonds are. She takes the colonel up to Pepe's room, where they are hidden in his guitar, returns to the elevator, and pushes the operator out. She runs the elevator into the top of its mechanism, dislodging the pulleys. The elevator crashes to the basement, killing Dolores and Balizar. Again referencing *Casablanca,* Paul Kenyon is at the airport being deported to Lisbon, where he will catch a plane to America. Rita rushes to join him and they start their journey together to the United States.

Maria had loudly and tenaciously exclaimed to anyone who would listen that in *Tangier* she finally had a part that would change her career. It did not. The saddest part was that while Maria handles the dramatic demands of the role adequately, she seems ordinary. Something she never did in the Neverland movies. The whole film seems like one of the hurried, second-rate B movies cranked out relentlessly by Universal prior to International signing on. Up-and-coming Universal contract player Ella Raines had been initially cast in *Tangier* but was withheld by the studio. Even so competent an actress as Barbara Stanwyck would have been challenged trying to make something of this movie, no matter who her co-stars were. In *Tangier* Preston Foster successfully projected the cultured swinishness expected of high-ranking screen Nazis, but Robert Paige as Maria's love interest and Kent Taylor as her tragically jealous dance partner were barely adequate. The only memorable aspects of the picture were the Travis Banton gowns, the spectacular elevator crash, and the always amiable Sabu singing "Polly Wolly Doodle" and "She'll Be Comin' 'round the Mountain" to hotel guests. Clearly, Universal saw the film as a way to get Maria to shut up. Not as a way to improve and expand the career of someone the studio considered a valuable asset.[51]

In short, *Tangier* appears recycled and simply screams "B movie." Screenwriting at Universal had traditionally been one of the weakest links in its film production. It actually named the agency chasing the evil Balizar the Allied Commission for the Recovery of Nazi Loot. Seriously, Nazi Loot. When a name was needed for a similar fictitious organization that dispatched Edward G. Robinson to track down a Nazi played by Orson Welles in *The Stranger* (1946), it was plausibly called the Allied War Crimes Commission. Set design could hardly have been more minimal and cheapjack in *Tangier*. The neon sign on the hotel simply spells out "Ritz"—a very pale imitation of the ornate "Rick's Café Americain" sign in *Casablanca*. The entrance to the hotel at the beginning is shown at night. There are none of the teaming, atmospheric, vaguely dangerous streets you see in the opening scenes of the Warner Brothers film.

Universal did nothing to help Montez establish the new persona she so desperately sought. No outside talent was brought in to write the screenplay or star opposite her to strengthen the movie. The reviewer for the *New York Herald Tribune* could not have been more accurate when he pointed out that Maria does not "get much help from the supporting players." Producer Paul Malvern picked contract director George Waggner to work from a M. M. Musselman and Monty Collins script. The fifty-day shooting schedule ran to fifty-six, and the budget ran $75,000 over the estimate. But despite all that, the film was no more than an adequate programmer. It cost $1,016,103 and barely broke even at the box office. Maria had accepted a suspension and left herself open to replacement by Yvonne De Carlo for a movie her studio treated as commonplace. It changed nothing.[52]

The critics did not rush to embrace *Tangier* after its April 23, 1946, opening. Even the trade papers saw it as needing a second feature to bring in crowds. *Variety* called it a "good romantic melodrama spiced with murder, mystery and Maria Montez glamor." The *Hollywood Review* warned fans that this was not the typical Montez Technicolor spectacular they might expect. Their reviewer also thought Universal would have to supply her with a stronger supporting cast if the studio planned to keep her in this type of role. Although noting that "once or twice she even makes her mark on the picture as an actress," as usual, it is Maria's opulent physicality that receives the most comment. The newspaper assures its readers that she is "quite as luscious" in black and white as she had been in Technicolor.[53]

The general newspapers were equally disappointed. The *Hollywood Citizen News* thought, "Maria Montez looks properly alluring in her expansive wardrobe," but the movie was "pretty much of a letdown." *Commonweal* agreed with the *New York Times*'s Bosley Crowther, who found *Tangier*'s themes "so tired and stale that it gets tiresome even with Maria Montez appearing as a Spanish dancer." She is as beautifully turned out as ever, and "fairly exudes glamour." But except for Travis Banton's gowns, the film "looks like a budget production." The *Independent Exhibitors Film Bulletin* thought this "confusing and cliché-bound spy melodrama" was for "Maria Montez fans only." In the "Now Playing" section in its Sunday edition, the *Kansas City Star* rated movies from bad to good with the illustration of a stick figure sitting in a chair, clapping in a chair, or standing up and clapping. For *Tangier* he is anchored to the chair, frowning. But in what had to be the most crushing review to Maria, Joe Pihodna in the *New York Herald Tribune* thought her portrayal of the leader of a group intent on finding the Fascist who murdered her family "is a bit too much for Maria Montez. A handsomely mounted girl, who can swish as engagingly as anyone in a negligee, Miss Montez finds the road to Tangier a tough one."[54]

All this was a far cry from the studio-generated publicity for the film. The one-sheet poster promised "the magnificent Maria Montez, playing her first modern role, with an important cast." Besides lots of photographs and articles about the stars and the making of *Tangier,* the press book provided a review of the movie for use by small-town newspapers. In the press book review, it is an "action-packed picture" that is "highly satisfactory from all viewpoints." Maria's acting ability is noted as "impressive" in the "first modern role of her career." This matched the studio's press handouts, which had "Maria Montez impressive in modern drama" and promised moviegoers they "will have a surprise when they see Miss Montez . . . in her first serious melodramatic role in '*Tangier.*'" There were also filler pieces about the twenty-eight different nations represented on the set, starting with Maria and Sabu.

Another color short piece was called "Auto Relic Has Role in Movie." The article claimed Maria was sure she had seen a car used in the filming before. It had very distinctive headlights and horn. Turned out it had supposedly been owned by Rafael Trujillo and she remembered it from Ciudad Trujillo.[55]

Maria had taken a huge risk by being so vocal and insistent about her aims. She made the same point over and over again for two years in a whole series of interviews. After finally getting the type of part she wanted in *Tangier* she was very explicit about what she hoped it would mean to her career in an interview with Virginia MacPherson of the United Press. "I am a happy woman at last. . . . And why? Because they have finally decided to let me do something besides show off my beautiful body. They are letting me act." MacPherson noted that Montez finally had the sort of part she had been demanding, "a picture where the public can see that she is also a great actress. A picture that didn't have a single Technicolor desert in it, or a horse, or those Queen of the Nile gauze costumes. . . . For years Miss Montez has been waging a one-woman campaign to get some clothes over her curves. But she didn't get far because Universal discovered it could sell almost any picture as long as it included the Montez body—scantily draped with transparent cheesecloth. . . . Hollywood is a show town . . . and like the pink-spangled circus queen who draws the eyes of all to the top of the big tent, Maria sparkled and spangled too." But now she had the chance to do more than merely sparkle. Montez told MacPherson, "I have made eight costume pictures and that is enough. By overusing the hen, you can stop the golden egg. And I don't want to stop that for a long time." *Tangier* was meant to be the gateway to this future, but it was not a success and only further convinced Universal that Montez did not fit into its future plans. Maria had loudly and tenaciously gambled and lost.[56]

There were two other dramas happening during the filming of *Tangier* besides Maria desperately wanting to change her Hollywood roles. The strike declared by the Conference of Studio Unions (CSU) against the International Alliance of Theatrical Stage Employees (IATSE) for control of set decorators had been in effect for six months when *Tangier* began filming in late September. It culminated in the pitched battle between strikers and workers who were trying to cross the picket lines at Warner Brothers on Black Friday, October 5, 1945. Eventually the CSU was accused of having Communist leadership and lost the fight with IATSE. The unions concentrated on the larger studios so Universal was able to keep filming with a mixture of strike-breakers and nonunion crew.[57]

The second drama was more personal to Maria and worked out very well for her. She was pregnant. As long ago as March 1944 she had told Louella

Parsons that she could not wait for Aumont to return so they could start on a family. As for Jean-Pierre, his experiences in the war had made him more determined than ever to have children. On his return from Europe, Aumont told an interviewer, "Far from being reluctant to raise a family in a world where there can be such turmoil, I am anxious to have children for I feel that what we are fighting for will bear fruit for them."[58]

The couple's hopes were realized when her pregnancy was confirmed in early June 1945. The previous few months had been tough for Maria. Not only was she on suspension from Universal, she also experienced a series of health problems. On June 30, 1945, she was admitted to St. Vincent's, the leading Catholic hospital in Los Angeles, suffering from diphtheria. She was recovering at home after July 2 and was well enough to attend Walter Wanger's July 20 party for England's major film producer, distributor, and exhibitor, J. Arthur Rank, who was in Los Angeles to discuss a possible merger with Universal Studios. Since Maria was not going to the lot, in July she and Jean-Pierre had a chance to escape to Big Bear in the local San Gabriel Mountains for a short vacation. After their return Montez soon found herself back at St. Vincent Hospital suffering from a severe cold.[59]

Nonetheless, Maria was a trooper. She was right on time for her first day on the set of *Tangier* on September 24, 1945. Universal was alerted as to her pregnancy and Maria had a letter from her pediatrician, Dr. Bernard Hanley, indicating that her work on the picture had to be completed no later than November 15 so she could get sufficient rest prior to giving birth. After her various illnesses in July, one of the great benefits of *Tangier* was that it was shot entirely on Universal City sound stages. All she had to do of a physical nature was change costumes and take a couple of close-up steps; her double did all the complicated dancing. There were no horses to ride, freezing pools to bathe in, or flimsy getups to wear. Plus, the kinds of dresses Maria was called on to wear in *Tangier* allowed them to be let out slightly during filming.

Look magazine took a photo of Maria working a telephone switchboard during her pregnancy for its article "How the Stars Would Cast Themselves." She's wearing a large smock loosely cinched at the waist. The magazine said she "camouflaged her famous curves for sake of decorum." Actually, she was covering her pregnancy. Universal found another way to get publicity out of the pregnancy without showing her in that state, which would have been very rare at the time. The studio issued a behind-the-scenes still for publication called "Stork Forecast." The photograph featured assistant director Charles Gould dangling a gold ring on a string over her stomach. If the ring goes in a circle, it will be a girl. If it hangs in a straight line, a boy. Gould's ring just

The new family at home on Tower Road. The sweater Maria is wearing must have been a favorite—it appears in photos over at least ten years.

hung there, indicating a coming male child. Maria firmly believed she was going to have a boy and urged Jean-Pierre to think up a suitable name.[60]

Well, so much for folk beliefs. Maria's last scene on *Tangier* was filmed on November 14 while her double, Doreen Mulvey, was kept busy until the 20th. On February 14, 1946, she was back at St. Vincent's Hospital. Maria gave birth by caesarian section to an eight-pound, three-ounce daughter she and Jean-Pierre named Maria Christina (after the mom and her great-grandmother). The baby's godfather was Charles Boyer. The godmother was Maria's sister

Lucita, who was married to French writer Jean Roy. The date was originally to be February 13, since that was Aumont's lucky number. He was overridden by Maria's astrologer Carroll Righter, who saw fourteen as a more astrologically propitious number. Jean-Pierre went along with the astrologer even though he was beginning to find him "a bit cumbersome." Within a month Aumont was trying to get permission to obtain enough wood (the material was still being rationed) to build a guesthouse on the existing ten-room Beverly Hills home that now contained a new baby to go along with two parents, two sisters, one visiting French journalist, and two dogs.[61]

When she was six weeks old, Maria Christina was whisked off to Universal to be introduced to her mother's co-workers and photographed for publicity releases. Further publicity came to her mother when Hedda Hopper noted that all of the gorgeous stars came to a huge party for Bing Crosby with the exceptions of the two new mothers Judy Garland and Maria Montez. Constance Palmer was one of the many journalists assigned to cover Maria's motherhood. She wrote an article for *Silver Screen* called "The Happy Aumonts." When Maria welcomed the writer to her home to meet the baby, the first thing she did was happily whack her diaphragm to show that she had lost her pregnancy weight, then Maria showed the scribe around and introduced her to Christina. Palmer found her ecstatic. "A woman hasn't lived until she's had a baby!" she tells the writer. Palmer tagged along when Maria, baby in arms, made quite a different entrance to the Universal commissary than the kind she was so famous for making six years earlier.[62]

Tangier opened in Los Angeles on April 23, New York on May 1, and across the country over the next two months. Universal, trying to go along with the program of declaring a new Montez in the film, proclaimed "The Modern Montez" on the snipe attached to one of the key Ray Jones portraits issued by the studio to publicize the film. The publicity department wrote, "Maria Montez, tired of being a sketchily-dressed Queen of Technicolor never-never lands, determined to capture a modern role in a story nearer reality. . . . The new Montez, therefore, as lovely as ever but this time lavishly dressed and not in Technicolor, can soon be seen in Universal's '*Tangier,*' a modern drama of intrigue and murder."[63]

As always, even as it publicized her new turn, the studio felt it had to find ways to placate Maria and keep her sufficiently in line to play the next role it had in mind for her. On March 14, publicity chief John Joseph wrote a memo to Maurice Bergman in Universal's New York office. The studio wanted to get Montez back into Technicolor following her brief foray into black and white. The new movie was *Pirates of Monterey* and Joseph saw trouble on the horizon,

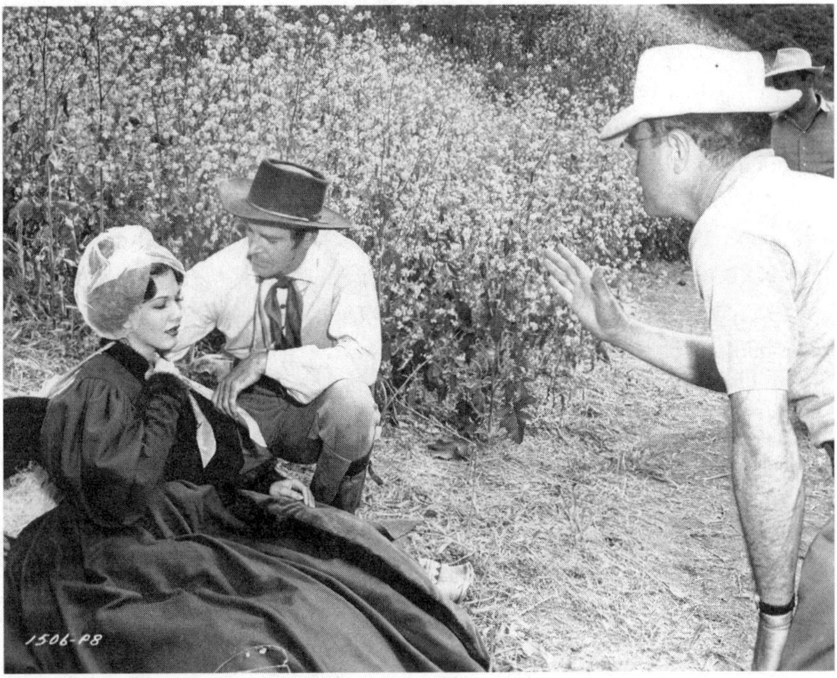

Director Al Werker rehearses Maria and Rod Cameron for a scene in the wildflower fields at Lompoc for *Pirates of Monterey.* The hair net protecting her coiffure will be removed when the cameras roll.

noting, "Confidentially, she doesn't like the script very well and I don't blame her." Proving the studio's rising belief that Montez had become that most dreaded of contract players, someone who was "difficult," Joseph warned Bergman that New York had better properly advertise her latest picture. He warned, "If '*Tangier*' is simply passed off in advertising for New York City, she is going to have fits and everybody will have that much more trouble getting her into the [next] picture." He noted that Maria was already convinced the advertising would be insufficient and had friends in New York who would monitor the newspapers for her. Joseph ended his memo with the warning, "There will be difficulty if nobody is able to send her any clippings about '*Tangier.*'"[64]

Whatever her qualms about the script for *Pirates of Monterey,* Maria showed up bright and early on April 26, 1946, for the first day of shooting. She was not the only one unhappy with the prospective movie. Seven different writers would not come up with a finished script until three weeks into the start of production. The budget would not be approved until May 25. The film's three major locations were Universal City, the beach at Palos Verdes, and Lompoc, California, with its completely restored (courtesy of the Civilian Conservation Corps) La Purisima Mission. Producer Paul Malvern signed on studio director Alfred Werker, who had helmed his first film in 1925. Cinematography would be in the experienced hands of Hal Mohr, whose credits included shooting the first talkie, *The Jazz Singer.* W. Howard Greene would be on hand as usual to consult on color photography. The picture wrapped on July 20, six days under its seventy-three-day schedule, by making extensive use of second-unit filming on the three shooting locations.

Even at that, the film cost $1,389,102.99, which was almost $140,000 over what had been a top budget for Universal. Maria's Universal salary topped out at $50,000 ($531,300 in 2021 dollars) plus a $5,000 bonus for her work on *Monterey.* As her contract stipulated, she received top billing, with her name in the largest print. Her salary was more than twice Rod Cameron's flat $22,500. Also, as usual, Maria's Travis Banton–designed clothes were by far the most expensive item to come from the costume department, at $11,500. The second female lead, Gale Sondergaard, was allotted $2,500 for her wardrobe. Like the rest of the women's dresses, Sondergaard's were designed by Universal's longtime designer Vera West. It would be her last wardrobe assignment in a twenty-year career. She committed suicide on June 29, 1947, two days after her forty-ninth birthday, leaving the cryptic and never fully explained note, "This is the only way. I am tired of being blackmailed."[65]

The various scripts submitted to the Hays Office found minor opposition from the censors. There was some concern that in the first draft submitted on March 11, 1946, a conversation between Phillip Kent and Maria "seemed offensively sex suggestive." This was rectified by the time a second script was submitted a month later. This time they were concerned with a fight scene that had Mikhail Rasumny repeatedly banging an enemy's head on the floor. Breen once again worried about Maria's cleavage, cautioning Universal "to make certain that her gown covers her breasts at all times." The next script came along two weeks after that, and it was deemed "unacceptable under the provisions of the Production Code because of the inference of a sex affair between the two leads." On June 6 all the objections had been met and the script finally received its okay from the Hays Office.[66]

Pirates of Monterey

In the opening of the movie a card comes up announcing, "The young republic of Mexico" will fight the "ravaging hordes of Royalist pirates to safeguard her richest jewel—California." *Pirates of Monterey* opens with American soldier of fortune Phillip Kent (Rod Cameron) leading a caravan through Mexican-controlled California in the early 1840s. He is bringing guns to the presidio in Monterey from Mexico City with his aide, Sergeant Pio (Mikhail Rasumny), to fight the Spanish royalists trying to reestablish control over California. Along the way they rescue Marguerita (Maria Montez) and her dueña, Filomena (Tamara Shayne), after their carriage crashes. Pio repairs it so the women can get to Los Angeles. Having missed the monthly stage to Santa Barbara, Marguerita and her duenna hide themselves in one of Kent's wagons. They are discovered en route and before long, Kent and Marguerita find themselves falling in love. They enjoy the Fiesta of the Harvest in Santa Barbara, but when Kent looks for Marguerita the next morning she is gone, making him fear she is a royalist spy.

Once he reaches the California capital, Kent delivers the rapid-firing rifles to the governor, his old friend Lieutenant Carlos Ortega (Philip Reed). They are needed in the fight against the Spanish royalist pirates who are trying to wrest control of California from the Mexican authorities. It turns out the reason Marguerita was so determined to get to Monterey was to fulfill an arranged marriage to Lieutenant Ortega. But she has fallen in love with Kent, who is loath to go behind the back of his old friend. Eventually Kent and Marguerita wind up together after escaping from the pirates and helping in the fight to defeat the enemies of Mexico. Ortega gives them his blessing and the couple rides off together in a carriage driven by Pio and Filomena.

Pirates of Monterey gave Maria a second, though less challenging, chance to stretch her acting skills. The movie may have been a historical piece, but at least she was not running around the screen in a sarong or diaphanous gown. Her accent even fit the part as she was playing a well-born lady from Mexico. She says a few words in Spanish in the film, even if it is only pronouncing California place-names. She sounds so melodic in Spanish in a way she never sounded in English. Maria always did imperious well and that was all that was called for in this movie except when she was flirting with Rod Cameron. It is indicative of her roles in her whole career that in the fight to overcome the royalists who have captured them, Montez doesn't just stand about while the men fight. She crowns the guard who bursts into their room with a candleholder so she, Kent, and Ortega can escape. She also got her wish as expressed to interviewer Pete Martin—Jon Hall and the rest of her established crew were nowhere to be found. One thing that did not change is that Maria again played an upper-class character who knew her mind and aggressively pursued what she wanted while two men loved her madly.

Never the passive bystander, Maria is about to crown an evildoer in *Pirates of Monterey.*

Her reviews remained much the same. As usual, Maria's lush physicality was lauded. Walter Winchell, who never cared for her performances but consistently admired her sensuality, noted of this one, "Maria's co-star is her torso." *Box Office Digest* said she "gives the proper decorative touch to the top role." The *Los Angeles Times* found her "sultry." *Variety* said she was "a gay and exciting eyeful." The *New York Times* actually rated her "bosomy." With the exception of the trades—*Daily Variety* lauded *Monterey* as having "all the ingredients of a top grosser"—reviewers saw the film as a barely acceptable, completely predictable action movie. Other than his positive words for Maria's breasts, Bosley Crowther at the *New York Times* summed up the general view of the movie, noting the script "was obviously ground out mechanically by an old typewriter on the Universal lot, set for 200 pages, while the writers played gin or slept." The performers did not rise above the trite material. "This swords-and-mantillas horse-opera is . . . walked through by bored and weary actors who have worn blisters on their feet in this same groove."[67]

The animosity in the Universal front office toward Maria and the obvious fact that Rod Cameron was the main character of the film did not diminish her centrality to virtually every review of *Monterey.* Alton Cook's review in the *New York World-Telegram* is a perfect case in point. He saw it as her movie regardless of who had more screen time. Nicely echoing Universal's position on Maria's career, Cook wrote, "Maria Montez' name has become symbolic of Technicolor extravaganzas full of lightly clad maidens for whom handsome heroes perform prodigious feats of daring-do [*sic*]. Her latest, *'Pirates of Monterey,'* runs true to formula except that Miss Montez is wearing much heavier clothing lately. Otherwise, the picture follows the same nonsensical pattern of all the rest of the Montez series." Noting that "the Montez fan is an indulgent soul," Cook claims that all that forbearance will be necessary "to get much more than the mildest of jolts out of her latest film."

Clipping services would have made it certain that Universal saw these reviews from around the country. But the *Hollywood Reporter* made it easy for them. It published a page titled "Critics Wield Cutlasses on *'Pirates of Monterey.'*" It contained ten negative reviews, from Bosley Crowther in the *New York Times* to Rose Pelswick of the New York *Journal-American*. She dismissed *Pirates*: "Starring Maria Montez, the picture resembles nothing so much as a fancy-dress ball." Even worse came from Jesse Zunser of *Cue* magazine. He condemned the waste of "a great deal of money and hard-to-get Technicolor film." Universal's own survey of thirteen women's organizations got a similar response. They agreed that an opportunity for a great epic of eighteenth-century California was "completely lost in their artificial, pseudo-historical social drama. . . . The entire production lacks reality and conviction." At best, they thought it might be okay for kids.[68]

The publicity machine at Universal tried to make moviegoers *Monterey* conscious, but it had to do so without Maria's help. The studio was able to get some mileage out of using Maria's younger sister Consuelo Gracia (billed as Julia Andre) in a small part as a noblewoman. At least Maria did not drive Maggy Maskel to distraction by telling interviewers that her latest movie was a "steenker." But as her alienation from Universal thickened, Montez expressed no interest in playing a personal role in publicizing *Monterey*. It must have seemed a step back for her. It was not the broad character she would have played in *Frontier Gal*, but neither was it the sort of modern, dramatic role she had set her heart on playing.[69]

You would never know any of this from reading Universal's *Pirates of Monterey* press book. Naturally it was all sunshine and light. There was an article on the La Purisima Mission at Lompoc, which had also been used in *For Whom the Bell Tolls*. Its natural white color would not register properly in Technicolor so it had to be painted a tan color and then repainted white after filming completed. There were several photographs of Maria and Rod

Maria on the set of *Pirates of Monterey* with her sister Consuelo. The snipe reads: "Maria is shown giving sister Consuelo a few pointers in the fine art of posing for 'cheesecake.' 'It's an important must in the career of any ambitious actress,' the established Montez informed her movie ambitious sister."

Cameron to express them as the prime love interest in the film. One of the longest articles was called "Here's How Maria Montez Fascinates the Male Sex." She suggests wearing perfume and perfectly done makeup, being sincere while wearing striking hats, and never wearing slacks. She had started working on being fascinating ever since her arrival in Hollywood, and

Universal could only conclude, "Judging from the results, she did a pretty good job of it."[70]

Rod Cameron carried the load when it came to live publicity. As previously noted, he appeared on Cal York's *Hollywood Tour.* He was also heard on *The Coast Guard Show* talking up the movie. Bob Rains, the executive in charge of radio promotion at Universal, dreamed up a tie-in with *Heart's Desire.* The idea of the show was to have listeners write letters about what their heart's desire would be, with the winner's wish being granted. The tie-in with *Pirates of Monterey* involved Universal buying and delivering a pony to the child who wrote the best letter explaining how this would improve his or her life. Rains thought this would be a prime way to advertise the movie since most of the action, "except the love making," takes place on horses. He suggested that the three ponies eventually given away be advertised as the offspring of the horses ridden by Maria and Rod Cameron in the movie. The only part Montez would play in this promotion was the mention of her "sponsoring" the giveaway.[71]

Maria still figured prominently in the publicity releases issued by Universal. An article with six illustrations called "Hollywood Looks to Europe for Century Old Fashions" detailed the extensive research that had been done by the costume department to make sure the look of both her clothes and hairstyles were authentic to 1840s California. Maria's often-stated desire to get away from skimpy costumes was poked fun at in another release titled "History Denies Itself Department." It noted she finally got her wish, but in the one-hundred-degree heat at Lompoc she regretted it. "This is one time I wish my costume was a sarong," Montez is quoted as saying. Maria's daughter was not neglected in the publicity. A release dated May 17, 1946, described a light starting to whine and then make a *wa wa* sound as Maria was to film a love scene with Rod Cameron. Montez quipped, "Sounds just like Maria Christina at feeding time." [72]

But there was no putting a smiley face on *Pirates.* Maria disdained the movie and, a far cry from the Neverland movies, it just barely broke even at the box office. The film looked great, from the opening scenes of the characters riding through wild flowers that come up to the horses' flanks to the haciendas at Monterey. But the whole movie brought meager compensation to Universal after all the *Sturm und Drang* of Montez's suspension and subsequent new contract. To the studio she had become difficult and unable to bring in the crowds to the non-Neverland films she insisted she now wanted to make. It was also aware her seven-year contract was nearing its expiration date.

Maria would not be back on Universal's lot for ten months after wrapping *Pirates.* Her next film would be *Siren of Atlantis,* the independent production assured in her contract filmed on the Goldwyn lot. After that she would be assigned to filming *The Exile* back at Universal. When it was finished, the studio could get rid of her.

9

The Exile

It is hard to think of a grade-B adventure film largely recommended for its vibrant Technicolor like *Pirates of Monterey* as the high point of Maria's last two years of her Universal contract. But it was. The rest of those two years was nothing but one failed project after another, a suspension, a lawsuit over one of the never-filmed movies, and two costly failures, with two more lawsuits that ended her American film career. This frustrating period would culminate in the Aumonts moving to France in August 1948. They would live there for the last three years of Maria's life.

This period of eventual disappointment started off very precipitously. *Tangier* had opened in Los Angeles on April 22, 1946. As she had insisted, Universal was promoting the film as featuring a new Montez. The snipe on the back of one of the most popular photographs distributed by Universal set out exactly what the actress had wanted the film to be. "What more appropriate role for the glamorous Dominican charmer, Maria Montez, than that of a Spanish dancer? That's her assignment in *'Tangier,'* Universal's new mystery-adventure film which gives Maria her first chance at a modern, dress-up role after a long series of Technicolor costume pictures." At least in print, the studio was going along with Montez's demands to escape Neverland.[1]

Following the completion of shooting *Pirates of Monterey* on July 20, 1946, Maria could turn her attention to planning her daughter's christening. As with everything else in the Aumont household, the christening would be an international event. From Jean-Pierre's side, his brother François Villiers flew in from Paris to join his father and stepmother. Maria's mother had heart problems and was unable to come north from Barahona, but her sisters were with her. (A considerable weight had been lifted from Maria's mind when she received word from her mother that all was good with her family after a series of earthquakes had rocked the Dominican Republic.) The theme music at the party was a lullaby for the baby composed in Paris by Louis Beydts and Jean Cocteau called "La fille des étoiles" (Daughter of the Stars).[2]

Montez sparred with Bob Hope again on his radio show on April 16. As usual she was a pure object of lust as Hope and Jerry Colonna vie for her favors as "a beautiful doll" of a dancer in a takeoff on *Tangier.* The independent production team the King Brothers were after her for *The Hunted,* in which she would play the kind of role she so coveted—a modern one with no animals in sight. As with all of the actors who were no longer constrained by a studio contract, Maria's price for her services escalated. Schallert in the *Los Angeles Times* reported she was being offered $150,000 plus 20 percent of profits by the brothers. Charles Rogers, who had known her at Universal and was now an independent producer, wanted both Maria and Jean-Pierre for *Queen of Hearts.* Montez had tried to interest her studio in the story, about the queen of Austria and the emperor Franz Joseph, for years. Her nonprofessional life was also going well. Her sister Consuelo married Maria's press agent, Kenneth Carter, at the 1100 Tower Road home on August 7. The Aumonts attended a welcome home party for Marlene Dietrich. Jean-Pierre had not seen her since their meeting in Italy during the war.[3]

With Maria Christina properly christened, Consuelo happily married, *Pirates of Monterey* being edited, and Jean-Pierre done with *Song of Scheherazade,* the Aumonts were finally ready to take their long delayed French honeymoon. The couple flew out of Los Angeles on August 26, 1946. The baby was left in the care of Lucita. The Aumonts first had a three-day stopover in New York. As always in Maria's life in the United States, there was work to be done, a career to boost. The Aumonts met the *New York Sun*'s Eileen Creelman for an interview at 21. The reporter got an earful from Montez about what was on her mind. As she had been two years earlier when speaking to May Mann, Maria was brutally honest when discussing her career and life. She spoke of Maria Christina, Paris, and movies while her husband "sat by and watched, with amusement and admiration." Maria explained that she felt she looked too "flamboyant" in color. She much preferred herself in black and white. Sadly, "I did only one picture in black and white; but it was not a good one, '*Tangier.*' Next time we shall get a good story; and then you will see." She noted her last picture, *Pirates of Monterey,* was in color and should "make a great deal of money. . . . The children will love it." While she was lamenting her return to color, Montez's old roommate Elizabeth Russell stopped by the table to greet the couple and admire her friend's hat. Maria told her that she meant to wear it in Cannes where she and Jean-Pierre were going for the motion picture festival.[4]

Returning to Eileen Creelman, Montez and Aumont said they had no plans to work in France; they were on a honeymoon. But there was some talk with French producers that they might make a picture there the following year called *Venetian Wedding*. Maria spoke of their daughter and how much she looked like her father, and of the Beverly Hills house filled with sisters, friends, an English teacher, and a secretary. Not surprisingly, given her family upbringing in Barahona, Maria said, "I like it that way, a big house filled with people." The couple was looking forward to making a film together. There may have been vague talk about a future French film, but the couple had definite plans to do *The Scarlet Feather*, about the pirate Jean Lafitte, for Charles Rogers at United Artists. Even if she was talking about working at another studio, for once Montez said something good about Universal. She claimed that since the merger with International, it was "the best studio now, the finest producers, the most able directors." She was ready and eager to work with these talented men because "my acting is so much improved. So, it is time that I have good acting parts. Three years ago, perhaps, I was not ready. Now I have worked and I have studied, and I am ready." She may have been finally embarking on a honeymoon after three years and two months of marriage, but her career was something she worked at all the time.[5]

The couple arrived in Paris on September 5, 1946. Maria Montez was one of the first Hollywood stars to visit France for anything other than a USO show since the war ended. Her great Neverland films were just being released in Europe and she was the wife of a national hero who gave up the cushiest of all possible positions to fight in the Free French Army. They were lionized wherever they went. Maria found a much different Paris than the one she had visited with her first husband a decade before. This time she was not just another foreign tourist, staying in the best hotels with her banker husband. Now she was an American movie star seeing the sights with a native hero who loved the city and knew it intimately. Not only was the couple welcomed by film fans wherever they went, to Maria's delight she met many of the French filmmakers and writers Jean-Pierre had been describing to her. Of particular import was her meeting with Jean Cocteau. Aumont immediately recognized the reason for their instant rapport. He thought both of them were as comfortable living with people as they were with a variety of spirits.

Maria was experiencing a much less complicated welcome from the French than she ever received in the United States. The French never knew her as the world's greatest commissary actress. Plus she was back in a Latin culture, openly admired for her beauty and feminine charms, speaking a language more familiar to her than English, and accepted as a great star without the constant complaint that her movies were ridiculous and she could not act. Also, as mentioned, she was married to a French national hero.[6]

Maria and Jean-Pierre arriving in France for their 1946 honeymoon.

Europeans welcomed the couple as Hollywood's representatives. They were exactly that in southern France on September 20 for the opening of the long-delayed first Cannes Film Festival. The original idea was to inaugurate the festival in September 1939. The German invasion of Poland and the subsequent declaration of war by France led to its cancellation. The 1946 Cannes Film Festival was as much a celebration of the promise of the postwar world as it was of current movies. Much of France was still in ruins, but Jean-Pierre Aumont and Maria Montez symbolized the glamour that could now return. Ray Milland and *The Lost Weekend* won the main awards.[7]

An article called "Montez and Aumont Tour Europe," published soon after the festival, is indicative of how the French viewed the couple. They are presented in the numerous photos as two people in love rather than strictly a pair of movie stars. The key photo of the piece shows Jean-Pierre wielding a gas hose to fill up the car's tank while Maria fumbles around in her purse trying to find the petrol coupons still necessary in postwar France. In Paris they are shown sipping wine at an outdoor café, walking in front of the Eiffel Tower and Arc de Triomphe, and buying ice cream from a street vendor whose cart guarantees "pure sugar." In Marseilles they were photographed in front of a large street-side poster of *Arabian Nights,* just released in that city.[8]

Maria wrote an article for *Photoplay* about the trip to southern France called "This Is My Husband." It is quite the chronicle of the joy she found with Jean-Pierre. Maria is pictured as the methodical one. She had a gown designed in Paris for an event while Aumont had to borrow a tux from a waiter as none were available. She had to make all the hotel reservations as her husband was happy-go-lucky and completely spur-of-the-moment. The car Jean-Pierre borrowed from his brother to show his wife the beauty of France kept breaking down. The two of them wound up pushing it into Cannes. The next day they took a very small airplane, arranged by Jean-Pierre, to the Brussels premiere of *Arabian Nights.* Maria could not have been happier being with her husband, no matter how precarious things might be at times. She concluded, "But for all the upset existence Jean Pierre and I have, I wouldn't dream of existence with anyone else. After all, wouldn't life be dull if Jean Pierre weren't in it to shake it up? And with him, life may be confused—but also it is quite, quite wonderful." It's no wonder *Screen Romances* noted about their relationship, "Were we planning to write a love story, we'd have great difficulty to keep from modeling our hero and heroine after two of the most fascinating people we know—Maria Montez and Pierre Aumont."[9]

According to Maria's idea of the fitness of things, in Cannes they naturally stayed at the Grand Hotel du Cap-Eden-Roc. They had lunch there with Erich von Stroheim, Marcel Dalio, and actress Denise Vernac. They posed in front of the neon "Festival du film" sign. When it was over, they flew to Brussels for the premiere of *Ali Baba and the Forty Thieves.* The proceeds went to a fund for children displaced and orphaned by the war. In this group of French photographs Jean-Pierre and Maria are portrayed as lovers on their honeymoon and movie stars in equal parts.

Several weeks after the Cannes Festival, Maria and Jean-Pierre traveled to London to participate in a royal command performance before King George and Queen Elizabeth on November 1 at the Empire Theater. They were invited to the event when they originally landed in Paris. Maria commented, "We were both thrilled to death." The event, called Cavalcade of the Movies, celebrated the history of films. *A Matter of Life and Death,* a British wartime fantasy film starring David Niven and Kim Hunter, was premiered. Ray Milland, Reginald Gardiner, Dorothy Malone, Joan Bennett, Walter Wanger, and Pat O'Brien sailed on the *Queen Elizabeth* to join Maria and Jean-Pierre in London. Walter Wanger, who was the immediate past president of the Academy of Motion Picture Arts and Sciences, spoke on that organization's role in the modern world of film. Pat O'Brien enacted a scene from *Front Page* and Ray Milland one from *Lost Weekend.* Maria was there as the Queen of Technicolor to represent the coming of color to motion pictures. British comedian Bud Flanagan introduced her and she in turn presented Jean-Pierre, who then made a speech to celebrate both his wife and the Technicolor process.[10]

Ignoring the talk of *Venetian Wedding* and *The Scarlet Feather,* while the couple was still in France, producer Seymour Nebenzal announced that he had signed Maria to a three-picture deal. The first film would be a new version of his 1932 film *L'Atlantide,* in which she would star with her husband. Nebenzal had joined the Society of Independent Motion Picture Producers in 1946 and would be releasing the film through United Artists. The movie would eventually be called *Siren of Atlantis* and was scheduled to go before the cameras in February 1947. It would be filmed in Hollywood on the Samuel Goldwyn lot. But the prospect of a return to their Beverly Hills home was becoming, in Aumont's mind, only temporary. France and the French film community had embraced both him and Maria and he wanted to return to them both. Jean Cocteau planned to do a film with them and producer Paul-Edmond Decharme wanted to put them under contract. To Jean-Pierre, the meeting between Maria and Cocteau was propitious. "From the moment of this first encounter not the slightest doubt remained: we were going to cancel our contracts with MGM and Universal and come to live in Paris as soon as we had finished our scheduled films."[11]

Under the terms of Maria's post-suspension contract with Universal, she had to make at least one more film with the studio and was allowed to make an outside project, for which she would be granted a formal leave by the studio's legal department. Her contract with Universal would be suspended both as to "services and compensation" until she returned to her home studio. The term of her contract was extended for a period equivalent to the entire period of her compensation by the other company. For the duration of the contract she would be paid $1,500 per week, with a $5,000 bonus when she made a film. Her language coach, Dr. Mitchneck, received $150 per week.[12]

Seymour Nebenzal wanted her badly for *Siren of Atlantis*, but others also sought her services. The brother team of producers Frank, Maury, and Herman Kozinsky (who changed their name to King) announced in January 1946 that they wanted her to play the role Hedy Lamar made famous in a remake of the 1933 Czech-Austrian film, *Ecstasy*. Clearly it would have called for an extensive rewrite to get the script past the Hays Office. Montez was no stranger to baths in movies, but it would be interesting to see how the famous nude scene would have been handled in a 1946 American movie. In April, after giving up on *Ecstasy*, the brothers approached her to play a modern role in *The Hunted*. It too was never filmed. There is no record that the brothers tried to enlist Maria as Annie in the movie they did make in 1949. The lead in *Gun Crazy* went to Peggy Cummins.[13]

Charles R. Rogers, the former head of production at Universal, had become an independent producer since his separation from the studio. In May 1946 he announced his desire to have Montez star in *Queen of Hearts* under his production deal with United Artists. Maria had wanted to play the role of Elizabeth of Austria for years. Jean-Pierre was cast as the emperor Franz Joseph. Montez's friend Alexis Thurn-Taxis was to direct. Maria had tried unsuccessfully for years to convince Universal to acquire the rights to Bertita Harding's *Golden Fleece*, a 1937 historical study of the royal couple. In January 1948, Rogers announced that *Queen* would finally start shooting at the end of the month.

Maria's pay rate as an independent actor would be considerably higher than her Universal rate, as was common in the postwar period. Maria was to be paid $100,000 for her role in *Queen of Hearts*. But this dream assignment was never to be. As the *Independent Exhibitors Film Bulletin* noted, "Charles R. Rogers . . . has yet to have a picture which lives up to its ballyhoo." The case of *Queen of Hearts* would be no different. The project fell through and it wound up in court, with Maria suing Charles Rogers for the contracted salary of $100,000. Initially she was going to sue him for $400,000, which included salary, money spent on costumes, and harm to her career. He had also expressed interest in her starring in *The Scarlet Feather* prior to making *Queen*. Nothing came of either project.[14]

In August 1947, a year after the failure of *Queen of Hearts*, Rogers formed a partnership with Seymour Nebenzal to produce three Technicolor films starring Maria. He had resurrected the idea of making *Scarlet Feather* and *Queen of Hearts* while Nebenzal would contribute *Atlantis.* On top of all this, according to a note in Philip Scheuer's *Los Angeles Times* film column, bandleader/actor Xavier Cugat also wanted Montez to star in a film about a Spanish dancer in Argentina. He supposedly had Mexican director Emilio Fernandez all lined up to film the South American adventure.

The picture that finally won out as Montez's outside Universal project was producer Seymour Nebenzal's *Atlantis,* in which she would star with her husband for the first time. The film had trouble right from the start. Because of the hectic schedule the Aumonts had while in France, a doctor recommended that Maria take a vitamin shot. Something went very wrong as she experienced swelling and intense pain. The shot had been administered to her posterior. This enraged la Montez even more. She told a writer, "Imagine! Me! Deformed there!" The couple had to attend the command performance in London despite how Maria was feeling. Then, to make matters worse, she could not wear any of her Paris gowns as the queen had decreed that everything be simple. So, as ill as she was, Maria had to go find another dress in London. She and Aumont sailed for New York the next day on the *Queen Elizabeth.* The ship's doctor told her she needed an operation as the shot was infecting her blood. She entered the hospital upon landing on November 11, 1946. Her doctor told her that if she had pressed on to Los Angeles to start *Atlantis* as she had planned she could have very well died of blood poisoning. The start date for filming had to be rescheduled while Maria recovered. She was finally given her official legal layoff from Universal to begin work on Nebenzal's film on February 17, 1947.[15]

First Filming of *Atlantis*

The *Atlantis* to star Maria was a remake of Seymour Nebenzal's *L'Atlantide,* which he produced in German, French, and English versions in 1932. Nebenzal was a well-traveled fellow. He was born to German Jewish parents in New York in 1899. His parents returned to Germany and Seymour followed to work with his father, who had created Nero-Film in Germany in 1926. He took over the studio as the world film industry transitioned from silent movies to sound. His most important German production was *M,* directed by Fritz Lang in 1931. He left Germany for France following the Nazis' rise to power. Nebenzal produced several films there before coming to Hollywood in 1939. He joined the Society of Independent Producers in 1946 with the idea of making American films outside the studio system to be

Celebrating the signing of the deal that Maria is to star in one picture a year for three years for producer Seymour Nebenzal. *Left to right:* Seymour Nebenzal, Harold Nebenzal, attorney Herbert Silverberg, Maria, her agent Louis Shurr, and Bernard Silbert of the law office of Greg Bautzer, Maria's lawyer. "Deal was completed at 5:45 p.m. sharp, because Miss Montez is a firm believer in astrology."

released through United Artists. He produced several films before deciding to remake two of his German hits. He eventually remade *M* based in Los Angeles in 1951, but first he meant to film the story of Atlantis being found in the Sahara Desert.

The story was a pretty grim one. Aumont plays a French Legionnaire looking for a lost expedition in the endless wastes of North Africa with his friend, played by Dennis O'Keefe. Instead they wind up in an underground complex in the Taureg Mountains that is the lost city of Atlantis, run by the vindictive, murderous Queen Antinea (Montez). She has a nasty habit of seducing men, tiring of them, killing them, then coating their preserved bodies with gold and putting the statues in her hallway. This would be both the old and a new Maria. As always, she would be royalty in a Neverland country, but she would finally have the chance for a meaty, black-and-white dramatic role. But a line of murdered golden guys in her lobby? This would be a brand-new Montez.

Atlantis did not suffer from lack of publicity. The fact that Maria and Jean-Pierre were finally going to do a movie together was a key part of the buildup of the upcoming film. Lupton Wilkinson wrote a piece for *Screenland* that detailed their wedding, marriage, child, and their starring in *Atlantis*. He remarked with some surprise how close the couple was. Comparing the former Dominican Dynamite with Montez as a wife, Wilkinson marveled, "No one who knew the magnificently and healthily self-centered Maria in her early days around the film capital could visualize a man who would be able to take Maria's mind off the wonderful Maria." The author is looking forward to seeing the completed *Atlantis*, as he knows all of Montez's fans will be. "This pair is the star couple in Hollywood to watch—the most brilliantly promising and the most intensely romantic husband-and-wife team on the screen."[16]

Nebenzal released his pictures through United Artists and that studio began issuing numerous publicity stills of the Aumont family at home with baby Christina as well as of the couple out on the town. UA also publicized the love in bloom on the *Atlantis* set. Hedda Hopper reported that not only were Montez and Aumont "pitching their usual woo," but their stand-ins got engaged to be married and French journalist Jean Roy, who was a technical advisor on the movie, announced his engagement to Maria's sister Lucita. She also reported on Harold Russell's visit to the set. An army sergeant who had lost his hands in a training accident, he had recently won the Best Supporting Actor Academy Award for his role in *Best Years of Our Lives* as well as a special Oscar for his inspiration to other veterans. Maria stopped production when she saw him and said, "This is one man with whom I want my picture taken."[17]

It is indicative of how strong a place Maria held in the collective national Hollywood mentality when psychoanalyst Dr. F. Bruce Russell's discovery of a stack of mummified bodies in a cave near the California-Arizona border wound up involving her. He claimed to have been led there by drawings on a grass mat he found in a similar cave in Mexico. All this was odd enough, but then he claimed they were proof he had found the lost continent of Atlantis. When questioned in his apartment "on the swanky Sunset Strip," he "hotly denied this had anything to do with Maria Montez' latest movie, *Atlantis*."[18]

The sets were another source of promoting the upcoming movie. Nebenzal hired Lionel Banks as set designer for the queen's chambers. Press releases noted he had done the Shangri-La sets for Frank Capra's *Lost Horizon* (1937). During the original shooting of *Atlantis* the elaborate sets for Queen Antinea's rooms were featured in the *Los Angeles Times* in 1947, while *Life* magazine ran an article about them after the film finally opened in 1949. It was clear from the title of the *Times* piece who the star of the film was. Philip Scheuer called his article "Weird Sets in *'Atlantis'* Reflect Beauty of Montez." It featured a page-wide photo of Maria and Jean-Pierre on Queen Antinea's bed in the middle of the ornate set. When Scheuer showed up on the set for his interview, he found her happily talking to her husband. Both were completely welcoming to the reporter. They talked about how nice it was to finally be together after the war's separation, their daughter, and how Jean-Pierre wanted to do for Molière and Racine what Olivier had done for Shakespeare. They also spoke at length about Maria's reaction to Cocteau's *Beauty and the Beast,* which she called "the most touching picture I have seen in my whole life."

In their discussion Scheuer found a Montez who, as always, understood her part. She said she was willing "to do the sex stuff people expect of me," but only as one aspect of what was asked of her. It was important to her to give a good dramatic performance, showing both the allure and the danger inherent in Queen Antinea. She realized that "the interminable succession" of fantasy films had made her studio a lot of money and assured her thousands of fan letters a month but, as she had been telling her studio for two years, she wanted to act in serious films. She wanted to prove her talent. "I cannot bear to be mediocre," she told the writer.[19]

The *Life* article came out soon after the film, now called *Siren of Atlantis,* finally opened nationwide in November 1949. The magazine ran a cropped version of the George Hommel photo used by the *Times* that featured the Aumonts sitting on the queen's bed along with three smaller pics, two of them by Peter Stackpole, of Maria in her various clinging dresses. This demonstrated the exotic look of the film. *But* the short paragraph accompanying the four photos summarized a failure. Although the reviewer noted, "According to one theory of movie-making, if you produce a film that deals with lust and cruelty in an exotic Kingdom, where gongs boom as slave girls dance and men's throats are slit in murky corridors, the world will beat a path to the door of the theater showing it," he did not expect this to be the case with *Siren of Atlantis.* He summarized the movie as a "sumptuous piece of nonsense," with "not much to be said for the acting, direction, script or anything else about this film."[20]

Very devastating stuff, but Harold Nebenzal, Seymour's son, who was involved with producing the film at its inception, maintained his father wanted badly to sign Maria for the remake. But Harold did not last long on the picture. He was still trying to come to terms with civilian life after serving in the Marine Corps as a Japanese translator. Harold was one of the guys standing by the cliffs on Saipan and Okinawa trying desperately to convince the islanders

The siren of Atlantis.

not to jump and commit suicide. He kept trying to assure them the Americans did not want to slaughter them all. Most did not listen and jumped, often with small children. It was several years before he could join his father's production company. Harold was associate producer on Seymour's 1951 American version of *M*, filmed on the streets of downtown Los Angeles and Bunker Hill.[21]

Seymour Nebenzal used Maria and her much-publicized physique to garner more publicity for the film. She was at her slimmed down best in the sexy costumes designed by Jean Schlumberger who, like Jean-Pierre, had been a member of the Free French forces. One of the key lures for the six Neverland movies was the revealing clothing Vera West designed to display Maria's delightful physicality. Though Schlumberger was best known for his jewelry design, the clothes he created for Maria helped garner considerable attention for the film. Five photos of the various costumes she would be wearing were featured in a piece prepared for Sunday papers on January 25, 1948. Nebenzal's photographer George Hommel was even sent out to Beverly Hills to capture a perennial nugget—Maria waking up in bed in a nightgown. Another of his photos was published in *Good Humor* magazine, which promised "Goofy Gags and Gorgeous Gals." An article titled "Humor from Hollywood" featured jokes and comic scenes from the film capital. It is illustrated by portraits of actors and pin ups of actresses. The other three women are in bathing suits. Maria is in her skin-tight *Siren* dress angled to show off what columnist Sidney Skolsky called "her best points" to perfection.[22]

A George Hommel photo taken for the production and published in *Esquire* features Queen Antinea lying in her tight black dress on a conch shell. The descriptor notes Maria is once again playing a royal character who puts numerous men under her spell with much hugging and kissing. The writer concludes, "All of this is hardly a surprise to Miss Montez to whom it has been happening regularly over the last five years, during which she has played queen of everything but the May." *Between Us* magazine ran the same photo in its inaugural issue. It was printed above Goya's famous painting of the Duchess of Alba nude. According to Sheilah Graham, Montez was to portray the duchess in an upcoming film. *Between Us* was skeptical that even as "conscientious" an actress as Maria would go the full Goya route.[23]

The original filming of *Atlantis* wrapped in early April 1948. Within two weeks Maria turned her attention to her last Universal contractual obligation. While Seymour Nebenzal and his film editor Gregg Tallas were cutting Karl Struss's cinematography, Montez would be back on the lot she knew so well. The film would be *The Exile*, where she would be once again playing royalty, albeit in a brief, twelve-minute part. It was to be independent producer Douglas Fairbanks Jr.'s second film after his return from distinguished wartime service in the US Navy. It was also written by Fairbanks and would be the first effort of his own production company. The movie told the story of English king Charles Stuart (Charles II), who had been deposed by Oliver Cromwell and the Roundheads in 1651 and wound up in exile in the Netherlands. It

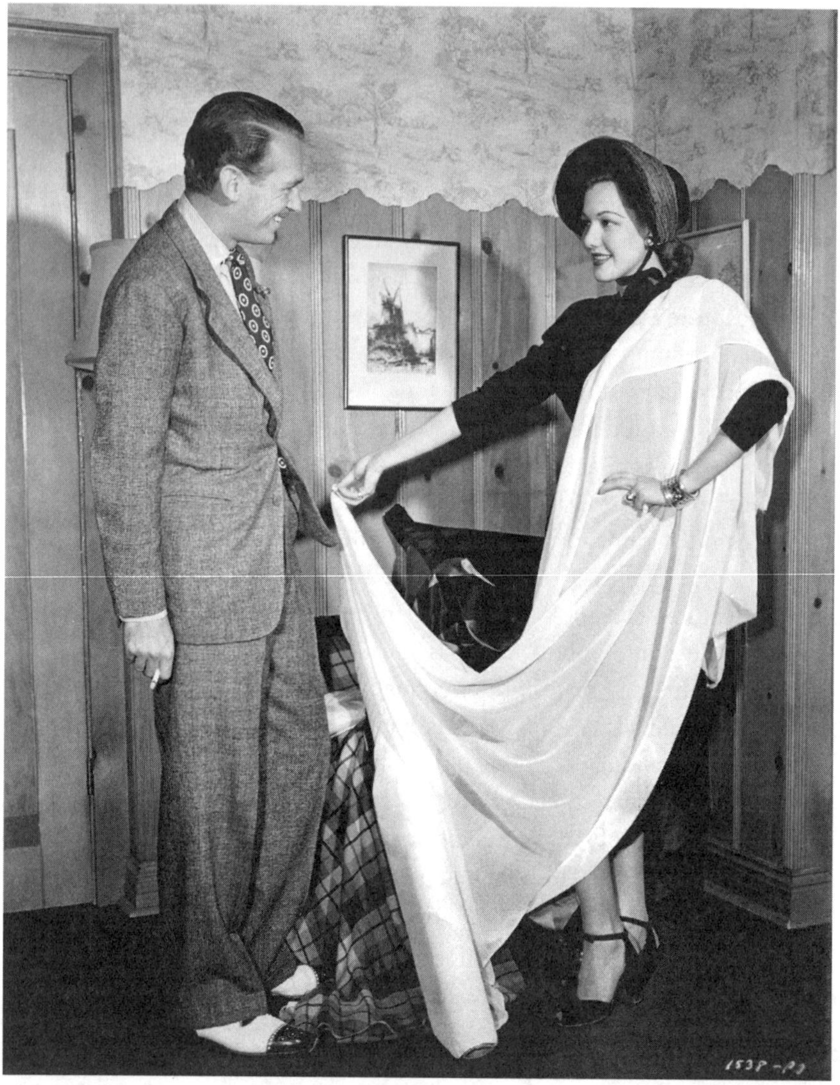

The producer and star of *The Exile,* Douglas Fairbanks Jr., goes over the fabric for the expensive dresses required for the actress he did not want and who did not want to be in the movie as they smile happily at each other. That's why they call it acting.

would be filmed on the Universal lot from late April to mid-July 1947. Maria's small part would be shot at the beginning.[24]

So where would Maria fit into all this English history? Nowhere, if Fairbanks had his way. His script was finished and director Max Ophuls's storyboards prepared. Like his film from the previous year, *Sinbad the Sailor,*

Fairbanks planned to make *The Exile* in Technicolor. Under his contract with Universal, the studio was to provide most of the cast, production facilities, distribution, and some of the money to complete the film. The bulk of the funds would come from Fairbanks himself. Universal was owed one more movie by Maria Montez and clearly the studio wanted her to be gone when her contract expired. She was forced on Fairbanks: take her or no financing. An April 2, 1947, memo from Universal to Fairbanks warned that the budget might have to be adjusted up for the "possible re-casting of the Countess." This was an understatement. Her time on set would be four and a half weeks for a fee of $42,875 plus a $5,000 bonus that would have to be absorbed by Fairbanks's production company. He would also have to pay $3,500 for the wardrobe involved with Montez's five setups. By comparison, the six setups of leading lady Paule Croset, who would play the owner of the inn, would cost $2,900 in wardrobe and her salary for the film would be $13,000. The script would also have to be rewritten to expand Maria's part of Countess Anbella de Courteuil. All this added cost attendant on Montez being in the film caused Fairbanks to have to cancel his proposed use of Technicolor. He could no longer afford it.[25]

Romanian actress Tala Birell was originally scheduled to play the part of the countess, but Fairbanks had entirely deleted the character from the script. With the signing of Montez, he was forced to re-create the character. The scene was expanded to have the countess pull up to the inn wearing a spectacular gown as she emerges from a very ornate coach. She sweeps through the plain lobby of the inn and up to her room. She is there to give her former lover Charles an expensive music box from the king of France. The countess flirts and talks to Charles while she bathes in a huge stand-up tub that completely encloses her. It was the last of the many baths Montez took on the screen and by far the least sexy. All you see is her head and shoulders. Her role is the perfect summation of what Fairbanks thought of Maria's abilities. She could play royalty and take a bath. That was all he could expect from her. The whole scene takes nine minutes. You see her in the morning in her carriage for three minutes saying good-bye to Charles, and returning past Katie in the tulip field after taking the wrong direction. She assures Katie that Charles "likes you very much" and he sold the music box she brought him to pay off her debts. And then she is gone.

Fairbanks was given no choice in this casting. He was told by the new heads of Universal, Bill Goetz and Leo Spitz, "We're not going to put up our share of the money unless you use Maria Montez." Fairbanks protested that the part no longer existed and "anyway, she's such poison that you're letting her go." But the studio had no other material for her coming up "and we want you to take her off our hands. So, you've got to take her." Fairbanks concluded, "They had me over a barrel." Then he not only had to rewrite the script but pay for her expensive costumes as well as find an ornate coach and bathtub. He also had to convince an actress he did not want in the first place to take a very small part she did not want. His opinion of Maria was low. He found her "silly. Shrewd, but not very bright . . . very affected and very difficult to persuade. She was quite rightly indignant over the whole idea, but there wasn't much she could do. They had her in a spot." As a neophyte producer, Fairbanks was coerced by Universal. It seems unlikely the studio could have pulled this trick with more experienced producers such as Mark Hellinger or Walter Wanger, who both had deals with Universal.[26]

Since Fairbanks could no longer afford to shoot *The Exile* in Technicolor as he had intended, he instead chose to film the entire movie in sepia tone, attempting to add what was called "mood tints" to the sepia. Love scenes were photographed in blue and the fight scenes in red. Using a green tone for the climactic storm scenes in an otherwise black-and-white movie had worked very effectively in David O. Selznick's *Portrait of Jennie* the previous year. But the mood tints just couldn't be made to work on *Exile.* Preview audiences did not understand the point of the varying tones and disliked the result. There was an added problem regarding toning the whole movie. Sepia called for using uranium as a principle ingredient, but uranium had not been available for five years because the government had exclusive rights to it for use in the atomic bomb program. George Seid, the head of U-I's camera department and laboratory, succeeded in creating a new way to make sepia, neatly sidestepping the problem caused by "the atom bomb's appropriation of uranium."[27]

George Seid's creativity notwithstanding, sepia certainly was not the producer's first choice. Fairbanks's previous film, *Sinbad the Sailor,* had been an action-adventure movie in full-blown Technicolor, and he was convinced this was one of the reasons it was so successful. He was also aware that 20th Century Fox's Technicolor release of *Captain from Castile* starring Tyrone Power at roughly the same time could considerably cut into the box office for *The Exile.* He was right. The film wound up barely breaking even and caused Fairbanks to fold his production company. He found sepia toning to be a very poor substitute for the Technicolor he lost due to the financial disruption of having to use Montez in the film. The movie came out about the same time as 20th Century Fox's *Forever Amber,* and was referred to as "Forever Dark Brown." Fairbanks carried a grudge for forty years. In an interview in 1988, he still had not forgiven Maria. When asked what his favorite films were,

Fairbanks replied they were *State Secret, Sinbad the Sailor, Gunga Din, Dawn Patrol,* and *The Exile*—"even though we were forced to hire Maria Montez for that."[28]

Fairbanks already had his cast in place prior to having to deal with Universal's demands concerning the part of the countess. Relative newcomer Paule Croset, who had been working at RKO in B movies as Rita Corday and would reemerge after *Exile* as Paula Corday in 1951—was to play Katie, a Dutch farmer and innkeeper who was Fairbanks's love interest. Henry Daniell was cast as the Roundhead assassin Colonel Ingram and Nigel Bruce, taking a respite from his continuing portrayal of Dr. Watson in Universal's Sherlock Holmes series, played the king's advisor Sir Edward Hyde. Ophuls was able to bring his favorite cinematographer, Franz Planer, into the production. Howard Bay, recently added to the U-I production design department, joined *The Exile.* It was a fine, experienced team and Fairbanks had high hopes for his production company's first effort.[29]

At least there would not be the added expense of having to take the filming of *The Exile* on the road. The whole movie would be shot on stage 12, Universal City's largest sound stage. Five indoor sets would be built. The first represented Dutch countryside, including a road, an inn with its barn and garden, a canal, and part of a farm. This set was used first and then dismantled in what Universal publicity called "one of the fastest set changes in history," replaced with forty-four tons of dirt to grow tulips and peach trees. The other sets included a canal with barges and a village in the background, a swamp scene with three full-sized windmills, and a marketplace with several buildings, a canal, and a roadway. All of this was accomplished by a variety of Universal-International crafts people working from the design of set directors Russell Gausman and Ted Offenbecker. It is a perfect example of what the studio system was capable of at its height and why Fairbanks needed to partner with one.[30]

The Hays Office was given the second draft of the script on March 17, 1947. Right from the start Breen wanted to "make certain that this story contains nothing that would give offense to the British." This would have been extremely unlikely in a production from arch Anglophile Douglas Fairbanks Jr. The censors also demanded that no suggestion be made in any way that the inn was also a brothel. When Croset's character yells, "Fire!" she is not to yell it in English "on account of the danger of upsetting audiences." But it was Maria's bathtub scene that aroused most of the censors' warnings. "This scene will be acceptable only if it is free of any sex-suggestive looks or inferences. Specifically, we assume the trick bathtub . . . will adequately cover the

Countess and that there will be no attempt to play on her nudity." Breen's demands were accepted and *The Exile* received its certificate of approval on September 23, 1947.[31]

The Exile

The plot of *The Exile* is quite straightforward. Charles Stuart is in exile in Holland while England is in turmoil under the rule of Oliver Cromwell. Charles meets a Dutch woman at the market and falls in love with her. He manages to get a job at her farm and inn. This helps in his effort to remain invisible to Cromwell's agents in Holland who are looking for him. But he is found, and a Roundhead assassin, Colonel Ingram, is sent to kill him. A French countess shows up, finds Stuart, and delivers a message of support from the king of France. She leaves the next day and the rest of the film is Stuart's ballet-like efforts to escape the murderous efforts of Colonel Ingram with the help of his advisor Edward Hyde and various others who support his return to the throne. After defeating Ingram, Stuart receives word that the British have overthrown Cromwell and want him to return to his rightful place as king of England. He, of course, cannot bring a commoner back to England as his queen. Stuart, now Charles II again, says a painful good-bye to Katie and, amid a phalanx of supporters, goes to the port to catch a ship back to England.

Two endings for *The Exile* were filmed. The American release featured the one described above. Edward Hyde kisses the king's royal hand as he walks out the door and down some steps to a waiting coach where a man and woman doff their hats. Left alone in the inn, Katie bows her head in sorrow and walks out of the room alone. In the European version there is no good-bye scene between the king and Katie, no explanation of why they cannot be together. This is supposed to emphasize more than in the US version how trapped by courtly pomp the king is. In both cases of Maria's final film on her seven-year Universal contract, she is long out of sight and of no consequence at its conclusion.

The Exile moves along at a good clip, but the story line is pretty arcane for American audiences. Other problems are the use of sepia toning for the film and the obvious fact that Douglas Fairbanks Jr. seems to be emulating the swashbuckling movies that made his father so famous. Initially it has to be explained why the king of England is in the Netherlands, then he must spend time wooing Katie or talking to the countess while she takes a bath before the real action can begin. Fairbanks then seems to be forever sword fighting and athletically climbing up anything taller than himself. It looks like a silent film from twenty-five years earlier. The whole derring-do thing worked much better in his Technicolor fantasy *Sinbad the Sailor.*

The Hollywood trade papers recommended *The Exile.* They liked Fairbanks's heroics and swashbuckling. *Daily Variety* found Paule Croset "a refreshing new personality" and thought that though Maria made only a brief appearance, she "makes her footage count." Edwin Schallert in the *Los Angeles Times* agreed that Maria "brightens the screen briefly as a yearning and exotic countess." He liked the sepia but thought the movie moved too slowly. The *Los Angeles Daily News, Hollywood Citizen-News,* and *Commonweal* magazine all thought the movie was okay at best. The *Citizen-News* agreed with Edwin Schallert that Maria's brief appearance "brightens the screen." "A.W." in the *New York Times* thought the film moved too slowly and was a pale reflection of the full-blooded swashbucklers of Fairbanks Sr. As was a tradition with his newspaper, A.W. dismissed Maria contemptuously.[32]

The *Canton (Ohio) Repository* thought the fight scenes were exciting and well staged. Fairbanks Jr. was lauded as fitting "the expected Fairbanks manner." Its reviewer, Wilkins Weber, also liked Paule Croset, finding her an "exceptionally attractive girl, sweet and especially talented." The sepia toning, he found, did not distract, but it "doesn't add anything either." He was of a like mind with the producer when it came to Maria's contribution. Weber wrote she "could have been skipped entirely when the film was being cast. But she gets star billing. She appears but briefly, her lines frequently are muddled and she adds practically nothing to the plot." You wonder if Fairbanks ever saw a clipping of this review. It would have validated everything he thought and probably driven him crazy as well.[33]

A major problem with the billing and advertising on the film reared its head when *The Exile* was largely completed. Maria had it written into her contract that she would get top billing in any film in which she appeared and her name would be in the largest print. It seemed odd to all concerned that her name would appear above that of the producer, screenwriter, and star Douglas Fairbanks Jr.—especially since she was on-screen for only twelve minutes. In the initial advertising for the film her name was not at the top as her contract held that it should be. One week after the movie's November 21, 1947, Los Angeles premiere, Universal-International, the Fairbanks Company, and Maria Montez announced litigation concerning the billing in *The Exile.* Maria sued for $280,000 for breach of contract. Judge J. F. T. O'Connor enjoined Universal from billing or issuing any publicity on the film. Maria had the stipulation as to billing down in black and white and there was little the studio could do about it. Conflicts over billing were nothing new in

Hollywood. Contemporary with *The Exile,* U-I had very definite legal instructions on the billing in Robert Montgomery's *Ride the Pink Horse.* But that was all worked out long before the film was released. What was unique about the *Exile* case was that the court had to decide if Montez or Fairbanks got top billing as both were guaranteed it in their contracts, although Universal claimed that Maria had waived her contractual right. An undisclosed settlement, reported by Philip Scheuer in the *Los Angeles Times* as between $15,000 and $30,000, was reached prior to the case going to court. Maria got top billing, and she withdrew her restraining order.[34]

The ad to be used in newspapers was the subject of a memo from the publicity department of Universal asking which of the four new designs would be agreeable to all parties. The winner featured Fairbanks, sword in hand, jumping over his name and the name of the film, both of which are in script. The text reads "Universal-International in Association With The Fairbanks Company Inc. Presents." Maria Montez is listed first, then the legend reads, "and Introduces Paule Croset." The two actresses' names are in the same large type. Underneath the leaping form of the producer is the legend "Douglas Fairbanks in *The Exile.*" His name is printed in the same size type as the two actresses' but appears right above the title and separate from them. His name is in script while the other actors' names are in normal print. His name also appears by itself next to the title of the film.[35]

Jimmie Fidler reported that Maria had won her suit and would receive top billing in the ads for *The Exile.* He argued it would be a Pyrrhic victory at best. He predicted the fans would not care. They only wanted a good movie that would entertain them. He did not think it would increase her status in her profession, either, "for the picture industry knows that the triumph was extorted." But the lasting harm would be her status within her own studio. "She's merely indicated, once more, that she can be a very difficult person to get along with when she gets in a belligerent mood."[36]

The billing dispute may have been resolved, but a month after the early May 1947 completion of *The Exile* Montez was no longer employed by Universal-International. Her contract had expired and it was not renewed. In the language of the time, "Universal failed to exercise its first annual option under a new contract . . . and she automatically became a freelance." The chief reason was that the studio no longer saw a place for her in the newly constituted Universal-International. She had been successful in the Neverland movies. But the war was over and that type of pure escapist movie largely ended with it. Universal-International did not believe she was capable of carrying the sort of modern, A-list films the studio was now to produce.

Harold Heffernan found another reason the studio did not renew her contract when he interviewed a U-I executive. The columnist wondered why Maria and the studio that had "groomed her from obscurity to high stardom have parted company." The executive explained, "She is too hep legally." The suit "over billing on '*The Exile*' was the last straw." The studio was convinced that not only was Montez a one-trick pony, she had become difficult in the extreme. Heffernan thought Universal might be acting precipitously in dismissing "one of its top money-makers." "From her start seven years ago, she made a study of unusual ways to attract attention. Included in her personally conducted ballyhoo campaigns were battles on the set, walkouts, scenes in night clubs, etc. The payoff was instantaneous and handsome. Miss Montez can now make pictures whenever she wishes, and at $100,000 a shot she's a fine buy, even in these tremulous days of studio retrenchments."[37]

Leo Spitz and William Goetz, who supervised production in Los Angeles, released the extremely truncated "Contract Talent Report" for Universal-International on June 21, 1947. Not only were Montez and her dialogue coach Simon Mitchneck missing, so were Susanna Foster, Gloria Jean, and the whole easterns crew. Deanna Durbin, for years the biggest star on the lot, retired completely from movies within the year, moved to France, and cut off all ties to Hollywood. By early 1948 Universal-International would have only sixteen contract players. The major studios as a whole had cut their rosters by half.

This just piled on the problems the Universal publicity department faced in advertising and exploiting *The Exile*. In a memo dated October 13, 1947, five weeks before the picture's scheduled Los Angeles premiere, the problems were spelled out. "Tie-ups on the picture are limited by the fact that Mr. Fairbanks personally does not approve of them for himself, because Miss Montez' cooperation is not forthcoming, and because Paule Croset is not yet well enough known." Besides being a neophyte, Croset was also very shy. In marked contrast to Montez at the start of her career, she would not walk into the Universal cafeteria without someone from the publicity department escorting her. Stills of both actresses would be released "to provide sex and romance to the campaign." But Universal concluded it was the swashbuckling nature of the film that seemed the best selling point and it was hoped to plant something in *Life* magazine about the film, perhaps in the "Pictures of the Week" feature. The studio also submitted the movie to the hour-long *Lux Radio Theater,* the most prestigious of the several programs that re-created movies for the radio audience. It was to star Fairbanks and Croset. No Maria. The proposal was turned down. *The Exile* was eventually accepted by the half-hour program *Screen Director's Playhouse* and aired on January 23, 1949.[38]

Several "tie-ups" had already been suggested by the Universal publicity department. There were obvious lines of promotion for the three stars. Fairbanks was part of a dynasty. Montez was taking a bath yet again in a movie. Croset was a new face and that should be exploited. Ray Jones had taken special "study portraits" of Paule Croset and they were being distributed to newspapers and fan magazines. The Association of Fur Coat Manufacturers would also choose her as its "Miss Cinderella." She would be awarded a sealskin fur coat and sent on a twenty-city personal-appearance tour at fashion shows held at leading department stores. The studio was also negotiating with cosmetic company Woodbury to develop a campaign for its facial cream featuring Croset. She was scheduled to be on the *Hollywood Star Review* radio show.

Other ideas for tie-ups for the movie included Montez—without Montez. Universal sent out a press release about Maria's latest bath. It noted her memorable baths from the past in *Arabian Nights, Gypsy Wildcat,* and *Ali Baba and the Forty Thieves.* Publicizing their soon-to-not-be-renewed actress, the release mentions the jump in fan letters written to Montez every time she took a bath. She is back in the bubbles for *The Exile,* but it "is the most modest bath in film history." Columnist Frederick Othman agreed. Remembering the glory days of Maria's bath in *Ali Baba and the Forty Thieves,* he wrote that this latest one proved to be "an anticlimax" and he was going to pass it up. Universal has Maria assuring her fans that even if she is locked up in a seventeenth-century copper stand-up tub that looks like a coffin, she will still make the scene as sexy as possible by vamping Fairbanks. Right to the very end Universal stuck to its policy of publicizing Maria's sexuality above anything else.[39]

The studio also did its level best to put a happy face on the fact that Maria is only in the movie for twelve minutes. It is interesting how positive Universal was about its soon-to-be-gone "problem" as it attempted to publicize the movie. In a two-page release, Don Reeve in the publicity department declared the studio might have started "an entirely new trend in film starring roles." They were sure Montez would make the best of her short time on-screen because "she isn't an average person—she's one of the smartest girls ever to hit the Hollywood shores. . . . She's also the gal whose pictures have been loading the coffers with gold pieces for about six years now." The release has Maria ecstatic about the role and Fairbanks very enthusiastic about having her in his movie. She sees herself as more like a European actress. "In Europe a star chooses parts by what they have to offer—not by the time they're on the screen." You wonder if Universal was trying to chase her out the door and off to Europe with that quote.[40]

Another proposed scheme featuring Maria without Maria was to put the ornate covered bathtub she used in the film in the window of Cedric Florists at Wilshire and La Brea Avenue in Los Angeles just south of Hollywood. Have it there for one week, then move it to another location. The studio would "try to secure services of a girl to pose in the bathtub, which would undoubtedly add to the appeal of the display." Or the studio could find a "very prominent bathroom fixture display company" to place the bathtub. There would be even more interest in the tub with a cutout still of Maria in it. A tub with a cutout of Maria in it seems like a bleak good-bye to someone who brought so much money to the studio. But when Clark Gable, the King of Hollywood, went to MGM one last time to collect his belongings, the only person to greet him was the gate guard. Hollywood studios rarely gave in to nostalgic gestures when shedding former stars, no matter how much time and effort they may have spent in building them up or how much money they may have made for that studio.[41]

The biggest promotion concerning *The Exile* had nothing to do with any of the stars of the movie and everything to do with where it supposedly took place. U-I set up a deal with the radio program *Heart's Desire,* which was carried on 436 stations of the Mutual Network Monday through Friday. The program would send the couple that wrote the best letter entitled "Why I would like a trip to Holland" on a ten-day, all-expenses-paid trip to the Netherlands given in the name of Douglas Fairbanks Jr. The contest would run from September 29 to October 10, with attendant publicity for *The Exile.* The winning couple would spend November 15–25 in Holland. While there, they would be taken on a tour of the towns lived in by King Charles II of England.

The winner of the contest was Charles Bowlby, principal of Amesbury, Massachusetts High School. Dutch airlines KLM was so taken with the idea that it threw in a third ticket so he could take both of his children with him. One of the towns on the tour was Zuidzande, whose school had been all but destroyed during the war. In a wonderfully American gesture toward a still-suffering Europe, Mr. Bowlby organized a campaign to gather two and a half tons of pencils, balls, soap, paper, clothes, and everything else kids would need to go to school and sent them to the schoolmaster at Zuidzande, who had spent the war in a German prison camp and was trying to put his school back together again. It was one of those rare examples when Hollywood ballyhoo had a larger impact than just selling the product.[42]

There was another reason beside the lawsuit over billing and the abandonment of Technicolor that Fairbanks wound up so frustrated with having Montez forced on him. The producer was very happy to have hired German-born

Maria sweeps into the inn in *The Exile.* Paule Croset is on the left.

director Max Ophuls to helm *The Exile.* He was a German Jew who left his homeland after the burning of the Reichstag in 1933. Initially he moved to France, finally arriving in the United States in 1941. *The Exile* was the first film he directed in America. He hoped to incorporate a favorite filming method of creating long continuous scenes where the camera would follow the actors.

Ophuls felt this approach, which used fewer cuts, pulled the audience more completely into the film. Paule Croset, who previously had had only a few small parts in RKO B movies, was able to handle the complex blocking and extended dialogue required for the long takes. Ophuls planned to use the technique the first time Montez arrived at the inn. The director blocked out the scene, determined where the camera would go, and carefully explained the process to Maria and what she had to do. They rehearsed the scene and attempted to film it several times to no avail. She just could not perform for the continuous take that Ophuls had mapped out. There was no question this held up the film and caused expensive delays. (On top of her difficulty with Ophuls's continuous takes, Maria came down with a cold and an eye infection in her short time on set. This caused further delay when she still looked ill when she returned to filming.) Ophuls never did get the sustained shot he'd planned. In the finished film Montez gets out of the coach and walks to the inn. Then she is inside the door, walks across the room, up the stairs to her floor and back down. She sees the fake king and is going to leave. Then she sees the real Charles and says, "We stay." The tracking shot had to be discarded. As filmed, the scene is broken up into several parts.

Ophuls had another long scene once the couple was in the countess's room. Fairbanks and Montez were to have an extensive dance sequence after talking. But neither one of them, especially Fairbanks, was a particularly good dancer. The scene was truncated to a few simple steps about the room with the original line of dialogue, "Do you still dance well, Charles?" changed to "Do you still dance as badly as ever?"[43]

Second Filming of *Atlantis*

With *The Exile* wrapped and the court case over billing decided so the film could be released, Montez found herself back on the Goldwyn lot on the set of Nebenzal's renamed *Siren of Atlantis* in late July 1949. The new name recognized that it was Maria's popularity that would bring people into the theaters. Despite all the trouble with the initial filming, Nebenzal remained very high on her. He was sufficiently impressed with her performance thus far that he was still keen on their deal for one movie a year for the next three years. But no matter how impressed the producer may have been with his actress, the original cut of the film performed disastrously in very limited release to preview audiences, and it was determined it would be necessary to film additional scenes. He managed to corral another $250,000 to reshoot several of the scenes and more completely develop others. Aumont and Montez were available for the new scenes, but director Arthur Ripley was not. John Braham was brought in to film the new scenes. Karl Struss, who received the first Academy Award for cinematography in 1929 along with Charles Rosher, returned to finish shooting the film. Morris Carnovsky was also unavailable, leading to his role being abolished and a new one created for Henry Daniell. The revised scenes took another two weeks to shoot. At first Maria refused to come back until she had been paid her deferred salary, but that issue was sufficiently resolved and she was back in Atlantis on July 12, 1948.[44]

A lot of work had been done since the original script arrived at the Breen office on February 13 and was declared "unacceptable under the provisions of the Production Code by reason of the improper treatment of illicit sex, the use of hashish and other details given below." Those details were lengthy. The response took three pages. Among the complaints were "The breasts of women" had to be fully covered; Maria "stretching luxuriously and lying back

St. Avit and Antinea enjoy the dancers and each other in the queen's chamber. This was one of the sets Douglas Sirk found insufficient to tell the chilling story of Atlantis.

on the divan . . . should be handled with great care"; "no indecent dance movements"; no indication of "illicit sex" between Maria and Aumont; no bare flesh between the garter and thigh can show; the count must not seem to be pimping; it is unacceptable to suggest there actually is a place like Atlantis, "otherwise it will be necessary to punish Antinea." Another objection came from Montez. She refused to do the scene where she whips Jean-Pierre. She told Louella Parsons, "That's no way for a wife to treat a good husband, even before the camera, and besides it would be a very bad example for our daughter." All these objections had been straightened out by the start of original filming. They were still in place as the second round of filming got started.[45]

The new scenes were aimed at making the film more coherent. The original preview audiences thought it "too philosophical," in Nebenzal's words. In American-speak that meant the characters spent too much of the movie just standing around talking to each other and engaged in far too little action. He therefore tried to simplify the story line, cut down on the philosophizing, pump up the romance between Antinea and St. Avit (the French Legionnaire played by Aumont), tone down the brutality, and in general make the film run more smoothly. St. Avit is exonerated in the first filming since the military inquiry board thought he hallucinated the whole episode with Antinea. He disappears into the desert when one of the queen's servants is taken into custody by the Legionnaires. In the second version he runs off into the desert and the last scene is of St. Avit dead in the desert as the blowing sand covers him. The censors would have required this. St. Avit had to pay for having killed his friend. The two-week shoot brought the cost of the film to $1,550,000.[46]

New scenes or not, once the film had been completed neither one of the directors wanted to take the credit. Instead film editor Gregg Tallas, who merged the two sections of filming, was credited as director. Originally Nebenzal had wanted fellow German Douglas Sirk to direct the film. He is best remembered for the series of melodramas he helmed in the 1950s. But in the 1940s he directed two films for Nebenzal, *Hitler's Madman* (1943) and *Summer Storm* (1944), and now the producer wanted to see what he could do with *Atlantis.* Sirk, however, was a big fan of *L'Atlantide,* the 1932 version directed by G. W. Pabst, and told Nebenzal he should reissue that film instead, especially since the producer planned to use some of the scenes shot in Algeria from the earlier movie. Sirk also felt it was imperative to have inspiring, fantastic sets if the remake was to stir viewers' imaginations the way the original had. He wrote a few scenes for the movie but had nothing else to do with it.

Nebenzal approached Sirk when the new footage was going to be produced, but again he said no. He had seen what had already been shot and was convinced he was right about the producer not having the money to create the sort of sets needed for *Atlantis.* Arthur Ripley had directed the first segment, and Sirk felt "for various reasons not to do with Ripley, but mainly with the cast, it did not come off. . . . And then Nebenzal asked me to 'salvage' it, but I didn't want to have anything to do with it anymore."[47]

Siren of Atlantis

French Legionnaire lieutenant André St. Avit (Jean-Pierre Aumont) is found after being lost in the Sahara Desert for three months. He and his friend Jean Morhange (Dennis O'Keefe) became separated from their companions while searching for a missing archeological expedition. They are found by the Tuaregs, a tribe of desert nomads, and taken to the lost city of Atlantis in the Hoggar Mountains of the Sahara. They meet Blades (Henry Daniell), an advisor to Queen Antinea (Maria Montez). He introduces them to several other European men who speak glowingly of the gorgeous queen. She takes many men as lovers, but has the drawback of having them killed, embalmed, and turned into golden statues when she gets tired of them.

St. Avit receives a summons to her bedchamber and quickly falls in love with the queen. Morhange, who has not met her, plans an escape with the court dancer (Milada Mladova). They are caught and the dancer kills herself rather than face Antinea's wrath. Morhange confronts the queen and is thrown in jail. Blades convinces St. Avit that the queen threw him over for Morhange. In a rage, St. Avit kills his friend and escapes into the desert. He is found by a rescue team and taken to his home fort. No one believes his story, concluding that the desert drove him to hallucinations. St. Avit starts to believe this himself until one of Antinea's bodyguards brings him her amulet. Still in love with her, he mounts a camel and rides off into the desert to find her. He is found dead, clutching the amulet.

Siren of Atlantis featured Maria Montez as royalty once again, ruling over the ultimate Neverland, as several of the reviewers noted. But this was sure not the Montez of the six Technicolor hits. This Montez was in a kind of fantasy film noir. It took place in ominous interiors of mountains in the Sahara Desert rather than the mean city streets, but it certainly used many of that genre's tropes. Not only were most of the sets as dark and ominous as some of the character's souls, Maria was literally a very fatale femme, turning guys into golden statues. Antinea was a much worse character than Naja, the evil twin in *Cobra Woman*. And there was no nice sister for Jon Hall to rescue, no Sabu to provide lighthearted, athletic moments and good fellowship. In *Atlantis* the queen had Morhange stay in her room, then opened the door so St. Avit could see him and fly into a jealous rage. St. Avit violently stabs him over and over again. He kills his best friend because of Antinea. *Siren of Atlantis* was dark, sinister, unforgiving, and had nothing at all like a happy ending. Montez could not be colder and had absolutely no soft edges. This was not a Maria her fans had much interest in seeing.

Nebenzal wanted to show the original cut of his film in a representative American city. Demonstrating his minimal understanding of the United States, he chose Las Vegas. It did not go well. It ran four days, from May 26 to May 29, 1948, and pulled in $900. The preview audience found it "too philosophical" and generally an incomprehensible mess—thus the decision to reshoot and develop new scenes. The second version, now officially titled *The Siren of Atlantis,* was slated to open in St. Louis, Indianapolis, and Louisville at the beginning of January 1949. The original plan to have Maria, Jean-Pierre, and Dennis O'Keefe make personal appearances at the premieres was abandoned. The movie opened at the four Fine Arts Theaters in Los Angeles on February 10, 1949. It closed on February 17.[48]

Maria crosses her fingers, perhaps because she is passing under a ladder or perhaps in hopes that the reshoots of *Siren of Atlantis* will cure the significant problems of the original filming.

The reviews of *Siren of Atlantis* had a dreary similarity of negativity. Even the usually positive *Hollywood Reporter,* while noting it had several "saleable angles," such as the lost continent idea and the inclusion of the desert scenes from the 1932 version, found that overall the movie's "spotty, episodic continuity reflects frequent changes of approach, and there is an overall confusion in development that makes the yarn difficult to follow." The *Reporter* thought the best thing the movie had going for it was "the angle of pulchritude," a concentration on Montez's "physical charms," which are amply displayed "in a series of form-fitting costumes." *Variety* just found the movie "floridly hokey, never for a moment to be taken seriously." The music and the set design were lauded, but as for the queen, "She is Nita Naldied to a fare-thee-well by Maria Montez."[49]

Newsweek thought Nebenzal certainly had no need to worry that this second version of his story would be "too philosophical" like the first. The reviewer wrote that this take subordinated the whole movie to "the exploitation of Maria Montez's affinity for striking and revealing costumes." *Time* just thought the movie was "a mess." Helen Eager in the *Boston Traveler* decided, "The thing is a fantastic absurdity." Philip Scheuer's review of the finished film in the *Los Angeles Times* was not enthusiastic. He realized Nebenzal was trying to capture the glory of his European effort *L'Atlantide,* but the current film was only "a shadow of its former self." He liked the Lionel Banks sets but was "disillusioned" to find "our old friend—bold, pouty, imperious Maria Montez, the 'siren' herself" in this gloomy environment with all the golden guys in the hallway. And it's a long hallway. The *Hollywood Citizen-News* found the movie "pretty much of a letdown," but it thought, "Maria Montez looks properly alluring in her expansive wardrobe."[50]

Things were no better around the country. Naturally the *New York Times* hated it. "Dull is the word for their adventures" is that paper's summation of the French Legionnaires' efforts in *Atlantis.* They engage "in endless palaver, none of which could be described as exhilarating." The lack of exhilaration extends to the principal performers. The reviewer is particularly harsh on the queen. "As the 'siren' of the piece, Maria Montez reveals her shapely limbs and little else." Fairfax Nisbet in the *Dallas Morning News* concentrated on Maria's role, as did most reviewers. He noted, "All films starring Maria Montez are designed to give the audience the feeling of having just indulged in a pipeful of opium laced with hashish. Application of the word fantasy to these films is strictly an understatement." He at least found both the movie and Maria "handsomely mounted."[51]

Criticism of the film came from all angles. Vernon Steele's review in the *Pacific Coast Musician* finds Michel Michelet's musical score extremely laudable, "as engaging a one as we have heard this season." The rest of the movie, "an indifferent production," does not live up to the score at all. Not a poor film, just an uninteresting one. It is one of those sadly common occurrences when "a fine musical score is set to an indifferent film." The *Harvard Crimson* never seemed to forgive la Montez for her 1941 visit. Reviewer Edward Sack notes that Maria rules her land "with an iron bosom." She "carefully avoids any acting and just stares blankly like a hungry cow." He did like Aumont as "the dashing legionnaire." Rather disappointing for a movie whose ads promised would be "Out Of This World! A spectacle Beyond Belief! never before . . . never again . . . Such Days Of Splendor And Spectacle!"[52]

Siren of Atlantis proved to be a complete box office disaster. Not only did Nebenzal lose his shirt, pants, and shoes on his investment in *Siren,* his house was foreclosed on by Joseph Schenck, former president of United Artists and chairman at that time of 20th Century Fox, due to an unpaid promissory note for $42,500. Nebenzal was forced to declare bankruptcy. Maria was also included as a defendant since she also claimed an interest in the house on Alpine Drive in Beverly Hills. All these money problems made him loath to complete the payments owed his star. This led to Maria's third lawsuit over her participation or nonparticipation in a film in two years. She started out this suit by saying she would enjoy the high salaries she was promised for her independent films—if she could only collect them. She sued Nebenzal for the $38,000 she was not paid on her $100,000 salary. The suit was filed in Los Angeles, so in April 1950 this necessitated Maria flying in from Rome, where she was shooting her first Italian film, *Thief of Venice.* The case was cheerfully covered in the local press. The *Los Angeles Times* described her testimony as "broken English expressions with foreign gestures." When the judge asked her name, she answered Maria Antonia Africa Gracia y Vidal Aumont. The *Times* described the judge as gasping and dropping his pencil. "You asked for it," Maria responded.[53]

Maria's performance on the stand was quite colorful. Not only did she explain why exactly Nebenzal owed her $38,000, she held up renderings of the clothes she bought in Paris for the next movie she was to do with the producer on their initial three-picture deal. She claimed the $5,000 purchase to be an economy move, as she would now have the clothes needed for the next movie. She read a letter she had sent Nebenzal telling him why it was such an excellent investment. "With all my clothes, furs and things we are going to make Rita Hayworth's $70,000 wardrobe in *Gilda* look sick and it will cost you less than the salary of a designer alone."[54]

Montez was back on the stand three days later. This time she explained how Nebenzal had screwed up the release of *Siren.* Astrologically speaking, "if the picture had been previewed before October 10, 1947 it would have been luckier—because Neptune squared is no good on pictures. . . . Obviously Mr. Nebenzal did not believe in astrology. Too bad for him. Unfortunate for all of us." Unfortunate indeed. Nebenzal had no response to his ignoring the astrological signs, but he did point out that the picture, which was produced at a final cost of $1,800,000, had by April 1950 gross returns of $335,000. He claimed that unless the gross receipts reached $3,500,000, it would not break even. It did better in Europe than the United States, but not $3 million better.[55]

Her testimony over, Maria flew back to Rome to complete *Thief of Venice*. On January 2, 1951, the court found in Maria's favor. Nebenzal claimed he had loaned Montez $17,084 to buy her costumes for their proposed next film. She denied that he had ever advanced her any money and the court went along with her. Nebenzal was required to pay her the entire $38,000 for which she sued.[56]

The years 1947 and 1948 had been disastrous for Maria Montez. *Queen of Hearts* was cancelled by Charles Rogers, which resulted in a lawsuit by Maria for $100,000 for nonpayment of wages. *The Exile* relegated her to a small supporting role and led to a lawsuit that stopped the advertising for the just-released film until the billing issue could be decided by a judge. This was followed by her release from her seven-year relationship with Universal. Then came the unmitigated disaster of *Siren of Atlantis,* which had been renamed to further feature Maria as its main attraction. The failure of the three movies and the lawsuits that resulted from them branded Maria with that most deadening word in the eyes of studios and producers—"difficult." They also strengthened producers' belief she was only welcomed by audiences in the Technicolor Neverland movies—and these had ended with Allied victory in the war and Maria's often and loudly proclaimed wishes to cease acting in them. The many ideas for films starring Montez floated by several producers dried up. Charles Rogers no longer wanted her for *Queen of Hearts* or *The Scarlet Feather.* Seymour Nebenzal lost all interest in doing the other films he had planned for Maria. The King Brothers gave up on the projects they had in mind for her.

In the midst of all this disaster Maria was honored once again by her most ardent supporters. Each year the Hollywood Independent Press Photographers picked their Queen of Glamour. In 1948 Jane Greer was queen, with Ava Gardner, Rita Hayworth, Linda Darnell, and Maria Montez as runners-up. It was one of the very few career bright spots in what was a very depressing time for la Montez. France seemed to be calling her and Jean-Pierre ever more insistently. They determined to respond.[57]

Hedda Hopper paid a visit to the Aumonts as they were preparing to move to France. She wanted to see the baby but wrote mostly about the happy household she found. English had to be the official language of the house because it featured such an international cast, with the two principals, three

Maria Christina happily plays with mom's earring at home in Beverly Hills, 1948. (Courtesy of the Wisconsin Historical Society.)

sisters, and friends coming and going. Maria was just back from the hospital, where she had received three pints of blood. "I told my doctor," Maria said, "no more Spanish blood; but some Dutch blood, please. It might calm down my temperament." Maria Christina was asleep, so Hopper had to rely on her mother's description of her. "She acts already, but I've come to the conclusion that she will be an artist, most likely a concert pianist." She explained to Hopper that she and Jean-Pierre were leaving soon for France to star in a film by Jean Cocteau. She was very excited. "Ah Paris. There I can do no wrong.

The Parisians even liked me in '*The Cobra Woman*.'" She and Jean-Pierre were going to start their own production company to make their own films in Paris. Hopper wished them luck on their new endeavor. She pointed out to her readers that Maria had "one of the shrewdest brains for business in Hollywood. She came here intent upon success and attained it through sheer effort while many of her contemporaries fell by the way. She knows what others have forgotten. Hollywood is a sucker for showmanship. She has it and deals it out with vast enthusiasm."[58]

For all the vibrancy of her home in Beverly Hills, the American movie market seemed closed to Montez at the moment. But Europe was making films again. Maybe she could find a new career in her husband's home country. Jean-Pierre's friend Jean Cocteau wanted to do a film about Orpheus starring the Aumonts. Maria Montez was dedicated to remaining what she had wanted to be her whole life—a movie star. If that had to be in European movies, so be it. *Screenland* described Montez's departure for Europe in a less than positive fashion. "Maria Montez is off to Europe in a bright red huff—she's had so many battles with producers over billing and roles and was so disappointed that Hedy Lamarr got the femme lead in 'Samson and Delilah' that she decided she'd go eat worms, uh, I mean Paris food and make her pictures there for a spell." Arthur Lubin, her director on *White Savage* and *Ali Baba,* advanced a more ethnocentric reason she was leaving for Europe. He believed Latin women had an exploding gene, activated by the time they turned forty, that caused them to gain weight. Maria was in her late thirties and had a child so the gene would be waiting right around the corner.[59]

But although Maria may have been running away from disappointments in the United States, she was also running toward Europe with high hopes. The last big party she and Jean-Pierre threw in their Beverly Hills home was to send off French designer Jacques Fath and his wife when they returned home. Every French actor in Hollywood attended the good-bye party. Maria's earnings for 1946 were reported as $78,375, more than Irene Dunne's $77,500 but considerably less than Deanna Durbin's $262,875. But this was now late 1948 and filmmakers in the United States had lost interest in the former Queen of Technicolor. Aumont had wanted to return to France ever since their honeymoon trip in 1946. Now there was a good reason.[60]

10

France

One of the chief lures that brought the Aumonts to France was a proposed film project with Jean Cocteau. Aumont had known him before the war and was proud to introduce him to his wife. The director and Maria hit it off immediately. "Maria and he belonged to the same race," Aumont observed. "Both of them were familiar with messages from the beyond, ghosts, and premonitions." Cocteau's desire to do a film with the Aumonts so excited Jean-Pierre that he determined to get out of his MGM contract and return to France to live. He felt that MGM's ardor for him had cooled after the war. "My French accent, which had been my greatest asset, had suddenly become my greatest handicap." He claims he got out of the contract by signing over all the money he was to make from *Atlantis* to MGM. He also erroneously claimed Montez was offered a new contract by Universal but turned it down since she wanted to live in Paris and make the film Cocteau was planning. She probably did want to make a movie with Cocteau, but Universal never offered her a new contract after her initial seven-year agreement expired.[1]

Cocteau wanted to do a contemporary take on the Greek myth of Orpheus, based on his ability to charm all living things with his music, his attempt to rescue his wife from death, and his own death by those who could not hear his divine music. In the film Orpheus would be a poet in modern Paris played by Aumont. Maria would play Death. Cocteau sent the screenplay to the couple as they were completing the shooting of *Atlantis*. They were enthusiastic about it, but two producers who were to provide the money for the filmmaking backed out of the project because they could not understand the script. It became evident the Aumonts would not be making *Orpheus* any time soon.[2]

A new project emerged from producer Pierre Baguenard while the Aumonts were still in the United States. He offered them *Wicked City*, a drama to be filmed in France as one of the first Anglo-French productions. Aumont spoke with Cocteau about the future of the stalled *Orpheus* as soon as they arrived in France. The director told him he was going to try to

With the Aumonts moving to Paris, French visitors to Los Angeles would no longer be welcomed to the city at Maria and Jean-Pierre's house on Walden in Beverly Hills, as actor Claude Dauphin was.

produce it himself with a crew that would be willing to share the financial risks. Aumont told him that he and Maria still very much wanted to do the film and would be available as soon as they completed *Wicked City.* Cocteau showed him some sketches the artist and designer Christian Berard had made for Maria's costumes as Death. But several weeks later Aumont read in the newspaper that Cocteau was making *Orpheus* with Jean Marais and

Maria Casares. Jean-Pierre was hurt by what he saw as a friend's betrayal. Maria, already disappointed by so many roles lost, said merely she would have liked to play Death. Aumont assured her she would have many more parts that were more like herself, "joyful and lovely and young. Smiling sweetly, she answered, 'But Death ought to be joyful and lovely and young.'"[3]

The retakes for *Siren of Atlantis* were finally completed on July 12, 1948. Charles Rogers's *Queen of Hearts* had been officially canceled and Maria's lawsuit against him had been proceeding in the courts since February. She was suing him for $400,000—$100,000 for being off the screen, $100,000 for loss of publicity, and $200,000 for compensation she would have received if the film was made. This was eventually narrowed down to the $100,000 she had been promised for starring in the movie. She and Jean-Pierre did not take up producer Richard Charlton's offer to appear in Noël Coward's play *Design for Living* for a twenty-eight-week run in Detroit. This cleared the track for the couple to return to France and finally film the first postwar Franco-American production, called *Hans le marin* (Hans the Sailor), in France and *Wicked City* in the United States and England.[4]

Jean-Pierre Aumont had read the novel *Hans le marin* by Edouard Peisson while he was recovering from shrapnel wounds received in Marseille in August 1944. The film had been in the works for two years and is an excellent example of the postwar effort to move outside the studio system to make films that were important to the makers. The novel took place in the French Mediterranean seaport of Marseille. Aumont began to work on the idea of filming on the streets of the city in the fatalistic style the French called poetic realism. Maria, Jean-Pierre and his brother François Villiers visited Peisson at his Provence home on their first trip to France in 1946 and arranged to purchase the film rights to his novel. The understanding was that Aumont would write the screenplay and star in the film along with Maria; Villiers would direct. At the press conference to announce the signing of an agreement with the author to make a film in Marseille of *Hans le marin* the point was stressed that the movie would demonstrate that Montez "is an actress as well as a manikin."[5]

In order to find the financing and get the film made, the Aumonts did what Douglas Fairbanks Jr. and many other Hollywood stars and directors did after the war. They formed their own production company. The Aumonts called theirs Christina after their daughter. French producer André Sarrut of Safia Productions in Paris agreed to put up 80,000 francs ($250,000) to pay the full production costs for what was then being called *The Last Port,* to be filmed in both French and English. That title was changed to *Wicked City* when it was pointed out the former was British slang for the final glass before

An elegant portrait of Maria by the French studio Harcourt.

closing time at pubs. Christina Productions was to deliver Montez, Aumont, and Lilli Palmer, as well as a bilingual screenplay, with the assurance that the company's costs would be paid off first out of receipts from the US release.

A Sunday features article prepared about the founding of Christina Productions for the *Wicked City* press book holds that the company was started because Maria was sick of always being a minimally costumed princess and the Queen of Technicolor. "It was once a princess always a princess. Jean Pierre and I decided to do something about it." So Maria "incorporated herself, risked some of her own money and traveled 6000 miles" to make a movie in which she would be required to act, not merely look great. It is quite the departure from

The Aumonts, Lilli Palmer, and her husband are on the same train as Winston Churchill on the way to Marseille for their new film *Hans le marin*.

her Universal roles. "Played with all frankness that censorship permits, her part is that of a cabaret girl in the more raffish portions of the port of Marseilles." The ever-loyal Louis Shurr assured the writer that his phone had been ringing off the hook. "Everybody wants Montez." But they could get her only for one picture at a time. She was no longer interested in any long-term contract.[6]

The filming stretched from September to early November 1948, with a crew of thirty in and around Marseille. The interiors were shot in Paris at Joinville Studios, the home of multi-language films. Many of the scenes featured the city's citizens, who were eager to be part of the filming. The benefit of filming in France was partially financial. The country had a long-established movie-making community that was eager and willing to work, the costs were 25 percent less than they would have been at a Hollywood studio, and the actual streets of Marseille were there for the filming. The drawback was the continuing shortage of all sorts of materials due to the war, and the need to send the exposed film all the way to Hollywood for processing. A long-term benefit for the French producers was the opportunity to get their films into the larger American theaters instead of the smaller "art" houses where their product was usually shown.[7]

Wicked City (*Hans le marin*)

Wicked City starts with an American freighter docking in Marseille. Hans (Jean-Pierre Aumont) and two other sailors head for the Kit Kat Club in the red-light district. Hans sees Dolores (Maria Montez) at the bar and falls irrevocably in love. They head off to her rooms. The next morning, on his way to his ship with Dolores, Hans is jumped and severely beaten by two men. Dolores just watches. After being released from the hospital, his ship having sailed without him, Hans goes back to the Kit Kat to find Dolores. He is told she has left with a rich man. He does not believe she is really gone since he is convinced she loves only him.

Hans gets a job as a hawker for a nightclub, returning every night to the Kit Cat to see if Dolores has returned. He becomes friends with Tania (Lilli Palmer), a gypsy fortune-teller who falls in love with him. But Hans is still obsessed with Dolores and keeps looking for her. He finds the two thugs who beat and robbed him. There is a fight and Hans kills one of the thieves and then leaves the scene. The police pick up the other thief and tell him if he cannot find Hans they will charge him with the murder. Tania hides Hans at the gypsy camp. He hears from a friend that his ship has returned. He returns to the Kit Cat again, this time finally finding Dolores. The second thief sees him at the club and calls the police. Dolores tells Hans she doesn't even remember him and laughs in his face. Later he waits outside her apartment and when she comes home he strangles her. He is arrested by the police.

The film was more popular with filmgoers than with critics in France. The criticism had more to do with the script than the actors. It fit in with the pre–World War II poetic realism style that had been so popular in France but was now on its last legs. Its roots had been in realist literature, and the films were often told from a working-class perspective and filmed in dark hues, as befit the prewar mood in a France just waiting for the increasingly inevitable conflict. In the United States, it was generally accepted as a French take on the American genre film noir. Aumont certainly fit the noir bill as the doomed good man. Maria was surprisingly effective as a film noir femme fatale. In the French version it was evident her character is a prostitute. In the American version she was like the Donna Reed character in *From Here to Eternity,* a "hostess" in a club. This was about as far as you could get from her Neverland princesses. It was much more reminiscent of the murderous leader of *Atlantis.* Her choice of role met with a similar reception from her fans in America—this was not how they expected to see Maria Montez.[8]

Fresh off his ship, sailor Aumont meets prostitute Montez in *Wicked City*.

This did not stop her from using the film to keep her name alive in Hollywood. In an interview with Earl Wilson, she presented the move to Europe not as a result of a series of disasters, but as part of a grand plan. Maria crowed that American producers had lost their nerve in the face of all the changes the film industry was experiencing. "They're all frightened," she said. "But Maria goes to Paris, produces her own film with a very meenimum expense, and shows them she can be a gewd actress. Hell, I am a woman of action." She also claims she finally had a chance to prove that she was a talented actress. She told Wilson she played a B girl in the movie. "B for bad." Again, criticizing her previous roles, she said, "Honey, it's the kind of role Hollywood never would give me. Every picture I get in Hollywood, it's a fantasy, and I'm queen of something. I said the hell with it." To Patricia Clary, Maria explained she was taking a six-thousand-mile trip "to get out of a rut. . . . There was nozzeeng wrong weeth zee peectyures I made at Universal. Nozzeng eff you like being prencess all zee time." She presented herself as having turned her back on being Queen of Technicolor to become a serious actress, although she had to go all the way to Paris to do it.[9]

From the first view of Maria's character in *Wicked City* it is very evident that we are no longer at Universal City. Hans has entered the Kit Cat with two shipmates. One of the working girls latches onto him. But Hans looks over to the bar. The camera does a slow crawl up Dolores, starting with her feet and ending with a very knowing look on her face. Hans sees the woman of his dreams. Dolores sees her next john and he's ripe for the plucking. They go to her room. The door closes. The camera lingers on the closed door. As he is leaving to return to his ship, Hans tells Dolores, "I hate it when other men look at you." She matter-of-factly replies, "You'll have to get used to it."

This is an entirely new Maria, and you completely believe she is a manipulative, high-priced prostitute who can read a man quickly and effectively and find the way to his fantasies and wallet. Patricia Clary was right. Maria had to go all the way to France to become a dramatic actress. The best acting Montez had ever done up to that time was in *Wicked City*.

Christina Productions closed after the completion of its one film. Producer Jacques Gauthier brought Maria's second French film to life. He had a script about a woman who loved manipulating men to attempt death-defying feats in carnival shows. Gauthier wanted some script revisions and he took it to Orson Welles and Charles Lederer. Welles had come to Europe after the failures of *Lady from Shanghai* for Columbia and *Macbeth* for Republic. When he got the proposed script for what was then being called *Portrait of an Assassin*, he and Lederer completely rewrote it. Welles was also slated to play the part of Fabius in the movie, but the role went to Pierre Brasseur. When Hedda Hopper originally heard of the possible pairing of Orson Welles and Maria Montez, she thought that it "could be the battlingest of the century." But in the end it became just another in Welles's impressively long list of unmade films. Gauthier rejected the script, refused to give the writing duo their last check, and wound up suing them for breach of contract.[10]

Peter Bogdanovich, discussing Welles's sojourn in postwar Europe in one of the many interviews that formed the book *This Is Orson Welles*, was inclined to skip right by *Portrait of an Assassin*, but Welles brought it up. Bogdanovich seemed somewhat taken aback when Welles lamented that the script he and Lederer wrote was never used because the film "had a great cast. Erich von Stroheim, Pierre Brasseur, Arletty, and Maria Montez." It seems Welles was a much bigger fan of Montez than his interviewer.[11]

Portrait of an Assassin

In *Portrait of an Assassin*, a man walks the rainy urban streets at night. As a woman is coming toward him, he shoots her and then returns to his trailer at a traveling carnival. Fabius (Pierre Brasseur) thought his victim was his wife,

Martha (Arletty), the attack motivated by his fear and angst generated by his job riding a motorcycle around the "Wall of Death." But then Martha walks through the door of his trailer. It turns out Fabius shot Christina de Rinck (Maria Montez), owner of the International Variety Agency. Learning who shot her, she turns up at Fabius's trailer and eventually tries to talk him into performing a double forward loop in a car, a stunt never before attempted.

Fabius is initially reluctant to do the stunt, but Christina persists, seducing him and appealing to his manhood. Eric (Erich von Stroheim) confronts Fabius, warning him not to trust Christina. They had been lovers but she turned her affection to his partner in their trapeze act, Antonio. The partner died trying a stunt she had dreamed up and Eric fell trying to save him; now he must wear a metal body brace to remain upright. But Fabius won't listen. He has fallen in love with Christina and she has convinced him to do the double loop with the car racing at sixty-five miles per hour down a forty-five-foot-high ramp. He has left Martha, who decides she must attempt the ride on the Wall of Death or she and Fabius's mechanic will be thrown out of the carnival. She is killed in the attempt, while Fabius is successful with the double loop. But he has killed Christina for heartlessly leading other performers and Martha to their deaths in her shows and trying to kill him too. After receiving the applause of the audience, he goes back to his dressing room to wait for the police beside Christina's body.

At least Maria's role in *Assassin* was a step up from being a prostitute. But this was still a far cry from Neverland. There is not one lighthearted moment in this film. As she had so many times before, Montez does play a wealthy, imperious woman. But here she is a scheming, heartless woman who enthusiastically uses her sexuality to get what she wants. Von Stroheim as the crippled Eric perfectly sums up her character when he says to her, "What you love in your lovers is that they are strong and full of life." She then finds a way to get them to die trying to perform some impossible stunt. She had used her sex to seduce first Eric and then his partner Antonio. The latter died trying to do an impossibly dangerous stunt and Eric broke his back trying to save him. When she is first introduced it is noted that her husband died under suspicious circumstances on their yacht. Her character in *Wicked City* used the sailor Hans cruelly, and Queen Antinea killed her former lovers and made them into statues. It seemed the Europeans, from Seymour Nebenzal on down, perceived Montez's proper role as a psychotic destroyer of men. She said she wanted modern, dramatic parts and the French certainly gave them to her. *Assassin* was successful in France. It was awarded the Grand Prix d'Art

Français, precursor to the Grand Prize at the Cannes Film Festival. The movie showed only in a handful of art house theaters in the United States.[12]

The film featured Maria's best on-screen kiss. She had been alternately vamping, complimenting, and belittling Fabius to do the double loop jump. She finally has him right where she wants him. He agrees to do the jump. The camera zooms in for a close-up as she prepares to kiss the emasculated daredevil. She looks at him with triumph as she opens her mouth slightly and pulls his head forcefully to her for the kiss. These types of passionate kisses would also feature in her Italian films. Europe perceived her as an aggressive, actively sexual, passionate woman who drove men crazy. This just was not how she acted with Jon Hall.

Another brief scene demonstrated how well Maria came to understand the camera and the possibilities inherent in a close-up. Fabius is talking to Christina in her office, expecting her to turn him over to the police for shooting her. In French, he says "les flics" should be arriving soon. "Les flics" was street slang for the police, like "cops" in English. But Christina was upper class. As far from a street person as you could get. Montez's face registers incomprehension. She says, "Les flics?" Fabius translates for her. It is one small part of a larger scene. But it perfectly sets up who Christina is and the social gulf between her and the man she is manipulating into risking his life. It is so subtle, but exactly what the scene required. Subtlety was certainly not encouraged in Neverland and was in general resolutely barred at the gate. Montez was finally being given a chance to act—and she rose to the occasion.

Portrait of an Assassin was made in early 1949. It proved to be an interesting insight into the France of that time. As was typical, scaring up the financing was not easy. American actors were common enough in Europe at the time. Orson Welles was to write, direct, and possibly star in the film. Maria Montez was popular in France due to her recently released Neverland films and her marriage to French war hero Jean-Pierre Aumont. Marcel Dalio played Fred, the man who designed and built the platform for the double forward loop. He had returned to France after playing the croupier who gives Captain Renault his winnings after he is "Shocked! shocked! to find there is gambling going on" in Rick's Café Americain in *Casablanca. Assassin* was French actress Arletty's first role since doing eighteen months under supervision for what was called at the time "horizontal collaboration" with her lover, a German Luftwaffe officer. Much of the film was shot on actual locations rather than expensive studio constructions. It continued the tradition of prewar French poetic realism. Like *Wicked City* and *Siren of Atlantis,* it also included the beloved French trope of *l'amour fou,* the hopeless, absolute, self-punishing love of a man for a woman who will just wreck him.

Maria has another very strong scene in *Portrait.* Von Stroheim is in Christina's office in his metal body cast, leaning on a cane, as she is hanging yet another photo on a very large wall labeled, "In honor of those who died so the show could go on." He knows she is looking forward to adding Fabius's photo to the wall. Von Stroheim launches into an angry, heartbreaking story of how Christina seduced both him and his partner. How she devised a nearly impossible trapeze sequence, resulting in Antonio the flyer missing the connection with Eric the catcher. Montez, cigarette in hand, asks if he did not catch his partner out of jealousy because of his relationship with her. He is pouring his shattered heart out about the death of his closest friend while she enjoys the spectacle and keeps pouring gasoline on the fire of his guilt and sorrow. She manipulates this crippled man who still loves her and she revels in his agony. It is similar to Montez talking about all her golden former lovers in *Siren of Atlantis.* But this scene is sublimely chilling in its heartless and joyous crushing of a man's soul. This is far more than imperiousness with an edge. This is cruelty for the sheer joy of it, and Maria pulls it off with obvious relish.

In 1949 the rights to Jean-Pierre Aumont's play *The Emperor of China* had been bought by the Theater Guild of New York. Leading American playwright Philip Barry had been hired for its English adaptation. What emerged was retitled *My Name Is Aquilon.* Lilli Palmer and Aumont were to play the leads. Maria read the adaptation and told her husband his play had been absolutely ruined and would be a failure. Aumont went to the United States seeking several rewrites to his play, but Maria was right. It ran at the Lyceum Theater from February 9 to March 7, 1949, only thirty-one performances, and was savaged by the critics. Maria flew in for the previews and opening of the play but had to return to Paris before the closing performance. Aumont was so depressed and embarrassed by its failure that he chose to go to the Florida Keys alone rather than head back to France and his wife.[13]

As he went from island to island in the Keys Jean-Pierre was writing a play that would become *L'ile heureuse* (The Happy Island). It concerned a film producer who buys a screenplay from its author and assures him it "will become a masterpiece on the condition that the title, action, characters, style, general idea, episodes, and all the lines are changed." His problems with Philip Barry certainly played a part in the frustration that led to Aumont writing this new play. It eventually became a play about taking a script by an idealist who wants to make the world a better place and turning it into a

United Artists snipe: "Movie star Maria Montez arrives at Idlewild Airport . . . where she recently completed a picture with her husband, Jean Pierre Aumont. Their 2 1/2-year-old daughter, Maria Christina, was on hand to meet the plane. The Aumonts plan to remain in New York for the next few weeks, during which their latest picture 'Siren of Atlantis' will open on Broadway, and Aumont's play, 'The Emperor of China,' will be presented by the Theater Guild."

South Seas island epic with the leading female character running about in a sarong. He had written the play for his wife.

When he finally returned to Paris, after picking up his daughter, who had been staying with Aumont's father and stepmother in New York, he found a very unhappy Maria. She was angry that he had gone off to the Keys instead of coming back to her. They had a bitter argument and the word *divorce* came up. Word of their marital problems broke in the United States on March 23, 1949, between the completion of *Portrait of an Assassin* in France and the start of *Thief of Venice* in Italy. Louella Parsons quoted the cable she received from Montez in Paris: "I want you to be the first to know that, unable to get along, Jean Pierre Aumont and I have filed legal separation procedure. Best love . . ." Parsons wrote that she "couldn't be more surprised." She, along with everyone else, thought the Aumonts' had been one of the strongest marriages in Hollywood. It was a commonly held belief. Feg Murray put a bit in his Sunday cartoon *Seein' Stars* for April 4, 1947, that a letter had been received at the Hollywood Post Office from Vamos, Greece, addressed to "the Most Beloved Couple in Hollywood." It was delivered to the Aumonts and when they opened it, they found it was actually written to them. Louella could only conclude that the basis of the problem was career trouble. "Maria is a girl who loves the limelight. She was happiest at the height of her starring days at Universal when she was the 'Technicolor Queen,' giving out startling statements about her own beauty!"[14]

The Associated Press released a piece on the impending divorce on March 23, 1949, after interviewing Jean-Pierre. He is quoted as saying the couple "have awakened from their 'beautiful dreams of love,' and will be divorced shortly." The *Los Angeles Herald* went the AP one better when it reported, "Maria Montez to discard mate to wed director." Although the two had been "regarded in Hollywood as one of the happiest of screen couples," Aumont was on the way out so Montez could marry the French director F. H. Clouzot. It is hard to know where this bit of fantasy came from as Clouzot was very much involved with Brazilian actress Vera Gibson-Amado, whom he would marry in 1950.[15]

In the midst of the marriage problems, Hedda Hopper was walking her dog past the Aumonts' house in Beverly Hills when she noticed a tree had died. She found this symbolic of the couple's marriage. However, less than a month later it was being reported that the couple was back together again. Maria told columnist Harrison Carroll, "We kissed and made up. We are more in love than ever." She downplayed the incident, calling it a fight that "got out of hand and into the papers." It got into the papers, of course, because she wrote a note to Louella Parsons telling her. Aumont summarized the brief flare-up in their marriage in much the same way. Dorothy Kilgallen and Jimmie Fidler did not buy it. They both argued that what they described as the Aumonts' on again, off again marriage as "off once more." The debate now was over custody of Maria Christina.[16]

Paris news photo, stamped April 3, 1949. The snipe reads: "Actress Maria Montez registers shock, disbelief and sundry other emotions as she reads about divorce rumors between her and Jean Pierre Aumont. Miss Montez denied yesterday all reports that she and Aumont had filed legal separation papers, saying that they were 'amicably separated' on account of a quarrel over his adaptation of a play. . . . To rumors of a romance between herself and a Paris director, Maria replied, 'I don't even know his first name.'"

There was never any need to discuss which one of them would raise their child. This whole misunderstanding wound up being just a bump in the marital road. Perhaps a significant bump, but they got past it. Aumont remembered that horrible rift and its resolution. "We knew now that we belonged to each other. The truth was that in spite of our quarrels we were fiercely in love. This squall had been beneficial to us. The two last years we were to spend together would be the happiest of our lives. Our love was now more profound because we had nearly lost it."[17]

Soon after the two rededicated themselves to their marriage Maria, Jean-Pierre, and Charles Boyer were among the guests at what the *Los Angeles Times* described as "the most important social event in cosmopolitan Paris." It is indicative of the couple's place in Parisian society that they were guests at the Ball of Jewels at the mansion of the Marquise de Segur. All the women were expected to wear all of their best jewelry. It was estimated that $10 million ($108,451,681 in 2021 dollars) in pearls, diamonds, emeralds, sapphires, and rubies were worn by partygoers. There was also $5 million worth of sable, mink, and chinchilla furs. Princess Giovanni, Baroness de Cabrol, Countess Montesquire, and Duchess de Maille were all there. Maria Montez was the only actress in attendance. Two months later she was with Jean-Pierre and Charles Boyer at La Nuit del la Chancellerie (Night of the Ministry of Justice), chatting with Vincent Auriol, the president of France.[18]

Not long after the balls, Maria was off to Rome and the restored Scalera Studios to do an Italian-American production called *The Thief of Venice.* It was originally slated to start filming on August 12, 1949, but initial trouble in casting and continuing problems with finances caused the start date to be put off until November.

Orson Welles, in town doing reshoots for *Othello,* wanted to get together with his friend Maria Montez. Their friendship went back to his visiting the set of *Arabian Nights.* After that meeting she told columnist Sidney Skolsky, "He makes a woman feel very beautiful and desirable, and besides, he is every bit as spectacular as I am." Joseph Cotten was in Rome at the same time, finishing location shooting for *September Affair.* He and his comrade from the Mercury Theater had lunch together and Welles asked Cotten to have dinner with him that night at Harry's Bar, where he was dining with Maria. They had a great night. Cotten recalled, "Maria was a vibrant and beautiful girl. Her wit was sharp, her laughter uninhibited. Shyness was not Orson's strongest conscious trait, nor is it mine, and so our dinner was hilarious."[19]

Welles picked up the check and asked Cotten "to share the privilege of escorting Maria to her hotel on the Lido." When they got there the concierge told Cotten that he had won the tenth Venice International Film Festival's Best Actor award for *Portrait of Jennie.* Cotten told the concierge he had not been at the festival because no one invited him. The committee from the festival left the award with the hotelman, knowing he would see Cotten. His two friends congratulated him on his award and Maria, as always acting on her conception of the fitness of things, said, "You can't simply pick it up from the porter's desk without a presentation ceremony." The concierge got two waiters to clear one of the tables of the chairs piled on it, put a white cloth down, and bring out some champagne and glasses. The hotelman made a very poetic speech and Cotten accepted his award and bowed his thanks. "Maria kissed Orson and me goodnight, and I dropped him off at his location island, whose outline was beginning to take form in the rising sun." As he took the launch back to his hotel, Cotten thought about the awards ceremony at the hotel. "I saw a surprised and overwhelmed winner, a truly humble and dignified donor, all surrounded and endorsed by happy, unenvious friends."[20]

The Aumonts had a whole new problem to deal with back in Beverly Hills while Maria was waiting for the filming of *Venice* to commence. Their home had a lien placed on it by Paul Ross, a public relations man they hired to keep their names in American publications. He claimed the couple had not paid him $2,160 for the work he had been doing. This just escalated when Hedda Hopper received word that Maria had criticized the columnist's coverage of her. In 1940s Hollywood it was a really bad idea for an actor to find fault with anything Hopper did. She was known to be on the vindictive side. On March 19 Maria felt it was necessary to write a letter to the columnist to explain the situation. In the letter she basically blames the disgruntled public relations guy for spreading false rumors and tells Hopper that she would never criticize her writing and always appreciated that Hopper had "been kind and sweet to me." In her typically straightforward way, Maria noted, "Furthermore, I'm not a fool or a dope, why would I make an enemy of you? I like you very much and have always felt a kind of 'sisters under the skin' thing for you, being a Gemini." It all worked out. The columnist had always supported Montez and would continue to do so.[21]

Thief of Venice certainly was not without its problems. Initially it was to star Edmund O'Brien and his wife, Olga San Juan. Then Douglas Fairbanks Jr. got involved with the film. Finally, the producer settled on Maria and Paul Christian, who was hot off starring with the new Queen of Technicolor, Maureen O'Hara, in *Bagdad* (1949) for Universal. Jesse Lasky Jr. was hired to write the script. It was quite a different experience from his work at the affluent, highly organized Paramount back in Hollywood. He noted, "What we didn't have was enough money. Ever."

By 1950 the Italian movie industry was well into its postwar renaissance. The neo-realism films of Roberto Rossellini, Vittorio DeSica, and Luchino Visconti introduced an entirely new method of making films to the world. Not on sound stages, not with big stars, scarcely with a script. Realism. But Cinecittà, Europe's largest movie studio, had been put back together from its wartime bombing and life as a refugee camp. Italian filmmakers were using it as well as the streets of its cities to produce great sweeping historical dramas. American films would soon join in, giving Rome the nickname Hollywood on the Tiber. Where Maria Montez fit in all this was in the locally made historical dramas that were so popular with Italian filmgoers.

One thing that remained a major problem in the postwar Europe film industry was the financing of movies. *Thief of Venice* was no exception. Initially the filming was to start in August 1949. It finally started in November and ran through February 1950. More money had to be raised after the filming to bring Maria back from Paris to help with the extensive dubbing necessary on the Italian-American production in August. For once Maria did not own the franchise on accents. In *Thief* everyone had some sort of accent. There was the additional problem during the filming that the star very nearly drowned in one of Venice's canals. On January 24, 1950, the gondola Maria was being transported in ran afoul of a mooring cable off St. Mark's Square. Her gondolier, Oberdan Giorgetti, dived in and pulled her out.[22]

Lasky had never met Maria. In his experience, many actors tried to be anonymous in their private lives. "Not so Montez. She oozed patent, blatant allure. She was a panther of pleasure. . . . She glided into a room, undulating, her eyes like dark cauldrons in which the virtue of a saint could be dissolved." But as he got to know her better he realized, "Actually, she was a shrewd, hard-headed businesswoman, marketing a highly salable commodity: herself." He first met her for dinner in Venice with the producer and director. Generally, Italians presented Maria as a glamorous movie star as opposed to the French view of the woman in full. But this night as they left the restaurant a near riot ensued. A group of young Italian men were nearby. According to Lasky, Maria's naturally flirtatious manner ignited the crowd. Very quickly "the joyous cry lowered to a kind of carnal growl, no longer gay but ugly, even threatening. And not a *carabinieri* in sight." They jumped in their gondola and left the crowd behind. The only other time Lasky had seen such a response to an actress was Jean Harlow dealing with a "similarly overstimulated" mob in the other Venice in California. He was shocked when he heard a year after the incident that Maria had died. He thought, "Beauty can be a flame that consumes itself. To anyone who knew them, it would be hard to imagine the Jean Harlows and Maria Montezes as aging ladies."[23]

The Thief of Venice

The doge, or elected leader, of Venice is very ill. It is 1575 and the independence of Venice is threatened. He writes to the admiral of the Venetian fleet that Scarpa, the grand inquisitor (Massimo Serato), is poisoning him. The doge dies, the Turkish navy defeats the admiral, and Scarpa attempts to gain control of Venice. Part of his scheme is to marry the popular daughter of the admiral, Francesca (Faye Marlow). The one Venetian ship that escaped massacre by the Turks did so because the captain (Paul Christian) promised the slave rowers they would be freed if they could out-row the Turks. Scarpa refuses to honor the promise and the slaves blame the captain. They also blame him for the murder of the admiral by Scarpa's men. He goes to Angel's Roost, a café run by Tina (Maria Montez). The slaves are there and want to kill him. Tina persuades them to hold a trial. The captain is tied to a wheel and interrogated. She argues his case and he is found innocent.

Tina comes up with the idea of all the thieves of Venice stealing money from the rich so they can buy weapons and ammunition to overthrow the inquisitor. The inquisitor is hosting a large party when the thieves show up to rob everyone. The captain, who is now known as the Thief of Venice, escapes, but Tina is caught. She is tortured on the rack to try to get her to reveal who and where the thief is. She never does. The captain kidnaps Francesca and offers to trade her for Tina. The trade is made and Tina comes up with a plan to defeat Scarpa. Word goes out to all in Venice to arm themselves with anything they can for a general uprising on the day of the wedding of the inquisitor and the daughter. His barge is being rowed down the canal to the church when it is attacked by the thieves and half of Venice. There is a sword fight between the thief and the inquisitor. The thief wins. There is rejoicing throughout the city. The thief and Francesca happily watch the proceedings. Tina looks on sadly, for she had loved the thief and he chose another.

There are not too many places where you could make a film set in 1575 and not have to dress the streets and buildings very much. You could do that in Venice in 1950. Most of *Thief* takes place outdoors on the canals and in front of the buildings of the city. Jesse Lasky Jr. thought Venice was the true star of the film. It is used magnificently as a backdrop to this tale of duplicity by reigning offi-

Maria on the rack in *The Thief of Venice.*

cials and the heroism of the common people—of which Maria is one; she is not a princess. She runs a bar/restaurant. Montez never looked better. Her hair was always curly in her Italian films and it framed her face perfectly. She seems to have a freedom of movement in these films she never had at Universal. She is earthy and fundamental rather than imperious and above the fray. She joins right in the thieving and seduces men whenever necessary. The torture scene is very unexpected for Montez. She is stretched on the rack, burned with a hot iron, then dunked in the canal, her hands tied above her head, to revive her so she can be tortured some more. But she does not break and joins the thieves in the attack against the inquisitor. This is a tougher, grittier Montez than her fans in the United States ever saw. She plays the part very convincingly.

Thief, released Stateside by 20th Century Fox, was the last of Maria's movies to be reviewed in the United States. The reviews were generally quite positive. The *New York Times* set the template. Its reviewer praised how successfully director John Brahm moved the action along. The movie never lagged for a moment. The actors, including "the volatile Miss Montez," did a fine job, but the real star of the movie was Venice itself. The *Los Angeles Times* thought "'Spectacle' is the only word to accurately describe '*The Thief of Venice.*'" Venice itself is once again lauded. The reviewer wrote that Maria "gives a fine portrayal of a flirtatious, freedom-loving girl who knows just what she wants from life." *Motion Picture Daily* represented the exhibitors. Its reviewer also extolled the quick action and the beauty of Venice and thought the movie contained "the necessary elements for a healthy box-office." Particularly noted in the cast was Maria, who "turned in a zestful performance of the tempestuous peasant girl in love with handsome Paul Christian." The reviewer, stating that 20th Century Fox had indicated it intended to use a heavy advertising campaign, opined, "The combination of Venice, lots of colorful swordplay and Miss Montez should prove alluring to ticket buyers."[24]

Hedda Hopper continued to promote Montez in her column no matter where her films were made. On September 20, 1949, she reported Maria had signed to star opposite Michael Redgrave in *Queen of Sheba,* to be directed by Jean-Pierre's brother François Villiers in Egypt. On December 6 it was reported that Montez had registered the title *Mimi from the Folies Bergere* for a possible independent production. Neither of these films went anywhere. Instead, Maria was headed back to Rome to begin production on *City of Violence* (also called *Camorra*) in August 1950. Money was once again a problem and shooting continued on until November, including location work in Naples. Further complicating the production was that the funding came from German, Italian, and American sources and dubbing had to be created in all three languages.

City of Violence (*Camorra*)

City of Violence takes place in Naples in the late nineteenth century as Italy struggled to free itself from foreign occupation. The Camorra, the syndicate that controls Naples, had helped return the city to Italian control but soon became a criminal organization of graft and corruption. Pepe (Massimo Serato) has been railroaded into prison, but manages to escape. He tracks down Paolo, a member of the Camorra who grifted his girlfriend Dolores (Maria Montez), a singer at a local club, out of her jewelry. He is leading her down a lonely road to kill her when Pepe kills him first.

An army major (Alan Curtis) is sent by the king of Italy to smash the Camorra. Marco (Hans Sohnker), the syndicate's leader, determines to fight the major. Much to Dolores's dismay, Pepe falls in love with Marco's daughter (Mirella Uberti). The major shows up at their wedding and tells Marco that either the Camorra can surrender and be given amnesty, or the army, which is right outside, will kill all of its members. Marco decides to fight and is killed along with many of his men. His daughter and Pepe survive and plan to run off together. As Pepe returns to his apartment to pack his goods, he is greeted by Dolores, who begs him not to go. She entreats him to kiss her and when he won't, she pulls him to her and kisses him. When he again refuses to stay with her she stabs him to death. His final words are "All right, we belong together."

City of Violence certainly lives up to its title—it is a very dark movie. Like American films noir, much of it takes place at night, in ill-lit rooms or outside on city streets. The good guys and bad guys can be equally noble or duplicitous. The main difference is that the women are not femmes fatales. The Camorra leader's daughter is the classic good girl in a bad situation. Maria's Dolores is completely put upon. She was grifted out of her jewels by Paolo and would have been killed by him if not for Pepe, and then she loses her lover to another. In a very un-Montez-like situation, she throws herself at Pepe and begs him not to leave. His rejection leads to Dolores stabbing him to death. It is very interesting how the Europeans kept casting Maria.

Jesse Lasky Jr. was contracted by Hungarian producer-director William Szekely to write the script of *City of Violence.* This was his second time around with Maria Montez—he had scripted *Thief of Venice*—and the financing was even more complicated. He referred to the production as "a Tower of Babel." It was a co-production of German, Italian, and American companies. This involved not only three different languages, but also three different types of currency in those pre–European Union days. Lasky had little control over what happened to his script once it was accepted, so he had little to do with the financial roller coaster involved with the film. He had worked with Cecil B. DeMille on seven different films and the director wanted him to return to the United States to write his second take on *The Ten Commandments.* After all the multilingual fighting over financing of *City of Violence,* he was ready

The European star in Italy, August 1950.

to go. The film was never exhibited in the United States and is generally not listed on his résumé of scripts.[25]

Maria stayed in Venice in August and September for the Venice International Film Festival. Montez certainly understood she had to work as hard to become a part of the European film community as she had to become part of Hollywood's community. She reported early to the *City of Violence* set as she was scheduled to introduce Walt Disney's new film *Cinderella* at the festival on August 26, 1950. The Italian journalists, one of whom referred to her as a "French star," were as enthusiastic as their American counterparts with how la Montez reacted to photographers. She "is one of the few actresses who do not seek to cover their faces or otherwise escape the flashes of the photographers. She knows how to stay natural in her obligations and details. In Venice, the public has accompanied her to the door of her hotel."[26]

She is on the cover of *La settimana illustrata*'s (The Illustrated Week) forty-eight-page coverage of Festiva di Venezia smiling ecstatically at the greeting she received, looking every inch the movie star. She had good reason to be happy. Her friend Orson Welles was there, she had another Italian film in the final planning stages, and Jean-Pierre was completing *The Happy Island,* a play he had written for her. Two months after the Naples location work was completed for *City of Violence,* Maria was back in Paris for her first venture on the live stage. *The Happy Island* would open in January 1951 at the Edouard VII Theater. She would play a Latin American actress named Carlotta Goya who had a tough time in Hollywood.

If only *L'ile heureuse* had the happy denouement of the marital separation its writing led to. Aumont wrote it for her and hoped it would introduce her to a whole other aspect of acting. He was in Marseille touring with another play the night it opened. He called his wife at midnight and found out the power in the theater had gone out and the audience had to wait an hour and a half between the first and second acts before even partial power was restored. The play was not well received. *Variety* was running reports of the doings of American film people in Western Europe. Its review of *L'ile heureuse* could not have been more negative; the play was derivative and completely lacked the "crisp and funny" dialogue that might have saved it. Maria's performance got the exact same review her American films always earned. "Maria Montez undoubtedly has a beautiful pair of gams, but she is shy on the rudiments of acting." Aumont felt lousy for handing his wife such a poor part. "The character was a conventional Hollywood star. How I hate myself today [1976] for not having given Maria a deeper, more dramatic role."

Jean-Pierre was scheduled to take his play *L'homme de joie* (The Man of Joy) to Egypt late in February 1951. Maria was able to join her husband once *L'ile heureuse* closed. They toured Luxor and the Valley of Kings. Aumont suggested they stop in Athens on the way home, but Maria declined. She was so moved by her experiences in Egypt that she did not want to tarnish those memories by adding new ones from Greece.

Montez had returned from her tour of Egypt and was preparing for her upcoming role in *Revenge of the Pirates* when the House Un-American Committee was reconvening in Washington, DC. Its supposed task was to root out Communist influence anywhere in the country, but the committee concentrated on Hollywood because that's where the headlines were. Dozens of left-wing Hollywoodites were subpoenaed by the committee. They were all interrogated about their own affiliations as well as being asked to "name names" of other people they suspected were subversive. Even Maria was mentioned in the hearings.

Bella Lewitzky was born at the socialist commune Llano del Rio in California's Mojave Desert and went on to lead numerous dance scenes in the Neverland movies as well as many other Hollywood films. Her career came up during her testimony to the committee in 1951. It was established she had worked for RKO, MGM, and Universal Studios. She noted, "I was in most of the Montez films that had dance sequences in them." Representative McWheeler asked, "Are you referring to Maria Montez?" Lewitzky replied yes. Then the dreaded question: was the dancer a member of the Communist Party? Lewitzky took the Fifth on that one. As she did when asked about Henry Morgan, Mickey Ashton, and who was the secretary for her cell. She refused to incriminate herself or others and was blacklisted from Hollywood films. The committee at least had the sense not to spend further effort investigating Maria's political affairs.[27]

Revenge of the Pirates (*La vendetta del corsaro*)

Maria Montez's final movie was filmed in Rome at the refurbished Cinecittà Studios with her husband as co-star. Called *Revenge of the Pirates,* it is a slim effort indeed. Once again it is a historic epic, taking place in 1675 in the Caribbean Sea and Maracaibo, Venezuela. The naval war between Spain and the great naval powers has ended, but pirates are still very active in the Caribbean. Enrico di Roccabruna (Jean-Pierre Aumont) is the leader of a band of pirates that attacks and eventually boards a Spanish ship. It is carrying the Marquesa Consuelo (Maria Montez). In her last outing Maria is back to being a noble woman, this time Spanish. She and the pirate leader fall in love. It turns out that Luana (Milly Vitale), Consuelo's maid, is the long-missing sister of Enrico the pirate. While all this love is in the air, Enrico is trying to regain the riches that a wicked governor had stolen from him and to avenge the killing of his father. He is successful in winning Consuelo's heart, reunited with his sister, and wins back his gold and more from the

Poster for Maria's last film, *Revenge of the Pirates.*

governor. The film was released in Italy on October 18, 1951—a month after Maria's death. It was never released in the United States.

One of the few positive things to come out of *Revenge of the Pirates* was an example of how Maria was not completely forgotten in Hollywood. It was reported that Stanley Kramer wanted to see a print of the film. He was producing a picture called *The Juggler* that had a part for a very strong woman dedicated to building the state of Israel. Kirk Douglas as a Holocaust survivor was to fall in love with her. Kramer initially thought this might be a part for Montez until he saw and hired Italian actress Milly Vitale for the part.[28]

Maria certainly never gave up the idea of returning to America to resume her Hollywood career. Soon after completing *Pirates* and less than a month before her death, the Associated Press published an interview with her in Rome. The author wanted his readers to know, "The brown-eyed diplomat's daughter may have disappeared from American screens, but she's still one of the busiest actresses in the world," working in both France and Italy. Maria explained, "There are so many movies to be made." The writer thought this statement might "confound fellow stars who are bemoaning Hollywood doldrums." She had just completed a pirate movie starring with her husband and she claimed to have another film lined up with Dino De Laurentiis titled *Sensuality.* She noted the love story would probably have to be retitled for the United States. After that she wanted to takė a vacation. She worked so much in so many different countries that she scarcely had time to enjoy the five-bedroom house Jean-Pierre had recently given her in Paris. She told the interviewer that Louis Shurr kept after her to try television. After *Sensuality* and a vacation she planned to return to America where, she supposed, "I'll try it and see if I like it."[29]

Maria died not long after her Associated Press interview appeared in American newspapers. With the wretched insight that can come from hindsight, Jean-Pierre Aumont saw what should have been setting off alarms. He had been noticing how quickly Maria went along with anything he wanted to do. She began rising early in the morning, which was unusual. Her conversations with ghosts and revelatory dreams became more common. She was eager to accompany him to Trieste, where he was working on a film, just to spend time with him. She was reluctant to go swimming as her astrologer had always warned her to be wary of water. Maria told Aumont she sometimes could not feel her heart beating.[30]

Her longtime agent Louis Shurr had been in Paris that May. He had a large, boisterous dinner engagement with Maria, Bob Hope, and Hope's whole traveling troupe. Shurr remembered the night. "I had never seen her looking more wonderful, more full of life. . . . She was gay and lovely. She had everything to live for." He was planning to come back to Paris in October as he had a project for Maria, a movie called *Last Year's Show.* He never made the flight.

Maria never did get to film that last Italian movie, hear about the part in *Last Year's Show,* take a vacation, or return to America. On September 7,

Maria with Aumont and his father Alexandre Solomons and stepmother Anni at Orly airport, Paris. The International News photo, taken the night before her death, is captioned "Last Photo of Film Star Before Fatal Bath."

1951, as post-production was being completed on *Revenge of the Pirates* for its October release in Italy, Maria Montez went upstairs at her home in the Suresnes district of Paris to take a bath. Her husband was on a Parisian sound stage. Two of her sisters, Adita and Teresita, were downstairs. The trio was going out to lunch as soon as Maria finished her bath. Montez had been taking very hot baths with salt added as a reducing method for years. She took being a movie star very seriously and was not about to let weight get the best of her. She was thirty-nine by now and had borne a child. She had seemed to have put on weight in the harsh lighting of her French films, but had slimmed down for her Italian movies. She was still a star in Europe and hoped to return to work in the United States. She never let herself go and remained dedicated to watching what she ate, exercising, and taking the reducing baths.

This time something went drastically wrong. Adita finally got tired of waiting and went upstairs to see what was taking her sister so long. As she told the French police, "I climbed the stairs and looked in Maria's room but found nothing. I thought she could still be found in the bathroom a few steps away. I opened the door and almost fainted from the shock. Maria was completely submerged in the bathtub, with her forehead just out of the water filling the tub."

She screamed for Teresita to come help her. They pulled Maria from the water and rushed her to her bedroom. The Paris fire department was called and a medical team responded quickly. They worked to resuscitate Maria for three hours. But it was too late. Jean-Pierre raced back to their home from a film set in the Alfa Romeo sports car his wife had given him for their anniversary. But there was nothing he could do.

There was never an autopsy performed. The chief of Paris firefighters attributed her death to drowning. Either she fainted in the hot water and slipped under or she had a heart attack and slipped under. In either case, Maria Montez was dead at only thirty-nine years (although it was reported as thirty-one at the time due to the years Universal shaved off her life). Jean-Pierre sobbed through the night beside the body of his wife at the home she so loved in Paris. It was impossible to lead him from the room.

Her Catholic funeral mass took place four days later at Saint Pierre de Chaillot church in Paris. She was interred at Montparnasse Cemetery in the Isle-de-France district. A procession from the church to the cemetery wound its way through Paris. Thousands of her fans lined the streets, paying their respects. A photograph taken at the Saint Pierre mass ran in *Life.* Aumont appears in the front row, transfixed by grief. Next to him his sisters-in-law's faces are completely obscured by their black veils. Her sister Consuelo flew in from Los Angeles, but visa problems caused delays and she missed the funeral.[31]

Associated Press and United Press stories on Maria's death were featured on the front pages of newspapers across the United States. The AP described her as an "auburn-haired spitfire of the movies." The UP called her "raven-haired Maria Montez, 31, lovely inhabitant of Hollywood's Technicolored South Sea Isle and Oriental harems." The *Los Angeles Times* labeled her "vivacious, tempestuous," and went on to extensively quote Louis Shurr, who said, "It's such a shock. . . . I just can't believe it. She was one of the most vital persons ever to hit Hollywood." He went on to describe how happy she had been when he saw her in Paris in May. He had been working on reviving her Hollywood career and said he had an offer from Fidelity Pictures Corporation for her to star in *Last Year's Show.* Virginia MacPherson in the *Los Angeles Daily News* noted that Maria had "carved herself a million-dollar career as the most famous 'bathtub queen' since Claudette Colbert bathed in milk for 'Cleopatra.' . . . And it was bitterly ironical that the dark haired beauty who loved to take bubble baths in Technicolor should meet her death in just that way."[32]

Several other Hollywood people joined Louis Shurr in mourning Maria. Hedda Hopper remarked, "Maria Montez' death in France shocked everybody. She was so young and vital." Virginia Zanuck, who saw her in Monte Carlo a few weeks before her death, said she never looked more "vibrant and happy." Erskine Johnson had a section of his column called "Hollywood Is Talking About." On September 16, the talk was of Maria Montez's tragic death. "No matter what the doctors called it, her Hollywood friends knew she died of a broken heart, having failed in her crusade to re-capture her wartime title of movie glamour queen." [33]

Of all the Hollywood columnists, Bob Thomas wrote the most heartfelt piece. He had always enjoyed his time with her and his columns about Maria were inevitably bemused and positive. Thomas wrote, "Hollywood remembers Maria Montez as the girl who swore she would become a movie star—and did. . . . The prime factor in her success was—Maria Montez." He remembered her "knack for publicity" and what a regular visitor she was to both the Universal photo studio and the publicity department. He also recalled an enjoyable wartime "date" they went on so she could be seen out. He concluded, "Perhaps it was her great drive that caused her death. Because even when she became a leading star, she was not satisfied. Then she wanted to be a dramatic star."[34]

She certainly still had projects. In an October 1950 column Erskine Johnson wrote of an upcoming Montez film that would co-star Turhan Bey to be filmed in Germany, *The Belle of Naples.* Harold Heffernan was probably writing of the same film, only he called it *Earth of Love.* Besides this film and the De Laurentiis movie *Sensuality,* it seems there was a play in the works. John Carlyle, a small-time actor, gay gadabout, and friend of Judy Garland, had been traveling around Europe in 1951. When he was in Paris modeling for a French men's fashion magazine, he ran across British playwright, composer, actor, and general man about theater Noël Coward, who hailed him at a Left Bank café. As they drank, the actor listened to the playwright talk about *Stardust,* a play his secretary Cole Lesley was preparing for Maria Montez to perform on the London stage. It was a reworking and translation of Aumont's play *L'ile heureuse.*[35]

Coward had initially met Jean-Pierre and Maria at a party hosted by Laurence Olivier after the royal command performance on November 4, 1946. He found Aumont "sweet" and Maria a bit of a "show off." They met again on April 1, 1950, at a cocktail party in Paris just before Maria left to return to Los Angeles for the trial to recover her $38,000 from Seymour Nebenzal. Carlyle soon ran through his money and wrote a note to Coward asking if there might be a part for him in *Stardust.* He received a reply on November 9, 1951. "Dear John—Nothing at all is happening about that play yet as it was being done for Maria Montez and is now shelved till we can think of someone else to play the part which will not be yet awhile." He advised his friend to return to the United States and try to get some work in television. Coward certainly understood Aumont. After referring to Maria's death in his diary, he wrote, "Poor Jean Pierre will be demented."[36]

The loss was felt most keenly by her husband and family but was shared by so many in the film community as well as a world full of fans. The shock of it and the shared grief was summed up in a card sent by Jean-Pierre Aumont's stepmother thanking Golden Globes member Frank Yanosik, who had sent his condolences. She wrote, "Thank you my dear Frank for your kind letter which touched us deeply. I know how fond you both were of our dear Maria. Her death was a horrible shock to us."[37]

It certainly was a shock to Jean-Pierre. He was haunted by all those "if onlys" that seem so obvious in hindsight. He wondered, "Is it possible that fate is cruel enough not to make us understand these signs? . . . How many times since have I repeated to myself: 'If I'd only insisted that she see the doctor . . . If I'd stopped her from dieting . . . If she only hadn't taken such hot, long baths . . . If Maria Christina hadn't gone to lunch at my brother's . . .' There's no real answer. You have to believe in God or else go crazy."[38]

The grief did not end with Maria's funeral. A month after she died Cynthia Lowry wrote a piece describing Maria as the sixth star "claimed by untimely death." She was the latest in "a series of premature, tragic deaths of talented beautiful women who seemed to be fortune's favorites." The other five were Carole Lombard, Jean Harlow, Thelma Todd, Lupe Vélez, and Carole Landis. Three months after his wife's death, Jean-Pierre Aumont was photographed in a tuxedo escorting Margaret Truman, daughter of President Harry Truman, to the opening of *Caesar and Cleopatra* at the Ziegfeld Theater in New York. They are quite the study in contrast. Truman is beaming at the camera. Aumont is not. The caption noted, "Margaret Truman's smile contrasts with solemnity of her escort, French actor Jean Pierre Aumont." He was described as the husband of the late Maria Montez.[39]

Jean-Pierre remained haunted by Maria's death. A decade later Mamie Van Doren was having lunch with Aumont in a café in Argentina during the filming of *The Blonde from Buenos Aires.* Van Doren, who signed as a

Universal contract player in 1953, was familiar with Maria Montez's movies. A large photo of her still hung outside the studio commissary. Mamie was surprised when, with no prompting from her, Aumont talked lovingly about his late wife throughout their lunch together. He spoke of how much he missed her. The same thing happened every time the two ate together. Mamie was not sure why Aumont spoke so much about Montez to her. Maybe it was because they were in Latin America; maybe it was because Mamie was sympathetic. But it was clear to her that ten years after Maria's death her husband still missed her terribly.[40]

A French working-class pulp newspaper called *Radar* went into the greatest depth of any European or US publication on the death of Maria Montez. In its multi-page article, "Maria Montez, the Caribbean Cyclone: Victim Dies of Her Beauty," the immediate death scene was described. After specialists in artificial respiration failed to revive her, Dr. Dugonot declared her dead at 3:35 p.m. on September 7. He was certain she died by accident in water that was too hot— registered at 113 degrees Fahrenheit. "A Hollywood star was dead of her beauty," the writer argued. Dancers and actresses have to be thin, "which sometimes causes an accident."

A sidebar described in medical terms the detrimental effect hot water mixed with reducing salts can have on the heart. The main article explained in layman's terms that extremely hot baths can be dangerous enough, but salt baths in hot water can cause serious cardiac, pulmonary, or decalcification risks. The dissolution of the salts can raise the water temperature another twenty degrees. "Heart disease and even a simple fatigue of the heart is a consideration in all regimes of bathroom slimming." It was known that Montez had been recently noticing mild heart problems. It was what killed her father and would kill her brother Jaime at young age. *Radar* believed it was a combination of the extremely hot water with bath salts that led to her heart giving out and her drowning. The writer concluded, "A star is dead, victim of an ideal image required for the screen."

The newspaper advertised itself as "A Tour of the World in 150 Images." The cross-section of photographs and illustrations that accompanied the piece presented the view the French had of Maria—more complex than was ever the case in the United States. The French saw Maria as a woman in full rather than as the sultry Latin stereotype preferred by the American publications. The entire back page of the publication is given over to the life of someone the French clearly took to their national heart. The key photo in the written part of the article was of the actress in medieval formal dress from her final movie, *Revenge of the Pirates*. There followed a separate page of photos of

Montez. A full-face, smiling portrait is captioned, "The drama which has just taken away Maria Montez makes the stages of her young life even more sensitive . . .: glory, love, happiness. Our photos summarize this sparkly existence, laced with laughter and ended at its apogee by a stupid accident." There is a large photo of her lying down in her "eastern" finery from *Arabian Nights,* and a large illustration of her youngest sister, Teresita, running in a panic to get to the phone after finding her sister in the bathtub. There are four smaller photos of Maria and Aumont on the main set of *Atlantis;* the couple getting off an airplane, arms around each other; the two with their daughter Maria Christina labeled "An exquisite vision of calm happiness"; and Maria and her three sisters playing the piano and singing together.[41]

Festival, a pulp weekly French magazine, also mourned the passing of Maria Montez. She appears on the glossy cover in a full-color photograph, shot from below; she looks off to the right with a slightly melancholy expression. She is standing in a bountiful garden wearing an embroidered formal white dress with white gloves. The caption reads, "One of the last photos of the missed Maria Montez, gone so suddenly." *Le soir illustré* featured a cover photo of Maria and Maria Christina hugging each other with the caption, "The most recent photo of Maria Montez, the charming artist who has just tragically died." *Cine revue* did two articles on Maria's passing. The French published lots of pinups of Jane Russell and Ava Gardner, but the photos of Maria display a complete woman, both a very beautiful movie star and someone who was sincerely loved by her family.[42]

The most popular magazine in France in 1951 was *Paris Match,* roughly the equivalent of *Life* magazine in the United States. A color photo of Maria taken in France was on the September 22 cover with the title "The Dramatic End of Maria Montez." The essay within, titled "With Maria Montez Paris Lost Its Distant Princess," told of how she held a cherished place in the "hearts of thousands of strangers." As her funeral cortège made its way from the church to the cemetery, "Parisian crowds broke the barriers to say a last farewell to Maria Montez." She may have been a distant princess in Technicolor, "but nothing moves one more than the fate of a beauty fallen in full bloom."[43]

The authors went on to tell her life story, beginning with her family's home in the Dominican Republic, in "the natural splendor of their terrestrial paradise," where she was the favorite of her father. The fantasy of the convent school in the Canaries is told, and the article has American friends of her father taking her to New York, where she met a Universal producer. It speaks of her marriage to Jean-Pierre Aumont, his fighting in the Free French army, and their child, Marie Christina, now five. The family was so happy, Maria's

From first to last, French magazines always stressed what a loving couple the Aumonts were.

life so full—but it all ended so suddenly. "Apparently for no other reason than to remind us that destiny is sometimes jealous of happiness."

The four pages full of photographs covered the life of the "princess" even better than *Radar.* Like the other publication, *Match* made the effort to present the full woman the French admired so much, not just the movie star. The happy wife and mother, not just the Dominican Dynamite. In the largest photo she is shown in a demure white blouse sitting in the garden of her villa at Suresnes. The other two large photos show the parents with their daughter between them, "a radiant household of happiness," walking down the Avenue Carnot the previous winter, while the picture on the opposite page is of a devastated, crying Aumont at the cemetery with three of his sisters-in-law. There is also a series of smaller pictures of Maria in her wedding dress; at her Beverly Hills home playing with Maria Christina on the floor; with her three sisters at Farmers' Market in Los Angeles; in a mantilla at the Vatican to visit the pope in 1948; a 1949 photo of Maria in a striped dress that was said to be Aumont's favorite picture of her; a still featuring Montez as a barmaid in a roomful of men from the recently released *City of Violence.* The American newspapers reporting her death, by comparison, generally ran one of the early, sexy Ray Jones photos of a very languid-looking Maria with bare shoulders.[44]

Maria's will was not found until April 1952 when Aumont was cleaning up the garage at their Tower Road home in Beverly Hills that he was preparing to sell. It was handwritten and dated January 24, 1948. Her personal estate had been $14,000 in cash and $7,000 in jewelry in California. Her mother, Teresa, in the Dominican Republic received $10,000 from her insurance. Assuming she ever recovered the judgment from Seymour Nebenzal, $5,000 of it was to go to her sister Adita and $2,000 to her brother Aquilino. Her furs and clothing were left to her sisters Adita, Consuelo, and Teresita. All other property was divided between Jean-Pierre and Maria Christina. The house was held in joint tenancy and therefore went to her husband.[45]

Aumont continued in films in both Europe and the United States. On March 27, 1956, he married Italian-born actress Marisa Pavan at the Santa Barbara, California, courthouse. Her matron of honor was her twin sister, actress Pier Angeli, while Aumont's best man was MGM executive Benny Thau. Aumont had two sons with Marisa Pavan, Jean Claude and Patrick. Jean-Pierre Aumont remained active in film until five years before his 2001 death in France at ninety. Maria Christina would go on to become an actress in French, Italian, and American productions, known first as Tina Marquand after marrying actor/director Christian Marquand at seventeen, and later, after her divorce, as Tina Aumont. She was often asked about her mother but she was five years old when Maria died and remembered only how she looked and talked. What she knew of her mother's life came from conversations with her father and aunts. Tina passed away in 2006 and was buried at Montparnasse Cemetery next to her mother. Maria's loyal agent Louis Shurr died in 1967.[46]

Time moved on in Hollywood after Maria's death. Major stars like Clark Gable, Errol Flynn, Ronald Colman Myrna Loy, Betty Grable, or Rita Hayworth still resonate mightily with fans of Golden Age Hollywood. But even those fans might have trouble remembering exactly who Carole Landis, Anne Gwynne, or Maria Montez were. The wider society could not place them at all. *Sic transit gloria mundi* (thus passes worldly glory). Gable and the rest far outlived World War II in their careers. Maria Montez, not so much. She was a quick blazing thing for four years. A true Hollywood movie star who worked in European film for another three years in hopes of returning to Hollywood. But it was never to be. The courage to leave a secure life in the Dominican Republic, the Montez for Stardom Club, the endless time spent in Ray Jones's portrait studio, the triumph of the six Neverland hit films, finally having a family of her own, the lawsuits and disappointment of her last two years in Hollywood, and the loving reception she received in Europe were stopping points along her star's road. Then she took a hot reducing bath to maintain her movie star physique while her sisters waited for her to go to lunch.

Afterword

The six Neverland movies made Maria Montez the Hollywood star she had dreamed of being as a girl and young housewife in Barahona. For the first three years of her Universal Studios contract she was the world's greatest commissary actress, the tamer of Holly-wolves, one of the Sweater Girls, a serial dater, and the Mmmm Girl. For the last four years of her seven-year contract with Universal Studios she was a bona fide star, the Queen of Technicolor, top billed in her movies, a frequent radio guest, a feature in numerous national advertising campaigns, a loving wife, and eventually an expendable pain in the neck to her studio. Her movies were extremely popular with wartime audiences and made Universal millions of dollars. She was constantly mentioned in film-related newspaper columns all over the country as well as in the numerous movie magazines so popular at the time, ranging from a short note in a column to articles specifically about her, one of her movies, or her relationship with her husband.

She was also part of stories about groups of stars and what they did on their first date, what they thought about glamour, what they thought wartime wives should do with their time, how often they should write to their soldier husbands, photogs' favorite stars to photograph, or stars with red hair. She went to major parties, the Academy Awards, movie premieres, bond rallies, military bases, the Hollywood Canteen, and events at her studio. She displayed a nice sense of humor and timing as she performed on numerous radio shows as herself in spite of her accent. Her studio named her the Queen of Technicolor. When faced with a choice of studio all-star films it gave her a starring, first-billed role in its A-list, star-studded *Bowery to Broadway* (1944) rather than Olsen and Johnson's B-list *Crazy House* (1943). For a glorious four years she was not a kooky commissary actress willing to do anything for a photographer. She was a star.

It did not last long. Her studio grew sick of arguing with her over the direction of her career and the parts she was offered. Universal grew particularly weary of being sued by her. The men running the studio were convinced she had no place in the grittier postwar A films they planned to produce after their merger with International. Especially when they had Yvonne De Carlo under contract, who could do both exotic fantasies and modern dramas. With Montez in Europe, Maureen O'Hara quickly became filmdom's new Queen of Technicolor. The Good Neighbor Policy slipped into history along with the war that spawned it. The Cold War began on the heels of World War II and once again the United States felt it had to dominate Latin America to protect the hemisphere from the Soviet threat.

The whole studio system that had helped create and sustain her was crumbling. With television breathing down the studios' necks and the loss of their theater chains, they were all cutting their rosters of players. Universal was happy not to renew her contract. Independent producers considered Montez for many movies in the postwar period, but with the exception of *Siren of Atlantis* they did not pan out. She did continue to make movies in France and Italy, but their American distribution was minimal or nonexistent. Hollywood studios filmed dozens of movies in Europe after the war, but none of them featured Montez, who was already there.

Maria's fan base did not much care that she was no great actress so long as she was running around looking gorgeous in Technicolor in the six Neverland adventures. They did not want to see her in second-rate movies wanting to kill a Spanish Fascist, or as a crazed queen of an underground realm killing discarded lovers by the bushel. When trying to carry off these roles Montez simply did not have the acting ability to overcome the poor scripts or to win over her old fans or capture new American ones. She kept working and was popular in France and practically worshiped in Italy, but after three years abroad the memory of her was fading in the United States.

Then, after filming those five films in Europe, she died so young and so suddenly. Maria never had the chance to return to American films or to work on television. The list is long of Hollywood film actors whose career petered out, only to be revived on the small tube. Lucille Ball had a knockabout career in films, but she was the biggest star television ever produced. Marjorie Lord was in a few Universal B films and independent productions but gained fame as Danny Thomas's wife on *Make Room for Daddy* and *The Danny Thomas Show.* Barbara Hale was in several B movies for RKO and Columbia but will be forever remembered as Perry Mason's secretary and right-hand woman. Maria demonstrated such a flair for radio comedy. Who knows what she might have done in television?

Maria died before she could do anything to add to her legend. There was no autobiography, no *This Is Your Life* episode with Ralph Edwards, no sitting on the couch with Steve Allen, Jack Parr, or Johnny Carson discussing whatever new project she was involved with or to rehash her old films. She never had the chance to appear on *Murder She Wrote* with Angela Lansbury, a show that became such a home for Hollywood actresses of a certain age. There was no opportunity to speak with Ronald Davis of Southern Methodist University for one of his extensive interviews with Hollywood stars of the 1940s.

What little exposure Maria Montez did receive in the 1960s came by way of the gay community, which loved the camp and general outrageousness of her movies. Independent filmmakers Jack Smith and Kenneth Anger, Andy Warhol screenwriter Ronald Tavel, and Theatre of the Ridiculous founder John Vaccaro all loved her movies and her spirit. Smith in particular was affected by her exotic glamour found in what he called "musty" or "moldy" movies from the recent past that were dismissed by contemporary critics. These "secret flix" very much influenced his completely personal, very influential art films.[1]

Smith was a pioneer in "Queer Cinema," a leader in the movement dedicated to breaking free of any sense of convention. His multimedia work, while rarely seen outside a small group of artists at the time of its creation, has been preserved by the Museum of Modern Art in New York. His most complete appreciation of Maria's glamour—and his utter indifference to her minimal acting skills—is best expressed in his essay for *Film Culture,* "The Perfect Filmic Appositeness of Maria Montez." He summed up why he so loved her movies and thought everyone else should. "She believed and thereby made the people who went to her movies believe. Those who could believe did. Those who saw the World's Worst Actress just couldn't and they missed the magic. Too bad—their loss."

Maria is very much present in Smith's *Buzzards over Bagdad,* a reimagining of *Arabian Nights,* and *Flaming Creatures* (1963), which opens with a bit of dialogue from *Ali Baba and the Forty Thieves* and takes place in the Orientalist fantasy world the filmmaker loved. He even convinced his protégé drag queen, Rene Rivera, to take the stage name Mario Montez to honor his ideal. Rivera said he adapted her name because "she does everything with such fire—nothing is pretended." But Smith also makes the completely false and rather racist statement that she was, "Oily Skin dark and gave impression of being Dirty." It's great to appreciate the goofy grandeur of her Technicolor extravaganzas, but it is absurd to see her as oily and dirty.[2]

Maria cropped up all over the burgeoning gay culture of the 1960s and '70s. One of the characters in *Boys in the Band* (play 1968, movie 1970) proclaims Maria "was a good woman." She is a key player in Gore Vidal's novel

Myron (1974). The lead character, Myra/Myron, is sucked into a television set while watching one of her movies, *Siren of Babylon,* eventually trading places with Maria Montez in the endlessly repeating movie. Critic Rex Reed was another writer who helped keep Maria's name alive with frequent references, particularly to *Cobra Woman,* in his columns. This was certainly the movie that received the most attention from gay writers. Filmmakers like Smith and Kenneth Anger were interested purely in the exotic and overwrought images she projected in the Neverland movies. Smith in particular was far more interested in how Maria represented his artistic beliefs than in the reality of her life.[3]

Ronald Tavel, like Jack Smith, worked with Andy Warhol as the screenwriter for many of the films produced at the Factory. He was also obsessed with Montez and the Neverland films but made an effort to see her as more than an outrageous screen presence. His most complete writing on Maria was *Maria Montez: Anima of an Antediluvian World.* Equally obsessed with Maria and like Tavel a key member of the Theatre of the Ridiculous, John Vaccaro was also a friend of Jack Smith. All of them had fun with her accent. It was largely through them that "Give me the cobra jewel" became such a famous line. Eduardo Moreno was another writer interested in Montez. He summed up well her general standing in the gay community. "Maria Montez has become a cult figure, perhaps the most spectacular representation of screen camp and kitsch ever known."[4]

While Maria became a gay icon in the United States, the Dominican Republic honored its favored daughter in several ways. Barahona declared a day of mourning upon hearing of her death in 1951. A street was named in her honor. The house she shared with William MacFeeters in Barahona has been preserved. The house she grew up in was given a plaque to commemorate the fact, but was later torn down. The airport in her hometown was named the Maria Montez International Airport in 1996. In 1995 Montez was awarded the International Posthumous Cassandra award from the Dominican Republic Art Journalists Association. It was accepted by her daughter Tina Aumont. Classic dancer and writer Margarita Vicens de Morales, whose collection of photos and movie posters was featured at the Cassandra celebration, published a series of articles in the Santo Domingo newspaper *Listin diario* (Daily List) that became a full biography, *Maria Montez: Su vida* (Maria Montez: Her Life) in 1976. The book has been updated three times—in 1994, 2003, and 2013. Heavily illustrated, it provides photographs of Montez from her childhood in Barahona to her time in Europe. It is particularly strong in presenting her early life in the Dominican Republic. Vicens de Morales also published a series of articles and created a large exhibition in

Santo Domingo to celebrate her centennial. Maria was awarded a second Cassandra in 2010 along with Zoe Saldana to recognize actresses from the Dominican Republic.[5]

Montez has been the catalyst for two novels. Jean-Pierre Enard's novel *La Reine du Technicolor* (The Queen of Technicolor) was published in France in 1980. It concerns the work of a post–World War II detective in Paris investigating the death of an actress in her bathtub. The investigation is an introduction to the main story, which explores the detective's dysfunctional family. The novel was not a best seller and the author is best remembered for his earlier erotic novels. Len Levinson's *Cobra Woman: A Tale of Sexual Obsession* was published in the United States in 2019. Its protagonist Sam Wishnefsky is a twenty-six-year-old direct-mail advertising copywriter who meets a woman who looks just like Maria Montez at a TGIF party in Manhattan. He had an enormous crush on the actress as an eight-year-old after seeing several of her movies on television. He falls in lust with the look-alike, marries her, and finds out fantasy is not reality. All his eventual wife Gabriella has in common with la Montez is that she looks like her. Needless to say, things don't end well.[6]

The emphasis on her early life is also the case in the 2014 Dominican-produced, Spanish-language *Maria Montez: La pelicula* (The Movie), produced by and starring Celines Toribio as Montez. She admitted to having to guess at several aspects of her subject's life, such as her marriage to MacFeeters. The Dominican comes off as a paradise, Hollywood as a place of frustration. When asked why she wanted to make a movie about Montez, Toribio said she wanted to stress Maria's origins and the dedication she had to fulfilling her dreams. "Because she is a woman from my country and is a courageous Latina like myself. She was also an immigrant to the United States. I cling to role models like her. Maria Montez risked it all to dare to dream big. She was very persistent when it came to achieving her dreams, she motivated me a lot."[7]

Actress Dalia Davi created a one-woman show called *Maria Montez Queen of Technicolor* in 2011. Her mother was from the Dominican Republic and her father was Puerto Rican. The multi-media event was about a New York City actress who becomes possessed by the spirit of Maria Montez and gradually transforms into her. In the process she reconnects with both her Dominican roots and her mother and explores the strength of her spirituality while living in the South Bronx. Davi incorporated storytelling, two short films, and photo projections to present her show.[8]

The internet has presented several sites devoted to the Queen of Technicolor. The most complete is *Maria Montez: A Dominican Star* (www

.mariamontez.org), started in 2009 by Dominican natives Vivian Perez and Luisa Peguero. It is in both Spanish and English and includes not only a biography of Montez but also a list of all her films, an extensive bibliography, several of her poems, a gallery of images, and special sections on Jean-Pierre Aumont and Tina Aumont. Perez has also put several whole movies, the television show *Mysteries and Scandals* (originally aired May 26, 1998), which dealt with her sudden death, and cuts from her films on YouTube. The Maria Montez Fan Club preceded the website by five years. It published at least fifteen numbers of a magazine, edited by Richard Fellows, full of articles about Montez's career, what she meant to members of the club, what her outrageous acts really meant, and how generally underappreciated she was. Several other websites have presented biographies of varying accuracy.[9]

Realart film corporation, a subsidiary of Universal, began rereleasing Montez's films in the late 1940s. It is interesting to see her name listed with the key stars, even in *Invisible Woman,* where she appears in two brief scenes with no dialogue. By the early 1950s her movies began appearing on television. The six Neverland fantasies that made Maria's reputation have been reissued on DVD in all their Technicolor magnificence. Most of the other films from her complete oeuvre are available in various qualities from different small companies. Montez is no longer lost to the film community. The pictures that made her so briefly famous are available to be seen once again. The special effects featured in the movies look primitive by today's standards, but Technicolor was never used more effectively by Hollywood. The movies are exactly what they were meant to be in the mid-1940s. Nothing deep, just a lot of fun watching a beautiful woman cavort with various sidekicks to overcome travails in the end and live happily ever after. Jack Smith got one thing right. What difference does it make if Montez cannot act, sing, or dance? As Yvonne De Carlo said, you just have to enter her world, relax, and enjoy.[10]

Jean-Pierre Aumont had nothing but happy memories of their crowded house in Beverly Hills and his life with Maria. In his autobiography he summed up their days in a most human and poignant fashion. "People never seem to appreciate their blessings. The slightest problem overwhelms us with sadness or bitterness; we are singularly unconscious of our happiness, perhaps because we consider it our due. It has to be lost to be perceived. Later, I realized that the years spent in that house were among the most beautiful in my life. It's there that Lucita, then Consuelo were married, there that Maria Christina grew up, there that we lived the richest hours of our love."[11]

Maria may have died alone in a bathtub but her sisters were downstairs, her daughter was having lunch with her husband's brother, François Villiers, at his house nearby, and her devoted husband was just a few miles away on a sound stage filming the last scenes of *Les loups chassent la nuit* (Wolves Hunt at Night). Her mother, brothers, nieces, and nephews were back in the Dominican Republic. She had friends all over Paris, New York, and Los Angeles who were shocked and devastated by her death. She had a very full life and it was not a lonely one. The success she had experienced in the United States had waned, but her agent Louis Shurr was convinced it was not over. Noël Coward was preparing a play with her in mind, and a fourth Italian movie was being planned. When she died the streets of Paris were jammed as her funeral cortège made its way from Saint Pierre de Chaillot church to Montparnasse Cemetery. Newspapers and magazines all over the United States and France carried the shocking news of her premature death. She was a beloved movie star in her time whose name brought a smile to her fans wherever her movies had been shown. She was a wartime ambassador of goodwill between the Americas and the original Queen of Technicolor. No matter how convoluted and unique her journey, Maria Montez achieved what she set out to do in the Dominican Republic. She had a stable, happy home life and became a true Hollywood movie star.

ACKNOWLEDGMENTS

This biography of Maria Montez has been a long time coming. I first got interested in her while doing a book about Universal's chief portrait photographer Ray Jones with his son John Jones. He told me all sorts of stories about his father, the people he photographed, and the studio he worked for. John is one of the very few people I ever found who had actually met Maria—and not only met her, he sat on her lap. Several decades later he remembered every second of it. Tom Maroudas brilliantly put color to Ray Jones's black-and-white portrait for the cover.

Christina Rice, the senior librarian for the Los Angeles Library's Photographic Collection and the author of biographies of Ann Dvorak and Jane Russell, not only urged me on with my writing but came up with several research sources I'd never heard of. Roger Hatheway is the greatest researcher I know. He got interested in Maria and asked me if I had ever used Geneology.com because she was all over the place there. He sailed as man before the mast in his youth and never lost his interest in boats. It was through him I found out what little there was to know about the *Mako II*. Michael John Sullivan has both a photographic memory and a huge interest in Hollywood history. He was always very insightful in placing Maria in her overall role in Hollywood and lamented that Max Steiner never created music for her. Vivian Perez, who developed the original and most complete Montez website, was particularly helpful in guiding me through Maria's early life in the Dominican Republic. Dominican author Margarita Vicens de Morales has updated *Su vida*, her biography of Maria, three times and produced several articles about her, which she has been sending out for several years.

Gregory William Mank had extensively interviewed Elizabeth Russell and was very generous is sharing what he learned and telling me about the screenplay she wrote about her friend Maria. I was unable to find a single copy of the screenplay until I spoke to one of the research librarians at the

Academy of Motion Picture Arts and Sciences' Margaret Herrick Library who said, "Maybe she copyrighted it. Try the Library of Congress." I did and found the only known copy of the manuscript. I had to go to Washington, DC, to read it, but it was absolutely worth the effort. One word of advice. If you are from Southern California and you have to go east to do research, read the weather reports. If it says it is going to be ninety-two degrees and 96 percent humidity, prepare for suffering and disorientation. Have cab money if you need to go further than four blocks. If you get on a practically empty New York subway car, do not congratulate yourself on your luck. The air-conditioning will be broken and you will be a soaking mess after three stops. Life is tough when you're from L.A. and you have to face actual weather. When even the locals are complaining, somebody from L.A. doesn't have a prayer.

Anyone doing research on the history of Hollywood must visit the Margaret Herrick Library of the Academy of Motion Picture Arts and Sciences. It has the finest collections and the best librarians you could possibly hope for. Ned Comstock at the University of Southern California's Cinematic Arts Library led me to many sources that had never occurred to me. The same was true of the librarians at the Wisconsin Historical Society's archives at the University of Wisconsin, Madison, which houses the Walter Wanger Collection, and the University of Utah, which houses the May Mann Collection. Stephen Duckham searched the Noël Coward Society's records to find his involvement with Maria. There is no Maria Montez Collection anywhere so these peripheral collections were extremely valuable.

Maria Montez was quite the citizen of the world. Many of the sources were not in English. I must say, Google Translate has improved markedly over the past decade. But I have been very lucky to know Amie Kosberg for help with Spanish and Yolande Freimuth and Dominique Abensour for French. Nancy Spitz helped me understand Latin American wedding traditions. The magnificent Andria Litto introduced me to her father George, who had been friends with Louis Shurr, who in turn connected me with Raina Paris, daughter of Maria's youngest sister Teresita. Marjorie Lord spent an afternoon talking about her time at Universal Studios during World War II and specifically about how it was to work with Ray Jones.

Everyone at the University Press of Kentucky have been extremely helpful in making the original manuscript about Maria better in every way. Ashley Runyon, Sarah Olson, Victoria Robinson, and Jewell Boyd all helped enormously in preparing the book for publication.

Los Angeles researchers have to be grateful to the *Times* for putting its newspapers going back to 1881 in a historical archive available online. Geneology.com and Newspapers.com have radically changed what is available to researchers. They were particularly helpful with research on Montez, as she was very popular with the many Hollywood-related columnists publishing all over the country during the 1940s.

NOTES

Abbreviations

AFI	American Film Institute Catalog of Feature Films
MHL	Margaret Herrick Library, Motion Picture Arts and Sciences, Beverly Hills
MPPC	Motion Picture Production Code (Hays Office), files at Margaret Herrick Library, Motion Picture Arts and Sciences, Beverly Hills
TZC	Tom Zimmerman Collection
USC	University of Southern California Cinematic Arts Library
WWC	Walter Wanger Collection, Wisconsin Center for Film and Theater Research, Wisconsin Historical Society, University of Wisconsin, Madison

Introduction

1. In one of the first articles published about Maria, she spoke of her initial plans for getting attention in Hollywood. When the article was published, it was key to her landing her first leading role in *South of Tahiti.* But in spite of all the craziness to get attention, the author pointed out she always had a plan and believed she behaved with dignity. There was a source for her believing so strongly in herself. "Her father, says Maria, was a very wise man, and her greatest inspiration until his untimely death several years ago. 'He taught me a great deal,' she said. 'Most of all, he taught me how to think things out for myself.'" Tom DeVane, "Glamour Is Her Dish," *Hollywood,* January 1942, 38.

2. "It Has Three Million Followers Who Live by the Stars," *Life,* December 30, 1946, 45–46; Robert Wallace, "Stargazer to the Stars," *Life,* April 5, 1954,143–55. Maria is prominent in both articles.

3. "U. S. Military by the Numbers," nationalworldwar2museum.org.

4. Michelle Pautz, "The Decline in Average Weekly Cinema Attendance, 1930–2000," *Issues in Political Economy* 11 (2002); "1946: The Year for Movie Going," ew.com/article/1994/04/29; Jeanine Basinger, *The Star Machine* (New York: Knopf, 2007), 466.

1. The Dominican Republic

1. An excellent history of the Dominican Republic is Frank Moya Pons, *The Dominican Republic: A National History* (Princeton: Marcus Wiener, 1995). For a

history of the Trujillo government at the time Maria would have been most involved with it, see Eric Paul Roorda, *The Dictator Next Door: The Good Neighbor Policy and the Trujillo Regime in the Dominican Republic, 1930–1945* (Durham: Duke University Press, 1998). To put that government's relation to Maria Montez in the context of the Good Neighbor Policy, see 28–31, 221–22.

2. The *Detroit Free Press* noted, "Her mother was the daughter of a Dutch political refugee ("News Pictorial, Rotogravure Section," May 23, 1943, 20.

3. Margarita Vicens de Morales, *Maria Montez: Su vida* (Santo Domingo: Republica Dominicana, 1992), 25–26, 35; Raina Paris, personal interview, September 8, 2014. For photos of the family and a young Maria, see Vicens Morales, *Su vida,* 25–33.

4. Charles Samuels, *Motion Picture,* January 1946, 36, 102; Charles Samuels obituary, *New York Times,* May 8, 1982.

5. Jean-Pierre Aumont, *Sun and Shadow: An Autobiography* (New York: Norton, 1977), 172. Six photos of Aumont's visit with Maria's family are in Vicens de Morales, *Su vida,* 215.

6. The best reference for Maria Gracia's life in the Dominican is Vicens de Morales, *Su vida,* 17–34. (For her birth certificate, see 26; marriage license, 31.) This period is also covered in Pablo Clase Hijo, *Maria Montez: Mujer y estrella* (Santo Domingo: Editorial del Norte, 1985), 15–20. He repeats the fallacies of her supposed education in the Canary Islands and her father being a diplomat.

7. William MacFeeters is mentioned briefly as living near the family and falling in love with and marrying the eldest daughter, Maria. Vicens de Morales, *Su vida,* 17, 30. Ancestry.com has numerous mentions of MacFeeters. See: Ireland, Census, 1911, U. S. Naturalization Record Indexes, 1791–1992; San Juan, Puerto Rico Passenger and Crew Lists, 1901–1954; U.K., Outward Passenger Lists, 1890–1960; New York, Passenger Lists, 1820–1957; California Passengers and Crew Lists, 1882–1957; England and Wales, Death Index, 1916–2007. William MacFeeters died in London, age seventy-five, in June 1968.

8. "The Life Story of Maria Montez," *Picture Show,* November 8, 1943,11.

9. Samuels in *Motion Picture,* 102.

10. Personal letter from Vivian Perez, founder of the *Maria Montez: A Dominican Star* website, January 24, 2009.

11. Ancestry.com, William MacFeeters, Mary MacFeeters: San Juan, Puerto Rico Passenger and Crew Lists, 1901–1954; U.K., Outward Passenger Lists, 1890–1960; New York, Passenger Lists, 1820–1957.

12. "A Star in Gemini" has a very poignant aspect. Russell wrote it after her son John died in 1993. The screenplay is told by him, called Jim in the play, as he remembers his "Tia Maria." They are described as being very close. Maria was very kind and loving toward him. The screenplay ends with Russell's son on the beach in the south of France. A beautiful young woman is hit with a beach ball and her friend summons her father, who turns out to be Jean-Pierre Aumont. Jim/John recognizes him and realizes it is Tia Maria's daughter who was hit with the beach ball. He introduces himself and shakes hands with Aumont. The last scene is of Russell's son and Maria's daughter dancing together in France. How badly Russell misses her friend Maria is

palpable throughout the screenplay. Elizabeth Russell, "A Star in Gemini" (screenplay, Copyright Office, Library of Congress, Washington, DC, 1999).

13. Jewell Dean, "Maritime News," *Cleveland Plain Dealer,* April 21, 1939, November 9, 1939, March 30, 1940; "Prominent American Angler on Visit Hopes to Hook Tarpons and Marlins," *Kingston Gleaner,* April 5, 1939, 8; Alan Whitneym, "The Role of the Camera in the Navy," *All Hands,* in *The Bureau of Naval Personnel Career Publication,* no. 561 (October 1963), 2–6; *Portland Oregonian,* December 5, 1948, 95; Bud Harvey, "Mexico City Report of Donnelley, Miss Gracious Marriage Confirmed," *Palm Beach Post-Times,* September 16, 1948. I contacted Thorne Donnelley's son, who told me his father left no diary or memoir and he did not know anything about his father's life before he married his mother in 1948. Donnelley died in April 1963 at sixty-seven years of age. For the *Mako II,* see "Many Yachts and Other Craft Arrive in Port," *Key West Citizen,* 1; *Palm Beach Post,* January 22, 1939, 10, and April 22, 1939, 7; *Chicago Chronicle,* April 9, 1939, 94; "Southward Ho!" *Motor Boating Magazine,* March 1944,60. Maria MacFeeters: Ancestry.com, U. S. Subject Index to Correspondence and Case Files of the Immigration and Naturalization Service, 1903–1959; Russell, "A Star in Gemini."

14. Vicens de Morales, *Su vida,* 18; glamourgirlsof thesilverscreen.com/mariamontez.

15. US Treasury Department, Bureau of Customs, *Merchant Vessels of the United States, 1945* (Washington, DC: Government Printing Office, 1945); Jake Rackman, "Spotlight 2nd Reel," *Omaha World Herald,* August 26, 1939, 111; "Many Yachts and Other Craft Arrive in Port."

16. Gregory William Mank, *Women in Horror Films: 1940s* (Jefferson: McFarland, 1999), 98, 211; Randy Vest, "Elizabeth Russell," *Films in Review,* May 1980, 289–93; Elizabeth Russell file, MHL.

17. "Her Picture Gallery," *Maria Montez: A Dominican Star,* mariamontez.org.

18. Gertrude Steinman, "Galaxie" (typewritten proposal for a book about Schurr's agency), MHL.

19. George Lozzi, personal interview, February 22, 2010. He noted Louis received as high a compliment as Hollywood could pay an agent. In *Golddiggers of 1935* the chorus girls go up to Barney Hopkins's office to see if he got the funding for his proposed show. On the door under Barney's name is painted, "Louis Shurr, Secretary." In its obituary for Shurr, the *New York Times* printed an oft-told story. The question would be heard, "Who is that man with the stunning girls? That? Oh, that's Louis Shurr. He's always accompanied by the best looking girls in town, the answer would inevitably follow." *New York Times,* November 3, 1967, 48; Donald Spoto, *A Girl's Got to Breathe: The Life of Teresa Wright* (Jackson: University Press of Mississippi, 2016), 33, 36, 40. Ava Gardner quote: Pete Martin, *Hollywood without Makeup: Favorite Stars as They Really Are* (New York: Bantam Books, 1949), 30.

20. Lucius Beebe, "New York Speaking," *Cleveland Plain Dealer,* September 8, 1940, 59 refers to Ferry's Monte Carlo as "the densest imaginable concentration of glamour, wealth and chic." Lucius Beebe, "New York Speaking," *Cleveland Plain Dealer,* July 6, 1941, 44; Danton Walker, "Walker's Broadway," a piece on the founding of the "New York Is a Friendly Town" committee, Gen.com, December 8, 1941; *Maria Montez: A Dominican Star;* Joe Pasternak, *Easy the Hard Way* (New York: Putnam's,

1956). Pasternak waxes on for pages about discovering and developing Deanne Durbin while never mentioning Montez at all.

21. Douglas Gomery, *The Hollywood System* (New York: St. Martin's, 1986).

22. Alan Woll, "Hollywood's Good Neighbor Policy," *Journal of Popular Culture* 3, no. 4 (Spring 1980): 278–93. Good Neighborism was stressed by the government to Hollywood. Of "the six basic themes that pointed a way toward a better understanding of this war," number 3 was "The United Nations and Peoples." "The Framework of the Government Information Program," WWC, box 14, folder 17; "Suggested Working Program for the Motion Picture Society for the Americas," WWC, box 14, folder 4; "An Open Letter from Hollywood to Mr. Nelson Rockefeller, Coordinator of Inter-American Affairs," WWC, box 14, folder 4. In the *Handbook of Industry Committees Organizations* (Hollywood: Publicity Directors Committee, 1942), the board of directors of the Motion Picture Society for the Americas was headed by Chairman Y. Frank Freeman and Executive Secretary Walter Wanger. All of the studios had representatives on the board. Cliff Work represented Universal: WWC, box 52, folder 27.

23. Jay Sexton, *The Monroe Doctrine: Empire and Nation in Nineteenth Century America* (New York: Hill and Wang, 2011). For the role played by the Dominican in the Roosevelt Corollary, see Pons, *The Dominican Republic,* 287–91.

24. Woll, "Hollywood's Good Neighbor Policy"; "Pix Vital to U. S. in S. A. Relations," *Hollywood Reporter,* January 15, 1941, 1+; "Whitney Asks True Pictures for Latins," *Variety,* November 18, 1941, 3; "Heavy Building in South and Central America, Says Daff," *Motion Picture Daily,* January 10, 1944,8. Alfred Daff was Universal's foreign sales supervisor. True to the company, he wrote, "They like to hear the natural voices of popular American stars. . . . Maria Montez is one of the most popular American stars." Debra Walters, "Hollywood, World War II and Latin America: The Hollywood Good Neighbor Policy as Personified by Carmen Miranda" (Ph.D diss., University of Southern California, 1978), 108. Jimmie Fidler interviewed an Argentinian visiting Hollywood. He quoted him, "What would it be if 'Gone With The Wind' was made in Rio or Lima, Peru by people who had never been to Georgia?" Fidler argued it was folly to keep trying to make movies about Latin Americans that just insulted them with US ignorance of their countries and customs. Fidler column, Gen.com, March 7, 1943. Miranda booed: Smithsonian Year of Music, "Carmen Miranda," music.si.edu/carmen-miranda.

25. J. D. Spiro, "Latin Beauties Rise in Films," *Milwaukee Journal* (Screen and Radio, Sunday supplement), December 22, 1940, 8–9.

26. Gaizka de Usabel, "The High Noon of American Films in Latin America" (Ph.D. diss., University of Wisconsin, Madison, 1982), 145–65.

27. Ancestry.com, U. S. Subject Index to Correspondence and Case Files of Immigration and Nationalization Service, 1903–1959, June 5, 1939. Elizabeth Earl would eventually marry broadcasting executive Pat Weaver and become the mother of Sigourney Weaver.

28. "Crop of Screen Sirens," *Variety,* October 21, 1940, 226, October 29, 1941, 17; "New Film Faces, *Variety,* January 8, 1941, 48. See also Harold Heffernan, "Bonfire Starlets of 1942: Directors Say These Six 'Bonfires' Have Best Chance for Stardom," *Omaha World Herald,* December 14, 1941, 46. The "stars" were Maria Montez, Janis Carter, Ava Gardner, Suzanne Ridgeway, Faith Dorn, and Aline Brandes. Sheilah

Graham, "Younger Girl Players Now Get Film Breaks," *Hartford Courant,* December 13, 1942, A18; Dee Lowrance, "Cinema Cinderellas Get Their Chance," Gen.com, January 3, 1942.

2. Universal City

1. Bernard Dick, *City of Dreams: The Making and Remaking of Universal Pictures* (Lexington: University Press of Kentucky, 1997); Michael Fitzgerald, *Universal Pictures: A Panoramic History in Words, Pictures, and Filmographies* (New Rochelle: Arlington House, 1977); Clive Hirschhorn, *The Universal Story: The Complete History of the Studio and Its 2,641 Films* (New York: Crown, 1983); Douglas Gomery, *The Hollywood Studio System* (New York: St. Martin's, 1986), 147–60; Thomas Schatz, *The Genius of the System: Hollywood Filmmaking in the Studio Era* (New York: Pantheon, 1988).

2. Dick, *City of Dreams,* 95–110; Gomery, *The Hollywood Studio System,* 150–52.

3. "Universal Studio Sale Forecast," *Los Angeles Times,* November 2, 1935, 1; "Studio Sold by Laemmle," *Los Angeles Times,* March 15, 1936, 1, 11.

4. Mark Vieira, "Darkness, Darkness: The Films of Val Lewton," brightlightsfilm.com, November 2005; Mark Vieira, *Hollywood Horror: From Gothic to Cosmic* (New York: Harry Abrams, 2003); Gregory William Mank, *Women in Horror Films: 1940s* (Jefferson: McFarland, 1999), 97–99, 103; Randy Vest, "Elizabeth Russell," *Films in Review,* May 1980, 290; Salka Viertel, *The Kindness of Strangers* (New York: Holt, Rinehart, Winston, 1969), 139.

5. Universal Studios biographical data sheet, TZC.

6. Santo Silas, from her mother's side, was often added on to Montez's name. Margarita Vicens de Morales lists all the various names that were applied to Maria in *Maria Montez: Su vida* (Santo Domingo: Republica Dominicana, 1992), 17. Maria did enthusiastically support Universal's reduction of her age. In an article called "Should a Woman Tell Her Age?" *Photoplay,* April 1946, 52–53, Joan Fontaine answered, "Certainly," Clifton Webb "Why hide it?" Anne Baxter "Very definitely," Dorothy Lamour "It's immaterial," Cornel Wilde "Stop worrying about it." Maria said, "It's nobody's business. . . . Besides, a woman's life is centered around a man in most cases. . . . Every man wants to think the light of his life is young. I think it's silly to do anything that would take away any part of that mystery."

7. Universal Studios, "Maria Montez Biography, 1940," TZC.

8. Hedda Hopper, "Hedda Hopper Says," *Los Angeles Times,* November 7, 1943, E3.

9. Tom Zimmerman, *Light and Illusion* (Los Angeles: Balcony, 1999); Universal-International, Universal City, Calif., "Ray Jones—A Biography," two-page mimeographed sheet, c. 1952, TZC. Jones was certainly a hometown-boy-made-good to Superior, Wisconsin: "Ray Jones, Superior Photographer, Is Head of Hollywood 'Still' Studio," *Superior Evening Telegram,* May 3, 1938, 1, 3.

10. Zimmerman, *Light and Illusion;* Paul Harrison column: Gen.com, December 9, 1941. Ray Jones's one argument with Maria took place when she threw a tantrum in the studio. He explained to Bob Thomas that it was due to her having taken a series of vitamins she was allergic to. Bob Thomas, "Veteran Cameraman Hangs Blast on

'Skinny Movie Queens,'" *Boston American,* April 9, 1952, 2; *Albuquerque Journal,* July 5, 1942,14.

11. TZC; *Los Angeles Examiner* Collection, Los Angeles Public Library Photography Collection. In the Universal system the negative to be printed would be marked in ink on the bottom with the subject's initials; portraits were simply numbered consecutively, Publicity photos were labeled PUB and a number, and F for fashion followed by the number of the photo within the code. The numbering is a truer indicator of when the photo was taken than the date at the bottom of the released photo, as a 1940 photo might not be released until 1942.

12. For the do's and don'ts of the movie still censors, see the photo created by Paramount's Whitey Schafer in Zimmerman, *Light and Illusion,* 21. For the Hays Office, see Thomas Doherty, *Hollywood's Censor* (New York: Columbia University Press, 2007).

13. The Gloria Jean photo is GJ-138, 1944, TZC. Richard Hays, "Gloria Jean Grows Up," *Seattle Daily Times,* July 2, 1944, 27.

14. "Tall Gals," *Screenland,* August 1944, 42–43+. The photo is fashion #118, used to publicize *White Savage.* The magazine chose to airbrush out a column that made her look even taller in the original. This issue contains quite a lot about Montez. There is a photo of her with Joan Fontaine wearing Lily Dache hats on p. 54 and a May Mann article called "Maria Montez' Frank Advice to Movie Struck Girls" on pp. 46–47+.

15. Universal release, Gen.com, June 28, 1941; for more nicknames, see "Meet the Service Men's Sweethearts," *Laff,* June 1944, 18–19; "Queen of Technicolor: Title Is Found for Dominican Starlet Maria Montez," *See,* January 1944, 10–11.

16. AP release, Amy Porter, "Real Rio Uncovered in Latin American Quiz," Gen.com, February 27, 1941; *Oakland Tribune,* Gen.com, March 9, 1941; Dorothy Kilgallen, Gen.com, July 10, 1940; Sheilah Graham column, Gen.com, March 8, 1941; Jimmie Fidler column, Gen.com, November 7, 1942, August 4, 1943; Sheilah Graham column, Gen.com, April 19, 1941.

17. *Los Angeles Times,* June 9, 1940, D4; Harrison Carroll column, Gen.com, November 8, 1940; Jimmie Fidler column, Gen.com, November 22, 1940. Auer can be seen playing the piano with grapefruits in RKO's *Around the World* (1943). Maxine Bartlett, "Death Valley Riders to Foregather Today," *Los Angeles Times,* November 3, 1940, E9.

18. *Variety,* October 21, 1940, 11; Jimmie Fidler, "Maria Montez Is Incredible for This Era," Gen.com, August 7, 1943; "Maria Montez: The Female Vic Mature; Hollywood's Most Spectacular Young Actress—This Temperamental Latin," *Silver Screen,* November 1942.

19. Hedda Hopper, "Hot Copy," *Modern Screen,* August 1945, 106; Howard Sharpe, "The High Cost of Maria Montez," *Liberty,* May 15, 1943, 39, 53. In 1950 Rogers would join with Warren Cowan to form one of the leading public relations firms, Rogers and Cowan.

20. Jeanine Basinger, *The Star Machine* (New York: Knopf, 2007), 507.

21. Only Maria's height, five foot seven, and weight, 122 lbs., were asked for on the biographical sheet, and were repeated on her September 1940 studio-issued biography. By the time of her August 1943 studio bio, her measurements were listed as 35–24–36, and her shoe size as 5. In April 1944, *Esquire* listed her as 34–23–36. Still with a size 5 shoe.

22. Montez, quoted in George Hadley-Garcia, "New Generation of Fans Smitten by Allure of Actress Maria Montez," *Los Angeles Times*, February 13, 1992, 3.

23. Anne Gwynne: WWC, box 90, folder 24; Ava Gardner: Pete Martin, *Hollywood without Makeup: Favorite Stars as They Really Are* (New York: Bantam Books, 1949), 29–30; Evelyn Keyes: Evelyn Keyes, *Scarlett O'Hara's Younger Sister* (New York: Fawcett Crest, 1977), 19. Cecil B. DeMille told her when he initially interviewed her, "That Southern accent must be eliminated at once. . . . You don't want to play nothing but southern girls all your life, do you?" Julie Adams: telephone interview, February 21, 2009.

24. "Hollywood Fights Its Slowdown," *Click*, March 1943, 15; Hedda Hopper, *Modern Screen*, July 1945, 52; "Maria Montez: The Female Vic Mature"; Hedda Hopper column, Gen.com, February 13, 1944.

25. Pete Martin, "Dominican Dynamite," *Saturday Evening Post*, July 28, 1945, 29.

26. Anne Gwynne: *Variety*, October 21, 1941, 11, quoted in Mank, *Women in Horror Films*, 153. Rosemary de Camp: Ronald Davis Oral History Collection, Southern Methodist University, #250, July 13, 1982, MHL.

27. *Office of War Information, War Manpower Commission*, August 17, 1943, WWC, box 14, folder 18.

28. Vern Haugland column, Gen.com, October 4, 1942.

29. Marjorie Lord, personal interview, September 24, 2005; Kyle Crichton, "Born to Act," *Collier's*, April 4, 1942, 17, 54.

30. Dee Lowrance Sunday column, "They Won't Ration Glamor," Gen.com, August 16, 1942, 57; Louella Parsons, Sunday column, *Washington Post*, September 20, 1942, L1.

31. John Franchey, "Caprice Espanol: How the Senorita from Santo Domingo Made Hollywood Dance to Her Music," *Movies*, July 1943, 62; "The Great Montez," *Look*, February 23, 1943, 29. See also "Good News," *Modern Screen*, October 1942, 85: "There isn't an eye in the room that can rip itself off Maria when she goes into her act. . . . She's a smart girl that Montez. She'll be famous someday." Ed Hartmann, who as screenwriter played a part in the comedy films of both W. C. Fields and Abbott and Costello, perfectly expressed the lament of the people behind the cameras. He remembered lunchtime tourists visiting the studio would walk into the commissary. "They were looking for Turhan Bey and Maria Montez and Donald O'Connor. . . . They'd wander past the tables staring, and they'd pass my table, and look and say, 'Oh, he's a nobody.'" Max Wilk, *Schmucks with Underwoods: Conversations with America's Classic Screenwriters* (New York: Applause Theater and Cinema Books, 2004), 236.

32. John Franchey, "Latin, Lissom and Lethal," *Silver Screen*, March 1942, 42–43+; Louella Parsons noted, "I've watched her stage entrances into various Hollywood night spots and they are Academy Award performances." "Perdon the Hahvahd Accent!" *Washington Post*, December 13, 1941, 16. Parsons announced that Maria was finally going to have a significant role in *South of Tahiti*. She wrote, "Red headed Maria Montez who has had more night club publicity than movie roles, is going to get a picture at last at Universal where they've been secretly grooming her. She will be a big attraction on a South Sea island." Louella Parsons column, Gen.com, August 24, 1941, 58.

33. USC, Universal Studios Collection, "Articles, Maria Montez" folder.

34. Sheilah Graham, "When Stars Mingle with Their Public," Gen.com, April 6, 1941, July 7, 1941. The suspicion spread about Maria's origins. Columnist John Truesdell described her as "the blonde Brooklyn girl who went Latin and developed a nifty South American accent." Gen.com, August 27, 1941.

35. *Hollywood,* September 1942, 38.

36. In the space of two weeks Harrison Carroll has Maria involved with three different men. In his column for December 29, 1941, she is with Teddy Stouffer; on January 7, 1942, it is agent Bill Burnside; and on January 13 she is with Stuart Barthelmess, all Gen.com. Gene Schrott, "Who's Afraid of Hollywood Wolves?" *Motion Picture,* December 1941, 23, 60–61.

37. Maria Montez, "Are Men Such Fools?" *Stardom,* September 1942, 40–41, 48; Maria Montez as told to Gladys Hall, "Me and Men," *Screenland,* July 1943, 36–37, 86–87; Tom DeVane, "Glamour Is Her Dish," *Hollywood,* January 1942, 38; Jimmie Fidler column, Gen.com, December 29, 1941. This is still one year before Maria's breakout in *Arabian Nights.*

38. Maria Montez, "How to Dress for a Man," c. 1944, University of Wisconsin, Madison, Wisconsin Historical Society, Clippings file: "Maria Montez."

39. *Motion Picture,* March 1942, 20; "Romance Is Rationed," *Motion Picture,* December 1942), 38.

40. H. Allen Smith, "La Montez Tells Women in General of Holly-Wolves," *El Paso Herald-Post,* November 10, 1941, 7; Harrison Carroll column, October 23, 1941, Gen.com.

41. Sheliah Graham column, Gen.com, June 23, 1941; May Mann column, Gen.com, February 7, 1943.

42. Robert Myers, AP, "I'm Sensational, Maria Montez New Movie Glamour Girl, Admits," Gen.com, November 8, 1942.

43. "The Great Montez, "*Look,* February 23, 1943, 28–30.

44. "*Life* Spends a Day with Sidney Skolsky," *Life,* May 3, 1943, 102–5.

45. Jimmie Fidler column, Gen.com, February 18, 1943; Erskine Johnson column, Gen.com, April 17, 1943.

46. "Letters to the Editor," *Look,* April 16, 1943, 8.

47. "Hollywood Inside," *Variety,* March 1, 1943, 2; Elizabeth Wilson, "'Perhaps I Am Too Egotistical,' Admits Maria Montez," *Movie Show,* March 1943, 38–39+; Robin Coons, "Maria's Gonna Quit Bragging," *Baton Rouge Advocate,* August 24, 1942, 5.

48. Basinger, *The Star Machine,* 504. Andrew Dowdy in his excellent study of social meanings in movies, *Films of the Fifties: The American State of Mind* (New York: Morrow, 1975), has a chapter devoted to what he called "The Tit Culture." The book was originally published in 1972 as *Movies Are Better Than Ever.*

49. "Movie Memos," *Motion Picture,* July 1943, 8. John La Gotta did an article on best body parts and chose Maria as having "the most beautiful back in America." The Hollywood writer for the *Amarillo New-Globe* was fairly amazed by this: "There are good reasons why Maria Montez, the Technicolor beauty, seldom has her back toward the camera." Dorothy Kilgallen column, Gen.com, March 24, 1944.

50. On Howard Hughes's obsession with Jane Russell's breasts, see Christina Rice, *Mean, Moody, Magnificent! Jane Russell and the Marketing of a Hollywood Legend*

(Lexington: University Press of Kentucky, 2021). The author quotes an astoundingly revelatory eight-hundred-word memo from Howard Hughes on the subject (150–51). Elizabeth Russell, "A Star in Gemini" (screenplay, Copyright Office, Library of Congress, Washington, DC, 1999). You cannot quote directly from a manuscript in the Copyright Office, but it seems evident that when Russell has Maria talking about her breasts, she was inspired by Ingrid Bergman in *Saratoga Trunk.* When Curt Bois as Augustin Haussy nervously tells Ingrid as Clio Dulaine that she is "very beautiful," she responds, "Yes, isn't that lucky?" Exactly how Maria commented on her breasts in the screenplay. *Screenland,* May 1941, 76.

51. Ida Jean Kain, "Your Figure Madam," Gen.com, March 20, 1943.

52. A cropped photo of Maria by Peter Stackpole was published in "Hays Office Cracks Down on Cinema's Sweater Set," *Life,* April 14, 1941, 32–33. Hurrell photograph, TZC.

53. *Modern Screen,* February 1942, 56.

54. Gene Lester, *When Hollywood Was Fun: Snapshots of an Era* (London: Robert Hale, 1993), 208–10.

55. Pete Martin, "Dominican Dynamite," *Saturday Evening Post,* July 28, 1945, 29+; Earl Wilson column, Gen.com, September 27, 1944. The Earl Wilson Papers are at the University of Wisconsin, askarchives@wisconsinhistory.org.

56. Sidney Skolsky, *Hollywood Citizen-News,* May 24, 1944.

57. *Modern Screen,* May 1945, 72; Weston East, "Here's Hollywood," *Modern Screen,* June 1946, 64.

58. Maria Montez and, May Mann, "Maria Montez' Frank Advice to Movie Struck Girls," *Screenland,* August 1944, 46–47+. The original article is at USC, Universal Studios Collection, "Maria Montez Articles" folder. A considerably reduced version of the article was published in the *Atlanta Constitution* on September 19, 1944, 10.

59. Jimmie Fidler column, Gen.com, December 2, 1941.

60. Sheilah Graham agreed with Maria's advice about legs, "Legs Are Running Riot Again," Gen.com, January 17, 1943. She noted, "Even the more sedate celluloid queens like Greer Garson and Barbara Stanwyck are pitting their pretty underpinnings against those of Betty Grable, Maria Montez and Judy Garland." See also Ted Gill, "Action Seen in Leg Art," *Portland Oregonian,* May 30, 1941, 4; *Variety,* February 7, 1941, 6.

61. The best place to read about Maria's individual films is the American Film Institute's Catalog. The Movie Data Base is also a good source. Short descriptions of all her films are in Hirschorn, *The Universal Story.*

62. *Invisible Woman* finances: USC, Universal Studios Collection, *"Invisible Woman."*

63. John Johnson, "How Three Strip Technicolor Worked," August 19, 2019, hometheaterhifi.com/editorial.

64. Jane Lenz Elder, *Alice Faye: A Life beyond the Silver Screen* (Jackson: University Press of Mississippi, 2002), 144–47.

65. Donald McCaffrey, *Bound and Gagged in Hollywood* (Lanham: Scarecrow, 2006), 10.

66. As befits her eleventh place on the cast list and the fact that she is not a Fox contract player, Maria is not mentioned on any of the posters for *That Night*

in Rio, nor is she in the press book. It was Universal that advertised her part in the film.

67. Maria's screen test for Dona Sol is on YouTube: *Test de camera de Maria Montez para "Sangre y arena."*

3. National Stage

1. Sheilah Graham column, Gen.com, July 7, 1941.

2. "Latin Ladies: Hollywood is Invaded by Talent from South of the Rio Grande," *Life,* February 3, 1941, 50–52. See also Edith Lindeman, "Latin Names Now Plentiful in Hollywood," *Richmond Times Dispatch,* July 30, 1942, 7; Fairfax Nisbet, "Real Latins Getting Big Play in Films," *Dallas Morning News,* August 3, 1942, I4; "Films Have Latin Influx," *Seattle Daily News,* August 17, 1942, 67.

3. Peter Stackpole, *Life in Hollywood, 1936–1952* (London: Mainstream, 1992).

4. "Hays Office Cracks Down on Cinema's Sweater Set," *Life,* April 14, 1941, 32–33.

5. "Funnyman W. C. Fields Has His Own Way of Keeping Himself Fit," *Life,* May 12, 1941, 104–9.

6. *Harrison's Reports,* April 19, 1941, 4.

7. MGM map: bing.com/images; Carole Landis was one of the major Sweater Girls. She worked out a gimmick, the Carole Landis Sweater Club, whereby she would send a new one every month to members. But one of the qualifications was that the girl must meet the challenge of being able to wear a Carole Landis sweater. Quite the challenge. "Carole Landis Sweater Club," *Silver Screen,* June 1942.

8. Hedda Hopper column, Gen.com, February 13, 1941, March 22, 1941, April 22, 1941. Jimmie Fidler, Gen.com, April 23, 1941. In the "Mutterings" section of his column for March 15, 1941, Fidler noted, "Financial Ambition: To own a sweater shop and have Lana Turner as a model" (Gen.com). Gag: "Sweater Sweethearts," *Movie Life,* June 1941, 47. Jimmie Fidler also contributed a "Sweater Ban Poem": "I've applauded the Hays office fretters / for railings which made us their debtors / But they're going too far when they set out to bar / Girls who keep us so warm with their sweaters." Gen.com, May 7, 1941.

9. Sheilah Graham column, Gen.com, July 7, 1941; Sheilah Graham, Sunday column, Gen.com, April 18, 1943; Louella Parsons column, Gen.com, August 21, 1941.

10. Robert Myers Associated Press Sunday column, "I'm Sensational,' Maria Montez, New Movie Glamour Girl, Admits," *Boston Herald,* November 8, 1942, 60. There is a book of mounted photos from the cruise at the University of Southern California, Warner Brothers Collection, *"The Sea Wolf"* folder, file box 604B.

11. *Film Fun,* June 1941, 16–17.

12. "14 Stars Here Tomorrow on Way to Valley of the Moon," *San Francisco Chronicle,* May 21, 1941, 9; "Premier at Sea Upsets Writers," *Los Angeles Times,* March 23, 1941, A14; "A Premier and a Pilgrimage," *San Francisco Chronicle,* March 23, 1941, 61; Frederick Othman, "Hollywood, Like the Marines, Puts on Show by Land and Sea," *San Diego Union,* March 25, 1941, 7; "America's Movie Premiere: A Hollywood First—Onboard America's Finest," freepages.history.rootsweb.ancestry.com; "Soiree at Sea," *Movie Life,* June 1941, 13.

13. *Silver Screen,* June 1941, 52–53.

14. Herb Caen, "It's News to Me." *San Francisco Chronicle,* March 24, 1941; "May Mann's Going Hollywood," *Ogden Standard-Examiner,* March 27, 1941, B4, tells of Mann and her friends doing the town from the Mocambo to watching L.A.'s premier stripper, Betty Rowland, "the Ball of Fire," downtown at the Burbank Theater after flying back from the premiere.

15. Jimmie Fidler, "In Hollywood," *Los Angeles Times,* December 30, 1940, 11; Erskine Johnson column, Gen.com, April 9, 1941.

16. Harrison Carroll column, Gen.com, July 25, 1941; Hedda Hopper column, Gen.com, July 29, 1941; Jimmie Fidler column, *Los Angeles Times,* June 9, 1941, 14; Associated Press blurb, "Actress Learns Fiancé Is Nazi War Prisoner," Gen.com, August 13, 1941. For photo, see "Has Bad Luck in Large Doses," *Hagerstown Daily Mail,* November 18, 1941, 5.

17. " Beware of Carbon Copies," *Screen Guide,* February 1942 (part of group of articles without further attribution, purchased on eBay); Jimmie Fidler column, Gen.com, March 17, 1942; "Magic Maria," *Movie Life,* April 1942, 54–55. Besides the photo where Maria is sitting next to a photo of Claud Strickland, the article mentions she "created a sensation in a sarong" in *South of Tahiti.* She is glad she is doing *Marie Roget* next so she won't get type cast. Jaik Rosenstein, *Hollywood Leg Man* (Los Angeles: Madison, 1950), 53.

18. "To the Rear of the Class, Baron Munchausen," *New York Times,* August 23, 1942.

19. Jimmie Fidler column, Gen.com, September 17, 1943; "Fearless: The Truth about Hollywood's Man Scramble," *Photoplay,* May 1943, 28–30.

20. James Robert Parish and Don Stanke, *The Glamour Girls* (New York: Arlington House, 1975), 47; "I Look Sexy—but Sweet: Notes on Mario and Maria Montez," *Mediático,* March 17, 2014, Sussex.ac.uk.

21. Louella Parsons column, *Washington Post,* September 20, 1943, L1.

22. May Mann published "Second Love for Maria" under her nom de plume Mary Jane Manners in *Silver Screen,* July 1943, 34–35, 68–71.

23. Jimmie Fidler column, Gen.com, March 17, 1942. For a photo of the two of them at the Mocambo, see Erskine Johnson, "Hollywood Newsreel," *Hollywood,* March 1942, 6; *Photoplay,* October 1943, 86.

24. Teddy Stauffer, *Forever Is a Hell of a Long Time: An Autobiography* (Chicago: Henry Regnery, 1976), 144–45, 164, 193; Harrison Carroll, "Behind the Scenes Hollywood," Gen.com, December 29, 1941; Ken Morgan, "Hollywood Keyhole," Gen.com, April 16, 1942. Photo: "Good News," *Hollywood* Magazine, March 1942, 55.

25. "Magic Maria," *Movie Life,* April 1942, 54–55; "Good News," *Modern Screen,* October 1941, 60.

26. "Claud Hugh Strickland, F/O Claud Dobree Strickland," in *Burke's Peerage and Baronetage,* 107th ed., ed. Charles Mosley (Wilmington: Burke's Peerage, 2003), 1034; "Lady Marguerite Tangye," *Telegraph,* October 16, 2002, Telegraph.co.uk /10/15/2002; "Strickland, Claud Dobree," unithistories.com; photo of Strickland on the wing of his Hurricane II fighter aircraft, TZC via H. Houterman, Netherlands.

27. Hedda Hopper column, Gen.com, July 29, 1941.

28. "List of RAF Aircrew in the Battle of Britain," Wikipedia.org; Royal Air Force History, "History of No. 615 Squadron," raf.mod.uk/history.old/h615; "Operations

Record Book, 615 Squadron, R.A.F.," June 1, 1937 to August 18, 1941, National Archives of the United Kingdom, Kew, Richmond.

29. "615 Squadron's Log Book," October 27, 1941, National Archives of the United Kingdom.

30. Strickland's death and Maria's relationship with him was reported in: Charles Samuels, "Femme Fatal," *Motion Picture,* January 1946, 104. In his extensive interview with Maria, Samuels noted, "Maria has given out more versions of her life story than there are systems to beat the races." One aspect of her life he did believe was her agony upon learning of Strickland's death. "Despite all her high jinks and showoff theatricals, Maria is essentially a passionate, deeply emotional woman. Her grief was very real, deep, violent. For days she lay in bed, unable to get up, feeling as though her heart had been ripped out."

31. Dennis Sprague, "Lush, Latin and Lethal," *Photoplay,* June 1943, 41, 64. The article erroneously has MacFeeters owning "several plantations," and dismisses him as the forty-year-old who married the seventeen-and-a-half-year old.

32. Hedda Hopper column, Gen.com, September 21, 1945.

33. "Ann Sheridan Sharpshoots at Lampy; Calls Harvard Humor Sheet Sad Rag," *Harvard Crimson,* March 6, 1940, April 10, 1940, thecrimson.com.

34. Bertram Benedict, telephone interview, July 19, 2005.

35. Ibid.; photographs, TZC. After wartime service Benedict returned to college. He got a Ph.D. and went on to become a major social anthropologist and chairman of the University of California, Berkeley, Department of Anthropology. Benedict did a wonderful oral history of his life for the University of California's Calisphere. The Montez story is in the "Educational Experiences of World War II" section, cdlib.org. *Film Daily,* October 30, 1941, 2; *Film Bulletin,* November 17, 1941, 32.

36. Hedda Hopper column, Gen.com, November 10, 1941; the *Boston Herald* noted Maria arrived at South Station "with a bag of fruit in her arms," remembering what happened to Marjorie Woodworth (October 31, 1941, 23). One of the young men at the hotel was a Cuban student named Jose Rodriguez. This gave her a chance to speak Spanish with another native speaker.

37. Renan Moreira, "Maria Montez Visits Tech Campus; Regards Students 'as Typical College Men,'" Georgia Tech, *Technique,* November 21, 1941, 1. The photo of Moreira interviewing Montez is titled "Chiquita Mia—Si, Si!"

38. Georgia Tech, *Technique,* November 26, 1941, 4.

39. *Showmen's Trade Review,* November 8, 1941, 12, 38.

40. Gene Schrott, "Who's Afraid of Hollywood Wolves?" *Motion Picture,* December 1941, 23, 60–61; see also Maria Montez as told to Gladys Hall, "Me and Men," *Screenland,* July 1943, 36–37, 86–87.

41. Maria had just received her first royalty check for $14.50. "Chaparral Poets Hold Conference Tomorrow in Hollywood," *San Pedro News-Pilot,* May 14, 1943, 5; "Anne Atwood to Address Poet Group," *Riverside Daily Press,* May 12, 1943, 4; Elizabeth Bemis, "The 5th Freedom," *Movie-Radio Guide,* February 6–12, 1943, 5, 36; "This Way to Charm," *Screen Romances,* May 1943, 16. The author did not understand Spanish but noted, "The stanzas, in the pure Castilian spoken by Maria, were like music in the rhythm of the lovely, liquid, rippling notes." Maria did not really speak Castilian

Spanish, but in the few recordings there are of her speaking her native tongue she is as richly melodic as the language is famous for. "The Cheering Section," *Screen Romances,* December 1943, 6: the writer noted of Montez, "With people she trusts, she drops the professional mask of Maria, the actress and talks about the thing Maria the individual, likes. Poetry, perhaps, tops the list. She herself has had poems published in Spanish, has recently written several in English. She read two poems at the '21 Club' party that was given by Universal for her and Jean Pierre Aumont." Song: Bee Bangs, "Hollywood Earful," *Silver Screen,* September 1945, 8.

42. "Poetess Montez, Who Wows 'Em with Song," *New York Sunday Mirror,* May 3, 1943, reproduced in Margarita Vicens de Morales, *Maria Montez: Su vida* (Santo Domingo: Republica Dominicana, 1992), 148. Several of Maria's poems are reproduced in *Maria Montez: A Dominican Star,* "Poems," mariamontez.org.

43. Kelly, quoted in Dennis, "Lush, Latin and Lethal."

44. Maria's brief life as a blonde can only be seen in *Moonlight in Hawaii,* pre-shooting photos for *Raiders of the Desert,* and several Ray Jones portraits in TZC.

45. AFI, "*Moonlight in Hawaii*"; *Film Bulletin, Weekly Variety, Hollywood Reporter,* all October 10, 1941, MHL Production Files, "*Moonlight in Hawaii*"; Universal press book, "*Moonlight in Hawaii.*"

46. "Traffic Problem," *Jewish Criterion,* July 4, 1941, 24.

47. *Weekly Variety,* July 8, 1941; "Pair Invade Film Desert," *Los Angeles Times,* July 9, 1941, A16.

48. *Weekly Variety,* July 8, 1941; "Pair Invade Film Desert." At this point Turhan Bey was just getting started at Universal and was almost completely unknown. He was listed in *Bombay Clipper*'s credits as "Turban" Bey. After he appeared in *Dragon Seed* with Katherine Hepburn in 1944, it was quite a different story. See Inga Arvad, "Ladies Knight," *Photoplay,* December 1944, 46–47+.

49. MPPC files, "*Bombay Clipper.*"

50. *Hollywood Reporter,* January 22, 1942; *Variety,* January 21, 1942; *Motion Picture Herald,* January 27, 1942, MHL Production Notes, "*Bombay Clipper.*"

51. Snipe on *Los Angeles Examiner* photo, July 25, 1941, TZC; "Maria Montez: Rising Screen Personality Takes a Holiday," *Spot,* November 1941, 38–39.

52. Tom Weaver, Michael Brunas, and John Brunas, *Universal Horrors: The Studio's Classic Films, 1931–1946* (Jefferson: McFarland, 2007), 338.

53. *Variety,* May 23, 1941, 1; *Spot,* January 1942, cover.

54. "'Battle of Sarongs' on in Film City," *Oakland Tribune,* August 28, 1942, D20.

55. *Film Bulletin,* October 18, 1941, 2; *Cleveland Plain Dealer,* December 23, 1941, 17.

56. MPPC files, "*South of Tahiti.*"

57. Universal press book, "*South of Tahiti,*" TZC; *Variety,* September 24, 1941, 5; *New York Times,* November 10, 1941; *Film Bulletin,* November 1, 1941, 10, agreed with the *Times;* for the spread of sarong usage, see Edith Lindeman, "Sarong Business Booming in Hollywood," *Richmond Times Dispatch,* October 26, 1941, 58.

58. "Maria Montez at Lux," *Boston Traveler,* November 27, 1941, 34.

59. "The Box Office Slant: *South of Tahiti,*" *Showmen's Trade Review,* October 25, 1941, 18, 22.

60. Paul Harrison, "Trainer Defends Her Catty Friends," Gen.com, September 22, 1941.

61. Series of photos released by Universal in TZC. There was a chimp named Joe Maria had to deal with in *Tahiti*. They appeared together again in *Arabian Nights*. Universal released a photograph of the two of them. According to the imaginative snipe on the back of the pic, the studio made a gift of Joe to Maria, who happily took him home (TZC).

62. "Beware of Carbon Copies! Montez Shows Lamour That Two Can Play at That Game," *Screen Guide*, February 1942, 44–45. The copy editor for the *Oakland Tribune* titled the review of *Tahiti* "'Battle of Sarongs' on in Film City: Maria Montez New Challenge to Dorothy Lamour," August 28, 1941, D20. Erskine Johnson column, Gen.com, October 24, 1941. Paul Harrison explained in his column that the Hays Office demanded the sarong be no higher than three inches from the knee and no lower than a normal evening gown, Gen.com, October 21, 1941.

63. Tom DeVane, "Glamour Is Her Dish," *Hollywood*, January 1942, 38.

64. New York Public Library, Performing Arts Library, "Maria Montez" file.

65. Sidney Skolsky, "Puts Her Best Points Forward," *Hollywood Citizen-News*, May 25, 1944.

66. *Screen Guide*, April 1943, 27; Keith Wilson, "Who's Queen of the Smokies?" *Omaha World Herald*, August 16, 1942, C26.

67. Richard Hays, "Along Film Row," *Seattle Times*, September 22, 1941, 11.

68. *Variety*, April 22, 1941, 3.

69. *Variety*, December 5, 1941, 7; Peggy Moran Koster: Ronald Davis Oral History Collection, Southern Methodist University, #271, July 21, 1982, 30–31, MHL. She was listed as playing Marie Roget when the cast list was published in *Film Daily*, December 8, 1941, 7.

70. Louella Parsons column, Gen.com, December 10, 1941.

71. Weaver, Brunas, and Brunas, *Universal Horrors*, 283–89.

72. *Weekly Variety*, August 3, 1942; *Hollywood Reporter*, August 3, 1942; *New York Times*, May 5, 1942.

73. Weaver, Brunas, and Brunas, *Universal Horrors*, 285.

74. Teddy Stouffer, *Forever Is a Hell of a Long Time* (Chicago: Henry Regnery, 1976), 149–50.

4. *Arabian Nights*

1. Warren Harris, *Clark Gable: A Biography* (New York: Three Rivers, 2002), 69–70.

2. Louella Parsons column, Gen.com, April 17, 1942.

3. Mike Fitzgerald, "Western Clippings," westernclippings.com; Mimi Couch, "Book Reviews: *Light and Illusion*," *American Eagle News*, June 18, 1998, 5–6.

4. 'Sarong Goes at U," *Variety*, March 2, 1942, 3 (Maria "will be a South Seas princess"); "Production Chart," *Variety*, April 10, 1942, 5.

5. "Studios Preparing Crop of Musicals as War Antidote," *Trenton Evening Times*, March 29, 1942, 29.

6. Jimmie Fidler column, Gen.com, March 25, 1942; *Seattle Daily Times,* February 14, 1942, 4, March 9, 1942, 14. Studio blurb: Richard Hays, "Along Film Row," *Seattle Times,* March 27, 1942, 10; Bernard Dick, *City of Dreams* (Lexington: University Press of Kentucky, 1997), 113–16, 132–34.

7. Matthew Bernstein, *Walter Wanger* (Berkeley: University of California Press, 1994), 176–84; Tino Balio, *United Artists: The Company Built by the Stars* (Madison: University of Wisconsin Press, 1976), 202–3, 228–29, 186–89; Tom Vallance, "Turhan Bey: Actor Who Worked with Hepburn and Montez," *Independent,* October 12, 2012, independent.co.uk. For Alfred Hitchcock's experiences with *Saboteur* as an independent producer at Universal, see Joel Finler, *Hitchcock in Hollywood* (New York: Continuum, 1992), 50–52.

8. Bernstein, *Walter Wanger,* 186–88; Mildred Martin, "Hollywood Producers Have Jitters about War Films," *Philadelphia Inquirer,* April 30, 1944; James Agee, "So Proudly We Fail," *Nation,* October 30, 1943, decries the blatant unreality of war films produced during the conflict. Reprinted in "Voices from the Grave: So Proudly We Fail," flagerlive.com, May 27, 2019.

9. WWC, box 62, folder 32. The difficulty and the glory of using Technicolor is discussed by a Universal art director in Robert F. Boyle, oral history, 51, Academy of Motion Picture Arts and Sciences, 1998, MHL.

10. "Screen News Here and in Hollywood," *New York Times,* March 24, 1942, L25. The accompanying photo was of Jon Hall. Richard Hays, *Seattle Times,* March 27, 1942, 10; Edwin Schallert, "Southern California Pageant to Be 'Shot,'" *Los Angeles Times,* April 1, 1942, 16.

11. Edwin Schallert, *Los Angeles Times,* July 13, 1942, 8; December 24, 1942, A13; *Showmen's Trade Review,* July 11, 1942, 25.

12. *Screenland,* August 1942, 90.

13. John Rosenfield, "Maria Montez Makes Good Publicity Agent," *Dallas Morning News,* January 31, 1943, ix, 1, 4.

14. Ibid.

15. Elizabeth Russell, "A Star in Gemini" (screenplay, Copyright Office, Library of Congress, Washington, DC, 1999). Prior to this, columnists were trying to stoke up a feud between Maria and Marie "The Body" McDonald over who got more attention from the Universal publicity department. "Arabian Nights," *Silver Screen,* (November 1942, 50–51+. Acquanetta: WWC, box 62, folder 28; Tom Weaver, Michael Brunas, and John Brunas, *Universal Horrors: The Studio's Classic Films, 1931–1946* (Jefferson: McFarland, 2007), 343.

16. *Milwaukee Journal,* July 20, 1942, L5; United Press, "Billed as 'Venezuela Beauty': Indian Girl Hoaxed Filmdom," Gen.com, July 19, 1942; "Venezuelan Volcano: Fiery Burnu Acquanetta Flare Up in Harem," *Life,* August 24, 1942, 57–60.

17. WWC, box 14, folder 4.

18. The 1930 Production Code is reproduced as appendix 2 in Mark Vieira, *Sin in Soft Focus: Pre-Code Hollywood* (New York: Harry Abrams, 1999), 215. "Hollywood Jungle Girl," *Jet,* February 14, 1952, 58–62; *Los Angeles Sentinel,* July 1950.

19. Erskine Johnson column, Gen.com, September 5, 1942; Sheilah Graham column, Gen.com, January 17, 1943; Louella Parsons column, Gen.com, September 20, 1942.

20. "Hollywood Jungle Girl"; Gregory William Mank, *Women in Horror Films, 1940s* (Jefferson: McFarland, 1999), 202–21.

21. Dick Mook, "Pictures on the Fire," *Silver Screen,* November 1942, 14.

22. Pamela Hutchinson, "Shadow Dancer," *Sight and Sound,* April 2017, 12–13; "Jeni LeGon," rogerebert.com, January 23, 2013.

23. John McElwee, "Before She Accused Flynn Peggy Satterlee Was a Universal Starlet," greenbriarpictureshows.blogspot.com, March 21, 2014; AFI, *"Arabian Nights."* One casting decision that never went beyond the Wanger offices was that of Nina Matleva. There were two memos from Walter Wanger concerning her and wanting to know why she was not on the set list as he asked. He wanted to stress "that she is to work wherever and whenever possible" as she is "the perfect type for background on this picture and is in real need of work." You wonder what the backstory might be. *"Arabian Nights,"* inter-department communications from Walter Wanger, July 1, 1942, WWC.

24. *Arabian Nights* program available in theaters showing the movie, TZC; "Movie Classic Close-ups: *Arabian Nights,*" twelve-page handout brochure about the film, TZC; Walter Wanger to Maurice Bergman, October 19, 1942, *"Arabian Nights"* Correspondence, WWC. Given how prevalent photos of Peggy Satterlee are in these programs, you wonder what Universal had in mind for her before the trial destroyed her in Hollywood.

25. Philip Leibfried, *Star of India: The Life and Times of Sabu* (Albany, GA: Bear Manor Media, 2010), 4–5, 15–17.

26. "Star Dreams Up Perfect Harem for the Movies," *New Orleans Times-Picayune,* January 31, 1943, 53; "Leif Erickson," togetherweserved.navy.com.

27. Russell, "A Star in Gemini"; AFI, *"Arabian Nights,"* 1942; Universal press book *"Arabian Nights,"* TZC; Bernstein, *Walter Wanger,* 175.

28. Universal press book *"Arabian Nights,"* TZC; Jean Herrick to Walter Wanger, August 3, 1942, "*Arabian Nights*" Correspondence, WWC.

29. Universal press book *"Arabian Nights,"* TZC.

30. Ibid.

31. Right from its 1936 inception Wanger's concept for the story was "a very clear and simple plot . . . with strong popular appeal." He wanted the rightful caliph to be usurped and need to rely on the common people to get his throne back. The plot "should be presented to the public very lightly through plenty of comical characters and situations. Shahrazade is the only one who believes in him supplies romance and love story." At least four writers had a go at the script but the general idea always remained. *"The Arabian Nights,"* September 24, 1937, WWC, box 14, folder 18.

32. USC, Universal Studios Collection, *"Arabian Nights"* folder, box 269.

33. Ibid.

34. *Variety,* July 17, 1942.

35. John Jones, personal interview, June 20, 2020.

36. MPPC files, *"Arabian Nights."*

37. Bernstein, *Walter Wanger,* 441.

38. *Hollywood Reporter,* December 18, 1942; *Variety,* December 18, 1942; MHL, Production Notes, *"Arabian Nights."*

39. *Showmen's Trade Review,* December 26, 1942, 9.

40. *Pittsburgh Post-Gazette,* December 16, 1942, 9; Don Short, "*Arabian Nights,*" *San Diego Union,* December 27, 1942, 27; *Dallas Morning News,* February 6, 1943, 18; *Cleveland Plain-Dealer,* March 4, 1943, 8.

41. "In *'Arabian Nights'* She Does the Dance of the Single Veil," *Life,* September 28, 1942, 69–70; "*Arabian Nights,*" *Time,* January 1, 1943, 88; *Photoplay,* March 1943, 94; "*Arabian Nights,*" *Modern Screen,* February 1943, 12–14; "Streamlined Fantasy," *Hollywood,* December 1942, 46.

42. Walter Wanger to Byron Price, Director of Censorship, Washington, DC, January 20, 1943, 2, WWC, box 14, folder 18; *New York Times,* December 26, 1942.

43. Jimmie Fidler column, Gen.com, June 4, 1943.

44. Maria Montez and May Mann, "Maria Montez' Frank Advice to Movie Struck Girls," *Screenland,* August 1944, 46, 74.

45. Barbara Hall, Alexander Golitzen Oral History #108, Academy Oral History Project, 1992, MHL; Pauline Rawlway, "Cooking Made Clear," *Motion Picture,* February 1942, 54+; "Are You Star Material?" *Motion Picture,* December 1942, 28–29.

46. "Fame for Maria," *Silver Screen,* September 1942, 52–53.

47. Sheilah Graham column, Gen.com, January 26, 1943.

48. Sheilah Graham, "Younger Girl Players Now Get Film Breaks," Gen.com, December 13, 1942; Dee Lowrance column, Gen.com, December 27, 1942; Kate Hollidax, Associated Press, *Baton Rouge Advocate,* January 4, 1943, 6.

49. "Glamour Girls Will Pose for Amateur Photographers," *Los Angeles Times,* June 7, 1942, 15.

50. Universal-issued photograph, TZC. Every production has its small problems. In the case of the winner of the Miss Victory contest appearing in *Arabian Nights,* journalist H. C. Caltaney threatened to publish a piece accusing Universal of using the contest for crass publicity "in our emergency." The company pointed out that the whole idea of the tie-up with the movie was Victory House's. The winner has been signed to appear in the film, so what was Caltaney complaining about? Miss Foley from Lou Smith, July 16, 1942, "*Arabian Nights*" Correspondence, WWC.

51. "Sea Wolf," *Silver Screen,* June 1942, 52–53; John Franchey, "Latin, Lissom and Lethal," *Silver Screen,* March 1942, 41–42+; John Franchey, "Fame for Maria," *Silver Screen,* 52–53.

52. *Variety,* March 11, 1943, 8, March 17, 1943, 6. Universal released a photo of Maria handing out the trophy to Johnny Mac Brown, TZC.

53. *Ay Jalisco:* "Roosevelt Theater," cinematreasures.org.

54. "My First Date," *Cosmopolitan,* November 1943, 40–41; "Going Hollywood," *Collier's,* November 14, 1942, 12; "M-mm-mmm Girl Montez," *Movie Stars Parade,* November 1942, 54–55. Painting: Edwin Schallert, *Los Angeles Times,* November 21, 1942, A7. Universal released several photographs of the event featuring Maria and the painting and Frederick Sprague, TZC; Trio: *Variety,* July 15, 1942; Philip Schallert, *Los Angeles Times,* July 13, 1942.

55. Louella Parsons column, Gen.com, April 17, 1942.

56. George Hadley-Garcia, *Hispanic Hollywood: The Latins in Hollywood* (New York: Citadel, 1990), 115.

57. The Anne Frank wall is illustrated in Tom Zimmerman, *Light and Illusion: The Hollywood Photographs of Ray Jones* (Los Angeles: Balcony, 1999), 29.

58. Paul Harrison column, Gen.com, July 9, 1942.

59. Frederick Othman column, Gen.com, November 5, 1943; "Maria Montez: The Girl Who Couldn't Last," *Screen Guide*, April 1943, 23. *Liberty* magazine tried to go along with the program but called it a slendang. Wrong movie. Howard Sharpe, "The High Cost of Maria Montez, " *Liberty*, May 15, 1943, 37. There is an excellent color photo of a bare-chested Jon Hall hugging Maria in her sheerong on p. 37.

60. *Photoplay*, July 1943), 101; *Motion Picture Daily*, May 18, 1943, 6; Elizabeth Wilson, "'Perhaps I Am Too Egotistical,' Admits Maria Montez," *Movie Show*, March 1943, 38–39.

61. Arthur Lubin, oral history by James Desmarais for the Directors Guild of America, 67, January 1977; Arthur Lubin: Ronald Davis Oral History Collection, Southern Methodist University, #353, July 15, 1985, 15–16, MHL. One other incident occurred during the late filming of *White Savage*. Lon Chaney Jr. was filming *Son of Dracula* on the lot at the same time. He had a major problem with alcohol and couldn't stand Maria. One night, seized by drink, he threw feces at her bungalow. Later in the shooting he broke a vase over director Robert Siodmak's head. Curt Siodmak, *Wolf Man's Maker: Memoirs of a Hollywood Writer* (Lanham: Scarecrow, 2001), 277.

62. Douglas Daniel, *Tough as Nails: The Life and Films of Richard Brooks* (Madison: University of Wisconsin Press, 2011), 26–27.

63. MPPC files, "*White Savage*."

64. *Variety, Motion Picture Daily, Hollywood Reporter*, all April, 9, 1943, MHL Production Files, "*White Savage*"; *Jefferson City News and Tribune*, May 2, 1943, 10; *Canton (Ohio) Repository*, May 13, 1943, 20; *Dothan, Alabama Eagle*, May 2, 1943, 10; Richard Hays, "*White Savage*," *Seattle Daily Times*, June 7, 1943, 12; *Omaha World Herald*, May 28, 1943, 1; Rudolf Elie Jr., "White Savage," *Boston Herald*, June 2, 1943, 14. Ads: *Motion Picture Daily*, April 9, 1943, 6, August 27, 1943, 13.

65. Lee Mortimer in the *Daily Mirror* reached the same conclusion. "After an epidemic of war films, '*White Savage*' is what the public has been yelling for" (April 9, 1943, 6); Don Short, "New Spreckels Offers Change from War Films," *San Diego Union*, June 10, 1943, 11.

66. Cal York, "Inside Stuff," *Photoplay*, February 1943, 14; "Hollywood Newsreel," *Hollywood*, March 1943, 17, noted, "Maria Montez, who can get along very well without Jon Hall, finally got the best of him in their celluloid feud" when she got to push him in the water in *White Savage*.

67. Ethan Mordden, *The Hollywood Studios: House Style in the Golden Age of the Movies* (New York: Knopf, 1988), 353–55.

5. Queen of Technicolor

1. Universal, "Maria Montez Biographical Sheet," 1943, p. 1, TZC; "'Queen of Technicolor': Title Is Found for Dominican Starlet Maria Montez," *See*, January 1944, 10–11; four-page full-color ad spread on *White Savage* starring Maria Montez in her sheerong with the title "This Is She." *Showmen's Trade Review*, April 17, 1943, 7–10.

2. "Star Arrives in Technicolor," *New York Sun,* February 8, 1943; USC, Universal Studios Collection, "Articles, Maria Montez" folder.

3. "Star Arrives in Technicolor."

4. *Boston Herald,* February 10, 1943, 17.

5. "Julia McCarthy, "'Sarong' or 'Sheerong,' Maria Montez Is It," *New York Daily News,* February 13, 1943.

6. Ibid.

7. Hyman Goldberg, "Maria Montez Wants to Do a Movie with Clothes On," *New York PM,* March 7, 1942, 6; photographs from Sherry Netherland, TZC.

8. When confirmed Manhattanite columnist Earl Wilson heard the comment about Brooklyn, he just noted that Hyman Goldberg writing in *Yank* magazine had the best explanation of Brooklyn's failings. When told of Maria's complaint, Goldberg observed, "Nobody ever told her because it would take so long." Earl Wilson, "It Happened Last Night," *Tucson Daily Citizen,* September 27, 1944, 8.

9. *Riverside (California) Daily Press,* April 22, 1943, 5.

10. Edwin Schallert, "Drama and Film," Los Angeles *Times,* May 5, 1943, A16; *Showmen's Trade Review,* November 6, 1943, 49; 1951 film *Flame of Stamboul,* AFI.

11. Camp Cooke also was used as an army training base in the Korean War. In 1956 it would be transferred to the air force and eventually renamed Vandenburg Air Force Base. It became the premier West Coast launching facility for space craft and missile testing.

12. "Today's Radio," *San Antonio Express,* March 2, 1943; *Variety,* March 9, 1943, 9.

13. Teddy Stauffer, *Forever Is A Hell of a Long Time: An Autobiography* (Chicago: Henry Regnery, 1976), 204–5.

14. Theta Sigma Phi: *The Matrix,* April–May 1943, University of Washington, Special Collections, Association for Women in Communications Collection, letter from Gina Kessler Lee, Librarian, April 23, 2013, womcom.org/about _us/history. Maria returned to Theta Sigma Phi on November 9, 1948, when members were invited to meet "Hollywood's most publicized actress." Snipe on back of *Herald Examiner* photo, Los Angeles Public Library Photo Collection, photo #00110844. "Romantic twosome": *Los Angeles Examiner,* March 25, 1943.

15. MPPC files, *"Cobra Woman."*

16. A good survey of South Seas films is Luis Reyes, *Made in Paradise: Hollywood's Films of Hawaii and the South Seas* (Honolulu: Mutual, 1995).

17. Sheilah Graham column, Gen.com, May 11, 1943.

18. *New York Times,* May 18, 1944.

19. Donald McCaffery, *Bound and Gagged in Hollywood* (Lanham: Scarecrow, 2006), 10. John Jones heard the same story from his father: John Jones, personal interview, June 20, 2020. Jimmie Fidler heard the story. He wrote, "It's censorship that keeps filmville columnists from reporting the hilarious reasons for the feud twixt Maria Montez and the head property man." Fidler column, Gen.com, May 25, 1943.

20. William Weaver, "Hollywood," *Motion Picture Daily,* May 4, 1943, 8.

21. *Sight and Sound,* Autumn 1959, 181.

22. Robbin Coons column, Gen.com, June 20, 1943.

23. *Council Bluffs Nonpareil,* September 25, 1943, 9.

24. Ted Gill, "Heat Turned on, Peter Returns Home," *Portland Oregonian,* July 11, 1943, 48.

25. Bosley Crowther, "*Cobra Woman,*" *New York Times,* May 18, 1944; W. Ward Marsh, *Cleveland Plain Dealer,* July 7, 1944, 13; *Showmen's Trade Review,* April 21, 1944, 10; John Rosenfield, *Dallas Morning News,* July 7, 1944, I10.

26. *Variety,* April 21, 1944; *Hollywood Reporter,* April 21, 1944; MHL Production Files, "*Cobra Woman.*"

27. Universal Studios press book, "*Cobra Woman,*" TZC, quoted in *Ardmore (Oklahoma) Ardmorite,* September 17, 1944, 13; Lee Mortimer, *New York Daily Mirror,* April 24, 1943, 13.

28. *New Orleans Times Picayune,* June 1, 1944, 26.

29. USC, Universal Studio Papers, "*Cobra Woman*" file; Philip Leibfried, *Star of India: The Life and Films of Sabu* (Albany, GA: Bear Manor Media, 2010), 149–53.

30. USC, Universal Studio Papers, "*Cobra Woman*" file.

31. *Baton Rouge State-Times,* October 11, 1943, 9; Universal, "*Ali Baba and the Forty Thieves*" press book, TZC.

32. Universal, "*Ali Baba and the Forty Thieves*" press book, TZC; Hedda Hopper, "Looking at Hollywood," *Los Angeles Times,* August 30, 1943, A14.

33. "La Montez Dives into Bubble Bath for Film," *Cleveland Plain Dealer,* November 14, 1943, B18; two-page ad for *Ali Baba, Variety,* January 31, 1944, 5–6. With *The Exile,* Universal released an extensive description of Maria's various baths over the years. The list included *Arabian Nights, Ali Baba, Gypsy Wildcat,* and *The Exile.* USC, "*The Exile*" file, folder 2176. Sheilah Graham column, Gen.com, September 18, 1943; *New York Journal American,* August 24, 1943. *Screenland* reported that a sailor watching the action stopped the show by shouting, "Stand up Maria, and take a bow." "Hot for Hollywood," April 1944, 6.

34. Erskine Johnson column, Gen.com, October 24, 1943; Frederick Othman column, Gen.com, January 1, 1944.

35. *Omaha World Herald,* August 24, 1943, 20.

36. MPPC files, "*Ali Baba and the 40 Thieves.*" *Ali Baba* was the subject of a two-part essay in *American Cinematographer:* Richard Schmidt, "'*Ali Baba and the Forty Thieves*': A Romantic Fantasy in the Sand," October–November 1994, 83–91.

37. *Hollywood Reporter,* January 4, 1944; *Motion Picture Daily,* January 7, 1944; *Variety,* January 7; 1944 MHL Production Files, "*Ali Baba and the 40 Thieves.*"

38. *New York Times,* March 16, 1944, 17; Philip Scheuer, "Montez '*Ali Baba*' Eyeful," *Los Angeles Times,* January 21, 1944, A9.

39. John Rosenfield, "Miss Montez' Heart Belongs to Bagdaddy," *Dallas Morning News,* March 24, 1944, I10; Edith Lindeman, "'*Ali Baba*' Just Follows Set Pattern: Maria Montez Needs No Change of Style," *Richmond Times Dispatch,* February 25, 1944, 12.

40. "Screen in Review," *New Orleans Times-Picayune,* March 3, 1944, 7.

41. "Universal Answers U. S. Long Tax Form," *Seattle Daily Times,* March 3, 1944, 18; Paul Malvern interview by Raymond White, October 13, 1983, February 7, 1987, MHL, 38, 205. Hall: Richard Schmidt, "'Ali Baba and the Forty Thieves': A Romantic Fantasy in the Sand" (part 2), *American Cinematographer,* October 1994, 92.

42. John Robert Parish, *Hollywood's Great Love Teams* (New Rochelle: Arlington House, 1974), 612–13, argues *Ali Baba* was the best of the Montez-Hall series.

43. Maria Montez, "Jean Pierre Aumont: The Man I Love," *Photoplay,* November 1943, 52–53+.

44. Elizabeth Russell, "A Star in Gemini" (screenplay, Copyright Office, Library of Congress, Washington, DC, 1999).

45. Raina Paris, personal interview, September 8, 2014.

46. Jean-Pierre Aumont, *Sun and Shadow: An Autobiography* (New York: Norton, 1977), 80–81.

47. Cruiser *Los Angeles:* Acme news photo, taken June 30, 1943, released to publicize upcoming wedding, July 9, 1943, TZC; All photos, TZC.

48. Cal York, "Inside Stuff," *Photoplay,* October 1943, 4; photo: TZC.

49. Louella Parsons column, Gen.com, March 11, 1943; May Mann column, Gen.com, March 25, 1943; Frederick Othman column, Gen.com, March 17, 1943.

50. Jimmie Fidler column, Gen.com, March 23, 1943, April 4, 1943, April 9, 1943, April 22, 1943, April 28, 1943.

51. Cal York, "Inside Stuff," *Photoplay,* August 1943, 12; Walter Winchell column, Gen.com, May 21, 1943; Louella Parsons, Gen.com, June 14, 1943; Sheilah Graham, Gen.com, June 23, 1943.

52. The most complete story of the wedding is in Fredda Dudley, "Romance in the Grand Manner," *Movieland,* October 1943, 19–21, 68–72. Several photos of the wedding are in *Screenland,* November 1943, 57. A photograph of the happy couple accompanied "Actress Montez Will Wed French Soldier," *New York Journal American,* April, 7, 1943; Montez, "The Man I Love"; Aumont, *Sun and Shadow,* 81–82; "Montez Finds Her Man: Three on a Match Lit the Way to Maria Montez Romance," *Screen Guide,* June 1943, 52–53; "Montez Loses Her Man: Pierre Aumont Is Leaving Maria—To Fight for Free France!" *Screen Guide,* September 1943, 22–23; wedding photos: TZC.

53. Aumont, *Sun and Shadow,* 82–83.

54. Nancy Winslow Squire, "13 Is Lucky for Love," *Modern Screen,* October 1943, 62–63, 93–96.

55. Doug McFarland, *Forties Film Talk: Oral Histories of Hollywood* (Jefferson: McFarland, 1992), 324.

56. Interview with James M. Cain: Doug McFarland, *Forties Film Talk: Oral Histories of Hollywood* (Jefferson: McFarland, 1992), 324; Schmidt, "'Ali Baba and the Forty Thieves."

57. MPPC files, *"Gypsy Wildcat."*

58. Universal-released nylons photo: TZC; this photo and a positive review: *San Diego Union,* October 26, 1944, 13.

59. *New York Times,* October 5, 1944; *Seattle Daily Times,* October 18, 1944; *Portland Oregonian,* November 2, 1944, 14.

60. Philip Scheuer, *Los Angeles Times,* September 8, 1944, A11; *Los Angeles Times* review, August 4, 1944, A10; Sheilah Graham, "Maria Montez Wages Battle with Bosses: Torrid Latin Wants Dramatic Roles and Not Opposite Hall," Gen.com, May 27, 1944. For more on the animosity between Montez and Hall, see Jimmie Fidler column, *Portland Oregonian,* April 30, 1944, 40.

61. Universal Studios press book, *"Gypsy Wildcat,"* TZC; *Anniston* (*Alabama*) *Star,* January 26, 1945, 9; *San Diego Union,* October 26, 1944, 13.

62. *Variety,* August 3, 1944; *Hollywood Reporter,* August 3, 1944; MHL Production Files, *"Gypsy Wildcat."*

63. Frederick Othman column, Gen.com, November 13, 1944.

6. *Sudan*

1. Universal did protect the contract players whose future they believed in. The studio had seven Donald O'Connor films on the shelf to be slowly released during his time in the army to make it seem like he never left. He still received his studio salary of $350 a week, making him one of the better paid privates in the US Army. His contract was held in abeyance while he was in the service, starting again the day he reported back to the studio after his discharge. "Donald O'Connor," *Variety,* February 4, 1944, 9; MPPC files, *"Bowery to Broadway."*

2. USC, Universal Studios Collection, *"Bowery to Broadway"* box, "Disbursements" file.

3. Universal press book, *"Bowery to Broadway,"* TZC; Associated Press blurb, Gen.com, September 17, 1944. You'll see it's true if you watch the movie; her mouth does not synchronize with the song lyrics.

4. *Hollywood Reporter,* October 20, 1944; *Variety,* October 20, 1944; MHL Production Files, *"Bowery to Broadway."*

5. "Maria Plays a Modern Girl," *Pittsburgh Press,* December 26, 1944. 10.

6. *Bismarck Tribune,* January 4, 1945, 12; January 6, 1945, 8; *Athens Messenger,* December 24, 1944, 8; *"Bowery to Broadway," Middletown* (*New York*) *Times-Herald,* January 4, 1945, 5.

7. Walter Winchell column, Gen.com, December 5, 1944; Erskine Johnson column, Gen.com, September 19, 1944, December 9, 1944.

8. Edwin Schallert, *Los Angeles Times,* May 10, 1944, A11.

9. "Ernst Van Leyden," tate.org.uk; Raina Paris, personal interview, September 8, 2014.

10. *Pageant* did a full-color article on the making of *Sudan* to celebrate Technicolor. The last picture is a full pager of Maria, captioned "Maria Montez reached star status in two years. Young, lovely, her role in *'Queen of the Nile'* is another bid for the 'Queen of Technicolor' crown." "Behind the Scenes in Technicolor," *Pageant,* February 1945, 97–114.

11. *Variety,* 11th Anniversary Issue, October 16, 1944.

12. MPPC files, *"Sudan."*

13. Bey: *Mysteries and Scandals,* Maria Montez, E Channel, April 26, 1998. Malvern: Frederick Othman, "Maria Montez Wishes the Public to See Her Spiritual Qualities," *Winnipeg Free Press,* August 16, 1944, 4. Captain: Howard Caheyn, "Gentle Palomino Popular with Movieland Actors, "*Portland Oregonian,* June 25, 1950. Navajos for Egyptians: Arthur Lubin #353, Ronald Davis Oral History Collection, Southern Methodist University, July 15, 1985, p. 16, MHL.

14. Frederick Othman column, Gen.com, August 9, 1944; "Prosecutor Steps into Dorsey Row," *Trenton Evening Times,* August 10, 1944, 3; *Hayward (California) Review,* August 5, 1944, 1; "D. A. to Take Role in Fracas of Dorsey, Hall and Others," *Madison (Wisconsin) State Journal,* August 10, 1944, 4; United Press, "Mrs. Dorsey Talks Today to Attorney," Gen.com, August 15, 1944; Frederick Othman column on nose fix, Gen.com, September 14, 1944; "Jon Hall Expected Back for Finish of *'Nile'* Next Week," *Variety,* August 9, 1944; Frederick Othman, "Director, Hall and Montez Are All Cripples Nowadays," *Winnipeg Free Press,* August 19, 1944, 4. Producer Paul Malvern hurt his leg and was limping, Jon Hall's face still had one piece of plaster from the fight, and Maria's ear was infected, causing one side of her face to swell.

15. Arthur Lubin #353, Ronald Davis Oral History Collection, Southern Methodist University, July 15, 1985, p. 16, MHL. Lubin summed up Maria, "She was very temperamental. She was very lovely" (15). Anne Gwynne agreed with Lubin: "Jon Hall and Maria Montez never got along." Gregory William Mank, *Women in Horror Films, 1940s* (Jefferson: McFarland, 1999), 156.

16. Ellis Amburn, *Olivia de Havilland and the Golden Age of Hollywood* (Guilford, CT: Lyons, 2018), 152; Brent Lang, "How Olivia de Havliland Took on the Studios," *Variety,* July 27, 2020, variety.com.

17. Othman, "Maria Montez Wishes the Public to See Her Spiritual Qualities."

18. *Hollywood Reporter,* March 1, 1945; *Variety,* March 1, 1945; *Motion Picture Daily,* March 1, 1945; MHL Production Files, *"Sudan."*

19. Jake Rachman, "Maria Montez Needs No Sound," *Omaha World Herald,* March 9, 1945, 9. One interviewer praised Jon Hall's role in all this Technicolor extravagance: Inez Wallace, "Jon Hall Hailed as No. 1 Star of Tropical Movies," *Cleveland Plain Dealer,* February 6, 1944, 4.

20. Bosley Crowther, "The Screen: Out West in Egypt," *New York Times,* April 19, 1945; Edwin Schallert, *Los Angeles Times,* April 14, 1945, A5; Jimmie Fidler column, Gen.com, May 23, 1944.

21. *Film Bulletin,* April 30, 1945, 20; "Reviews," *Photoplay,* June 1945, 123. In the same group of reviews, *Salome—Where She Danced* is rated "a goodie" (122).

22. *Los Angeles Examiner,* April 15, 1945.

23. Raina Paris, personal interview, September 8, 2014; Russell, "A Star in Gemini"; Ed Estabrook photos, TZC. The snipe on the back of one of the Pasadena photos reads, "Maria Montez, known as the Technicolor Queen at Universal studio, met her three sisters at the station to welcome them to the gay movie city."

24. Virginia Tomlinson, "Now Maria Is 4!" *New York Journal American,* May 12, 1945.

25. Maria Montez, "My Sisters and I," *Photoplay,* n.d., Wisconsin Historical Society, University of Wisconsin, Madison, "Maria Montez" folder; "Maria Brings Three Sisters Here," *Los Angeles Times,* October 26, 1944, A2.

26. Gladys Hall, "I Thought How Remarkable She Is," October 27, 1944, Gladys Hall Collection, MHL, published as "Advice For Her Kid Sisters," *Silver Screen,* February 1945, 30–31, 83–86.

27. Louella Parsons column, Gen.com, September 30, 1944.

28. fandango.com/alexisthurn-taxis-673439/biography; Movie Data Base, Alexis Thurn-Taxis.

29. "Celebration: Hollywood Goes Formal for Elsa," *Life,* October 9, 1944, 91–93; "French Colony Celebrates on Studio Stages," *Variety,* August 24, 1944, 8.

30. "Pix 50th Anniversary Gets Send-off with Star Turnout," *Variety,* November 1, 1944, 10. Golden Apple Award: Edwin Schallert, *Los Angeles Times,* December 14, 1944, A11; *Boston Herald,* December 19, 1944, 6; Philip Scheuer, *Los Angeles Times,* December 14, 1944, B1.

31. Herald Heffernan column, Gen.com, August 29, 1944.

32. Inga Arvad column, Gen.com, November 21, 1943; *Motion Picture Daily,* November 23, 1943; *Variety,* December 13, 1943, 4; *Cleveland Plain Dealer,* January 20, 1944.

33. Yvonne De Carlo got immediate attention from the fan magazines when signed by Universal: "Salome Modern Version," *Pic,* December 19, 1944, 24–25. Ethnic change: Fred Stanley, "The Hollywood Digest," *New York Times,* December 17, 1944, X5.

34. D. M. Giangreco, *Hell To Pay: Operation Downfall and the Invasion of Japan, 1945–1947,* rev. ed. (Annapolis: Naval Institute Press, 2017); Ian Toll, *Twilight of the Gods: War in the Western Pacific, 1944–45* (New York: Norton, 2020), 645–48, 674, 681. Purple Hearts: D. M. Giangreco and Kathryn Moore, "Are New Purple Hearts Being Manufactured to Meet the Demand?" historynewsnetwork.org; D. M. Giangreco and Kathryn Moore, "Half a Million Purple Hearts," americanheritage.com.

35. Associated Press blurbs, Gen.com, May 10, 1945, October 15, 1945; Sheilah Graham column, Gen.com, July 18, 1945.

36. Rosalind Shaffer, "Turhan Bey to Real War," *Omaha World-Herald,* May 13, 1945, 52; Associated Press, "Screen Actor Turhan Bey, Veteran of Café Battle, Will Soon Be off to War," Gen.com, May 18, 1945. The "Café Battle" referred to a fight he had with Lana Turner. Universal distributed a photo of Bey in uniform saying goodbye to Montez on the set of *Tangier,* TZC. He had not been to her house since Aumont left for North Africa, though he had been there quite often before that because "It's just not done in his book of rules." Kirtley Baskette, "Turks Are No Jerks," *Modern Screen,* November 1944, 107.

7. Maria on the Home Front

1. Mary Ryan, "The Stars Shone for Maria," *New York Journal-American,* January 29, 1944. The article presents Maria as just another war wife always waiting to hear from her husband overseas.

2. There are several studies of Hollywood during the war. See Christian Blauvelt, *Hollywood Victory: The Movies Stars and Stories of World War II* (Philadelphia: Running, 2021); Colin Shindler, *Hollywood Goes to War: Films and American Society, 1939–1952* (Boston: Routledge, Kegan Paul, 1979); Clayton Koppes and Gregory Black, *Hollywood Goes to War: How Politics, Profits and Propaganda Shaped World War II Movies* (New York: Free Press, 1987); Thomas Doherty, *Projections of War: Hollywood, American Culture and World War II* (New York: Columbia University Press, 1993). For a contemporary look at the subject, see Editors of *Look, Movie Lot to Beachhead: The*

Motion Picture Goes to War and Prepares for the Future (New York: Doubleday, 1945); Hollywood Victory Committee for Stage, Screen and Radio," *The Radio Annual, 1943* (New York: The Radio Annual, 1943), 919; "Committee Mission Statement, Hollywood Victory Committee for Stage, Screen and Radio, February 27, 1942," MHL, "Hollywood Victory Committee" file; *America's Town Meeting on the Screen: How Should the Movies Aid National Defense?* (Los Angeles: America's Town Meeting of the Air, 1941). Hollywood's view of its wartime duty and dedication was best summed up in Joe Schoenfeld's broadside "Dedication to a Cause," originally published in *Variety* on March 3, 1943. In the first paragraph three names are given of entertainers who died serving their country: Carole Lombard died in a plane crash returning to Los Angeles after a bond tour on January 16, 1942; Roy Rognan and Tamara Drasin were killed in a plane crash at Lisbon on a USO tour on February 22, 1943.

On the back cover of the *Second Annual Report of the Hollywood Victory Committee* (Los Angeles: Hollywood Victory Committee, 1943) is written:

> I am the spirit of all actors. My name might be Jolson or Brown; Francis or Raye; Benny or Hope, Cantor or Landis, Kelly or Adler. My name is Carole Lombard . . . Roy Rognan . . . Tamara.
>
> I am an acrobat; a singer; a comedian; a dancer, and a tragedian. I am the soubrette; the ingenue; the juvenile, and the leading man, I am the modest performer and I am the star.
>
> At this moment I am playing in a tin hut somewhere in Alaska . . . a camp in Australia . . . a makeshift theater in the Caribbean. I am slogging through mud in North Africa; I am in the Solomons; in Ireland; in England, and in Iceland—wherever there's an American soldier, sailor or marine.
>
> Let no cloistered thoughts mourn for me. I am a living spirit. It is not for tears that I serve my country. That is my duty as a heritage.
>
> If I persuade a man to buy his limit in war bonds; if I inspire a worker to quicken his lathe; if I brighten the lot of the lonely soldier—then these are my contributions to an America at war. It would be cause for lament only if my efforts failed.

For this work I ask no plaudits; no eulogies. I am a soldier in greasepaint, serving a free country and freedom-loving men. This service is the actors' imperishable memorial.

3. Bruce Torrance and Lisa Mitchell, *The Hollywood Canteen* (Duncan, Okla.: Bear Manor, 2012); Gary McMaster, *Hollywood Canteen: Hollywood's Famous Club for World War II Servicemen* (self-published, 2009; available at the Camp Roberts National Guard store); "Hollywood's War Effort," *Hollywood,* January 1943, 22–23.

4. Photo and snipe, *Herald-Examiner* Photo Collection, Los Angeles Public Library, Maria Montez file.

5. "Pin-up Girl—Maria Montez," *Motion Picture,* December 1943, 54. Maria as representative of the Good Neighbor Policy cropped up in a photo of her with two lion cubs used to advertise *Arabian Nights.* It was a nationally released photo from Universal captioned, "Maria Montez, the Little Dutch Girl, Plays the First Good Neighbor—Scheherazade." The text pointed out that Maria "symbolizes Latin America's alliance with

the United States in the war against the dictators." *Oakland Tribune,* August 2, 1942, Sunday supplement. Maria was on the cover of *True Romance,* April 1947. The note on the "Cover Girl" extolled her continuing work as a Good Neighbor. "There's been much talk about what we are doing to further friendly relations with South America. Now we're hearing about some of the things she's doing about the Good Neighbor Policy."

6. *Los Angeles Times,* October 22, 1943, 1; October 27, 1943, 8.

7. Dominican Republic Order of Juan Pablo Duarte, Order of Trujillo, Wikipedia.org; Raina Paris, personal interview, September 28, 2014.

8. Invitational Postal Telegraph telegram to event from Ismael Aviles, Dominican Consul of Los Angeles, October 19, 1943, TZC; Universal Pictures press release, n.d., TZC.

9. *Los Angeles Times,* October 22, 1943, 1; Marjorie Dean, "Foods of Our Allies," *Modern Screen,* March 1944, 96–97; Helen Holmes, "It's a South American Custom," *Modern Screen,* February 1942, 78; Feg Murray, "Seein' Stars," Gen.com, January 2, 1944; "Topics for Gossip," *Silver Screen,* May 1944, 56.

10. Jimmie Fidler, "Hollywood Visits America," Gen.com, June 18, 1943. Pan-American: Chapin Hall, "What Goes On," *Los Angeles Times,* April 9, 1943, 21; "Pan-America Model for World, Says Hull," *Los Angeles Times,* April 15, 1943, A1. Photo of Maria at celebration: Margarita Vicens de Morales, *Maria Montez: Su vida* (Santo Domingo: Republica Dominicana, 1992), 37. A story was put out by Maria following the Corpus Christi celebration. Pushing her father as a diplomat, she claimed that Nasa Kuri, a nurse who supposedly cared for her father when he fell sick on a diplomatic mission from Spain to Casablanca, Morocco, invited Maria to come pay a visit. Ken Morgan, "Hollywood Keyhole," Gen.com, May 1, 1942.

11. "Four Movie Stars to Be at Bond Show," *San Francisco Chronicle,* September 25, 1942, 6; "War Bond Show: Giant Pageant of the Theaters Ready to Go!" *San Francisco Chronicle,* September 28, 1942, 8; "War Shows: Two All-Star Revues to Be Staged This Week at Civic Auditorium," *San Francisco Chronicle,* September 29, 1942, 7 (Montez and crew would be at the auditorium on Wednesday; Hope and Crosby were coming on Saturday); "War Bond Show: Citizens Star as Purchasers with Night's Total of $1,250,000," *San Francisco Chronicle,* October 2, 1942, 6.

12. Gloria Jean, telephone interview, December 16, 2004.

13. *Boston Herald,* January 17, 1943, SA2; January 19, 1943, 22; January 20, 1943, 26; Gloria Jean, telephone interview, December 16, 2004; *Boston Traveler,* January 21, 1943, 1, 5; January 19, 1943, 5.

14. *Variety,* January 15, 1943, 9; January 20, 1943, 6.

15. Photographs in TZC.

16. "Regional News from Correspondents," *Showmen's Trade Review,* February 13, 1943, 14.

17. Memo sent from Universal to *Screen Guide,* June 26, 1943, USC, "Maria Montez Articles" folder.

18. Alison Bell, "Racetrack Has a Wartime Story," *Los Angeles Times,* November 8, 2009, latimes.com/archives/la-xpm-2009-nov-08.html; "Santa Anita Assembly Center," Wikipedia.com.

19. "Santa Anita Ordnance Training Center," Wikipedia.com.

20. "13,000 Theaters Open Stamp Drive for $130,000,000," *Film Daily,* July 1, 1943, 1, 6.

21. "13 Is Lucky for Love," *Modern Screen,* October 1943, 62–63, 93–96; Cal York, "Inside Stuff," *Photoplay,* August 1943, 6; Jimmie Fidler column, Gen.com, September 4, 1943; George Owens, "French Hero," *Hollywood,* January 1943, 50; Gladys Hall, "'Before I Go,' Pierre Aumont's Farewell to Civilian Life," *Silver Screen,* February 8, 1943, manuscript form, MHL, Gladys Hall Collection, folder 22; photo: TZC.

22. Symposium, war wives: USC, "Maria Montez Articles" folder.

23. Maria Montez, "My Most Thrilling Moments," *Screen Stars,* July 1944, 13.

24. Franklin Delano Roosevelt Presidential Library and Museum, Hyde Park, New York, "President's Birthday celebration, 1944" folder. Eleanor Roosevelt wrote her February 1, 1944, "My Day" column on the birthday parties (Franklin Delano Roosevelt Presidential Library and Museum, "My Day" columns folder). Regarding her guests, Eleanor stated, "On Sunday we had lunch at the White House for all the movie stars and as usual, showed them around. I am always impressed by the historical sense which actors and actresses seem to have so much more strongly than people who do not project themselves into other peoples lives as an everyday occurrence."

25. "Stars Blanket U. S. for Bonds," *Variety,* January 17, 1944, 9. The eight major drives and the endless small and neighborhood sales of bonds amounted to $187.7 billion of securities. Duke University Libraries digital collections: "Brief History of World War II Advertising Campaigns War Loans and Bonds; "Stars Cluster Again at Birthday Balls," *Life,* February 14, 1944, 34.

26. *Cleveland Plain Dealer,* January 18, 1944, 11; Thompson Products, Inc., *42nd Annual Report* (April 1944). Maria is noted in the *Cleveland Plain Dealer* as one of "the famous guests that have inspired us." The photograph is in TZC; Jimmie Fidler column, Gen.com, December 2, 1941.

27. *Cleveland Plain Dealer,* January 19, 1944.

28. *Variety,* February 2, 1944, 8. Universal released a photo to mark her visit to the Stage Door Canteen.

29. *The President's Birthday Ball, 1944* (Washington, DC), TZC.

30. Montez, "My Most Thrilling Moments"; Hedda Hopper column, Gen.com, February 23, 1944.

31. Bill Henry, "By the Way," *Los Angeles Times,* February 2, 1944; *New Orleans Picayune,* April 9, 1944, 59.

32. *Variety,* February 2, 1944, 8, 19.

33. Universal released a photo to note Maria's visit to the Press Photographers Association that featured her in a tight sweater with vertical stripes, her arms pulled sharply back. TZC.

34. *Variety,* March 3, 1944, 5.

35. The US Army Signal Corps sent a group of photos to John Joseph at Universal, noting, "Thought you would be interested in a few prints because of Maria Montez." USC, "Maria Montez" folder. *Los Angeles Times,* February 17, 1944, 2; February 28, 1944, 9; *Variety,* March 3, 1944, 5.

36. *Mail Call,* May 30, 1944, available from Old Time Radio, OTRCAT.com, TZC.

37. *Variety,* April 7, 1944, 9; May 25, 1944, 1; *Picture Daily,* April 10, 1944, 10.

38. James Hilton, "Salute to the Hollywood Canteen," *Photoplay,* November 1943, 84; "Super-Duper Epic: Hollywood Canteen," *New York Times,* October 17, 1943; "Hollywood Canteen," *Movies,* December 1944, 20–21 (there is a photo of Maria sitting with Irene Dunne and several members of the French military enjoying the entertainment, also TZC). There's an odd take on the canteen; several stories are told about what dopes some of the soldiers are with the actresses—"Hollywood Canteen," *Liberty,* January 23, 1943, 26–28; Jane Lockwood, "Hollywood Canteen," hostess's personal diary, MHL Special Collections.

39. Edwin Schallert, "Star Sings Ko-Ko Role since 1934," *Los Angeles Times,* August 29, 1954, D3.

40. Universal Studios, "Maria Montez Pin-up Nominations," TZC.

41. Dee Lowrance, "Leave Us Phrase It," Gen.com, April 30, 1944.

42. United Press blurb, Gen.com, January 24, 1944.

43. Evelyn Keyes was one of the workers in the Pin Up Industrial Complex. Of her service she wrote, "We females spent hours posing in bathing suits, negligees and shorts, jumping out of candy boxes for Valentine's Day. Posing with turkeys for Thanksgiving, sleighs for Christmas. We donned our sexiest threads and visited Army camps always with a photographer present who had elected us 'girl of the week—month—year.' 'The one to be with on a deserted island.' (I was elected 'Miss Tastiest Dish.')" Evelyn Keyes, *Scarlett O'Hara's Younger Sister* (New York: Fawcett Crest, 1977), 54–55; see also "Cheesecake Graduate (Janet Blair)," *Hollywood,* February 1943, 28.

44. Ted Gill, Associated Press Sunday article, Gen.com, May 30, 1943. See also Sheilah Graham, "Legs Are Running Riot in Movie Circles Again," *Hartford Courant,* January 17, 1943, A7; "They're Still in Style," *Omaha World Herald,* March 14, 1943, 36; Marjorie Lord, personal interview, September 24, 2005.

45. Graham, "Legs Are Running Riot."

46. There are several letters and V-mails addressed to Montez in the TZC. Donna Reed kept several hundred letters written to her by soldiers during the war: Larry Rohter, "Dear Donna: A Pinup So Swell She Kept G. I. Mail," *New York Times,* May 24, 2009, nytimes.com/2009/05/25/arts; Irene Dunne, personal interview, November 20, 1982.

47. "Action Seen in Leg Art," *Portland Oregonian,* May 30, 1943, 41; "The 'most' Girls of Hollywood!" *Screen Guide,* January 1944, 44–47; "Gals, Gags, Giggles," *Eyeful,* Spring 1944, 22–23.

48. *Hartford Courant,* October 10, 1943, SM2.

49. Frederick Othman, "Maria Montez Wonders," Gen.com, August 14, 1942.

50. "First Pin-up Exhibit Opens in Hollywood," *Los Angeles Times,* November 27, 1944, A1; "Pin-up Exhibition," *Los Angeles Examiner,* December 4, 1944, Los Angeles Public Library Photo Collection, *Herald-Examiner* Collection, #00045485. Academy exhibit: Tom Zimmerman, *Light and Illusion: The Hollywood Photographs of Ray Jones* (Los Angeles: Balcony, 1999), 30–37; Hal Hall, "The Academy Still Show," *American Cinematographer,* January 1944, 9, 27. The Superior, Wisconsin, hometown folks were always proud of Ray Jones. "Superiorite's Photo Is No. 1 Pin-up," *Superior Evening Courant,* December 2, 1943, part 1, p. 5.

51. "Pin Up Girl No. 8," *Movies,* January 1943, 43–44; "Pin Up Girl," *Motion Picture,* December 1943, 54; "Pin Up," *Close-Up,* December 1942; January 1943, 3; *Movie-Radio,* September 1943; *War Laffs: Fun for the Fighting Men,* December 1943, 57. Maria's portrait was in a compendium of favorite pin ups in *Movie Play,* Winter 1944, 38. "Pin Up," *Physical Culture,* July 1945, 56; *Yank,* November 29, 1942, 18; *Stars and Stripes,* December 9, 1942, 4.

52. "Yank," *Life,* November 15, 1943, 123; Leo Hofeller and Allen Churchill, *Pin Me Up: A Book Full of Pin-up Girls* (New York: Melrose, 1944). Two other photos of Maria appeared in *Yank.* The much-reproduced photograph of a doctor patching her knee after a fall at Fort Knox appeared in the March 21, 1943, issue on p. 13; a photo of Maria and her three sisters arriving at the Pasadena train station appeared in the November 24, 1944, issue on p. 19.

53. *Brief,* August 29, 1944, 14; *Caribbean Breeze,* July 1944. *Sheppard Field Facts* (Army Air Force, Sheppard, Texas), January 15, 1944, 4, featured two drawings by Corporal Bill Sully. The first was a perfectly shaded, sensual portrait of Montez. The second was a leggy drawing of her in costume for *Ali Baba and the Forty Thieves.* "Eagle Eye Pin-up Girl of the Week," *Eagle Eye* (Army Air Force, Eagle Pass, Texas), October 20, 1944. Another big year for Maria in military publications was 1945: *Mid Pacifican,* March 31, 1945, back cover; *Powder Horn* (Panama and Central America), January–February 1945, 29; *Navy News* (Guam), August 18, 1945, 3. *Sudan* was playing at the post film exchange at the same time. Writing for the military page of the *Laredo Times,* Gene Joffe commented that the three fantasy figures for the soldiers he knew were Lana Turner, Bette Grable and Maria Montez, "Off the Beam," July 1, 1943, 7.

54. "American Beauties, Western Style," *Esquire,* April 1944, 58–59.

55. Roger Carroll, "He Glamorizes Glamour," *Motion Picture,* March 1942, 27–34; Key Hurrell photograph is in TZC.

56. Published nationally on Sunday, August 12, 1945. See *New Orleans Times-Picayune,* section 2, p. 11.

57. Hildegarde Fillmore, "Give Yourself Vitality," *McCall's,* June 1944, 105; "Maria Montez Is Economically Independent," *Pic,* July 21, 1942, 30–33.

58. *Silver Screen,* June 1942, 16; two photos of Maria applying the leg makeup are in TZC. Her Universal contract mate Marie McDonald also posed applying the makeup.

59. Dee Lowrance, "Factory Girls Balk at Cast-off Overalls," *Omaha World Herald,* September 28, 1942, 3, Nationally syndicated through Newspaper Editors Association.

60. Bells: photo published nationally on Sunday, June 28, 1942, Gen.com; photo is in TZC. For Brownie, see "Foxbrownie," vintagefashionguild.org/label-resource/foxbrownie. For Hurrell, see: Whitney Stine and George Hurrell, *50 Years of Photographing Hollywood: The Hurrell Style* (New York: Greenwich House, 1983); Mark Vieira, *George Hurrell's Hollywood: Glamour Portraits, 1925–1992* (New York: Running Press, 2013).

61. Photos released by Universal Studios, TZC.

62. "Going Hollywood," *Collier's,* November 14, 1942, 12.

63. All photos in TZC, issued by Universal.

64. Hollywood Bowl photo and poster to build the cruiser *Los Angeles* is in TZC. "Build the Cruiser 'Los Angeles' Campaign," *Movieland,* October 1943, 14–15; "Here's Hollywood," *Screenland,* October 1943), 58. Photos of Hollywood Bowl rally: *Motion Picture Daily,* July 1, 1943, 4; "Drive to Build Cruiser Will Start Wednesday," *Los Angeles Times,* June 27, 1943, A2; "Cruiser Drive Opens Today," *Los Angeles Times,* June 30, 1943, A1. Funds raised: *Los Angeles Times,* June 30, 1943, A1.

65. Victory House: Universal Studios–released photo, TZC; *Cleveland Plain Dealer,* July 5, 1942, 2; additional photos in TZC.

8. Suspended

1. Hedda Hopper, "Wives Don't Wait," Gen.com, March 28, 1945; Jean-Pierre Aumont, *Sun and Shadow: An Autobiography* (New York: Norton, 1977), 119–20.

2. The Jean-Pierre Aumont Papers are at the Cinemathèque in Paris, but none of the wartime letters are included. Maria's nice Raina Paris cannot remember ever hearing about a cache of letters from or to her aunt existing in the family. A wartime photo of Maria sitting alone at the Clover Club was printed in *Screen Romances,* November 1944, 110. It is captioned, "Maria Montez, bespangled, bejeweled, be-yutiful. Dreaming of her Jean Pierre." Bee Bangs, "One-Man 'Zweetie,'" *Movie Show,* March 1945, 24–25+; Maria Montez, "Promises I Made My Soldier Husband," *Motion Picture,* January 1945, 47, 69; "My Maria?" Hedda Hopper column, Gen.com, July 31, 1944.

3. Louella Parsons, "Maria Montez and Jean Pierre Aumont," *San Francisco Examiner,* June 3, 1945; Hattie Bilson, "Jean Pierre Comes Home," *Screenland,* March 1946, 48, 74–75.

4. Bob Thomas, "Hollywood Sights and Sounds," March 26, 1945, MHL Biography Files, "Maria Montez" file.

5. Gladys Hall, "I Thought, 'How Remarkable She Is,'" October 27, 1944, Gladys Hall Collection, MHL, published as "Advice to Her Kid Sisters," *Silver Screen,* February 1945, 30–31. As one of three presenters on books about Hollywood stars, I met Peter Coe's sixth wife at the Los Angeles Central Library and interviewed her by telephone on September 22, 2014. She told me Coe claimed to have had an affair with Maria during the filming of *Gypsy Wildcat.* She also told me he said he was a swimmer in the 1936 Berlin Olympics and served with the Marine Corps in the South Pacific. Both are lies. In fact, she referred to him as a "pathological liar" and a complete drunk by the time she knew him. Their marriage was annulled in 1969 after two years, when she was nineteen. She also noted he hated women, generally boiled over with anger, and hated himself. It was quite an odd interview. I see no reason to believe his claim. This is simply not the sort of man Maria was ever interested in.

6. Gladys Hall, "Reunion," *Photoplay,* July 1945, 27+.

7. Ibid.; "Aumont Returns from War Area," *Los Angeles Times,* April 12, 1945, MHL Biographic Files, "Jean Pierre Aumont" file.

8. *Silver Screen,* September 1945, 6, 8; Harrison Carroll column, Gen.com, April 1, 1945; Louella Parsons column, Gen.com, April 11, 1945; Sheilah Graham column, Gen.com, April 21, 1945.

9. "My Easter Prayer," *Photoplay,* April 1945, 42–43.

10. Aumont, *Sun and Shadow,* 119; Philip Scheuer, "Hollywood G.I.s Find Themselves Richer from Experiences of War," *Los Angeles Times,* October 7, 1945, B1, 3.

11. "With Only 6 Dache Hats," *Chicago Sun,* April 10, 1945, 1.

12. Ibid.; snipe on Acme News Photo, Chicago Bureau, "Alak! Two Hats!!" April 9, 1945, TZC; "2 Daches Lost, Montez Boils," *New York Journal-American,* April 10, 1945; "Hollywood Inside," *Variety,* June 26, 1945, 2.

13. Jesse Henderson, "Home to Hollywood," *Movies,* July 1945, 26–27+.

14. Universal teams: Bernard Dick, *City of Dreams: The Making and Remaking of Universal Studios* (Lexington: University Press of Kentucky, 1997), 129–34; Thomas Schatz, *The Genius of the System* (New York: Pantheon Books, 1988), 352–53.

15. Edwin Schallert, *Los Angeles Times,* February 16, 1944, A10; George Hadley-Garcia, *Hispanic Hollywood: The Latins in Motion Pictures* (New York: Citadel, 1990), 117.

16. Pete Martin, "Dominican Dynamite," *Saturday Evening Post,* July 28, 1945, 29+, reprinted in Pete Martin, *Hollywood without Makeup* (New York: Bantam, 1949) 36–44.

17. Ibid.

18. Erskine Johnson, "In Hollywood," *Baton Rouge Advocate,* May 25, 1943, 4.

19. Jimmie Fidler column, Gen.com, May 2, 1945. Louella Parsons had earlier remarked that Maria risked suspension over rejecting *Frontier Gal.* Gen.com, April 17, 1945. Wanting to change image: Edwin Schallert, "Miss Montez: She Only Wants to Learn the Ropes," *Los Angeles Times,* April 18, 1945, C3; Erskine Johnson, "It Happened in Hollywood," *Riverside Daily Press,* April 22, 1944, 16; Hedda Hopper, "Maria Montez Finds out How Well It Pays to Advertise," *Los Angeles Times,* February 13, 1944, C1; Jerry Mason, "Fair and Sultry" (prepared for Sunday supplements to newspapers all over the country), USC, Constance McCormick Collection, "Articles—Maria Montez" folder. See also Jerry Mason, "Maria Montez Has Changed in the Last Year—She Says . . ." *Boston Herald,* March 12, 1944, 25; Edwin Schallert, "Maria Montez Will Quit Sarong Roles," *Los Angeles Times,* August 17, 1944, A10; Julia McCarthy, "Black and White Films Reveal Montez 'Flame,'" *New York News,* September 22, 1944; Charles Samuels, "Montez: Last of the Sirens," *Motion Picture,* October 1947, 33+. In late December 1943, a photo of Maria sitting fetchingly on a divan showing some leg was distributed for publication nationally by Universal. The caption read, "Although actress Maria Montez has been hungering to do dramatic roles, studio won't oblige her. Seems as though she's destined to be a South Sea siren as long as she can look like this." See, for example, "South Sea Eyeful," *Greensboro Daily News,* December 23, 1943, 12.

20. Pam Munter, "Edmund O'Brien: The Prince of Noir," edmundo'brien.com.

21. Hedda Hopper column, Gen.com, March 28, 1948; "Chatter," *Kansas* City *Star,* February 3, 1946, 56; Constance Palmer, "The Happy Aumonts," *Silver Screen,* August 1946, 35; Dianne Scott, "Mythical Maria," *Photoplay,* January 1946, 44–45, 81–83; "Hectic Haven," *Movie Show,* September 1947, 24–25, 66–69.

22. Edwin Schallert, "Yvonne De Carlo Stands out Again as 'Threat Girl,'" *Los Angeles Times,* June 3, 1945, B1.

23. "Yvonne DeCarlo, Popular West Coast Showgirl," *Laff,* October 1942, cover; Jake Rachman, "Salome Dances in Technicolor," *Omaha World Herald,* July 20, 1945, 22.

24. "Yvonne DeCarlo, Popular West Coast Showgirl"; Rachman, "Salome Dances in Technicolor"; "*Salome Where She Lives,*" *Silver Screen,* March 1945, 33.

25. The letter from the bomber squadron actually came from De Carlo's cousin Kenny, who was a bombardier trainee in Saskatoon. Yvonne De Carlo, with Doug Warren, *Yvonne: An Autobiography* (New York: St. Martin's, 1987), 89. For the studio version, see "Bombardiers Choose Salome," *Movie Show,* March 1945, 23.

26. "Salome Up to Date," *Silver Screen,* April 1945.

27. Rosalind Shaffer, "Yvonne DeCarlo Grabbed Chance and Won Fame," *Richmond Times-Dispatch,* August 19, 1945, 51; Matthew Bernstein, *Walter Wanger, Hollywood Independent* (Berkeley: University of California Press, 1994, 190–91; WWC, "*Salome*" file: John Joseph to Charles Huy, June 2, 1944, "*Salome Where She Danced*" campaigns; Pete Daily to Walter Wanger, May 11, 1944, on indirect plantings; Charles Huy, "*Salome Where She Danced,*" May 10, 1944, "Search for the 'Most Beautiful Girl in the World'"; letter from Dan Kelly, Executive Assistant in Charge of Talent, "Suggested Letter to All Leading Photographers, Models, Singing Dancing and Charm Schools and Others." The reviewer for the *Washington, DC, Times-Herald* was less impressed. He opined that "Miss DeCarlo is a sort of poor man's Hedy LaMarr," WWC, box 90, folder 25.

28. Owenbey: Universal Studios–released photograph and snipe, TZC; "Lift Operator Gets Test for Film Lead," *Los Angeles Times,* August 6, 1944), A3; Ray Jones photograph released by International News, De Carlo combing Owenbey's hair, WWC, box 90, folder 25, published in the *Los Angeles Times,* November 13, 1944, A10; De Carlo and Warren, *Yvonne,* 85–92.

29. Tom Zimmerman, *Light and Illusion: The Hollywood Photographs of Ray Jones* (Los Angeles: Balcony, 1999). *Salome* ad: *Los Angeles Examiner,* Sunday edition, April 15, 1945, TZC. Photos and snipes of De Carlo are in TZC.

30. "Wanger flopped": The quote may have come from columnist Erskine Johnson, "In Hollywood," Gen.com, June 23, 1945. In a later column about her suspension from Universal over *Frontier Gal,* he noted, "Universal is now known as 'Maria—Where She Pouted.'" Gen.com, June 7, 1945. The reviewer for the *Washington, DC, Times-Herald,* May 26, 1945, was so disappointed in the movie he wrote, "Mr. Walter Wanger is the producer, and the more I see of Mr. Wanger's latter-day output, the more I wonder how much he really had to do with '*The Long Voyage Home.*'" WWC, box 90, folder 25. De Carlo and Warren, *Yvonne,* 102. De Carlo's understanding was that Montez "did not want Rod Cameron or Jon Hall to be her leading man and did not like the idea of playing mother to a young girl who might very likely upstage her." At that point she had not met Maria and had no idea of her two-year fight to change her image and the type of movies she made. Michael Sheridan, "Venus DeCarlo," *Motion Picture,* May 1945, 27+.

31. Hedda Hopper column, Gen.com, May 24, 1945; Charles Samuels, "Femme Fatale," *Motion Picture,* January 1946, 36; Rosalind Shaffer, *Richmond Times Dispatch,* August 19, 1945, 51.

32. Edwin Schallert, *Los Angeles Times,* June 3, 1945, B1.

33. De Carlo and Warren, *Yvonne,* 116. On the set of *Scheherazade,* after her third Technicolor movie, De Carlo started to express a desire to leave the exotic behind.

She "plaintively" told Sheilah Graham, "I'd like to be a modern woman in black and white." Sound familiar? Sheilah Graham column, Gen.com, February 3, 1946.

34. De Carlo and Warren, *Yvonne,* 116–17.

35. Hadley-Garcia, *Hispanic Hollywood,* 123–24; Kathryn Bishop-Sanchez, *Creating Carmen Miranda: Race, Camp and Transitional Stardom* (Nashville: Vanderbilt University Press, 2016).

36. Universal published an ad in the business pages of newspapers called "Entertainment for the Millions" that featured a section called "Financial Progress." It noted the net profit as well as charted the gross income from operations at Universal from $17.41 million in 1936 to $51.05 million in 1945. *Boston Herald,* January 30, 1946, 17.

37. Dick, *City of Dreams,* 138–41; Schatz, *The Genius of the System,* 464–66.

38. "Film Groups Form New Companies," *Los Angeles Times,* November 28, 1945, 1; Dick, *City of Dreams,* 139–40.

39. Copies of ads featuring Montez: TZC; *Maria Montez: A Dominican Star,* mariamontez.org; Margarita Vicens de Morales, *Maria Montez: Su vida* (Santo Domingo: Republica Dominicana, 1992), 208. Three-wheeled car: Acme Newspictures, Los Angeles Bureau photograph, distributed nationally September 13, 1945, TZC.

40. Leo Simon to Maria Montez, USC, "Maria Montez" file, box 606, file 18208.

41. Ormiston: USC, *"Tangier"* file. Serta mattresses: Leo Simon to Maria Montez. 108th Regiment: "*'Arabian Nights'* Is Southtown Feature," *Springfield Daily Illinois State Journal,* April 4, 1943, 18. Serta: USC, *"Tangier"* file.

42. Radio: USC, "Maria Montez" folder, concerns Universal's approval process for Maria to appear on the shows. Maria's appearance on *The Old Gold Comedy Theater, Bob Hope Show,* and *The Edgar Bergen and Charley McCarthy Show* are available from Old Time Radio, OTRCAT.com, TZC; *Edgar Bergen and Charlie McCarthy Show,* March 11, 1945, Museum of Television and Radio, Beverly Hills.

"Maria Montez on the Air," *Old Gold Comedy Theater, She Loves Me Not,* TZC.

43. Mitchneck certainly got publicity for teaching such a famous client; see "Maria's Speech Coach Masters Dozen Tongues," *New Orleans Picayune,* November 26, 1944, 3; "There's Glamour in Speech," *Movieland,* May 1946, 56–57+. He worked with Jean Gabin at 20th Century Fox before he met Maria: "Who Is This Great Lover?" *Modern Screen,* July 1941, 42–43.

44. USC, *"Pirates of Monterey"* file, "Correspondence" folder, *Coast Guard Show.*

45. Hedda Hopper column, Gen.com, April 23, 1945.

46. Erskine Johnson column, Gen.com, June 23, 1945; *Strange Woman* was eventually filmed in 1946 with Hedy Lamarr in the role for Hunt Stromberg Productions.

47. *Los Angeles Times,* August 27, 1945, 8. A group of wedding photos including Maria are in May Mann Papers (MSS 1449), Brigham Young University Special Collections, "May Mann personal photographs, undated" folder.

48. "Universal," *Independent Exhibitors Film Bulletin,* February 6, 1948, 2.

49. Louella Parsons column, Gen.com, June 27, 1945.

50. MPPC files, *"Tangier."*

51. AFI, *"Tangier."*

52. *New York Herald Tribune,* March 7, 1946; MHL Production Files, *"Tangier."*

53. *Variety,* March 6, 1946; *Hollywood Reporter,* March 6, 1946.

54. *Hollywood Citizen-News,* April 24, 1946; *Commonweal,* May 17, 1946, MHL Production Files, *"Tangier"*; *New York Times,* June 7, 1946; *Independent Exhibitors Film Bulletin,* March 18, 1946, 13; "Now Playing," *Kansas* City *Star,* April 7, 1946, 66; *New York Herald Tribune,* March 7, 1946, 9.

55. Universal Studios one-sheet and press book, *"Tangier,"* TZC.

56. Virginia McPherson, United Press, "Maria Montez Has New Movie Role—With Clothes and Calm Disposition," USC, "Maria Montez Articles" folder, or *Baton Rouge Advocate,* October 19, 1945, 16; "Maria's a Spy in *'Tangier,'"* *Movie Show,* February 1946, 12.

57. "Black Friday," October 5, 2012, patriahysell.wordpress.com; "Hollywood Black Friday," Wikipedia.org; "Strikes Stud U.S.," *Life,* October 15, 1945, 38.

58. "Jean Pierre Aumont Notes" for proposed 1946 article, MHL, Gladys Hall Collection, folder 23, published as Gladys Hall, "Reunion," *Photoplay,* July 1945, 103.

59. United Press, "Says Maria Montez Now out of Danger," Gen.com, July 2, 1945; Louella Parsons column, Gen.com, July 24, 1945.

60. Photo and snipe released by Universal, TZC.

61. Aumont, *Sun and Shadow;* "Louella Parsons' Good News," *Modern Screen,* May 1946, 60.

62. Palmer, "The Happy Aumonts"; Virginia MacPherson, "Maria Montez Boasts That Hers Is World's Most Beautiful Baby," *Rockford Morning Star,* June 6, 1946, 10. Maria Christina "wrote" an article called "I Like My Parents," *Movieland,* August 1946, 30–31. It had Maria Christina exclaiming how lucky she was to have a home full of parents and aunts who loved her. Bob Thomas did a column on the problem for Universal: "Two of the company's top stars, Deanna Durbin and Maria Montez, are making pictures while expecting babies." Bob Thomas, "Montez, Durbin Happy about Their Babies but Universal Studio Isn't," *Omaha World Herald,* November 4, 1945, 62; Rae Lynn, "Hectic Haven," *Movie Show,* September 1947, 24–25, 66–69.

63. Universal Studios released photograph with descriptive snipe on verso, TZC.

64. USC, *"Tangier"* file.

65. USC, *"Pirates of Monterey"* file, "Production Budget"; USC, "Vera West" folder.

66. MPPC files, *"Pirates of Monterey."*

67. Walter Winchell column, Gen.com, December 23, 1947; John Scott, "*'Pirates of Monterey'* Old California Thriller," *Los Angeles Times,* December 17, 1947, A9; Bosley Crowther, "The Same Old Story," *New York Times,* December 17, 1947; *Variety,* November 12, 1947; MHL Production Files, *"Pirates of Monterey"*; USC, *"Pirates of Monterey"* file.

68. " Critics Wield Cutlasses on 'Pirates of Monterey,'" *Hollywood Reporter,* December 22, 1947, 8; USC, *"Pirates of Monterey"* file, "Reviews."

69. Universal released a set photo of Maria checking her sister's makeup with a snipe explaining their relationship, as well as other photos with her sister, TZC; USC, *"Pirates of Monterey"* file, "Publicity Releases" folder.

70. Universal Studios press book, *"Pirates of Monterey"* TZC; USC, *"Pirates of Monterey"* box, "Disbursements" folder. Also in this file is a note about the two wardrobe girls and two hairdressers who had to leave Universal with Montez to get to the

Palos Verdes location where J. A. Smith, police chief of the Palos Verdes Estates Police Department, would collect $218.75 to protect the site.

71. Publicity: USC, *"Pirates of Monterey"* file, "Correspondence" folder. "Heart's Desire": USC, *"Pirates of Monterey"* file, "Correspondence" folder.

72. USC, *"Pirates of Monterey"* file, "May 17, 1946.

9. *The Exile*

1. Universal Studios released photograph to advertise the film, with snipe on verso, TZC.

2. Earthquake: Sheilah Graham column, Gen.com, August 23, 1946; Christening: USC, *"Pirates of Monterey"* file, "Correspondence" folder, letter to Hedda Hopper from Universal Publicity Department.

3. King Brothers: Edwin Schallert, *Los Angeles Times,* April 17, 1943, 10. Terence Young filmed *Mayerling* in 1968 with Ava Gardner as the empress Elizabeth and James Mason as the archduke Joseph in a completely different story of the royal couple.

4. Eileen Creelman, "Picture Plays and Players: Maria Montez and Jean Pierre Aumont Talk of Films Before Flying to Paris," *New York Sun,* August 31, 1946, USC, "Maria Montez" folder.

5. Ibid.; Rae Lynn, "What's a Crowd?" February 26, 1947, manuscript at USC, folder "Articles, Maria Montez"; "Scarlet Feather," *Film Daily,* February 6, 1948, 3.

6. "Montez and Aumont Tour Europe," part of a fan's collection of clipped articles purchased on e-Bay. Sadly, in most such cases the fans were not history majors and did not attribute the articles. "J. P. Aumont Presents Paris to Maria Montez" (translated), *Pour tous films,* no. 4, September 24, 1946, 4–5, has seven photos of the couple at the Arc de Triomphe, with members of the French film community, eating ice cream from a street vendor, etc. Their arrival in France was covered by Universal newsreel in its feature "Personalities of the Screen." *Maria Montez, Lou Costello Rare 1946 Newsreel,* YouTube.

7. "First Cannes Film Festival," history.com/first-cannes-film-festival; "U. S. Movies Abroad," *Los Angeles Times,* November 27, 1946, A4; "Festival of Cannes Is Open" (translated), *Pour tous films,* no. 24, September 24, 1946, 2, concerns how to get to the festival and the films being shown.

8. Unattributed article, from fan's collection purchased on e-Bay.

9. Maria Montez Aumont, "This Is My Husband," *Photoplay,* August 1947, 64–65, 108–9, USC, Constance McCormack Collection, "c. 1948–1948" folder.

10. United Press, "Film Stars on Their Way to Perform for Royalty," *New York Times,* October 21, 1946; C. A. LeJeune, "Bulletins from London," *New York Times,* November 24, 1946, 85; William Eythe, "Royal Command Performance," *Photoplay,* February 1947, 62–65, 118.

11. Jean-Pierre Aumont, *Sun and Shadow: An Autobiography* (New York: Norton, 1977), 126.

12. For comparison, Broderick Crawford and Andy Devine made $1,500 per week, Deanna Durbin $2,750, and Abbott and Costello $5,000. USC, "Contract Talent Reports" folder, July 1–December 31, 1946.

13. "Ecstasy": Louella Parsons column, Gen.com, January 28, 1946; Jimmie Fidler column, Gen.com, February 12, 1946; Edwin Schallert, "King Brothers Will Take a Fling at '*Ecstasy*,'" *Los Angeles Times*, January 30, 1946, A3. "Hunted": Edwin Schallert, "Montez to Chameleon Way out of Fantasy," *Los Angeles Times*, April 20 1946, A5.

14. Louella Parsons, "More Excitement! Maria Montez Seeking Jack on '*Queen of Hearts*' Deal," *San Diego Union*, February 8, 1948, 60; Ralph Wilk, "Hollywood-Vine Yard," *Film Daily*, August 18, 1947, 8; Louella Parsons, "Maria Montez Sues for Share of '*Queen of Hearts*,'" Sunday column, *Waterloo Courier*, February 3, 1946, 19; "$400,000 Asked for Film Role That Simply Vanished," *Los Angeles Daily News*, February 5, 1948; *Film Daily*, August 18, 1947, 8; "Studio Size-ups," *Independent Exhibitors Film Bulletin*, June 10, 1946, 19.

15. Nebenzal: Harold Nebenzal, telephone interview, January 13, 2016; AFI, "*Siren of Atlantis*"; MHL Biographical Files, Seymour Nebenzal; "Seymour Nebenzal, Obituary," *Variety*, September 27, 1961; "Seymour Nebenzal Obituary," *New York Times*, September 25, 1961; J. A. Aberdeen, *Hollywood Renegades: The Society of Independent Motion Picture Producers* (Los Angeles: Cobblestone Entertainment, 2000); Patrick McGilligan, *Fritz Lang: The Nature of the Beast* (New York: St. Martin's, 1997), 145–46, 173.

16. Lupton Wilkinson, "Maria and That Man," *Screenland* (1946), 25, 72; "Maria Montez, United Artists Star," *Good Humor*, July 1948, 13; Jim Marshall, "The Strange Embarrassment of Madame Aumont," *Collier's*, June 28, 1947, 12–13.

17. Hedda Hopper column, Gen.com, March 19, 1947, March 25, 1947.

18. Bruce Russell: United Press, "Should Have Waited for Proof of Prehistoric Men," Gen.com, August 5, 1947.

19. Philip Scheuer, "Weird Sets In 'Atlantis,'" *Los Angeles Times*, March 9, 1947, B1.

20. "*Siren of Atlantis*," *Life*, January 31, 1949, 54–55.

21. Harold Nebenzal, telephone interview, September 8, 2016.

22. "Wisconsin Historical Society, University of Wisconsin, "Maria Montez" file; Hommel photograph, TZC.

23. "Maria on the Half Shell," *Esquire*, December 1947, 11; "Plum for Maria," *Between Us*, December 1949, 11.

24. USC, "*The Exile*" file 1538; Douglas Fairbanks Jr.: Ronald Davis Oral History Project, Southern Methodist University, #28, October 7, 12, 14, 1982, 75–77, MHL.

25. Ibid., 78.

26. Ibid., 79–81.

27. USC, "*The Exile*" file 14941, memo dated October 9, 1947.

28. USC, "*The Exile*" file 14941, memo dated October 14, 1947; Brian Connell, *Knight Errant: A Biography of Douglas Fairbanks* (Garden City: Doubleday, 1955).

29. Ron Alexander, "Douglas Fairbanks, Jr. Tells His Story (Some of It, That Is)," *New York Times*, April 20, 1988, C4. According to Harold Nebenzal, the son of "*Siren of Atlantis*" producer Seymour Nebenzal and husband of Paule Croset (Rita Corday), his wife never forgave Maria for what she saw as the ruining of her career. Harold Nebenzal, telephone interview, June 13, 2016.

30. MPPC files, "*The Exile*" file, "Preview" folder; Hedda Hopper, "Hollywood Owes Set Makers Much," Gen.com, August 31, 1947.

31. MPPC files, "*The Exile*" file; Robert Osbourne, introduction to *The Exile,* Turner Classic Movies, January 23, 2012.

32. *Variety,* October 15, 1947; Edwin Schallert, *Los Angeles Times,* November 22, 1947; *Los Angeles Daily News,* November 22, 1947; *Hollywood Citizen-News,* October 25, 1947; *Commonweal,* January 39, 1948; MHL, "*The Exile*" production files; *New York Times,* December 26, 1947.

33. "Doug Pleases as Dashing Exile," *Canton Repository,* March 25, 1948, 24.

34. Philip Scheuer, "Problems of Prestige Give Showmen Grief," *Los Angeles Times,* December 21, 1947, C1; Thomas Brady, "Another Action," *New York Times,* August 3, 1947, X3; "Maria Montez Wins Court Writ," *Los Angeles Times,* November 27, 1947, A1; "U-I Asks Court Rule on Billing Tangle," *Motion Picture Daily,* June 23, 1947, 7; Harold Heffernan, "Maria Montez Makes Ballyhoo Really Pay Off," *Hartford Courant,* March 7, 1948, A9.

35. USC, "*The Exile*" file, folder 14941; Display ad for *The Exile,* TZC. All of the display ads for the film are reproduced in *The Exile* press book published by Universal.

36. Jimmie Fidler column, Gen.com, September 10, 1947.

37. Harold Heffernan, Sunday column, Gen.com, March 7, 1948.

38. USC, "*The Exile,*" file, folder 14941.

39. USC, "*The Exile*" file, folder 677/2176J; Frederick Othman column, Gen.com, May 24, 1947.

40. USC, "*The Exile*" file, folder 411/12 GA3, May 15, 1947.

41. USC, "*The Exile*" file, folder 14941, "Odds and Ends."

42. USC, "*The Exile*" file, folder 411/12693.

43. Lutz Bacher, *Max Ophuls in the Hollywood Studios* (New Brunswick: Rutgers University Press, 1996), 104–7.

44. AFI, "*Siren of Atlantis.*"

45. MPPC files, "*Siren of Atlantis*"; Louellla Parsons column, Gen.com, January 2, 1947; Thomas Brady, *New York Times,* March 2, 1947, X5.

46. Wisconsin Historical Society, University of Wisconsin, United Artists Collection, "*Synopsis of 'Atlantis,'*" box 5, folder 6; "Finally," *New York Times,* January 2, 1949.

47. Jon Halliday, *Sirk on Sirk* (Boston: Faber and Faber, 1997), 85–86.

48. Wisconsin Historical Society, University of Wisconsin, United Artists Collection, "*Atlantis,*" box 5, folder 6. Typical of the train wreck *Siren of Atlantis* became, when United Artists tried to fill a contract with the navy for three 35mm and twenty-one 16mm prints of the movie, it only had the negative for the first shooting, which was called *Atlantis,* and had no negative to work from for the upgraded *Siren of Atlantis.* The studio was about to lose the $7,500 contract. "Office Rushgram," H. D. Buckley to Robert Hilton re: "*Siren of Atlantis,*" University of Wisconsin, United Artists Collection, box 6, folder 5.

49. *Hollywood Reporter,* December 13, 1948; *Variety,* December 13, 1948; MHL Production Files, "*Siren of Atlantis.*"

50. *Newsweek,* February 21, 1949; *Time,* January 13, 1941; *Boston Traveler,* February 9, 1949, 16; Philip Scheuer, "La Montez Queens It Up in Atlantis," *Los Angeles Times,* February 11, 1949, 19; "Maria Montez an Exotic Queen Indeed!" *Hollywood Citizen-News,* February 11, 1949.

51. A.W., "2 Legionnaires Learn about Atlantis," *New York Times,* August 22, 1949; *Dallas Morning News,* April 15, 1949, I22.

52. Vernon Steele, "Sound Track," *Pacific Coast Musician,* March 6, 1948; Edward Sack, "The Moviegoer," *Harvard Crimson,* February 11, 1949, thecrimson.com; display ad for *Siren of Atlantis, Los Angeles Times,* February 10, 1949, B8. John Robert Parish and Lennard DeCarlo nicely summed up *Atlantis* in *Hollywood Players: The Forties* (New Rochelle: Arlington House, 1976), 415, writing, "It sunk lower than the fabled lost continent."

53. The bankruptcy also held up payment money made on ticket sales in Europe where the film performed better than in the United States. The French francs were impounded pending disposition of the claims of Nebenzal's creditors against that money. University of Wisconsin, United Artists Collection, O'Brien, Driscoll, Raftery and Lawlwer to Seymour Nebenzal, December 4, 1950, box 5, folder, 6.

54. "Film Actress Goes to Court," April 17, 1950; "Believes in Stars: Maria Montez Tells Court about Astrology," April 22, 1945, both in UCLA *Los Angeles Daily News* Collection, box 812, folder "Maria Montez, 1947." Jimmie Fidler quipped, "When people talk about Maria Montez' 'new suit,' you never know whether it's wearing apparel or another court battle." Jimmie Fidler column, Gen.com, October 23, 1948. "Maria Montez in Rush to End Salary Hearing," *Los Angeles Times,* April 18, 1950, A17; "Maria Montez Tells of Purchases for Film," *Los Angeles Times,* April 19, 1950, A1.

55. "Maria Montez Tells Court about Astrology"; "Failure to Heed Stars Blamed for Film Flop," April 21, 1950, UCLA, *Los Angeles Daily News* Collection, box 812, folder "Maria Montez, 1947."

56. Thomas Brady, "Montez Wins Suit for Unpaid Salary," *New York Times,* January 3, 1951; "Maria Montez in Rush to End Hearing," *Los Angeles Times,* March 18, 1950, A17; "Maria Montez Victor in $38,000 Salary Suit," *Los Angeles Times,* January 3, 1951, A12.

57. *Variety,* April 26, 1948, 4.

58. Hedda Hopper, "Aumonts' Life Pivots on Baby," *Los Angeles Times,* March 28, 1948, C1. Several other writers commented on the very full, very happy Montez-Aumont home: Inez Wallace, "Hollywood Personalities: Fireball Maria Montez Keeps Eight Servants Busy," *Cleveland Plain Dealer,* November 3, 1946, 22; Erskine Johnson, "In Hollywood," *Baton Rouge Advocate,* January 26, 1947, 4.

59. "What Hollywood Itself Is Talking About," *Screenland,* October 1948, 55; Ronald Davis Oral History Collection, Southern Methodist University, Arthur Lubin, #353, July 15, 1985, MHL.

60. International News Service, "Mayer Heads Salary List; Durbin, Gable Lead Stars," Gen.com, February 20, 1948.

10. France

1. Jean-Pierre Aumont, *Sun and Shadow: An Autobiography* (New York: Norton, 1977). 126.

2. Ibid., 128.

3. Ibid., 132.

4. Bob Thomas column, Gen.com, February 20, 1947.

5. George Thomas Jr., "Filming in Paris: Notes on First Franco-American Projects," *New York Times,* December 12, 1948, X6.

6. Christina Productions, *"Wicked City"* press book, p. 3, TZC; *New York Journal-American,* July 1, 1947.

7. Thomas, "Filming in Paris." There is an excellent synopsis and history of *Wicked City* in noiroftheweek.com/wicked city.

8. *Wicked City* did less business in France than either *Sudan* or *Siren of Atlantis.* The latter was a big hit in France, no matter what a disaster it was in the United States: boxofficestory.com/France-949.

9. Earl Wilson column, Gen.com, December 30, 1948; Patricia Clary, "Maria Montez Sets Modern Travel Record," *Baton Rouge Advocate,* January 4, 1949, 2.

10. Hedda Hopper column, Gen.com, January 3, 1949.

11. Orson Welles and Peter Bogdanavich, *This Is Orson Welles* (New York: DaCapo, 1998), 222–23.

12. Review of *Portrait of an Assassin:* lefilmguide.com/review/portrait-d-un-assassin-1949.

13. *"My Name Is Aquilon,"* playbill.com; Aumont, *Sun and Shadow,* 133–35; ibdb.com/broadway/my-name-is-aquilon.

14. USC, Louella Parsons, *Los Angeles Examiner,* March 23, 1949; "Dreams End: Actor Aumont to Divorce Maria Montez," *Los Angeles Times,* March 23, 1949, A24; UCLA, *Los Angeles Daily News* Collection, box 812, folder "Maria Montez, 1947."

15. "Maria Montez to Discard Mate to Wed Director," *Los Angeles Herald,* March 23, 1949.

16. Louella Parsons, "Maria Montez Seeks Separation from Jean," *New York Journal-American,* March 23, 1949; Hedda Hopper column, *Los Angeles Times,* March 26, 1949, A8; Dorothy Kilgallen column, Gen.com, April 24, 1949; Harrison Carroll, "Maria Montez Patches Quarrel with Actor Mate Aumont," *Los Angeles Daily News,* April 1, 1949; Jimmie Fidler column, Gen.com, July 7, 1949.

17. Aumont, *Sun and Shadow,* 136.

18. "Lavish Paris Soiree Blazes with Jewels," *Los Angeles Times,* May 18, 1949, A17; *Springfield Daily Illinois State Journal,* July 26, 1949, 18 (photograph); Sidney Skolsky, "Puts Best Points Forward," *Hollywood Citizen-News,* May 25, 1944.

19. Joseph Cotten, *Vanity Will Get You Somewhere: An Autobiography* (San Francisco: Mercury House, 1987), 104–6.

20. Ibid.

21. "Montez Home Attached by Flack," *Los Angeles Daily News,* September 20, 1949; Jimmie Fidler noted the hiring of the Hollywood-based P. R. man in his column for July 30, 1948, Gen.com. MHL, Hedda Hopper Collection, Maria Montez file, folder 1844 September 20, 1950.

22. *Los Angeles Times,* January 25, 1950; "Maria Montez Saved by Pilot in Boat Mishap," *Los Angeles Daily News,* January 24, 1950. Italian film industry: Shawn Levy, *Dolce Vita Confidential* (New York: Norton, 2016).

23. Jesse Lasky Jr., *Whatever Happened to Hollywood?* (New York: Funk and Wagnalls, 1973), 275–78. Aumont writes of the Italian devotion to Maria in *Sun and Shadow,* 139. Another prime example of funding of films in Italy was Orson Welles's *Othello.* Due to financial problems the filming was stopped three times, starting again when money was found. See Welles and Bogdanovich, *This Is Orson Welles,* 224–38. For Italian presentation of Maria, see *La settimana illustrata* (The Illustrated Week), no. 34 (August 26, 1950), cover; "Venice Enthusiastic for Maria Montez," *Hollywood,* November 4, 1950, cover; *Bis: Tuti gli spettacoli* (Bis: All the Shows), no. 41 (October 14, 1950); "Maria Montez Wants Adventure," *Cine illustrado* (Cinema Illustrated), no. 43 (October 22, 1950), cover, 8–9.

24. *New York Times,* November 28, 1952; "Spectacular Film and Musical Coupled," *Los Angeles Times,* May 14, 1953, B11; "Motion Picture Daily Feature Reviews" *Motion Picture Daily,* November 14, 1952, 8.

25. Lasky, *Whatever Happened to Hollywood?* 279–83.

26. *Italian Movies,* August 26, 1950.

27. *Hearing before the Committee on Un-American Activities, House of Representatives, 82nd Congress, First Session, 1951* (Washington, DC: Government Printing Office, 1951), 2122–26. I queried the FBI under the Freedom of Information Act to see if there was a file on Maria. There was not.

28. *Screenland Plus T-V Times,* February 1953, 55.

29. Associated Press, "Foreign Films Tie Up Maria: Actress Busy in France and Italy," *Portland Oregonian,* August 11, 1951, 44. A 1941 Ray Jones photo of Maria in a dark, midriff-baring top was released by Wide World on August 12, 1951, with this snipe on the verso: "It's been three years since Maria Montez has done a film in Hollywood, but she's still one of the busiest actresses in the world. She's made a few movies in France, a few in Italy, done a stage play in Europe that took her on tour through France, Belgium and Luxemburg, and right now she's in an Italian film about a bunch of dashing pirates." In another effort to remind America that Maria was still around, a Wide World photograph of her dining with Van Johnson, called "Stars Dine in Rome," was released and published in the *Los Angeles Times* on July 5, 1951, 20. Maria never did do any television: David Inman, *Performers' Television Credits,* vol. 2, *G-M* (Jefferson: McFarland, 2001).

30. Aumont, *Sun and Shadow,* 142–43.

31. *Life,* September 24, 1951, 58. The caption said Aumont "registered deeper grief than any role could possibly demand." The same scene photographed from the left shows the sisters in black with veils over their faces and Jean-Pierre with his face in his hands, from a fan's collection of clippings, *Silver Screen* (1951): United Press, "Aumont Weeps at Maria's Death," *San Diego Union,* September 9, 1951, 16; "Mate Sobbed at Side of Dead Montez," *Los Angeles Daily News,* September 8, 1951; United Press, "Maria Montez Buried in Old Paris Cemetery," *Los Angeles Times,* September 12, 1951, A20. Six photos of the funeral are in Margarita Vicens de Morales, *Maria Montez: Su vida* (Santo Domingo Republica Dominicana 1992), 134. There is always the dissenting voice. On the E Channel's Maria Montez episode of the series *Mysteries and Scandals* Mexican-born actress Linda Christian, who said she was Maria's friend, was sure she had killed herself because "she just didn't want to grow old." She claims Maria Christina Aumont showed her a despairing letter her mother wrote to her just

before she died. Raina Paris, interviewed right after, disputed this, saying her mother and aunts all said it was impossible that Maria killed herself. She had never been happier.

32. The Associated Press story appeared in the *New York Times* as "Maria Montez, 31, Dies Suddenly After Reducing Bath in Paris Home," September 8, 1951, 8; the United Press story appeared in the *Los Angeles Times* as "Maria Montez Dies In 'Scalding Bath,'" September 8, 1951, 1. Virginia MacPherson, "Died in Paris Bathtub," *Los Angeles Daily News,* September 8, 1951.

33. "Movie Colony Shocked by Montez Death," *Los Angeles Times,* September 8, 1951, 3, accompanied by a photo of Maria holding hands with Jean-Pierre at a Hollywood premiere; *Los Angeles Times,* September 10, 1951, B6. In the *New York Call Bulletin* for September 7, 1951, her death was announced on page 1 above the fold with a red banner headline at the top of the page, "Maria Montez Drowns in Bathtub," accompanied by an early photo of her in an off-the-shoulder black dress without a bra looking young and hot. UCLA, *Los Angeles Daily News* Collection, box 812, folder "Maria Montez, 1947"; "Maria Montez Found Dead in Bathtub in Paris," *New York Post,* September 8, 1951, 1—the article stressed that she was a "Champion Bath Taker" in her movies and died in one.

34. Bob Thomas, "Maria Recalled as Girl with Tireless Drive," *Hollywood Citizen-News,* MHL, "Maria Montez" file. Thomas talked about the date and how enjoyable it was in the *Mysteries and Scandals* episode on Maria, which aired April 26, 1998.

35. Erskine Johnson column, Gen.com, October 6, 1950; Harold Heffernan column, NP.com, October 6, 1950; John Carlyle, *Under the Rainbow* (New York: Carroll and Graf, 2006), 87–88.

36. Carlyle, *Under the Rainbow,* 87–88; email responses from Stephen Duckham, Noël Coward Society, December 23, 2020, December 27, 2020, quoting from Coward's diary.

37. TZC.

38. Aumont, *Sun and Shadow,* 142–43.

39. Cynthia Lowry, "Miss Montez Is Sixth Star Claimed by Untimely Death," *Hartford Courant,* September 30, 1951, 18. In a similar vein, an article was published comparing dead stars Maria Montez, Carole Lombard, and Carole Landis versus the living Yvonne De Carlo, Linda Darnell, and Yolande Donlan: "Screen's Sultriest Sirens—Departed or Current," *Glance,* April–May, 1952, 26. The reader was urged to look at the six photos and to "*Glance* and decide" who was the sultriest. The caption of Maria's photo, in which she wears a sarong, stated, "Maria Montez, who dieted her way to death, was the undeniable queen of the Sultan's sultry sirens"—a year and a half after her death she still set a standard. Columnist Danton Walker noted that Monique Van Vooren was "being groomed as another Maria Montez": Danton Walker, "Hollywood on Broadway," *Screenland and T-V Land,* March 1953, 70. Associated Press photograph, *Los Angeles Times,* December 21, 1951, 10.

40. Mamie Van Doren, telephone interview, August 23, 2005. Ellis Amburn worked for several American publishers and edited and wrote many biographies and autobiographies of American film stars. He knew Jean-Pierre and noted, "When I knew him he was happily married to Marisa Pavan, Oscar-nominated for her part as Anna Magnani's

daughter in *The Rose Tattoo,* but he'd never stopped loving his late wife Maria Montez." *Olivia de Havilland and the Golden Age of Hollywood* (Guilford, CT: Lyons, 2018), 239.

41. "Maria Montez, the Caribbean Cyclone: Victim Dies of Her Beauty" (translation), *Radar* (France), September 16, 1951, 10.

42. *Festival* (France), no. 119 (1951); *Le soir illustré,* no. 1003 (September 13, 1951); *Cine revue:* "The black series continues. . . . Maria Montez, who was one of the queens of glamour, is no longer" (translation), no. 37 (September 14, 1951), 25, "These four photographs are the last we did of Maria Montez" (translation), no. 42 (October 25, 1951), 23.

43. Patrick Kessel and Maurice Jarnoux, "With Maria Montez Paris Lost Its Distant Princess" (translation), *Paris Match,* September 22, 1951, 10, 16, 133, 136. Maria had graced a previous *Match* cover when the magazine covered the fiftieth anniversary gala for Maxim's restaurant: *Paris Match,* June 4–11, 1949.

44. The photo most often used in US publications is a 1940 Ray Jones portrait labeled MM-13, TZC.

45. "Maria Montez Leaves U. S. Property to Her Family," *Los Angeles Times,* February 15, 1952, A7; "Will of Maria Montez Probated; Mate in Court," *Los Angeles Times,* March 7, 1952, A3.

46. Jean-Pierre Aumont very eloquently sums up his last days with Maria in *Sun and Shadow,* 140–44. Edwin Schallert, "Aumont Redesigning Full Life Following Wife's Tragic Death, " *Los Angeles Times,* April 13, 1952; "Jean Pierre Aumont and Marisa Pavan Marry," *Los Angeles Times,* March 28, 1956, A1; Philip Scheuer, "Hollywood Family—2nd Generation," *Los Angeles Times,* March 15, 1966, C10; findagrave.com/Tina Aumont.

Afterword

1. "Maria Montez, Queen of Technicolor," Downtown Pop Underground, dsps.lib.uiowa.edu.

2. David Parkinson, "Jack Smith's Technicolor Muse: Maria Montez," *Guardian,* September 23, 2011; Matt Singer, "The Perfect Filmic Appositeness of Arnold Schwarzenegger," indiewire.com, August, 2012; Jack Smith, "The Perfect Filmic Appositeness of Maria Montez," *Film Culture* (Winter 1962–1963): 28–36; Edward Leffingwell, *Flaming Creature: Jack Smith, His Amazing Life and Times* (New York: Lookout Books, 1997); Gary McColgen, "The Superstar: An Interview with Mario Montez," *Film Culture,* no. 45 (Summer 1967): 17–20; "'I Look Sexy but Sweet': Notes on Maria and Mario Montez," Mediatico.com, March 13, 2014; *"Arabian Nights,"* p. 2, moviediva.com/arabiannights; "Maria Montez Queen of Technicolor."

3. Eduardo Moreno, "Maria Montez," *Films in Review,* no. 32 (1981): 223. Jonathan Rosenbaum, "More Vidal" (Review of *Myron*) is essentially a reprint of a review written for the *Village Voice,* November 14, 1974, posted February 8, 2019, jonathanrosenbaum.net.

4. "Ronald Tavel, His Life and Work: Celebrating the Life of an Accomplished Entertainer," ronaldtavel.com; "John Vaccaro: The Downtown Pop Underground," dsps.lib.uiowa.edu; "Maria Montez, Queen of Technicolor."

5. "Se exhibition fotos y objectos de la actriz dominica, vida de Maria Montez," *Allegria!* December 29, 2013, 11B; "Soberano Awards," en.wikipedia.org; nochelatina/articles/7019; Margarita Vicens de Morales, *Maria Montez: Su vida* (Santo Domingo: Republica Dominicana, 1992); liquisearch.com/maria_montez/legacy_and_afterdeath. Margarita Vicens de Morales published a series of articles about various aspects of Maria's life and career over a decade in the early 2000s in the Santo Domingo newspaper *Allegria!* in the "Hoy" section.

6. Jean Pierre Enard, *La reine de Technicolor* (Paris: Presses de la Renaissance, 1980); Len Levinson, *"Cobra Woman": A Tale of Sexual Obsession* (www.roughedgepress, 2019).

7. *Maria Montez: La pelicula* is available on YouTube from Indiewire.com (2015); *Maria Montez: The Movie,* Movie Data Base, imbd.com.

8. Davi: peppernegron.blogspot.com; bronxarts.org/documents/091511/daladavi.

9. The Maria Montez Fan Club publication can be found at MHL.

10. George Hadley-Garcia, "New Generation of Fans Smitten by Allure of Actress Maria Montez: Popularity of '40s-Era Star Rises, Thanks to Cable TV and Video," *Los Angeles Times* (*nuestro tiempo* edition), February 13, 1992, 3.

11. Jean-Pierre Aumont, *Sun and Shadow: An Autobiography* (New York: Norton, 1977), 120.

SELECTED BIBLIOGRAPHY

Interviews

Adams, Julie. Telephone interview, February 21, 2009.
Benedict, Bertram. Telephone interview, July 19, 2005.
Jean, Gloria. Telephone interview, December 16, 2004.
Jones, John. Conversations, 1998 to present.
Lord, Marjorie. Personal interview, September 24, 2005.
Lozzi, George. Personal interview, February 22, 2010.
Nebenzal, Harold. Telephone interview, September 28, 2016.
Paris, Raina. Personal interview, September 8, 2014.
Van Doren, Mamie. Telephone interview, August 23, 2005.

Books and Manuscripts

Alpi, Deborah Lazaroff. *Robert Siodmak.* Jefferson: McFarland, 1998.

Amburn, Ellis. *Olivia de Havilland and the Golden Age of Hollywood.* Guilford, CT: Lyons, 2018.

Aumont, Jean-Pierre. *Sun and Shadow: An Autobiography.* New York: Norton, 1977.

Bacher, Lutz. *Max Ophuls in the Hollywood Studios.* New Brunswick: Rutgers University Press, 1996.

Basinger, Jeanine. *The Star Machine.* New York: Knopf, 2007.

Bernstein, Matthew. *Walter Wanger, Hollywood Independent.* Berkeley: University of California Press, 1994.

Bishop-Sanchez, Kathryn. *Creating Carmen Miranda: Race, Camp and Transitional Stardom.* Nashville: Vanderbilt University Press, 2016.

Burr, Ty. *Gods Like Us: On Movie Stardom and Modern Fame.* New York: Pantheon, 2012.

Cotten, Joseph. *Vanity Will Get You Somewhere: An Autobiography.* San Francisco: Mercury House, 1987.

Daniel, Douglas. *Tough as Nails: The Life and Films of Richard Brooks.* Madison: University of Wisconsin Press, 2011.

De Carlo, Yvonne, with Doug Warren. *Yvonne: An Autobiography.* New York: St. Martin's, 1987.

de Usabel, Gaizka. *The High Noon of American Films in Latin America.* Ann Arbor: University Microfilms, 1987. (Originally published as a Ph.D. dissertation, University of Wisconsin, Madison, 1982.)

Dick, Bernard. *City of Dreams: The Making and Remaking of Universal Studios.* Lexington: University Press of Kentucky, 1997.

Doherty, Thomas. *Hollywood's Censor: Joseph I. Breen and the Production Code Administration.* New York: Columbia University Press, 2007.

———. *Projections of War: Hollywood, American Culture and World War II.* New York: Columbia University Press, 1993.

Fitzgerald, Michael. *Universal Pictures: A Panoramic History in Words, Pictures and Filmographies.* New Rochelle: Arlington House, 1977.

Gans, Eric. *Carole Landis: A Most Beautiful Girl.* Jackson: University Press of Mississippi, 2008.

Gomery, Douglas. *The Hollywood Studio System.* New York: St. Martin's, 1986.

Hadley-Garcia, George. *Hispanic Hollywood: The Latins in Motion Pictures.* New York: Citadel, 1990.

Hijo, Pablo Clase. *Maria Montez: Mujer y estrella.* Santo Domingo: Editorial del Norte, 1985.

Hirschhorn, Clive. *The Universal Story.* New York: Crown, 1983.

Hofeller, Leo, and Allen Churchill. *Pin Me Up: A Book Full of Pin-up Girls.* New York: Melrose, 1944.

Kiser, Brett. *The Pin-up Girls of World War II.* Duncan: Bear Manor Media, 2012.

Lake, Veronica. *Veronica.* deanstreetpress.co.uk, 2020. (Originally published by Citadel, 1970.)

Lamour, Dorothy. *My Side of the Road.* Englewood Cliffs: Prentice-Hall, 1980.

Lasky, Jesse Jr. *Whatever Happened to Hollywood?* New York: Funk and Wagnalls, 1973.

Leff, Leonard, and Jerold Simmons. *The Dame in the Kimono: Hollywood Censorship and the Production Code from the 1920s to the 1960s.* New York: Grove Weidenfeld, 1990.

Leibfried, Philip. *Star of India: The Life and Films of Sabu.* Albany: Bear Manor Media, 2010.

Lester, Gene. *When Hollywood Was Fun: Snapshots of an Era.* London: Robert Hale, 1993.

Longworth, Karina. *Seduction: Sex, Lies and Stardom in Howard Hughes's Hollywood.* New York: Custom House, 2018.

Mank, Gregory William. *Women in Horror Films, 1940s.* Jefferson: McFarland, 1999.

Martin, Pete. *Hollywood without Makeup.* New York: Bantam Books, 1949. (Originally published as "Dominican Dynamite." *Saturday Evening Post,* July 28, 1945.)

McEuen, Melissa. *Making War, Making Women: Femininity and Duty on the American Home Front, 1941–1945.* Athens: University of Georgia Press, 2010.

McFarland, Douglas. *Forties Film Talk: Oral Histories of Hollywood.* Jefferson: McFarland, 1992.

Mordden, Ethan. *The Hollywood Studios: House Style in the Golden Age of the Movies.* New York: Knopf, 1971.

Parish, James Robert. *Hollywood's Greatest Love Teams.* New Rochelle: Arlington House, 1974.

Pons, Frank Moya, *The Dominican Republic: A National History.* Princeton: Marcus Weiner, 1995.

Reyes, Luis. *Made in Paradise: Hollywood's Films of Hawaii and the South Seas.* Honolulu: Mutual, 1995.

Rice, Christina. *Mean . . . Moody . . . Magnificent! Jane Russell and the Marketing of a Hollywood Legend.* Lexington: University Press of Kentucky, 2021.

Russell, Elizabeth. "A Star in Gemini." Screenplay, Copyright Office, Library of Congress, Washington, DC, 1999.

Schatz, Thomas. *Boom and Bust: American Cinema in the 1940s.* Berkeley: University of California Press, 1999.

———. *The Genius of the System: Hollywood Film Making in the Studio Era.* New York: Pantheon Books, 1988.

Siodmak, Curt. *Wolf Man's Maker: Memoirs of a Hollywood Writer.* Lanham: Scarecrow, 2001.

Spoto, Donald. *A Girl's Got to Breathe: The Life of Teresa Wright.* Jackson: University Press of Mississippi, 2016.

Stackpole, Peter. *Life in Hollywood, 1936–1952.* London: Mainstream, 1992.

Stauffer, Teddy. *Forever Is a Hell of a Long Time: An Autobiography.* Chicago: Henry Regnery, 1976.

Steinman, Gertrude. "Galaxie." Margaret Herrick Library, Academy of Motion Picture Arts and Sciences.

Vicens de Morales, Margarita. *Maria Montez: Su vida.* Santo Domingo: Republica Dominicana, 1992.

Weaver, Tom, Michael Brunas, and John Brunas. *Universal Horrors: The Studio's Classic Films, 1931–1946.* Jefferson: McFarland, 2007.

Zimmerman, Tom. *Light and Illusion: The Hollywood Photographs of Ray Jones.* Los Angeles: Balcony, 1999.

Periodicals

Alexander, Ron. "Douglas Fairbanks, Jr. Tells His Story (Some of It, That Is"). *New York Times,* April 20, 1988, C4.

"Are You Star Material?—Test Yourself for Stardom." *Motion Picture,* December 1942, 28–29.

Aumont, Maria Christina. "I Like My Parents." *Movieland,* August 1946, 30–31.

Bangs, Bee. "Maria Montez: One-Man 'Zweetie.'" *Movie Show,* March 1945, 24–25, 64–65.

Baudin, Anne. "Maria Montez Guest Editor Tells You How to Go to the Head of Your Glamour Class." *Rexall,* September 1942, 8–9.

"Beware of Carbon Copies! Montez Shows Lamour That Two Can Play at That Game." *Silver Screen,* February 1942, 44–45.

"Carroll Righter; Stargazer to the Stars." *Life,* April 5, 1954, 143–55.

"Celebration: Hollywood Goes formal for Elsa." *Life,* October 9, 1944, 91–93.

Chicago Sun. Color pin up of Jon Hall and Maria Montez from *Cobra Woman.* November 14, 1943.

"Cover Girl—Maria Montez." *True Romance,* April 1947, 3.
Crichton, Kyle. "Born to Act." *Collier's,* April 4, 1942, 17, 54. (Reprinted in "It's Simple if You've Got What It Takes." *Reader's Digest,* July 1942, 17.)
Dean, Marjorie. "Foods of Our Allies." *Modern Screen,* March 1944, 96–97.
DeVane, Tom. "Glamour Is Her Dish." *Hollywood,* January 1942, 38.
Doyle, Neil. "Maria Montez: 'I Am So Beautiful.'" *Classic Images,* no. 318 (December 2001), 10–15.
Dudley, Fredda. "Romance in the Grand Manner." *Movieland,* October 1943, 19–21+.
Eythe, William. "Royal Command Performance." *Photoplay,* February 1947, 62–65, 118.
"Fame for Maria." *Silver Screen,* September 1942, 52–53.
"Farewell to Art: Illustrators and Models Fete McClelland Barclay as He Joins the Navy." *Click,* September 1941, 50–51.
Franchey, John. "Latin, Lissom and Lethal." *Silver Screen,* March 1942, 42–43+.
"Funnyman W. C. Fields Has His Own Way of Keeping Himself Fit." *Life,* May 12, 1941, 104–9.
"Glamour Issue." *Motion Picture,* March 1942, 33.
"Going Hollywood." *Collier's,* November 14, 1942, 12–13.
Gostick, Patricia. "McClelland Barclay: More Than Beautiful Women." *Illustration,* Fall 2009, 8–67.
Graham, Sheilah. "Maria Montez—She's One Smart Girl." *Portland Oregonian,* April 18, 1942, 50.
"The Great Montez: A Flaming 'Female Victor Mature,' Maria Picks Hollywood as Her Personal Oyster." *Look,* February 23, 1943, 28–30.
"Gypsy Wildcat." *Movie Story,* September 1944, 44–45, 101–7.
Hadley-Garcia, George. "New Generation of Fans Smitten by Allure of Actress Maria Montez: Popularity of '40s-Era Star Rises, Thanks to Cable TV and Video." *Los Angeles Times* (*nuestro tiempo* edition), February 13, 1992, 3.
Hall, Gladys. "Advice to Her Kid Sisters." *Silver Screen,* February 1945, 30–31, 83–86. (Original manuscript, "I Thought How Remarkable She Was." Gladys Hall Collection, Margaret Herrick Library, Academy of Motion Picture Arts and Sciences.)
———. "Overseas Report on Jean Pierre Aumont." *Photoplay,* May 1944, 54–55+.
———. "Reunion." *Photoplay,* July 1945, 27+.
Haugland, Vern. "Maria Puts on Best Show without Benefit of Camera Work." *San Diego Union,* October 6, 1941, 7.
"Hays Office Cracks Down on Cinema's Sweater Set." *Life,* May 14, 1941, 32–33.
"Hollywood Fights Its Slowdown: Wage-Ceiling Starlets Will Solve the Shortage of Stars." *Click,* March 1943.
Holt, Struthers. "Waiting for Jean Pierre." *Modern Screen,* August 1944, 54–55+.
Hopper, Hedda. "Hot Copy." *Modern Screen,* August 1945, 52–53.
———. "Maria Montez Had to Get Attention Before She Got a Career." *Modern Screen,* July 1945, 52.

———. "Montez the Magnificent." *Chicago Sunday Tribune Magazine,* February 22, 1948, 13.

"How the Stars Would Cast Themselves." *Look,* February 19, 1946, 76–84.

"In 'Arabian Nights' She Does the Dance of the Single Veil." *Life,* September 28, 1942, 69–70.

"I Will Not Deal In Scandal! Says Maria Montez." *Stardom,* February 1943, 30–31.

Johnson, Erskine. "In Hollywood." *Trenton Evening Times,* April 20, 1943, 14.

Kessel, Patrick, and Maurice Jarnoux. "With Maria Montez Paris Lost Its Distant Princess" (translation). *Paris Match,* September 22, 1951, 10, 16, 133, 136.

"Latin Beauties Rise in Films." *Milwaukee Journal,* December 20, 1940, 8–9.

"Latin Ladies: Hollywood Is Invaded by Talent from South of the Rio Grande." *Life,* February 3, 1941, 50–52.

"Let's Gossip with Maria Montez." *Motion Picture,* July 1945, 28–29+.

"*Life* Spends a Day with Sidney Skolsky." *Life,* May 1943, 102–5.

"Lightning Can Strike More Than Once in the Same Family." *Yank,* November 24, 1944, 19.

"Magic Maria." *Movie Life,* April 1942, 54–55.

"Make Way for Montez." *Movie Land,* May 1945, cover photo, 22+.

"Manhattan Project." *Movie Life,* December 1946, 40.

Mann, May. "Yes, Maria Loves Publicity—Latin Beauty Is Ambitious." *Ogden Standard Examiner,* February 7, 1943, B13.

Manners, Mary Jane (May Mann). "Second Love for Maria." *Silver Screen,* July 1943, 34–35, 68–71.

"Maria Montez." *Films in Review,* April 1981, 213–25.

"Maria Montez Is Economically Independent." *Pic,* July 21, 1942, 30–31.

"Maria Montez, the Caribbean Cyclone, Victim Dies of Her Beauty" (translation). *Radar* (France), September 16, 1951, 10+.

"Maria Montez: The Female Vic Mature; Hollywood's Most Spectacular Young Actress—This Temperamental Latin," *Screen Guide,* November 1942.

"Maria Montez: The Girl Who Couldn't Last." *Screen Guide,* April 1943, 123.

"Maria's a Spy in 'Tangier.'" *Movie Show,* February 1946, 12.

Marshall, Jim. "The Strange Embarrassment of Madame Aumont." *Collier's,* June 28, 1947, 12–13.

Marvin, Courtenay. "South of the Border." *Screenland,* May 1941, 58–59+.

Mason, Jerry. "Fair and Sultry." *Los Angeles Times,* March 12, 1944, F15.

McColgen, Gary. "The Superstar: An Interview with Mario Montez." *Film Culture,* Summer 1967, 17–20.

"M-mm-mmmm Girl Montez." *Movie Stars Parade,* November 1942, 54–55.

Montez, Maria. "Are Men Such Fools?" *Stardom,* September 1942, 40–41, 48.

———. "Jean Pierre Aumont: The Man I Love." *Photoplay,* November 1943, 52–53.

———. "Me and Men." *Screenland,* July 1943, 36–37, 86–87. ("As told to Gladys Hall.")

———. "My Most Thrilling Moments." *Screen Stars,* July 1944, 13.

———. "This Is My Husband." *Photoplay,* August 1947, 64–65, 108–9.

Montez, Maria, and May Mann. "Maria Montez' Frank Advice to Movie Struck Girls." *Screenland,* August 1944, 46–47+.

"Montez Finds Her Man: Three on a Match Lit the Way to Maria Montez Romance." *Screen Guide,* June 1943, 52–53.

"Montez Loses Her Man: Pierre Aumont Is Leaving Maria—to Fight for Free France." *Silver Screen,* September 1943, 22–23.

Movie-Radio. September 1943. Pin up of Maria.

"My Easter Prayer." *Photoplay,* April 1946, 42–43.

Myers, Robert. "'I'm Sensational,' Maria Montez, New Movie Glamour Girl Admits." *Boston Herald,* November 8, 1943, 60.

Palmer, Constance. "The Happy Aumonts." *Silver Screen,* August 1946, 46.

Parsons, Louella. Sunday column, *Washington Post,* September 20, 1942, L1.

"Pierre's Romantic Good-bye to Montez." *Movie Life,* January 1944, 20–23.

"Pin-up Girl—Maria Montez." *Motion Picture,* December 1943, 54.

Piva, Richard. "Maria Montez: A Vindication." *Maria Montez Fan Club,* no. 8 (2004). (Available at the Margaret Herrick Library, Academy of Motion Picture Arts and Sciences.)

"Plum for Maria Montez." *Between Us,* December 1949, 11.

"Portrait of Hollywood." *Pic,* December 21, 1940, 10–13.

"Promises I Made My Soldier Husband." *Motion Picture,* January 1945, 47, 69.

"Queen of Technicolor: Title Is Found for Dominican Starlet Maria Montez." *See,* January 1944, 10–11.

Rosenfield, John. "Maria Montez Makes Good Publicity Agent." *Dallas Morning News,* January 31, 1943, section 4, pp. 1, 4.

Rubello, David. "Hollywood Photographer: The Jack Albin Story." *Photogram* (Michigan Photographic Historical Society), February–March 2009.

Samuels, Charles. "Femme Fatale." *Motion Picture,* January 1946, 36–37+.

———. "Montez: Last of the Sirens." *Motion Picture,* October 1947, 33+.

Schrott, Gene. "Who's Afraid of Hollywood Wolves?" *Motion Picture,* December 1941, 23, 60–61.

Scott, Dianne. "Mythical Maria." *Photoplay,* January 1946, 44–45, 81–83.

Sharpe, Howard. "The High Cost of Maria Montez." *Liberty,* May 15, 1943, 36–37+.

Sheridan, Michael. "Venus DeCarlo." *Motion Picture,* May 1945, 27+.

"A Sight to Sea." *Film Fun,* June 1941, 16–17.

"'Siren of Atlantis.'" *Life,* January 31, 1949, 54–55.

Smith, Jack. "The Perfect Filmic Appositeness of Maria Montez." *Film Culture,* Winter 1962–1963, 28–36.

"Soiree at Sea." *Movie Life,* June 1941, 13.

Sprague, Dennis. "Lush, Latin and Lethal." *Photoplay,* June 1943, 6, 41.

Starr, Steve. "Starlight: Maria Montez." Chicago *Art Deco Society,* Fall 2008–Winter 2009, 4–5.

"There's Glamour in Speech." *Movie Land,* May 1946, 56–57+.

"13 Is Lucky for Love." *Modern Screen,* October 1943, 62–63, 93–96.

"To the Rear of the Class, Baron Munchausen." *New York Times,* August 23, 1942.

"Tropical." *American Magazine,* June 1942, 46.

Vermilye, Jerry. "Maria Montez." *Screen Facts* 3, no. 13 (1965): 1–27.
War Laffs: Fun for Fighting Men. Pinup. December 1943, 57.
"Who Is That Dame?" *Pic,* December 10, 1940, 10–11.
Wilson, Elizabeth. "'Perhaps I Am Too Egotistical,' Admits Maria Montez." *Movie Show,* March 1943, 38–39+.
Yank. Pin up. November 29, 1942, 18.

INDEX

Page numbers in italics refer to photographs.

SCREEN CLASSICS

Screen Classics is a series of critical biographies, film histories, and analytical studies focusing on neglected filmmakers and important screen artists and subjects, from the era of silent cinema through the golden age of Hollywood to the international generation of today. Books in the Screen Classics series are intended for scholars and general readers alike. The contributing authors are established figures in their respective fields. This series also serves the purpose of advancing scholarship on film personalities and themes with ties to Kentucky.

Series Editor

Patrick McGilligan

Books in the Series

Olivia de Havilland: Lady Triumphant
Victoria Amador

Mae Murray: The Girl with the Bee-Stung Lips
Michael G. Ankerich

Harry Dean Stanton: Hollywood's Zen Rebel
Joseph B. Atkins

Hedy Lamarr: The Most Beautiful Woman in Film
Ruth Barton

Rex Ingram: Visionary Director of the Silent Screen
Ruth Barton

Conversations with Classic Film Stars: Interviews from Hollywood's Golden Era
James Bawden and Ron Miller

Conversations with Legendary Television Stars: Interviews from the First Fifty Years
James Bawden and Ron Miller

You Ain't Heard Nothin' Yet: Interviews with Stars from Hollywood's Golden Era
James Bawden and Ron Miller

Charles Boyer: The French Lover
John Baxter

Von Sternberg
John Baxter

Hitchcock's Partner in Suspense: The Life of Screenwriter Charles Bennett
Charles Bennett, edited by John Charles Bennett

Hitchcock and the Censors
John Billheimer

A Uniquely American Epic: Intimacy and Action, Tenderness and Violence in Sam Peckinpah's The Wild Bunch
Edited by Michael Bliss

My Life in Focus: A Photographer's Journey with Elizabeth Taylor and the Hollywood Jet Set
Gianni Bozzacchi with Joey Tayler

Hollywood Divided: The 1950 Screen Directors Guild Meeting and the Impact of the Blacklist
Kevin Brianton

He's Got Rhythm: The Life and Career of Gene Kelly
Cynthia Brideson and Sara Brideson

Ziegfeld and His Follies: A Biography of Broadway's Greatest Producer
Cynthia Brideson and Sara Brideson

The Marxist and the Movies: A Biography of Paul Jarrico
Larry Ceplair

Dalton Trumbo: Blacklisted Hollywood Radical
Larry Ceplair and Christopher Trumbo

Warren Oates: A Wild Life
Susan Compo

Improvising Out Loud: My Life Teaching Hollywood How to Act
Jeff Corey with Emily Corey

Crane: Sex, Celebrity, and My Father's Unsolved Murder
Robert Crane and Christopher Fryer

Jack Nicholson: The Early Years
Robert Crane and Christopher Fryer

Anne Bancroft: A Life
Douglass K. Daniel

Being Hal Ashby: Life of a Hollywood Rebel
Nick Dawson

Bruce Dern: A Memoir
Bruce Dern with Christopher Fryer and Robert Crane

Intrepid Laughter: Preston Sturges and the Movies
Andrew Dickos

Miriam Hopkins: Life and Films of a Hollywood Rebel
Allan R. Ellenberger

Vitagraph: America's First Great Motion Picture Studio
Andrew A. Erish

Jayne Mansfield: The Girl Couldn't Help It
Eve Golden

John Gilbert: The Last of the Silent Film Stars
Eve Golden

Stuntwomen: The Untold Hollywood Story
Mollie Gregory

Otto Preminger: The Man Who Would Be King, updated edition
Foster Hirsch

Saul Bass: Anatomy of Film Design
Jan-Christopher Horak

Hitchcock Lost and Found: The Forgotten Films
Alain Kerzoncuf and Charles Barr

Pola Negri: Hollywood's First Femme Fatale
Mariusz Kotowski

Sidney J. Furie: Life and Films
Daniel Kremer

Albert Capellani: Pioneer of the Silent Screen
Christine Leteux

Ridley Scott: A Biography
Vincent LoBrutto

Mamoulian: Life on Stage and Screen
David Luhrssen

Maureen O'Hara: The Biography
Aubrey Malone

My Life as a Mankiewicz: An Insider's Journey through Hollywood
Tom Mankiewicz and Robert Crane

Hawks on Hawks
Joseph McBride

Showman of the Screen: Joseph E. Levine and His Revolutions in Film Promotion
A. T. McKenna

William Wyler: The Life and Films of Hollywood's Most Celebrated Director
Gabriel Miller

Raoul Walsh: The True Adventures of Hollywood's Legendary Director
Marilyn Ann Moss

Veit Harlan: The Life and Work of a Nazi Filmmaker
Frank Noack

Harry Langdon: King of Silent Comedy
Gabriella Oldham and Mabel Langdon

Charles Walters: The Director Who Made Hollywood Dance
Brent Phillips

Some Like It Wilder: The Life and Controversial Films of Billy Wilder
Gene D. Phillips

Ann Dvorak: Hollywood's Forgotten Rebel
Christina Rice

Mean . . . Moody . . . Magnificent! Jane Russell and the Marketing of a Hollywood Legend
Christina Rice

Fay Wray and Robert Riskin: A Hollywood Memoir
Victoria Riskin

Lewis Milestone: Life and Films
Harlow Robinson

Michael Curtiz: A Life in Film
Alan K. Rode

Ryan's Daughter: *The Making of an Irish Epic*
Paul Benedict Rowan

Arthur Penn: American Director
Nat Segaloff

Film's First Family: The Untold Story of the Costellos
Terry Chester Shulman

Claude Rains: An Actor's Voice
David J. Skal with Jessica Rains

Barbara La Marr: The Girl Who Was Too Beautiful for Hollywood
Sherri Snyder

Buzz: The Life and Art of Busby Berkeley
Jeffrey Spivak

Victor Fleming: An American Movie Master
Michael Sragow

My Place in the Sun: Life in the Golden Age of Hollywood and Washington
George Stevens, Jr.

Hollywood Presents Jules Verne: The Father of Science Fiction on Screen
Brian Taves

Thomas Ince: Hollywood's Independent Pioneer
Brian Taves

Picturing Peter Bogdanovich: My Conversations with the New Hollywood Director
Peter Tonguette

Carl Theodor Dreyer and Ordet: *My Summer with the Danish Filmmaker*
Jan Wahl

Wild Bill Wellman: Hollywood Rebel
William Wellman Jr.

Clarence Brown: Hollywood's Forgotten Master
Gwenda Young

The Queen of Technicolor: Maria Montez in Hollywood
Tom Zimmerman